THE ECONOMIC ORGANIZATION OF AGRICULTURE

The Economic Organization of Agriculture

THEODORE W. SCHULTZ

PROFESSOR OF ECONOMICS
UNIVERSITY OF CHICAGO

NEW YORK · TORONTO · LONDON

McGRAW-HILL BOOK COMPANY, INC.

1953

THE MAPLE PRESS COMPANY, YORK, PA.

To
Esther Werth Schultz

PREFACE

This study is based on two fundamental beliefs about which I want to be explicit. There is the belief that the community prefers a developing economy to one that is stationary, and it prefers economic stability to large, sudden changes in prices and employment. This is to say, economic development is good, stagnation is bad. A steady level of prices and full employment are good, whereas large, short-term movements of prices and mass unemployment are bad. The other belief is that the concept of economy is an organizing value, which means that to economize is good, and that it is necessary for a community to organize to achieve economy. Should it be true that either or both of these two beliefs were invalid—that is, if the community were to prefer stagnation or were indifferent about it, or preferred economic instability; or if the community were to place no value whatsoever on economy, or if it could achieve economy without organization—a study such as this would be quite meaningless.

Agriculture can make, as it has in some countries, important contributions to economic development. Agriculture also finds it necessary to make major adjustments as a consequence of economic development. These particular contributions and adjustments do not come easily, quickly, or automatically. Whether the contributions are large and whether the adjustments are made satisfactorily are dependent in large measure upon economic organization. So that a community may choose with greater assurance the path it wishes to take in relating its agriculture to the development it wants to achieve, I have devoted a major part of this study to these organizational possibilities.

I am also concerned about economic instability in relation to agriculture. This instability has attributes, some of which are general to the economy as a whole and some specific to agriculture where the demand and supply schedules are highly inelastic, where large and abrupt shifts of the demand schedule occur frequently, and where weather causes some large year-to-year variations in production. In this study I have made an attempt to find ways of improving the existing economic organization by eliminating or reducing the instability, or where this does not seem to be the solution, by adapting the economy to the instability.

Unfortunately, most studies of economic organization deal either with the functions of particular firms and households, in microanalysis, or with general social and political issues, which are all too often represented solely as problems in valuation and of methodology. Nor has macroanalysis as currently practiced lived up to its promise or prospects. Nevertheless, economics can contribute much to the art of national housekeeping; to do so, however, it will be necessary to rediscover *political economy*. This means that the student should go beyond the organization of firms and households although not neglect the important role that they play in a community which places a high value on decentralization in its organizational structure. Factor and product markets should not be taken for granted as is now common practice. In the case of agriculture, in adjusting to economic development, as I have shown in this study, the performances of the factor markets are of critical importance. Then, too, one should not leave out the integrating functions borne necessarily by the social and political processes.

I look upon this study as a progress report for I have carried forward the essential ideas of my *Agriculture in an Unstable Economy*. Meanwhile, I have drawn heavily upon new research, some of which has been done by my colleagues. I have come to see more clearly the implications of the analysis not only for communities that are rich but also for those that are exceedingly poor in the collection of resources and in the income at their disposal. Nor do I view this as a definitive study. Much remains to be done and this has led me to formulate at many different points what I deem to be the best hypothesis for explaining the particular behavior. To test these hypotheses calls for much hard work. My hope is that some of these hypotheses will challenge other workers sufficiently for them to put particular hypotheses to test and thus hasten the process of rejecting or establishing the explanation that I have tentatively advanced.

For data I have turned again and again to members of the staff of the Bureau of Agricultural Economics. Everyone whom I burdened has been exceedingly generous in helping me. There are, however, two important sets of data which governmental agencies have failed to produce, namely, data on rewards to factors used in farming and on how these rewards compare to those received by comparable factors in other sectors of the economy, basic as such data are in analyzing the efficiency of agriculture, and data on the personal distribution of income within agriculture. A few research workers located mainly in the South and in the Plain States have undertaken studies related to uneven economic development of agriculture and to yield and price uncertainty. I have benefited from these.

I saw fit to offer for publication two chapters: "Reflections on Poverty within Agriculture," which appeared in the *Journal of Political Economy* and "The Declining Economic Importance of Agricultural Land," in the *Economic Journal.* I am grateful to the editors for permission to use these chapters in this study as was my plan.

I am deeply indebted to my colleague, D. Gale Johnson, as will be clear to any reader as he proceeds. Not all of the research already completed by Johnson is presently available. The results, however, from our major research enterprise at the University of Chicago, made possible by two generous grants from the Rockefeller Foundation, will in due time be presented to the profession as a treatise by Johnson.

The difficult set of tables appearing in Chaps. 12 and 13 is the work of George Coutsoumaris. He also checked most of the tables and references in other parts of this study. The painstaking hand and intelligent efforts of Mrs. Janet Weider throughout and especially in correcting proof represent a contribution which has saved me much grief.

It is my privilege, however, to bear full responsibility for what appears and to invite criticism from others as part of the larger endeavor of advancing our still very limited insights about economic development and economic stability.

T. W. Schultz

CHICAGO, ILL.
OCTOBER, 1952

CONTENTS

PART I. ECONOMIC DEVELOPMENT AND AGRICULTURE

By way of classification and procedure. Four elementary representations of developments related to agriculture. A population increase, an increase in income, a new technique employed by consuming units, and a new output-increasing agricultural technique.

Equal rates of shifts to the right. Demand for farm products in the forefront. Supply of farm products out ahead.

Focal points of demand for farm products. Conditions affecting long-term shifts of the demand. Some pitfalls in ascertaining shifts in demand for farm products. Shifts in demand of selected farm commodities, 1875 to 1929.

Relevant population and food aggregates. High food drain (Type I), intermediate food drain (Type II), and low food drain (Type III). The population variable in relation to the food economy. Population as a within variable and as an outside variable. Some demand effects of Types I and II. Population growth and United States agriculture.

Income elasticity—an appeal of cross-sectional data. Income elasticity—use of time series. Clues from consumer studies of consumption of food over time. An evaluation of income elasticity estimates. Income elasticity of farm products from Tintner's model. Clues from crude expenditures for farm products. Income elasticity of services added to farm products. Income elasticities of particular food groups. Classification of industries. The rise in the level of income.

Increasing the efficiency of food: supply effects. Demand effects of nutrition. Correcting nutritional imbalances.

Changes in the supplies of inputs. Outcome with 1946–1948 input prices and outcome with 1910–1914 input prices. New and better production techniques. Industry and agriculture compared. "Producing" and distributing new techniques. Agricultural research: expenditures and returns. Gauging the value of the inputs saved. 1910 techniques for 1950 production. 1940 techniques for 1950 production. Labor force and its distribution.

Agriculture relative to the whole economy. Relative position of land as an input in producing farm products. Land as an economic variable.

A hypothesis. Implications of hypothesis.

Simplifying empirical propositions. Economic development can bring about increasing disparity in income. Conditions related to the increasing disparity in income. Proportion of population that contributes to income. Conditions that determine the abilities of a population to produce. Conditions that impede factor-price equalization.

PART II. ECONOMIC INSTABILITY AND AGRICULTURE

Hypothesis explaining the price instability of agriculture. Shifts that are large. Elasticities that are relatively low.

Fluctuations in yield by location. The Pacific region is placid. The turbulent West Central regions, both North and South. Location of yield instability in the United States. Fluctuations in yield by products.

more complete information, and farm enlargement programs. Land reform.

No marked short-term movements in the employment of resources in agriculture. Yield instability in farming. Functioning of the economy in relation to yield instability. Improvements in organization to cope with yield instability. Organization to adjust to yield instability.

Reducing the instability of farm prices. War and peace with less economic instability. Gradual and small versus abrupt and large shifts of the demand. Reducing the variations in agricultural production. Increasing the price elasticity of the supply. Increasing the price elasticity of the demand for farm products. By way of accommodations. Organize farms more capable of coping with price instability. Safeguarding income of agriculture in depression. Possibilities by storage.

LIST OF TABLES

LIST OF FIGURES

xix

PART ONE

ECONOMIC DEVELOPMENT AND AGRICULTURE

1

AGRICULTURE IN A DEVELOPING ECONOMY

Part One is a study of development and of agriculture where the two join. The economics of development would be incomplete unless it could explain the emergence of new and better production possibilities in agriculture and the effects of developments, from whatever source, upon agriculture. The economics of agriculture, in turn, would be incomplete unless it could explain this same economic behavior. And one would expect the two explanations to be consistent one with the other.

Agriculture may limit severely or contribute importantly to the development of a particular economy. When the niggardliness of nature is real, and new and better production possibilities in agriculture come hard, the prospects for economic development are not bright. When technical advances in agriculture make possible a cornucopia, the stage is set for a more rapid development. When the agricultural sector and the rest of the economy become maladjusted as a consequence of the process of development and it becomes necessary to transfer many resources into agriculture, a *food* problem usually puts in its appearance. When it becomes necessary to transfer many resources out of agriculture, a *farm* problem is likely to arise.

Part One of this study, dealing with development and agriculture, is an endeavor to provide a foundation for an analysis of economic organization, which is undertaken in Part Three, where the organizational objectives are twofold: (1) to *induce* development and (2) to *adjust* to it. These objectives, when restricted to agriculture, indicate two sets of problems. There are the problems of the agricultural sector adjusting to developments whether they originate within agriculture or in the rest of the economy. There are also the problems of a community endeavoring to induce development where this is possible and preferred.

But when is a particular development possible and preferred? This question raises some difficult issues: What is economic development? How may it be studied? Is there an accepted theory of economic development?

Clearly, there is no received theory explaining economic development comparable, for example, to the theory of the firm (the firm under static conditions). The economics of development, at this stage of our knowledge, is more akin to a collection of ideas and studies representing different approaches. Some approaches are cast in a biological mold and concentrate on the "growth" attributes of the economy; some single out the economic effects of specialization; some place a particular class of entrepreneurs in the role of key innovators; some trace the economic effects of changes in particular factors, be it population, capital, or land; there is the magnificent approach to economic progress of the older English economists (the classical school); there is the particular interpretation of economic history of Marx; and then there are the various bits and pieces from static analysis involving time and from process analysis.[1]

In Part One of this study we shall bring several of these approaches to bear. Much of it is an endeavor to determine the economic effects of changes in fundamental factor supplies and in product demands upon agriculture. It is possible to gauge these effects without explaining the underlying changes. This does not mean that none of the changes in fundamental factor supplies and in product demands can be explained. Again and again, as we proceed, the question will arise: Are these changes beyond economics, and must we, therefore, forgo any explanation whatsoever and simply take them as they appear from statistical and other empirical studies and restrict ourselves to a study of the economic consequences that flow from the particular observed changes? We would have no choice on this point if each and every change in factor supplies and product demands were wholly independent of the existing economic system. In that event we would of logical necessity be forced to treat them as strictly outside (exogenous) variables that are not influenced in any way by price or income. Yet, we know that most, if not all of these changes not only influence price and income and other inside (endogenous) variables but these developments are also influenced by them. Moreover, we would put ourselves in a position of not using a great deal of valuable information about these changes over time if we were to treat each of them as outside and beyond economic analysis. We need to take a page from the work sheets of Ricardo, Malthus, Mill, and their colleagues who in their broad conception of economic progress introduced the growth in population as a development that was dependent upon the food supply, which in turn was subject to the diminishing returns against land. Although the growth in population in some Western countries has come to behave as if it were quite independent of the

[1] For a useful survey and systematization, see William J. Baumol, *Economic Dynamics* (New York: The Macmillan Company, 1951).

supply of food, this earlier formulation is still exceedingly useful in explaining the growth of population in many parts of the world.

Surely enough information is at hand to indicate that the accumulation of additional capital, the development of new techniques, and the improvement of skills affecting factor supplies are not entirely independent of price and income considerations. A similar observation is in order for some of the basic developments affecting product demands. In later chapters we shall take advantage of some of this information and incorporate it into our inquiry because it will help us at least partially to explain some important factors underlying economic development.

BY WAY OF CLASSIFICATION AND PROCEDURE

Changes in fundamental factor supplies are possible as a result of (1) discovery of additional resources, (2) accumulation of additional capital, (3) new and better techniques, (4) growth in population, (5) improvements in skills, and (6) other institutional and organizational modifications. These are changes from which one commonly abstracts in static analysis.[2]

Equally basic changes in product demands are possible from developments in (1) population, (2) income, (3) taste, (4) techniques applicable within consuming units, and (5) other institutional and organizational arrangements. This classification gives a clue to the materials and organization of later chapters.

Each of these changes affecting elementary factor supplies and product demands may be viewed as a particular development and as such each may be elaborated. Most of them may be further refined and classified into subgroups. For example, new techniques are usually specific to a particular industry; hybrid corn belongs to agriculture where it is re-

---

[2] Professor Jacob Viner, in his distinguished article "Cost Curves and Supply Curves," points out that the Austrian School assumes that the supplies of the elementary factors of production are given and independent of their rates of remuneration while the English School stresses the dependence, notably of labor and waiting, on the rates of remuneration. Other restricting assumptions are frequently made. While these need not detain us, there is a good deal of substance in R. F. Harrod's lament, *Towards a Dynamic Economics* (London: Macmillan & Co., Ltd., 1948), Lecture 1, p. 2, "I find much that is unsatisfactory in the tendency to narrow the scope of statics, by imposing ever more numerous and rigorous restrictions on the alleged sphere and validity of that branch, with the consequent danger that what is true, valuable and of practical moment in the traditional static theory may escape attention and pass out of view."

stricted to the corn-producing areas; the assembly line belongs to industry and to specific types of manufacturing and processing. New techniques, also, may be classified in accordance with their effects upon particular factors, that is, whether they are labor, capital, or land "saving" because in practice a new technique usually has the effect of increasing the supply of particular resources or inputs. On the demand side, one might take the growth in population to illustrate the possibilities of and gains from subgrouping. Not all segments of a population increase at the same rate. The aged may increase more rapidly than the rest of the population. The rate of growth of the population in agriculture is usually greater than that in urban centers. Significant differences, therefore, may arise among age groups, between sexes, and in geographical and occupational distributions.

While it is useful to study singly and in the small the effects of a particular change in the supply of a factor or in the demand of a product, it is important to collect and bring these effects together. For farm products, we shall attempt to aggregate these effects into supply and demand shifts. The next chapter is based on these concepts in which three sets of shifts of the two schedules are indicated to determine whether the shifts make it necessary to transfer resources into or out of agriculture.

We shall, also, from time to time, as we proceed, reach out for a more generalized analysis. To do this, we shall endeavor to represent the emerging possibilities and the path of the preferences of the community as a whole. By this means, it will be possible to explain in broad outlines the declining economic importance of agricultural land and of the farm and food sectors in a developing economy.

As has been said, the economics of development is not one of the more elegant compartments of economics; it is not neat and tidy, for it is not of one theoretical piece; instead, it represents a collection of insights obtained by a variety of approaches. We shall employ, as has been indicated, more than one of these as we proceed. The question, however, remains: Exactly what is meant by economic development? What is a development?

Because of the different approaches underlying the study of the economics of development, one would expect the concept of development to have acquired different meanings, as has been the case. To make room for particular studies analyzing only a segment of economic activities in the small, it is convenient to look upon any change affecting fundamental factor supplies or product demands as a development. This means that on the side of factor supplies each of the following represents a particular development, that is, the discovery of additional (natural) resources, the accumulation of additional capital, new and better techniques, growth in population, improvement in skills, and better economic organization. Changes affecting basic product demands provide a parallel list of developments. There will follow in this chapter a simple, brief representation of four of these developments to indicate approximately how each is related to the problem of resource allocation in agriculture.

It is also important to study the economic effects of these changes in the large to gauge their meaning as aggregates. Here, however, we come up against the difficulty of passing from individual values to social choice, a difficulty which one may neglect in considering some small changes. The idea of "economic progress," when defined as an improvement in the means used to achieve a given end, which is to say, improving the ratio of the end achieved to the means used, is not a way out of this difficulty. Unfortunately, the end to be achieved, the social choice, is not objective; it cannot be determined by casual observations or from introspection. There are no methods, leaving the possibilities of interpersonal comparisons of utility aside, of passing from individual tastes to social preferences which are wholly satisfactory.[3]

Nor it is possible to demonstrate that a development which gives rise to a much enlarged national product will necessarily result in a measurable improvement in social welfare.[4] Among other things, some people in the community may find their economic situation deteriorating as a consequence. We cannot, therefore, by economic analysis alone demonstrate that economic growth is in itself socially desirable because of the way the new production possibilities may affect the welfare of individuals and of families although it is clear that the Western community has sanctioned economic development and has favored it in many ways by its institutions.

These difficulties in the concept of social choice, however, do not justify, on the one hand, the use of crude and misleading indicators which so frequently appear in the literature on economic development, or on the other hand, the belief that no meaningful and approximate formulation is possible.[5] There is no excuse for identifying improvement in social welfare with increases in the ratio of industrial output to the

[3] Kenneth J. Arrow, "A Difficulty in the Concept of Social Welfare," *Journal of Political Economy*, Vol. LVIII (August, 1950). This problem will be considered further in Part Three.
[4] See Paul A. Samuelson's cogent analysis, "Evaluation of Real National Income," *Oxford Economic Papers*, New Series, Vol. II (January, 1950).
[5] D. H. Robertson, "Utility and All That," *The Manchester School of Economics and Social Studies*, Vol. XIX (May, 1951). A set of lectures full of wisdom on the latter point.

total; industrialization and urbanization with no other conditions specified; or with an enlarged rate of capital formation; or with increases in the national product with no restrictions on its distribution—as is so often the case.[6]

The classical concept of economic progress provides a bench mark to which we shall return from time to time in this study. Economic progress thus conceived meant a change in conditions which made possible a larger real output. The additional output, regardless of its source or of its magnitude, made possible and induced an equivalent growth in population and, therefore, the per capita output (income) settled to the (subsistence) level that existed prior to the development. In other words, economic progress meant a larger (national) income, with no restrictions on its distribution. But because of the assumed behavior of the population variable, the result was a constant level of per capita income at subsistence. The welfare prospects from economic progress under such conditions are far from bright; they are not a preferred outcome; the pessimism associated with this outcome is itself a bench mark in Western social thought.

There are three useful modifications in arriving at an *approximate* improvement in social welfare related to development. As the product of the economy (of a country or of a national economy) increases, the first of these requires a rise in per capita income. Many studies of economic development use this formulation as a sufficient criterion of an improvement in social welfare. It is, however, quite unsatisfactory, because it places no restriction whatsoever on the distribution of the larger (national) income. In this respect, it is even weaker than that implicit in the classical concept of economic progress. The per capita income of many countries and communities has increased measurably, as one may discover from the "puffing" that goes on in national statistics, while the poverty of large masses of people has become even more crushing than before. A second step, suggested by the preceding argument, is to specify that the increase in the national income and in the per capita income be so distributed that no segment of the population or that no community in the economy be worse off than it was before the development occurred. This criterion, with its restriction on the distribution of the enlarged income, comes appreciably closer to what may be an improvement in social welfare but it is, nevertheless, at best, a weak welfare standard. The third step is to require that the outcome

[6] Jacob Viner, *Lectures on the Theory of International Trade*, given at the Fundacão Getulio Vargas National University of Brazil, July–August, 1950, Princeton University (mimeo.). See Lecture VI.

of the development be such that in real terms every segment of the population or every community in the economy be at least somewhat better off than it was prior to the particular development. By taking the second and third steps, we have not resolved the difficulty in passing from individual values to social choice; we have, however, both a weak and strong standard which may be useful to approximate an improvement in social welfare.

Four Elementary Representations of Developments Related to Agriculture

Four different developments, each in the small, will be represented at this point: a particular population increase, an increase in income, and two types of improvements in techniques. These are the principal developments which we shall endeavor to gauge in subsequent chapters of Part One. None of the representations is taken to be complete. The purpose of introducing them at this stage is to indicate the direction (not always possible), but not the magnitude[7] of the effects of the particular development upon resource allocations within agriculture. We shall draw upon these representations in later chapters and in the process relax some of the simplifying assumptions and also take account of additional variables in interpreting such data as are available and appear relevant.

Let us divide the economy into two parts, one consisting of the agricultural sector and the other of the rest of the economy. To simplify, assume that firms and households in agriculture both buy factors and the services of factors from, and sell them to, producing and consuming units in the rest of the economy; while in the case of products, they buy only nonagricultural products (and services) and sell only farm products to the rest of the economy. The farm firms, therefore, produce a different set of products than do the other firms while factors are bought and sold and transferred from one to the other. More specifically, the agri-

[7] It is our belief that the best that economists can do on most dynamic problems is to infer the probable direction of the effect of a development and as long as, and to the extent that, this is true, it is exceedingly important to approach the problem of economic organization with this limitation of economic analysis firmly in mind. The implication of this belief is as follows: if it were possible to anticipate (determine) both the direction and the rate of such effects, the organizational structure could be designed to deal efficiently with the complete information; if, however, the best that we can do were to acquire insights on the direction alone, the appropriate organizational structure needs to have within itself the capacity to use new and more complete information as it becomes available.

cultural sector is taken to include all farms (and farm households) under the assumption that they produce only farm products and that the rest of the economy produces no farm products whatsoever. The agricultural sector supposedly takes in all economic activities that are subject to the decisions of farmers beginning with the purchase or sale of factors and services of factors by farmers from or to the rest of the economy and up to the point of first sales off the farm of the products which they produce. In addition, to begin with, let it be assumed that both the factor and product markets are free from imperfections and, at the time a development occurs, the economy is in long-run equilibrium.

1. *A Population Increase.* This particular increase in population, by assumption, is to be confined to the age groups which do not contribute to production so that elementary factor supplies remain unchanged. It also is assumed that the number of families and the income which each family receives are not altered while the size of each family increases, say, from four to five members. The demand effects of this development will, therefore, depend upon the behavior of these families as consuming units in response to the increase in the size of each family by one-fourth. One possibility, at one extreme, will arise if each family buys the same products in the same amounts as before and simply reallocate the products they purchase among members of the family. Given this behavior, there will be no demand effects whatsoever and, accordingly, the existing equilibrium will not be disturbed. On the other hand, if all families prefer to increase their purchases of one class of products (say, food) in proportion to the increase in the size of the family while curtailing another class of items (say, travel) enough to make this possible, these changes in demands will induce an expansion in agriculture and a contraction in transportation. Assuming that all production within all firms and industries is conducted under conditions of diminishing returns, the rewards per unit to factors that are specific to transportation will drop the most while those specific to agriculture will rise most.[8]

[8] The particular change in demand outlined above may be viewed as a *population effect* upon the behavior of the family which we take as the consuming unit. The population effect arises from an increase, in this case, in size of the family from four to five members with the income of the family and other conditions unchanged. One possibility, but not the only one and not the most plausible one, is a family preference which, when confronted by this population effect, the increase in family members of one-fourth, causes the family to increase its purchases of food by one-fourth, as has been indicated, and curtails its purchases of other items accordingly.

2. *An Increase in Income.* It is exceedingly difficult, if not impossible, to indicate a set of circumstances that would increase income without first introducing specific modifications in elementary factors. Let us suppose, however, that such a change were feasible by means of a set of technical advances throughout the economy which left the rewards (money payments) to all factors and to all families unchanged and which reduced all product prices without changing the price of one relative to the other and, thus, increasing the real income of all families by a given proportion, say by 10 per cent. With no changes in population and in taste and with other things remaining equal, what can be said about the effects of this development upon agriculture? We need to know, first of all, the income and price elasticities to explain the demand effects of this change. If the income elasticities of farm products of all families were zero and if food were in no way a substitute for other products, all the increase in demands would go for the products of the rest of the economy. Again, assuming diminishing returns throughout the economy, this change in demand would induce an expansion[9] in the nonagricultural sectors with rewards per unit to factors specific to these industries rising relative to the rewards to factors that can be transferred (say) out of agriculture, while the per unit rewards to factors specific to agriculture would drop more than would those that could be released and used in the rest of the economy. The new income situation postulated for development (2) therefore requires some contraction of agricultural production[10] before a new long-run equilibrium can be established. Relative prices of products will change in the process, depending in the short run primarily upon the price and income elasticities of the demand modified in the long run by basic costs conditions.

If, however, the income elasticity of farm products were high and that of products originating in the rest of the economy low (say, zero as an extreme), the same general analysis will apply but, of course, the consequences will run in the opposite direction with the demand for farm products increasing and with agriculture expanding; the rewards to factors will also take a turn about.

3. *A New Technique Employed by Consuming Units.* This new and better technique, let us assume, increases the want-satisfying capacity (really an increase in output) of one class of products (say, of food); furthermore, let us assume that all families adopt this technique and as a

[9] An expansion in addition to the increase in output resulting from the advances in technique postulated at the outset.

[10] A contraction in agriculture from the level attained as a result of the new techniques.

consequence with exactly the same purchases of food they all obtain, say, 10 per cent more nutrients and that nutrients measure fully the want satisfactions that they derive from such food. The new technique is taken to be costless, that is, it consists, in this instance, of new knowledge about nutrition that is freely available. Also, to simplify further, let us represent all food as consisting of one homogeneous product.

This development may be incorporated into either the demand for food at retail or the supply of food at the point of consumption. The supply of food at the point of consumption shifts to the right because it is assumed that a given collection of agricultural resources continues to produce the same quantity of food available at retail which now represents, because of the new technique, 10 per cent more food (nutrients) at the point of consumption than was the case formerly. On the other hand, the demand of the consuming unit may be represented as intersecting the supply of food at retail and, therefore, the production operations of the consuming unit including the adoption of this new technique will enter into and alter the (derived) demand for food at retail. We shall take this representation; however, in either case, the "normal" outcome would be that the price of food will fall at retail because not as many farm products are now required to give consumers as large an intake of food nutrients as they were accustomed to prior to the advance in their knowledge about nutrition. The demand effect of the fall in price may be divided into an income effect and a substitution effect. Since less of the family income will be required to buy as much food as formerly, some additional income will be available to buy other products and also more food than were purchased before. How this particular "savings" or increase in real income is allocated by consuming units will depend upon the existing income elasticities. In addition, to the extent that food can be substituted for other products, the fall in price will increase consumer purchases of food while decreasing that of others.

We can always be sure of the direction of the substitution effects because it will invariably result in an increase in purchase of food at retail. How much substitution takes place is, of course, exceedingly important. The price will always fall farther in the short run than the point where it will settle in the long run after food habits have had time to adjust[11] and after factor adjustments are made that are consistent with basic costs

[11] Consumers' habits may be viewed as a variable with taste remaining unchanged. These habits may be taken as fixed in the short run but as variable in the long run. Therefore, we need to take into account adjustments in food habits in moving to a new long-run equilibrium, and these adjustments will increase substitution and this will increase the price elasticity of the demand.

conditions. The income effect, however, can go either way, since some products are negative (inferior) while others are positive (superior) in terms of consumer response to changes in income. We cannot be altogether certain, therefore, about the direction of the combined substitution and income effects, although, except for rather unusual circumstances, the two effects together will increase the quantity taken.

Let us take, first, an extreme situation in which the income elasticity of demand for all products other than food is zero and in which the high income elasticity of food precisely counterbalances the additional efficiency of food. Suppose that people are very much underfed and prefer more food nutrients above all else, so much so that they buy exactly as much food at retail as they formerly did even though in consuming the food they now acquire more food nutrients. Under this very unusual situation, it should be noted, the only difference between the old and new equilibrium is that all families increase their intake of food nutrients by 10 per cent as a result of this particular technique.

Let us now turn to the other extreme and suppose that there is no substitution between food and other products and that people are so well fed that they have come to look upon food as an inferior product giving it a negative elasticity against income. In this case the substitution effect is zero and the income effect is negative; that is, instead of counterbalancing any or all of the improvement in nutritional efficiency of food which shifts the demand for food at retail to the left, the income effect contributes further to this leftward shift. The implications of this situation for agricultural production, its contraction, and for factor rewards and transfers are parallel to those already considered under developments (1) and (2).

4. *A New Output-increasing Agricultural Technique.* The economic effects of a new production technique are extremely complex. We shall restrict this representation to a new agricultural technique which increases the output obtained from one of the factors used in farming. Let us take the case where the factor affected is specific to farming and assume that the technique is costless to farmers, that all farmers adopt the technique, that agricultural production consists of a single product, and that it takes as many cooperating factors to produce a given output with the new technique as it did with the old one. What influences will this kind of change have upon agricultural production and income? The output of one of the elementary factors (say, land) is altered by this technique and the particular land is taken to be specific to farming, that is, none of it can be employed to produce any other products (or services). By assumption, all agricultural land continues to be employed and the same amount of labor and other cooperating factors is used as

formerly. The output increases as a consequence of the new technique (say) by 10 per cent. By assumption, land is in this case in the position of a residual claimant of total factor rewards in farming. If the demand for this farm product (food) has a price elasticity of unity, the larger supply will fetch the same total returns as formerly and in that event the rewards to land will not be altered and accordingly the income position of landowners will be unaffected by this technique. Consumers, however, will be better off, for they now acquire 10 per cent more food for the same total outlay on food as before because the price of food falls proportionally. The fall in price, however, brings about substitution effects reducing the price of substitute products and thus a long chain of price effects is set into motion which must work themselves out before a new long-run equilibrium becomes established.

The demand for food, however, is in fact quite inelastic and under these circumstances the larger total output sells for less, say for 10 per cent less than formerly. If the specific factor, land, were receiving 20 per cent of all factor income in farming prior to the introduction of the new technique, one of the consequences of the adoption of this technique will be a reduction of the rewards to all land by one-half. Landowners accordingly will experience a marked loss in income. To complete the sketch it will be necessary to trace the income effects of this loss upon other product and factor prices. Also, for consumers we now have, because of the fall in the price of food and the less than proportionate increase in purchases, in addition to the substitution effect an income effect that may be of substantial importance. However, we have already indicated how these effects run.

These four elementary developments do not, of course, exhaust the many kinds of changes that contribute to economic development. We have not attempted to represent such important processes as the accumulation of capital, improvement of skills, modifications of taste, and a better organization of the economy. Nor has this representation included all the possibilities, even for the four developments, since we have restricted the range of each case by a series of simplifying assumptions to a few, albeit salient, characteristics underlying the adjustment process toward a new long-run equilibrium. There is the further limitation that we have formulated each of these changes as if it were a unique event that occurred once and did not repeat itself. In the real world, however, we find some of these developments more akin to a flow rather than to a "once over" change to which the economy adjusts, but having done so, the decks are not clear because another similar change is upon it.

2

THREE SETS OF DEMAND AND SUPPLY SHIFTS

The concepts of demand and supply are both elementary and powerful in economic analysis. We shall now bring these into play. We shall continue to concentrate on the long view—on economic development and its consequences over a time span of decades—as we seek to explain the effects of such a process upon agriculture. While certain comprehensive structural changes can be represented usefully as results of new and better production possibilities and of changes in choice, a somewhat narrower focus is required, and this can be achieved by considering the growth of the demand and supply of farm products. We shall discuss briefly three sets of shifts and relate each set to the kind of empirical situation to which it appears to apply and indicate the kind of resource adjustments that will be required.

The following restriction is assumed, namely, that no resources are transferred into or out of agriculture, for it is our purpose to determine whether a transfer of resources is necessary and, if so, to detect the direction of the required transfer. The amount of resource transfer is also important but exceedingly hard to ascertain with existing tools and information.

We need, also, to keep in mind that in these three sets of demand and supply shifts, we are not dealing with large and abrupt shifts of these schedules which sometimes cause large short-term movements in food and farm prices (this particular problem of price instability will be examined in Chaps. 11 and 20). Nor are we dealing, at this point, with per capita changes. The shifts are all expressed in terms of aggregates; changes in any of the subaggregates, including per capita relationships, are not specified. Accordingly, the amount of food consumed per capita may be low or high; it may be falling or rising; or no change may occur as a consequence of underlying developments. The distribution of food is also not specified and therefore it, too, may undergo changes. All that is indicated at this point is that if, for example, the aggregate demand and supply schedules were to shift to the right at the same rate, the two schedules would continue to intersect at the same point, measured in terms of relative prices, in a kind of moving equilibrium.

Let us consider three situations, one in which the demand and supply of farm products each shifts at about the same rate, another in which the shifts of the demand to the right press hard against the niggardliness of nature, and a third where the shifts of supply schedule of farm products to the right exceed that of the demand schedule.

Set I. Equal Rates of Shifts to the Right

Suppose that the conditions bringing about a shift of the demand schedule are independent from those that cause the supply schedule to shift and that no resources are transferred into or out of farming. For example, if during the course of a decade the demand schedule for farm products as a consequence, say, of a growth in population, were to move to the right so that the quantity taken increases 10 per cent at the former relative price, and if during this period the supply schedule were to shift to the right, say, as a result of technical improvements in farming, so that the amount produced also increases 10 per cent at the old relative price, since the conditions bringing about the shift of each are presumed to be independent of one another and since the rates of shift are the same and with other things equal, no adaptation or adjustment problems would arise as a consequence of these increases in demand and supply of farm products.

The capacity of the economy to coordinate agricultural production and consumption does not undergo test whenever, under the above assumptions, developments increase the supply of, and the demand for, farm products at the same rate. Under these circumstances, no "farm problem," consisting of too many resources committed to farming, will put in its appearance; nor will a "food problem" with too few resources employed in agriculture arise.

We do well to guard against any superficial inferences to the effect that equal rates of shift in the supply and demand schedules of food is necessarily a desirable situation. This type of development carries no assurance whatsoever that diets will be improved. Equal rates of shift could check and even block economic progress. The one inference that is permissible, as already indicated, is that this type of development places no burden upon the capacity of the economy to transfer resources into and out of agriculture necessary to achieve a new equilibrium, because such a development does not disturb this aspect of the old equilibrium.

Set II. Demand for Farm Products in the Forefront

Take, next, a situation in which the demand shifts farther to the right than does the supply and as a result the demand schedule intersects the supply at a higher relative price. A rise in farm product prices sets the stage for a transfer of resources into farming. Two cases belonging to this set will be considered briefly.

Case 1. There is the Ricardo-Malthus-Mill formulation of economic progress. John Stuart Mill stated the conditions underlying this case succinctly, as follows:[1]

> Agricultural skill and knowledge are of slow growth, and still slower diffusion. Inventions and discoveries, too, occur only occasionally, while the increase of population and capital are continuous agencies. It therefore seldom happens that improvement, even during a short time, has so much the start of population and capital as actually to lower rent, or raise the rate of profits. There are many countries in which the growth of population and capital is not rapid, but in these agricultural improvement is less active still. Population almost everywhere treads close on the heels of agricultural improvement, and effaces its effects as fast as they are produced. . . . Agricultural improvement may thus be considered to be not so much a counterforce conflicting with increase of population, as a partial relaxation of the bonds which confine that increase.[2]

[1] At the time of Malthus, the British population was doubling itself in a half century. The question that troubled Malthus was simply this: Could the island produce enough extra food to feed this rapidly multiplying population? J. R. Hicks, in commenting upon the difference of the fate of England and Ireland in avoiding a serious want of food, adds: "As the problem appeared to the Malthusians, shortage of agricultural land was an insuperable obstacle; when once the population of any country had reached the point where shortage of land becomes acute, the people would be bound to suffer from poverty, poverty which could only be remedied by the population becoming smaller." *The Social Framework* (New York: Oxford University Press, 1942), pp. 55–56.

The implications of the growth of the demand for food pressing hard against the "niggardliness of Nature" for rent payments, the cost of food, and economic progress are well-known contributions of the older economists.

[2] John Stuart Mill, *Principles of Political Economy*, W. J. Ashley, editor, Book IV, Chap. III, Sec. 5, pp. 721–722. Mill goes on to say (pp. 723–724): "The economical progress of a society constituted of landlords, capitalists, and labourers tends to the progressive enrichment of the landlord class; while the cost of the labourer's subsistence tends on the whole to increase, and profits to fall. Agricultural improvements are a counteracting force to the last two effects; but the first, though a case is conceivable in which it would be temporarily checked, is ultimately in a high degree promoted by those improvements; and the increase of population tends to transfer all the benefits derived from agricultural improvements to the landlords alone."

The classical approach to economic progress is based on two fundamental assumptions, one pertaining to the technical conditions underlying production where the quantity of agricultural land is fixed, and the other pertaining to the behavior of the population variable where increases in production are absorbed by a growth in population. Agricultural land, an exceedingly important factor, representing at that time at factor costs about one-fourth of the income of the community, was taken as fixed; as additional inputs of labor and capital were applied, the returns to these and for all inputs of the community (against agricultural land) resulted in diminishing returns. In this formulation whenever better production possibilities emerge and the aggregate income increases, the per capita income of the (working) population, although it rises temporarily, settles to its former level, to the level of subsistence. The outcome, therefore, is for per capita income to remain unchanged.[3] This conception, as has been observed, is based on two rates of change, namely, that of production anchored in diminishing returns against agricultural land and that of the behavior of the population variable. The older English economists considered various increases in production, but under their formulation, it did not matter whether production increased gradually or took a sudden spurt, because the extra population soon took up the slack. In its main outlines, this approach to economic development is extraordinarily simple in its choice of assumptions and, while it represents special circumstances, it is a most useful tool whenever conditions are such that the growth in population absorbs all increases in production to the point that per capita income tends to remain constant; under such circumstances, and they appear to exist in many parts of the world, it necessarily follows that the rate of increase in production becomes the limitational factor not only of aggregate income but also of the growth of the population.

The process of economic coordination which the older economists envisaged is still instructive despite the shortcoming of the wage-fund doctrine and of other aspects of their analysis. They reasoned essentially as follows:

1. Additional production—whether from better economic organization, advances in technology, improvement in skills, extension of markets, or the accumulation of productive resources—increases the supply of capital.
2. The fund available to pay wages becomes larger as a consequence.
3. This increases the demand for labor, and wages rise.

[3] The real income of the working population expressed in terms of food tended to remain constant; the income of landowners and of the elite supported by property in land rose, however.

4. Higher wages induce a growth in the population and this increases the demand for food.

5. In response to this increase in demand, the production of food is enlarged by drawing poorer land into cultivation and by transferring some (additional) capital and labor into agriculture with diminishing returns to the additional capital and labor inputs.

6. And in the process rents rise, profits fall, real wages return to their former level, and landowners acquire a larger share of the (national) income.

Case 2. The circumstances affecting the demand and supply of farm products in the United States at the time of World War II may be viewed as a special case under this set. Take the period, for example, from about 1938 to 1948 when increases in the demand for food came to press hard against the available supply. Within the United States, from 1938 to the first quarter of 1948, wholesale prices of farm products rose about 50 per cent more than did the prices of products other than food. The old parity ratio of prices received and prices paid by farmers jumped from 77 in 1938 to 116 during the first three months of 1948. Food, as a consequence, became dear relative to manufactures and this placed a substantial burden upon most industrial-urban populations. This development, however, acted as a powerful inducement to expand agricultural production, and in the United States where the combination of new techniques and other resources were highly favorable, a very marked increase in output took place.

SET III. SUPPLY OF FARM PRODUCTS OUT AHEAD

The conditions underlying this set require a movement of the supply schedule to the right at a rate that exceeds the shift of the demand schedule in the same direction. A fall in farm product prices sets the stage, other things remaining equal, for a transfer of resources out of farming.

When this development occurs, a *farm problem* is likely to arise. Farm products become plentiful and relatively cheap, and land values and rent payments fall. The economic organization is faced with a transfer problem, that is, the task of moving some of the existing supply of resources out of agriculture.[4]

[4] John Stuart Mill, in the original text (1848) of the *Principles of Political Economy,* anticipated the possibility of the food supply gaining on the demand when he wrote, "[Agriculture] . . . so far as present foresight can extend, does not seem to be susceptible to improved processes to so great a degree as some branches of manufacture; but inventions may be in reserve for the

It is this set that has characterized the United States. It is a far cry from the hungry mouths wanting food and the niggardliness of nature which brought forth Malthus's gloomy predictions. It would be useful to trace economic history through the century and a half since Malthus wrote to discover what has happened that has so profoundly changed the Western outlook. The import of the change, however, has not gone unnoticed.[5] In Chap. 8 we shall examine the declining economic importance of agricultural land in this context.

The fundamental developments responsible for this set are (1) a slackening in the rate of increase of the population, (2) the relatively low income elasticity of farm products as people become richer, and (3) the large advances in techniques used in agricultural production.

These developments are to be viewed as secular changes; they do not occur abruptly but make themselves felt over the years; they occur not only in the economy of the United States but in the economy of some other countries as well. They may be hidden temporarily by mobilization and the waging of war and by major recoveries following a period of many unemployed resources. In the United States these developments, however, clearly had their head already prior to World War I; they moved on ahead persistently during the interwar years; and they are again in evidence as the fifties begin to unfold; and they are likely to continue to act as fundamental forces shaping the food and farm sectors of the economy.

---

future which may invert this relation." (Book IV, Chap. II.) This passage unfortunately was omitted in the fifth edition (1862) at the very time when important advances were being made in agricultural technology.

[5] We shall note only a few works on this subject: Alva Myrdal, *Family and Nation* (New York: Harper & Brothers, 1942); Alvin H. Hansen, "Economic Progress and Declining Population Growth," *The American Economic Review*, Vol. XXIX (1939); Joseph S. Davis, "The Specter of Dearth of Food: History's Answer to Sir William Crookes," *On Agricultural Policy, 1926–1938* (Stanford: Stanford University Press, 1939); Edwin Cannan, "The Need for Simpler Economics," *Economic Journal*, Vol. XLIII (1933).

3

FOCAL POINTS AND CONDITIONS AFFECTING
LONG-TERM SHIFTS OF THE DEMAND

Food at retail and farm food products at the farm are like the two end links in a long chain. The demand makes itself felt from the food end and it is transmitted from one link to the next until it reaches the farm product. We shall, therefore, first consider certain points and stages along this chain from consumers to farm production in gauging the demand for farm products. We shall then restate the circumstances that explain why it is that the long-term shifts of the demand for farm products to the right are slowing down and illustrate the effects of changes in population and income.

FOCAL POINTS OF DEMAND FOR FARM PRODUCTS

In a highly developed economy with long production processes, with much specialization in production, and where the final product is the result of many producers each adding some service to the product as is the case in the United States generally in food and in other consumer goods made from farm products, the demand for farm products can be taken at a number of different points and stages in the process from the farm to the ultimate consumer. The following points and stages may be observed:

Agricultural Products at the Point of Production

By definition this is the first stage in the process, for to go back of it is to become involved in the demand for specific factors or resources committed and combined with other resources in farming. Since we are endeavoring to get some notion of the changes in demand for farm products resulting from economic development in order to determine the implications of such changes for resource utilization within agriculture, this is the crucial focal point of our demand analysis throughout Part One. Even so, we are confronted by several points falling within this stage because of the nature of agricultural production. Various statistical series have been developed by the Bureau of Agricultural Economics in an attempt to reflect different points within this production stage. The following are important:[1]

1. *Gross Farm Production.* This is a measure of the total product realized during a year from all agricultural resources. It includes both the products that go eventually into human use, whether sold or carried forward on farms, and those products that are used as producer goods in farming. It measures, therefore, the total product of all land, other capital and labor resources employed in agriculture each year, including total crop production, pasture consumed by all livestock, and products added in the conversion of feed and pasture into livestock and livestock products for human use and into farm-produced power of horses and mules.

2. *Farm Output.* This concept is intended to measure the volume of agricultural production available for *eventual* human use through sales from farms or consumption in farm households. It does not include products used as producer goods in farming. It does include, however, products entering into inventories held on farms. The Bureau of Agricultural Economics calculates its index of *farm output* by subtracting from the quantity-price aggregate of gross production the quantity-price aggregate of farm-produced power (feed and pasture consumed by horses and mules plus the product added in converting this feed and pasture into animal power).

3. *Agricultural Production for Sale and for Farm Consumption.* This concept of production is intended to measure the *current* volume of farm products consisting of that part which enters into the marketing system and also that part which is used for human consumption on the farms where grown. In the long run (2) and (3) above are measures of the same things, that is, output of farm products for human use. But there are some yearly differences between them primarily because of year-to-year changes in farm inventories.

Agricultural Production for Sale. A simplified way of expressing this concept is as follows: agricultural production for sale and consumption [(3) above] minus consumption of home-produced products

---

[1] *Farm Production, Practices, Costs and Returns*, BAE, Statis. Bul. 83, October, 1949, Table 1, pp. 6–7. A more detailed explanation is provided in *Farm Production in War and Peace* by Glen T. Barton and Martin R. Cooper, BAE, 53, December, 1945, pp. 3–4 and 55–71 for methods.

used in farm households equals agricultural production for sale. Throughout Part One we shall neglect the income and price elasticities of the demand of farm people for the products they produce. Later in this study, when we come to consider certain short-run problems of supply, we shall attach considerable importance to these in relation to producers' supply. Suffice it to say that it appears that in the United States at this stage of its economic development, for farm people the income elasticity for home-produced farm products is not only low but may in fact be negative, that is, such products may have become for them inferior goods.

Agricultural Commodities at Wholesale. This stage can be formulated variously, depending upon the purpose of the analysis. If we assume that these commodities at this point have not been processed but are in their original form physically (except for location and the way they are grouped) and if our purpose is to examine the changes in demand for such services as interest and the carrying of risk and uncertainty when commodities are carried forward, the following concept is implied: Agricultural production marketed plus the value of the services added involving interest and the bearing of risk and uncertainty from the time of farm sales equals agricultural commodities at wholesale. Some of the most difficult problems in price analysis arise at this point in dealing with risk and especially with uncertainty considerations.

Food and Other Farm Products at Point of Consumption. As already indicated, agricultural production for sale excludes the consumption of home-produced farm products within farm households. Let us assume that every farm product sold by farmers has added to it some nonfarm services (resources) before it is consumed. The demand for this final product may, therefore, be viewed as consisting of two parts: the demand for the *services* that are the result of agricultural production and the demand for the *services* that are added after the product is sold by farmers. The following classification of combinations of these two types of services may be helpful:

1. Farm products with services added for which the income elasticity is less than it is for the services originating in agricultural production. Given this combination, an increase in incomes, with other things equal, results in a larger share of consumers' expenditures going to farmers. It is our belief that there are few, if any, farm products that fall into this class.

2. Farm products with services added which have for consumers an income elasticity that is the same as that for the services supplied by agriculture. Here the margins between farmers and consumers would not change over time as a result of the demand effects of increases in income, *ceteris paribus*.

3. Farm products with services added which have for consumers an income elasticity that is higher than that for the services produced by agriculture. Most farm products appear to fall into this class. An important implication of this combination is that as incomes rise the demand for the services added by nonagricultural producers increases relative to the demand for services of agriculture, and as a consequence, with other things unchanged, a diminishing share of consumers' expenditures is spent for the services produced by farmers.

CONDITIONS AFFECTING LONG-TERM SHIFTS OF THE DEMAND

Why is it that the demand for farm products in a relatively rich, technically advanced country like the United States does not shift rapidly to the right over the years as a consequence of economic development? The slowing down of the rate of increase is the consequence of changes in the fundamental conditions determining this demand. The chapters that follow examining the underlying conditions affecting the demand of farm products are based on the following empirical propositions:[2]

1. The growth in population is occurring at a diminishing rate although the early postwar period gave rise to a substantial upsurge.

2. The increase in income that comes with economic development is subject, in the case of farm products, to a relatively low income elasticity.

3. The additional demand to be had from better nutrition within the United States, while important on welfare grounds, is small in the aggregate.

Accordingly, if these propositions about our particular economic development and related social action are valid and if it is permissible to leave changes in taste and preferences aside in the belief that they tend to cancel out among the several foods, it follows from these changes in basic conditions determining the demand for farm products that it is subject (1) to a slow rate of increase and (2) to a diminishing rate of increase at this stage of economic development including social action to improve nutrition.

Before we turn to the data on population, income, and nutrition, we need to restate the purpose of this part of our study. Ours is the long view and our task is to explain the changes in demand and then to gauge at least roughly the claims that these changes in demand make upon agricultural resources and their utilization.

Up to this point, for the most part, we have taken food to represent

---

[2] These propositions do not, however, exhaust the conditions affecting demand over time.

the production of agriculture. This procedure has made it possible to maintain a link with the work of the older economists. Since our purpose, however, is to anticipate the changes that are likely to occur (say, during the next several decades) in the claims that the economy as a whole is likely to make on agricultural resources, it is necessary to shift to a more comprehensive formulation. The concept of food excludes a number of important commodities produced by agriculture; moreover, food usually refers to products and services at the point of consumption rather than to farm products at the point at which they leave agriculture. Obviously, agriculture supplies a number of major products, such as cotton, wool, jute, some wood products, and tobacco which are used as industrial raw materials and to satisfy wants other than food. Some feed is used to produce "animal power." Also, it is obvious that at the point at which food is purchased by consumers many nonfarm services have been added to the food (after it has left the farm). These nonfarm services are the result of inputs other than land, labor, and capital in agriculture. These nonfarm services probably do not create any additional demand for farm products as a whole. They do not represent claims on agricultural resources. Accordingly, we shall use the term "farm products" as including all agricultural products whether of crop or livestock origin, whether ultimately used for food or for nonfood purposes. "Farm products," as used in this study, are the products as and when they are sold by farmers. Thus defined, they give us a critical focal point in the pricing process at which the demand interacting with the supply makes its claim for the allocation of resources in agriculture. When we refer to food, it will be in the conventional context, namely, to goods and services used as food by consumers at the point when they are taken over by consumers.

It may be helpful to illustrate the importance of changes in population and income to the demand for farm products.

Situation 1. Suppose we take a decade during which the population were to increase 20 per cent (as it did fully no longer ago than 1900 to 1910) and during which the income per capita were to rise 25 per cent with the income elasticity for farm products at .75. Under these conditions, other things remaining unchanged, the demand for farm products will increase 42.5 per cent.

In this example, the growth in population and the income elasticity for food are characteristic of an early period in the development of this country, applicable perhaps to about the turn of the century. Under these circumstances, the increase in demand during the course of a single decade would be remarkably large, in fact even larger than the increase in agricultural production achieved in the United States during the forties. Let us now, however, take another situation and introduce conditions approximating population and income developments that appear to have occurred from 1940 to 1950.

Situation 2. Suppose that during the decade, the population were to grow 14 per cent (as it did from 1940 to 1950) and the income per capita were to increase about 33 per cent (as it did) with the income elasticity for farm products at .25.[3] Under these conditions, and again to simplify, with other things unchanged, the demand for farm products may be taken to have increased about 23.4 per cent.[4]

The very large shift of the demand schedule to the right, indicated in Situation 1, represents the outcome of a rapid growth in population and of a large rise in per capita income with the income elasticity of farm products relatively high. In Situation 2, the outcome represents a substantial growth in population (14 instead of 20 per cent but not the low

[3] If the income elasticity of farm products were as high as .5, the additional demand from the 33 per cent increase in income may be taken to have been about 18.8 per cent in the example above, and this plus the 14 per cent increase on the account of population would have given a total expansion of about 32.8 per cent. This makes evident the critical importance of the particular conditions affecting the income elasticity of farm products.

[4] The population in 1940 is taken at 131.8 million with a civilian population of 131.4 million compared to 151.1 million and 149.6 million, respectively, for 1950. Income per capita is taken at $1,075 in 1940 and $1,436 in 1950 in terms of prices during the first half of 1951. Accordingly, we have an increase in the civilian population of 13.85 per cent (rounded to 14 above) and an increase in income of 33 per cent. With an average income elasticity of .25 over the entire increase in income assumed, we have .25 × .33 × 114 = 9.4 per cent increase in demand arising from the increase in per capita income. Adding the 14 per cent for population and 9.4 per cent for income, we have an increase of 23.4 per cent. Total civilian utilization of food, however, only increased from 107.4 (index with 1935–1939 = 100) in 1940 to an index of 129.0 in 1950; this represents an increase of 20.1 or 3.3 less than that indicated by adding population and the demand effects of the rise in income with the income elasticity specified. It may be noted, also, that food production rose from 111 (1935–1939 = 100) in 1940 to 140 in 1950, an increase of 26.1 per cent. The difference between the increase in production (26.1 per cent) and that in food utilization by civilians (20.1 per cent) represents increases in commercial exports and in shipments abroad, food acquired by the military for the armed services and for civilian feeding and change in stocks. The differences between the 23.4 per cent increase indicated for the population growth plus that ascribed to the income rise and the 20.1 per cent increase in civilian utilization that occurred may be represented as the substitution effects of the marked increase in food prices relative to other consumer items.

increase of 7 per cent from 1930 to 1940) and a very large increase in per capita income (a record rise) but with the income elasticity relatively low. The very large relative rise in food production during the forties is small in relation to the demand shift represented in the first situation and large in relation to the second.

NOTE : SOME PITFALLS IN ASCERTAINING SHIFTS IN DEMAND FOR FARM PRODUCTS

A number of difficult problems present themselves when one endeavors to gauge shifts in demand that occur over time. Some of these problems are conceptual and others pertain to measurement. The demand schedule of a particular community for a particular product shows the quantity of the product that will be purchased by the community per unit of time at each price.[5] In comparing two demand schedules, separate in time (one for the recent past and the other for the more distant past), we may leave the elasticities of the demand schedules aside, provided the quantity taken by the group under each of the two sets of circumstances was purchased at the same relative price. Under these simplified conditions, the two points, one on each of the demand schedules, can be compared directly. However, even under this simplified approach, it is necessary to identify and measure the price and the product. Each of these tasks is exceedingly difficult in practice. Take first the product.

Farm products consist of a vast bundle of items, constantly changing in composition. As time goes on, some old products disappear and some new products put in their appearance. It would be rare indeed to find even a single product that did not undergo some change in its intrinsic properties during the course of a few decades under the impact of modern technological advances. We are inclined to speak of wheat, corn, cotton, and other agricultural commodities as if they remained unchanged and we think of them as being highly standardized (as specified in some futures contracts, for example) but this standardization is at best a conceptual and contractual achievement. It is not, however, to be confused with the properties of the product that is produced and offered for sale by farmers. The pig of today is a different model from the pig of thirty years ago; and so it goes for other farm products because of the changes that have come from better breeding, feeding, and other modifications in farming. Mere number of pounds or bushels do not tell us how much the composition of the product entering into these pounds or

[5] See Milton Friedman, "The Marshallian Demand Curve," *Journal of Political Economy*, Vol. LVII, No. 6 (1949), on alternative formulations and uses of the demand concept.

bushels has changed. On this point a brief reference to food is instructive. Total food consumption per capita measured in terms of its physical weight at retail has remained remarkably constant as the following data indicate:

Year	Retail weight in pounds equivalent
1909	1,576
1949	1,573

SOURCE: *Consumption of Food in the United States, 1909–48*, BAE, *Misc. Pub.* 691, August, 1949, Table 38, p. 120, as it was revised in the *Supplement to Consumption of Food in the United States, 1909–48*, September, 1950.

But the composition, as one would expect, has changed significantly (see Table 5–2, page 46, for this change).

A vast literature has accumulated on ways and means of constructing indexes for identifying and measuring the quanitity of farm products produced and consumed and a good deal has been achieved. Because of this work, one is spared many pitfalls and need not wander about aimlessly looking for clues. Nevertheless, we need constantly to be on guard because many imperfections still remain in the data and in any index, some of which are inherent in the underlying conditions and cannot be removed by any mode of measurement which entails aggregation.

A similar set of observations is in order with regard to the prices of farm products. Prices reported currently by the U.S. Department of Agriculture are undoubtedly more representative and accurate than are those available for earlier periods. But this is not the only difficulty: the prices reported from time to time are for quite different stages and points in the production process. The markets registering these prices vary from time to time in the kind and the extent of the "imperfections" affecting the pattern of prices in one direction or another. The experiences with gray markets during World War II made us keenly aware of some of these difficulties. Government subsidies and the effects of various farm programs shape and alter these prices in many ways, and the pitfalls, therefore, become many and serious when we try to estimate and interpret a farm product price. Here, too, the difficulties of weights in constructing an index cannot be fully resolved; they will always be with us.

NOTE : SHIFTS IN DEMAND OF SELECTED FARM COMMODITIES 1875 TO 1929

The exhaustive study of Henry Schultz, *The Theory and Measurement of Demand*, provides estimates of the elasticity and the shifts of the demand of a number of farm commodities. We are here concerned with the positive or negative shifts. These estimates show that the demand for cotton, for example, shifted to the right at a rate of 1.64 per cent per year on a per capita basis during 1875 to 1895 but shifted to the left, namely, at a —.75 per cent per year from 1915 to 1929. When adjusted for population changes, the demand for cotton grew 5.6 times as rapidly during the first of these periods as it did in the second period, increasing at the rapid rate of 3.87 per cent per year during 1875 to 1895 and at only .69 per cent per year during 1915 to 1929. Other major commodities appeared to have experienced similar marked declines in the rate at which the demand increased. Of the major commodities, corn suffered a complete reversal. Taking the per capita shift and the rate of increase in population, we find that the demand for corn shifted to the right at the strong rate of 2.55 per cent per year during 1875 to 1895, and then, despite an average annual increase in population of 1.44 per cent, during 1915–1929, the demand moved to the left at a yearly rate of —.69 per cent.

Product	1875–1895		1896–1914		1915–1929	
	Per capita	Population increase adj. added	Per capita	Population increase adj. added	Per capita	Population increase adj. added
Wheat[a] . . .	0.52	2.75 (1880–1895)	−0.76	1.01	−0.21[a] −0.50	1.23 (1921–1929) 0.59 (1921–1934)
Cotton . . .	1.64	3.87	1.40	3.17	−0.75	0.69
Corn . . .	0.32[a]	2.55	1.40	3.17	−2.13	−0.69
Sugar . . .	1.56	3.79	1.24	3.01	0	1.44
Potatoes . .	0.57	2.80	1.63	3.40	−0.15[a]	1.29
Barley . . .	2.13	4.36	3.28	5.05	−0.69 2.00	0.75 3.44 (1922–1929)
Rye	0	2.23	1.63	3.40	−7.66 6.26	−6.22 7.70 (1922–1929)
Buckwheat . .	−0.62	1.61	0	1.77	−3.20	−1.76

[a] Not statistically significant.

SOURCE: Henry Schultz, *The Theory and Measurement of Demand* (Chicago: University of Chicago Press, 1938).

4

POPULATION STILL UNCOILING

A few years ago, the economist might have begrudged the demographer his sureness as he plotted his population curves, but this is no longer the case. Received projections of population growth were rudely upset by what happened in the forties. The demographers are however, far from certain what interpretation to place on the recent upturn in population. It is hard to tell whether it is wholly real or partly apparent because not enough time has elapsed to determine how much of this recent growth represents a "borrowing" from future increases that were expected and how much is additional for the long pull. But not all of those who have come to criticize the demographers have been beset by such doubts.

Professor J. S. Davis, looking in on the demographers, ascribing to them an undue reluctance to admit their "errors," and not having their doubts as to the meaning of the new population data, has undertaken the task of awakening the nation to the significance of "America's tremendous population upsurge," which necessitates, so Davis contends, "a radical revision of prevalent views of our national growth and a reorientation of our economic thinking."[1] Although any ultimate test of Davis' "optimistic" population projection must wait on future developments, the historian looking back on the recent population increase in the United States is not likely to view it as "tremendous" or as requiring a "radical revision," for instance, of the relation of the demand and supply of food. The production of food expanded a strong 26 per cent from 1940 to 1950 whereas the population increased 14.4 per cent during that period.[2] The

[1] These quotations were drawn from a paper *Agriculture and the New Population Outlook* which Professor Davis gave before the National Agricultural Credit Association, Chicago, Illinois, Jan. 30, 1950; for a careful marshaling of his data, see *The Population Upsurge in the United States*, Food Research Institute, Stanford University, *War-Peace Pamphlet* No. 12 (Stanford) December, 1949.

[2] These crude data do not, of course, measure changes in demand and supply. Relative prices moved substantially in favor of farm products during this period and these changes in prices played an important part in the expansion in output.

demand effects of the marked rise in per capita income will be considered further in subsequent chapters.

RELEVANT POPULATION AND FOOD AGGREGATES

A population aggregate may be constructed for the purpose of determining one of many relations.[3] We are here concerned about the relation between food and population. The literature on this subject abounds with confusion, most of which is traceable to a failure to specify the structural conditions which determine the relation between food and population. The plethora of pamphlets raising the population scare following both World War I and II were fallacious because they related the food supply of the United States to the population of the world as a whole. Under "normal" conditions (leaving aside gifts of food and barring conquest), the populations of most of the world have no relevancy whatsoever to the demand and supply of food in the United States. For example, there is virtually no connection having any economic import between the population of India and the food of the United States except under emergency circumstances. In fact, in many countries, the population in one part of that country is normally completely separated from the food in other parts. This separation of one population from the food of another is a fundamental consideration in selecting and constructing relevant aggregates. Where a particular population and a particular "supply" of food are related, they are parts of the same economy. It is necessary, therefore, as a first step to make sure that the population under consideration is related to the particular food supply being studied.

The next step is to examine the characteristics of the relation between a population and the food on which it depends. There are two basic sets of relations: The first of these exists under conditions where the changes in the population can be explained, at least in large part, as a (within) variable dependent upon the (food) economy, that is, the population behaves like an endogenous variable of the economic system. The second set exists where the changes in population are determined by circumstances that appear to be outside the economic system; in this case the population behaves like an exogenous variable,

---

[3] The relation of population and manpower for military purposes is one; population and education is another; food and population is only one relation out of many that may be formulated and studied. See, John D. Black, "Coming Readjustments in Agriculture—Domestic Phase," *Journal of Farm Economics,* Vol. XXXI (February, 1949), for a penetrating discussion of relating a given population to the appropriate food supply.

although it does, of course, affect the economy in many ways, including the demand and supply of food.

Before we take up in somewhat more detail the determining conditions and the main variants of each of these two sets, it may be appropriate to suggest that the term "pre-industrial" frequently applied to certain populations is not a happy one. In the first place, it implies a counterpart, that is, an advanced industrial class including presumably all high per capita income populations, and this is quite misleading because a particular population can achieve a high ratio of outputs for its inputs of human effort without being strictly industrial. In the second place, it focuses attention on a vague institutional characteristic of a particular economy that cannot be readily classified into a meaningful series of gradations. There are a number of attributes that are more important and useful in this connection than that of "industrial" per se; among them is the ratio of output per man and closely related is the real per capita income of a population. More specific to the problem at hand and especially in light of the history of ideas associated with Malthus is the ratio of income spent for food by a particular population. We are inclined, therefore, to classify populations in accordance with the drain that food places upon their economies. Populations subject to a high food drain are those where a large proportion of the income is used for food. Following this lead, it will be convenient to classify populations along these lines.

High Food Drain (Type I). This type is taken to mean a situation where 75 per cent or more of the income of a population is normally used to acquire food. This is basically the situation covered by the Ricardo-Malthus-Mill formulation and sometimes referred to by students of population as the pre-industrial demographic class.

Intermediate Food Drain (Type II). This type may be taken to include those situations where less than 75 and more than 25 per cent of the income of a population is spent for farm products used as food (the focus here is upon the food services produced by farmers leaving aside those services that are added to food by other producers by the time the food reaches the consumer at retail). Here we have, for all practical purposes, the so-called transitional demographic class.

Low Food Drain (Type III). This type consists of those communities where 25 per cent or less of the income of consumers is spent on the farm-produced services that go to make up the food that is consumed. This is the demographers "incipient decline" or "advanced industrial" demographic class. The drain of food on income is so low and the dependence of the population variable on food so tenuous that the changes in population become essentially independent, and we shall, accordingly, treat the population in this situation as an exogenous variable.

THE POPULATION VARIABLE IN RELATION TO THE FOOD ECONOMY

The above classification is useful because it simplifies the task of organizing and interpreting a variety of data. Sight should not be lost of the fact, however, that it is the ratio of income spent for food to the growth characteristics of the population which is important and that this relation does not change abruptly in going from one set of circumstances to the next; instead the change is gradual and therefore small changes can be analyzed. The class intervals are intended to accomplish the following: where the population variable becomes "independent" of food, that is, acts like a variable *outside* of the (food) economy, it is conceived of as belonging in Type III; where its behavior makes it necessary to treat it as a variable *within* the economic system (restricted to the food sector of the economy), this classification places it in Types I and II. The distinction between Types I and II will be clarified below.

Population as a Within Variable. It is undoubtedly true that for most of the people of the world the growth of the population is still largely dependent upon food. Other variables in the economy, except as they affect the availability of food, are less important in this connection. These basic conditions continue to give the simple formulation of the relation of population growth and economic progress of Ricardo-Malthus-Mill wide applicability and usefulness although it cannot explain the situation which exists where people enjoy a high ratio of output per unit of input of human effort.

We shall throughout identify the *high food drain*, Type I, with the Ricardo-Malthus-Mill model. Type I is based on the following conditions: (1) a population with a level of income so low that a critically large proportion of the income is required for food (our hyphothesis is that when a population devotes as a matter of normal routine 75 per cent or more of its income for food, it is at this critical point) and (2) a population with established and stable cultural values determining and perpetuating this (low) level of living. There is implicit in these conditions the following behavior assumption: the cultural values determining the level of living are essentially stable and either or both the birth and death rates are flexible, and as a consequence, changes in these rates maintain an equilibrium between population and food, the population staying at a maximum consistent with the particular level of living and the particular food supply. Empirically, one observes that under these conditions the birth and death rates are normally very high (40 per thousand and higher) and that it is the flexibility of the death rate that is primarily responsible for maintaining the balance between population and food. From these restricted conditions, it follows that both the level and the stability of the population are dependent upon the level and the fluctuations in the food available to the particular population. At this point, one may distinguish among several variants of this high-food-drain type.

Type IA. Level and rate of food production constant; as a consequence, no change in population (a stationary equilibrium with regard to food and population).

Type IB. Gradual rise in the level of food production with the rate of output not fluctuating; gradual growth in the population equal to the rise in food production.

Type IC. The converse of Type IB (the consequences of a gradual fall in food production).

Type ID. The level of food output fluctuating with no change in the long-run level; the result is fluctuations in the size of the population but with no upward or downward drift. The effects of bad crops and the resulting famines and of periods of bumper crops and an upsurge in numbers of people fall under this subtype.

We shall now consider briefly the underlying conditions of the *intermediate-food-drain* structure. As already indicated, Type II also belongs to the set where the population is a variable *within* the economic system but it differs from Type I in that the dependency of the population on food is diminished; it diminishes as the proportion of the income required for food declines. It is our tentative hypothesis that Type II is normal for populations that "spend" somewhere between 75 and 25 per cent of their income for the farm-produced services of food, and as the lower limit of this range is approached, the population becomes an *outside* (exogenous) variable. In order to make the transition from Type I to Type II, it is necessary to modify one of the conditions outlined for Type I. The cultural values determining the level of living must be treated as a variable over time; the level of living rises gradually in response to larger aggregate production and thus sets the stage for a rise in per capita income; otherwise, all the gains in production would be reflected in population growth at some constant level of per capita income. Type II is required to explain the transitional demographic class of populations which characteristically start from high birth and death rates, and as economic (food) circumstances improve, there occurs a gradual rise in the level of living although at the outset most of the gains in output are absorbed by increases in population resulting from the fact that the death rate during the early stages declines more than does the birth rate.

Population as an Outside Variable. Clearly as the level of living rises and as the proportion of income spent for the farm-produced services in food falls, there comes a point where changes in the population cannot be explained by what happens in the agricultural sector of the economy. It is, of course, possible to redefine the economic component to include not only food but also the many additional expenditures such as medical care, education, and travel involved in rearing children and savings to be transferred to them and in so doing find that the proportion of the income spent for these purposes is of some use in "explaining" population growth.[4]

It is not our purpose in this chapter to outline a theory explaining the population variable under conditions where the income spent on food is so small that this expenditure by itself is no longer a factor in accounting for changes in population. It is our hypothesis that as a population reaches the stage where it spends 25 per cent or less of its income for the farm-produced services in food, it becomes an outside variable, that is, independent of the agricultural sector of the economy. Changes in population do, of course, affect the demand and supply of farm products but variations in the population are not dependent upon the economic circumstance surrounding the production of food. The United States and probably most countries of western Europe, once they recover from the worst effects of the war, appear to belong in this *low-food-drain type.*

Some Demand Effects of Types I and II. The growth attributes of the demand for food differ importantly from one type to another. In the case of Type I, there is no purpose in considering the income elasticity of food because under the conditions set forth, per capita income remains constant, and accordingly, other things remaining equal, there can be

[4] This approach can be pushed so far that the two become an identity which would simply tell us that per capita expenditures required to attain a given level of living (including savings to be accumulated) is equal to per capita income and the aggregate income divided by the per capita expenditures gives us the size of the population. Such statements are identities and in themselves are, of course, quite meaningless in explaining behavior. We shall later advance an hypothesis to explain why the birth rate has fallen less rapidly in some communities than in others during the same or similar stages of economic development by introducing a preference for property (wealth) and for children (including marriage) having particular substitution rates and relate this preference to the variations in (property) possibilities.

no increase in the per capita demand for food. Any increase in aggregate income is transformed into an equivalent increase in population by the social behavior[5] implicit in this type and, therefore, one need only ascertain the rate of growth of the population to determine the rate at which the demand for food is increasing. The causality, however, runs the other way, which means the increase in the supply of food comes first and the growth of the population occurs as a result.[6] One additional characteristic of the demand of Type I should be noted. A large part of any increase in aggregate demand is for food, simply as a consequence of the fact that the population uses 75 per cent or more of its income, and of any increase in aggregate income, to acquire food.

Very little of the demand for the farm products of the United States, especially for food, originates in populations falling into Type I. These populations and their demands are for all practical purposes separated from the supply of food of this country. By means of gifts and grants, some United States food is at times transferred to them in response to emergency situations. The exceptions are few, and where they exist, the economic linkage is fairly simple. To illustrate, the jute-growing population of Bengal may be viewed as belonging in Type I. Jute is exported in exchange mainly for rice; this demand for rice affects the demand for rice grown in this country. But any increase in the demand for rice on the part of the jute-growing population of Bengal depends upon their acquiring more income from the production of jute. Cheaper rice relative to the price of jute will, of course, improve their income position and presumably result in a commensurate growth in population. But, with other things equal, the quantity of rice that this population will take at a particular price will not increase unless, with the resources at its disposal, it can produce and sell more jute. To increase the production

[5] Two criticisms may be leveled against this behavior assumption: (1) The constant level of living presupposition results in an identity between the per capita expenditures for food and some given proportion of the per capita income when no variations are allowed for in the proportion of the income that is used for food and (2) no explanation is provided for variations in the income spent for food, say, between 75 per cent and some higher figure for this kind of outlay.

[6] There are here some interesting supply effects that depend upon the way in which economic progress occurs. For instance, if the increase in income were to originate from gains in output achieved in the nonfarm sector, it would be necessary to transfer some resources into agriculture to increase the production of food. The classical concept of economic progress, for example, as set forth in Book IV of the *Principles of Political Economy* by John Stuart Mill, envisages this kind of process.

possibilities, in this case of jute, is a process that normally occurs slowly, especially where there are no additional natural resources to be exploited. Circumstances as of the middle of the twentieth century indicate that an unimportant part of any increase in the demand for United States farm products is likely to originate in Type I food-population structures during the next decade or two.

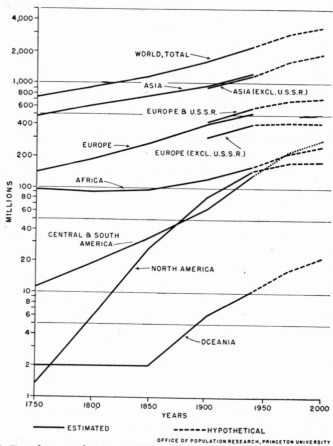

FIG. 4–1. Populations of major world areas, estimated 1750–1940 and projected.

In Type II, the increase in the demand for food consists of two parts, namely, that related to the growth in population which may occur at a rapid rate and that related to the rise in per capita income. We now need to know not only the rate of population growth, but, in addition, the rate of increase in per capita income and the income elasticity of food. It may be observed that during the early stages of this type the income elasticity of food is very high, approaching 1.0, and therefore the possibilities of the demand for food increasing are large both from the side of population and from that of per capita income as the income of the community rises.

It is far from easy to assess the prospects of Type II communities increasing the demand for United States farm products. Theoretically, it can occur and empirically it has done so. Countries of western Europe including the United Kingdom, during the time they were in Type II, drew heavily upon United States farm products for their food requirements. Countries in the early stages of industrialization may achieve a comparative advantage in making textiles and other fairly simple labor-absorbing industrial products to be exported for food. Japan would appear to be in this situation given her combination of agricultural and industrial resources and labor skills and the population growth that is underway.

It may be argued, for example, that because of recent advances in technology in growing wheat in the United States, this country has regained a substantial comparative advantage in this product in international trade, and meanwhile not only Japan but also Brazil and India as they enter upon industrialization may find it to their advantage to import food (some wheat) in exchange for certain manufactured products, thus creating a market and some additional demand for United States wheat. But the main stream of demand effects appears to flow in another channel. In the first place, most countries currently in Type II seem to find it necessary to draw primarily upon their own food-producing resources to satisfy increases in their demand for food. And second, as countries in Type II achieve an export surplus or acquire capital abroad, they appear to demand, in the first instances, mainly industrial equipment which is obtained from countries having a Type III food-population structure, where the population growth is basically independent of the (food) economy and where the income elasticity of food is already quite low.

Population Growth and United States Agriculture. In the preceding sections we have endeavored to explain the relation of food and population, and in doing so, we found that the demand for United States farm products is related primarily to Type III communities where the population variable is essentially independent of the (food) economy. There are, however, other important relationships, one of which arises out of the fact that rural communities have higher reproduction rates than do the urban areas, and closely related, there are the supply implications of this differential in reproduction for agricultural production and its adjustment to economic development.

The aggregate growth of the relevant population is fairly easy to describe, although some differences of opinion might exist in explaining the recent upturn. It certainly is true that the nightmare of overpopulation that oppressed Malthus and his contemporaries no longer troubles our minds, except as we look abroad and note the course of developments within Type I and II structures. The rate of population growth in the United States dropped rapidly from 1870 to 1920.

| | Per cent increase in United States |
Decade	population
1870–1880	26.0
1880–1890	25.5
1890–1900	20.7
1900–1910	21.0
1910–1920	14.9
1920–1930	16.1
1930–1940	7.2
1940–1950	14.4

SOURCE: *The Problem of a Changing Population*, National Resources Committee (Washington, D.C.), May, 1928, Table 1, p. 21, and *Statistical Abstract of the United States, 1942*, U.S. Department of Commerce, p. 5. The 1940–1950 datum is from *Current Population Reports*, Bureau of the Census, 1950.

Leaving the recent upturn in population aside for the moment, it is of interest to recall the anticipated increases in population as demographers interpreted the population experiences up to World War II. In the case of Europe, the following estimates were advanced:

	Per cent increase, 1950–1960
Europe (exclusive of USSR)[a]	1.4
USSR[a]	12.3

[a] Frank W. Notestein, Irene B. Taeuber, Dudley Kirk, Ansley J. Coale, and Louise K. Kiser in *The Future Population of Europe and the Soviet Union*, League of Nations Publication (New York), 1944, show that the population of Europe (exclusive of the USSR) in 1939 was 399 million and that the projected population for 1950 is estimated at 415 million, an increase of 4 per cent; and for 1960, at 421 million, an increase for the decade 1950–1960 of 1.4 per cent (Table 1, p. 45). The projected population for the USSR rises from 174 million in 1940 to 203 million by 1950 and to 228 million by 1960 (Table 2, p. 56). For estimates of population for the year 2000, see Notestein's paper, "Population—the Long View," *Food for the World*, edited by Theodore W. Schultz.

The population of Europe, however, experienced a new impulse to grow in the early postwar years, enough so to indicate that it will be necessary to revise upward the above estimate of 1.4 per cent for the decade of the fifties. When we take the recent increases in population of 15 western European countries, the total population rose 6 per cent

TABLE 4–1. GROWTH IN POPULATION IN FIFTEEN COUNTRIES IN WESTERN EUROPE
(Population in millions)

Country	1939	1949	
Austria	6.6	7.1	
Belgium	8.4	8.7	
Denmark	3.8	4.2	
Finland.	3.7	4.0	
France	41.3	41.2	
Greece	7.1	7.8	
Ireland	2.9	3.0	
Italy	43.1	46.0	
Netherlands	8.8	9.9	
Norway.	2.9	3.2	
Portugal	7.6	8.5	
Spain	25.5	28.0	
Sweden.	6.3	6.9	
Switzerland	4.2	4.6	
United Kingdom	47.8	50.3	
Total.	220.0	233.4	6 per cent increase
Germany (Trizone)	. . . . .	47.6	
Total.	. . . . .	281.0	

SOURCE: *Monthly Bulletin of Statistics*, Statistical Office of the United Nations (New York), May, 1950, Table 1.

from 1939 to 1949.[7] Observe, however, that this rate of increase was less than that of the United States during the thirties. The absolute increase of these 15 countries was only slightly above 13 million while in the United States there occurred a population growth of about 18 million during the same period.

[7] The population of Europe increased as follows in the interwar period:

Country	1920, in millions	1939, in millions	Per cent
United Kingdom and Ireland	47.1	50.9	8.0
West Central Europe	146.6	164.3	12.1
Northern Europe	17.9	20.1	12.2
Southern Europe	65.3	77.1	18.2
Eastern Europe	67.2	87.8	30.5
Europe (without USSR)	346.3	402.9	16.3
USSR	136.9	173.8	27.0

SOURCE: Dudley Kirk, *Europe's Population in the Interwar Years*, Office of Population Research, League of Nations (Princeton), 1946, Table 3, p. 24.

Notestein[8] in reviewing the excellent demographic analysis of the *Report of the Royal Commission on Population* of Great Britain observed:

[that the past war and recent] British experience is similar to that in much of Western Europe, the United States, and even in Japan . . . [and that the] major part of the movement of birth rates during and after the war can be explained in terms of the movement of marriage and the postponement and catching up of childbearing. Apparently, however, something more fundamental was occurring. If there had been no change in childbearing habits, the "expected" births might have been more numerous than those observed because some of the postponed births could never be made up by reason of war losses. Moreover, it seems probable that there was some delayed childbearing still to come after the end of 1948. On the other hand, it is possible that some of the births represent advances on the "normal" schedule of childbearing. The fact that actual births exceeded those expected suggests that by the end of 1948 there had probably been a slight real rise in marital fertility above the levels of the late thirties.

It is significant that in this report the high assumption about family size which results in a 6 per cent increase would yield a population for

POPULATION OF GREAT BRITAIN 1801-1947, PROJECTED 1947-2047

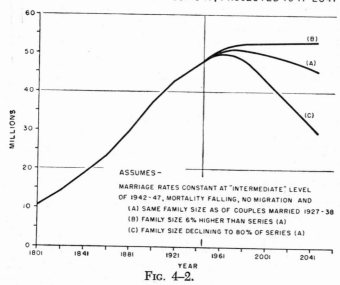

FIG. 4-2.

[8] *Population Index*, XV, (October, 1949): 306.

Great Britain only about 4 million larger than that of 1947 by the year 2000 and which thereafter would become stationary.

No hand can draw the precise growth curve of the future population of Europe or, for that matter, of the United States, not even for a decade ahead. It should not be amiss to point out that while demographers should be given credit for the real advances they have made in describing certain important aspects of the mechanism and in the measurement of population growth, they have not explained it. No meaningful explanation is at hand because no comprehensive theory has been developed for Type III, low-food-drain communities. For Types I and II we can still use the Ricardo-Malthus-Mill formulation with modifications to advantage.

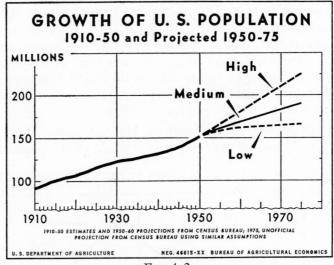

GROWTH OF U. S. POPULATION
1910-50 and Projected 1950-75

Fig. 4–3.

But as has been said, in countries like most of those of western Europe and in the United States, populations behave as an independent (exogenous) variable in relation to the (food) economy, and the indications are that other economic or noneconomic considerations are of major importance in explaining population changes. Nevertheless, the population data covering the depressed thirties and the prosperous forties, especially the data of the United States, suggest that the rate of population growth is affected substantially by such a drastic swing in the level of employment, production, and general economic activity.

On the descriptive level, looking carefully at charts and crude data—without theory to guide the analysis—one can prove, as Professor Davis has done, that the data of the late forties do not square with the data of the decade of the thirties. But all this does not tell one whether either set of data is relevant to the fifties and beyond. About all that can be distilled from the British population report and from the crude population data of western European countries and of the United States, including Davis's "tremendous upsurge," is about as follows: The rate of population growth for the near future will probably be somewhat higher than seemed likely to demographers during the early forties as they endeavored to interpret the population data of the interwar years. During the decade of the thirties, the United States population grew a little over 7 per cent and during the forties the upturn carried it back to fully 14 per cent.[9] Charts cannot penetrate the future; we know that the population is still uncoiling; unfortunately, however, there is no theory to explain why and how it uncoils under Type III circumstances.[10]

[9] The projected population (*Current Population Report*, U.S. Department of Commerce, Aug. 10, 1950) for total population resident in the United States, July 1, 1960, has been estimated as follows:

Low	161,241,000
Medium	168,933,000
High	179,839,000

The population indicated by the medium projection would represent an 11.7 per cent increase over the 151,240,000 of July 1, 1950. *Current Population Report*, U.S. Department of Commerce, Apr. 25, 1951.

[10] For a systematic discussion of the underlying issues in development and population, one turns especially to the contributions of Professor Joseph J. Spengler. See "Economic Factors in the Development of Densely Populated Areas," *Proceedings of the American Philosophical Society*, Vol. XCV (1951); "Measures of Population Maladjustment," *Proceedings of the Fourteenth International Congress of Sociology*, Vol. III (Rome, 1950); "The Population Obstacle to Economic Betterment," *Proceedings, American Economic Review*, Vol. XLI (May, 1951); and "Notes on France's Response to Declining Rate of Demographic Growth," *Journal of Economic History*, 1951. See also Kingsley Davis, "Population and the Further Spread of Industrial Society," *Proceedings of the American Philosophical Society*, Vol. XCV (1951).

5

GAUGING THE RELEVANT INCOME ELASTICITIES

Our task is to "estimate" the income elasticities of the demand for food and farm products. Available studies vary in results traceable to differences in techniques and data. We shall draw upon these studies and endeavor to interpret them as they bear upon the problem at hand. The task, however, is not an easy one because, as is usually the case whenever relevant economic information is sought, the data are stubborn. The information contained in the studies that have been reported is still fragmentary, and when one tries to use it, a good deal depends upon judgment which is always affected by "insights," experiences and events that go beyond the data and the formal analytical techniques employed.

One is obliged, therefore, to reveal his beliefs about this economic information so that others may be on their guard in evaluating the judgment and the evidence entering into the "estimates." When one takes the long view of economic development, as in this study, and restricts oneself to the effects of increases in income, as at this point, one assumes it to be true that people may choose the food they take in various forms not only as among farm products but also as among combinations of farm products and of services added after these products leave the farm. Where people are poor, the possibilities open to them are such that they choose farm products with few, if any, nonfarm services attached. Where people are very poor, as they are in many communities in the world, they are apt to consume primarily the cheaper energy foods, that is, very largely cereals, potatoes, and other plant foods rather than animal products, and to take their food mainly as farm products with few services added and to behave in relation to income in ways which indicate a high income elasticity for food, probably in the neighborhood of unity (1.0). As people become richer, it is probable that they will consume relatively more animal products and nonfarm services attached to the farm products entering into food; and what is exceedingly important, as they become richer the income elasticity of farm products for them will decrease, dropping to less than 1.0. We can imagine a community becoming so rich that the demand for farm products entering into food would no longer increase with income, and in that event, the income elasticity of such farm products would have become zero.

If we could determine these income elasticities for each of the major food-population types, it is our belief that we would find them about as indicated in Table 5–1.

TABLE 5–1. INCOME ELASTICITY RELATIONS AND EFFECTS

Type and attributes	All food	Farm-produced part of food	Nonfarm services added to farm-produced parts	
			When eating at home	When eating away from home
High food drain (Type I)	1.0	1.0	1.0	
Distribution, per cent	100	90–100	10–0	
Intermediate food drain (Type II) (in transition)				
Low food drain (Type III) . . .	0.5	0.25	0.625	1.25
Distribution, per cent (in transition)	100	50	40	10
Demand effects of a 10 per cent increase in income	5	2½	6¼	12½
Industries classified according to income elasticity	Composite	Primary	Secondary	Tertiary

By Type I we mean, as defined in Chap. 4, communities which use three-fourths or even more of their income for food. In these communities, we would expect most families to be quite self-sufficient and to consume farm products requiring in the main very little transportation and what processing is done would be the work of the consuming unit. The income elasticities of farm products, of the services added, and of the resulting food are about the same, and each is high, probably about 1.0. We may pass over Type II because it is simply an intermediate stage. Type III takes us to communities which spend a small fraction of their income for food; the figure of one-fourth or less is a convenient bench mark for this type. The composition of food has changed. It is no longer primarily farm produced. Nonfarm services are an important part, fully as large as is the part produced in agriculture. As incomes rise, the farm-produced part will contract relative to the nonfarm, with the services added when food is eaten away from home expanding the most. These relationships may be taken as "estimates" which represent the existing situation in the United States at this stage of economic development.

In untangling the demand effects of price and income, more depends upon the data that are used to measure the consumption of food than on the analytical techniques that are employed to explain the economic meaning of such data. The insights and wisdom of Adam Smith have stood the test of time and of modern studies so well that we are justified in quoting at some length. "The rich man consumes no more food than his poor neighbor. In quality it may be very different, and to select and prepare it may require more labour and art; but in quantity it is very nearly the same. . . . The desire of food is limited in every man by the narrow capacity of the human stomach."[1] People in the United States were substantially richer in 1949 than they were in 1909 but their consumption of food per capita, measured in terms of retail weight equivalent, was virtually the same (1,573 pounds in 1949 and 1,576 pounds in 1909). The composition of these two quantities of food changed very appreciably, however, during the four decades as the data in Table 5–2 indicate.

TABLE 5–2. RETAIL WEIGHT OF FOOD

Food group	Retail weight equivalent, pounds		
	1909	1949	Difference
Citrus fruit and tomatoes	44	98	+ 54
Dairy products (excluding butter)	388	429	+ 41
Leafy green and yellow vegetables	76	111	+ 35
Other vegetables and fruits	209	235	+ 26
Sugar and sirups	84	106	+ 22
Eggs	35	46	+ 11
Coffee, tea, and cocoa	10	19	+ 9
Fats and oils, including butter	59	65	+ 6
Dry beans, peas, nuts, and soya products	10	16	+ 6
Meats, poultry, and fish	161	159	− 2
Potatoes and sweet potatoes	204	116	− 88
Grain products	296	173	−123
Total	1,576	1,573	− 3

SOURCE: *Supplement for 1949 to Consumption of Food in the United States, 1909–48,* BAE, *Misc. Pub.* 691, September, 1950, Table 38 revised, p. 17.

While the total quantity of food consumed, as measured above, did not change (only 3 pounds), the quality did; presumably it improved as potatoes and grain products were replaced by other foods. But how is one to measure such changes in quality? Is there some unique and wholly dependable way of measuring this improvement in quality? The answer is clearly in the negative. Is there some satisfactory way? Here, again, the answer appears to be no. There are those who believe that

[1] Adam Smith, *The Wealth of Nations,* Edwin Cannan, editor (New York: The Modern Library series, Random House, 1937), p. 164.

food nutrients should give us such a measure. For example, "The most desirable index would be one with weights assigned to individual foods according to their nutritional importance, but no satisfactory basis has yet been found for combining nutrients."[2] Suppose it were possible to so combine nutrients; this achievement, nevertheless, would not measure all changes in quality because nutrients are at best only one attribute of the quality of food given the existing preferences of people.

The changes in nutrients available for consumption, per capita, per day are summarized in Table 5–3.

TABLE 5–3. CHANGES IN FOOD NUTRIENTS AVAILABLE FOR CONSUMPTION
(1935–1939 = 100)

Nutrient	1909	1949	Difference
Riboflavin	100	126	+26
Thiamine	113	134	+21
Calcium	91	112	+21
Iron	107	125	+18
Fat	95	107	+12
Ascorbic acid	91	104	+13
Vitamin A	94	105	+11
Niacin	114	125	+11
Protein	113	106	− 7
Food energy	107	99	− 8
Carbohydrate	113	94	−19

SOURCE: *Supplement for 1949 to Consumption of Food in the United States, 1909–48,* BAE, *Misc. Pub.* 691, September, 1950, p. 19.

These data on changes in the intake of food nutrients undoubtedly indicate, on the average, an improvement in diets. But how is one to handle a drop in the last three items in the above list in gauging the gains in the others and in evaluating the aggregate change? The task is an important one and a good deal of headway is being made by students of nutrition. But a solution of this difficulty will not resolve our problem, namely, that of measuring changes in the amount of food consumed which takes satisfactory account of all improvements in quality, including the purely nutritional aspects.

There are available, of course, other measures of changes in food consumption. Three such measures of per capita food consumption in the United States for selected years from 1909 to 1949 appear in Table 5–4.

[2] *Supplement for 1949 to Consumption of Food in the United States 1909–48,* BAE, *Misc. Pub.* 691, September, 1950, p. 88.

TABLE 5–4. THREE MEASURES OF PER CAPITA FOOD CONSUMPTION
(1935–1939 = 100)

Year	Retail weight equivalent		Per capita consumption of food, index	Per capita food expenditures, index
	Pounds	Index		
1909	1,576	104	99	
1914	1,528	101	97	
1919	1,519	100	98	
1924	1,545	102	102	
1929	1,550	102	102	102
1934	1,478	97	99	86
1939	1,553	102	104	106
1944	1,667	110	112	142
1949	1,573	104	111	141

SOURCE: *Consumption of Food in the United States, 1909–48* and *Supplement for 1949*
BAE, *Misc. Pub.* 691, August, 1949, and September, 1950.

Here we have three readily available measures of food consumption in the United States. In comparing these, we shall restrict ourselves to two dates, 1939 and 1949, because of certain shortcomings in the data on which the food expenditure series is based when one goes back of the late thirties. The comparison follows:

	Per capita increase from 1939 to 1949, per cent
Measures	
(1) Retail weight	1
(2) Consumption of food, BAE index	7
(3) Food expenditures divided by retail food prices index	33

It is the difference between (2) and (3) which accounts for most of the variations in the estimates of the income elasticity of food now available. We shall return to this problem of measuring food consumption after we have dealt with one or two preliminary matters.

When we try to use the concept of income elasticity to explain certain aspects of what is essentially a dynamic process, it is difficult to indicate and to ascertain what components are "safely" under control in our *ceteris paribus* compound in any particular situation. Certain elementary points need to be covered. Take, first, the most general property of the concept of income elasticity. It represents the relation between changes in income received by a particular consuming unit or some aggregate of such units and changes in the use to which the income is put. For example, when a family acquires 1 per cent more income and spends the additional income in such a way that the outlay of the family for a particular product increases 1 per cent, the ratio is 1:1; and, the income elasticity for this particular product for this particular family is unity (1.0), on the assumption that other things are equal. If, however, with a 1 per cent increase in income, the additional outlay for the product is less than 1 per cent, the income elasticity is less than unity and accordingly is referred to as "relatively inelastic" or "low in elasticity." Conversely, if the rate of outlay for the product is greater than the rate of increase in income, the income elasticity of the product is "relatively elastic" or "high in elasticity."[3]

We would expect, on a priori grounds, the marginal propensity to consume food to decrease with income. This means that as income rises the allocation of income by consumers is such that the proportion of the income spent on food falls while that allocated to some other item(s) rises. This effect of income upon the demand is often referred to as "Engel's law" because of a study which he published in 1888 (the income elasticity for food indicated by Engel was .7). The statistical work that he did on this problem was an important first step; yet it is a long way from providing an answer to the question: What is the income elasticity of farm products? In an expanding economy, with incomes rising and with technology in agriculture improving, it makes a great difference whether the income elasticity of farm products is less than .5 or substantially more, and whether, taking the community as a whole, it is falling slowly or rapidly as incomes rise.

We shall consider, first, the income elasticity of food and of farm products taken as a whole and then certain differences among farm products. It is well known that in the United States the income elasticity

[3] A particular income elasticity represents the slope at some point, or of a segment, or of an entire income-consumption schedule. The income-consumption schedule of a particular product for a particular population gives the quantity of the product that will be purchased by the population per unit of time at each level of income. The concept of income elasticity may be employed to express the elasticity of the entire income-consumption schedule (or of some relevant part of such a schedule) or to represent a given point on the schedule. A schedule for a particular group of consuming units (which may consist of a single individual as a special case) may conveniently have a constant elasticity throughout or what is more plausible, it may vary from one segment to another. A point elasticity for a particular group of consuming units may be composed of consuming units each having (conveniently) the same income elasticity or the group may be some kind of aggregate put together by weights or by some other procedure, composed of consuming units with different elasticities. We shall leave it to the context of the analysis to indicate the frame of reference specifying the income elasticity as we use it from time to time in this study.

of some fruits, vegetables, meats, and dairy products is high relative to that of most farm products, while potatoes, wheat and rye (for bread), and grain for cereals have not only a low but actually a negative income elasticity. Some farm products used for industrial purposes may show a high elasticity against income. All these differences are important in

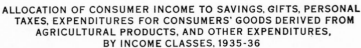

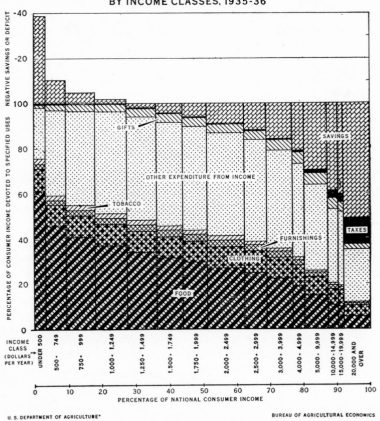

Fig. 5–1.

understanding the economic forces playing upon a particular farm product. Nevertheless, there is such a broad band of effective substitution in the use of agricultural resources in producing alternative farm products that much real insight can be had regarding agriculture from the over-all approach followed here.

Again, it is necessary to stress that we are concerned with the claims that the demand resulting from larger incomes may make on agricultural resources. It is the demand for the products as they leave agriculture, and not at a later stage, in which we are primarily interested. This distinction is important because it appears that the income elasticity of food, clothing, and of other goods made from farm products is higher than is the income elasticity of farm products because most consumers prefer relatively more services incorporated and attached to farm products as their incomes rise.

It is exceedingly difficult, however, to derive an estimate of income elasticity that meets the specifications of economic theory. The best that can be done with existing data and techniques is to acquire a few clues. These clues must suffice at this stage of our knowledge in our endeavor to gauge the income elasticity of farm products, food, and the services added to food by nonfarm firms. There are two main sources of information, namely, data collected over time and cross-sectional data.

INCOME ELASTICITY—AN APPEAL TO CROSS-SECTIONAL DATA

Budget studies have yielded higher income elasticities for food than have most studies based on time series and much effort has been expended to reconcile the two sets. But there are also variations in results among budget studies. We shall draw first on Tobin[4] in interpreting recent budget data and then consider briefly other related studies. The following five estimates are for food consumption in the United States adjusted to family size of 3.5 persons:

	Income elasticity
Tobin, 1941 budget data	.56
Rural nonfarm, 1935–1936	.55
Rural nonfarm, 1941	.53
Farm, 1935–1936	.37
Farm, 1941	.35

These budget data entail the following definitions: (1) *Disposable income* = disposable money income + rent imputed to owner-occupiers + other income in kind, including food. (2) *Food consumption* = money expenditure for food + value of food home-grown and received in kind as gifts, compensation and relief.

Tobin also reports results on eight additional sets of budget data.

[4] James Tobin, "A Statistical Demand Function for Food in the U.S.A.," *Journal of the Royal Statistical Society*, Vol. CXII, Part II (1950).

Three of these are based on (1) disposable income + imputed rent and (2) money expenditure for food:

Income elasticity

Urban, 1927–1928	.68
Urban, 1935–1936	.61
Urban, 1941.	.65

And, then there are five sets based on (1) disposable income and (2) money expenditure for food:

Income elasticity

Urban, 1918.	.57
Urban, 1941.	.64
Richmond, Va., 1947	.64
Washington, D.C., 1947	.59
Manchester, N.H., 1947	.59

Except for the behavior of farm families indicating an income elasticity that is significantly below that of nonfarm families,[5] these estimates are remarkably of one piece, when allowance is made for the differences in definitions of income and of food. The first three in the first set (.56, .55, and .53), which are based on essentially comparable budgetary data and which are also the most complete with regard to income and food consumption, appear to provide the "best" estimate now available from budget data.[6]

---

[5] The food which farm families utilize consists of two parts, that is, (1) home-produced food for which the income elasticity is at or near zero and (2) purchased food; the second part appears to have an income elasticity about the same as it has for urban families (see Chap. 14).

[6] Since this was written, the study by Karl A. Fox has appeared, "Factors Affecting Farm Income, Farm Prices, and Food Consumption," *Agricultural Economics Research*, Vol. III (July, 1951), Bureau of Agricultural Economics. Fox reports for urban families for the spring of 1948 the following expenditure elasticities for food:

Elasticity

A. Per family:
All food expenditures	0.51
At home	0.40
Away from home	1.12

B. Per family member:
All food expenditures	0.42
At home	0.29
Away from home	1.14

C. Per 21 meals at home:
All food (excluding accessories)	0.28

Other and earlier budget studies will be considered briefly, although they are, in the main, less satisfactory than those by Tobin. There are differences in the concepts of "income" and of "food" and the size of the family is usually not specified. Moreover, some of these studies overlap with those of Tobin where they draw on the same data. Allen and Bowley,[7] in 1935, summarized the results of a number of family-expenditure studies. In no case did they find the income elasticity of the demand for food, at the average expenditure level, to be as high as 1.0. In ten of their budget studies, food fell between .8 and .9;[8] in eight studies, between .5 and .7;[9] and in three, between .3 and .45.[10] Clark,[11] using United States data of nonfarm families, reports, "The average income elasticity of demand for food for the community as a whole is only .38, although it is clearly higher in the lower ranges of income.[12] For incomes from $0 to $3,000, the elasticity of food as calculated by Clark was .80, and for incomes $3,000 and larger, it was .14.[13] The 1935–1936 Consumer Purchase Study in the United States was undoubtedly the most comprehensive ever attempted. Mack,[14] using this study, derived an income elasticity for food of .52. Kaplan,[15] also drawing on this study, found that the expenditure elasticity of food, at the mean, was as follows: for wage-earner families, Chicago, .636; for wage-earner

[7] R. G. D. Allen and A. L. Bowley, *Family Expenditure, A Study of Its Variation* (London: P. S. King & Staples, Ltd., 1935), Table A, pp. 32–33.

[8] *Ibid.*, Liverpool, 1929, workers, .9; Belgium, 1928–1929, workers, .8; Germany, 1927–1928, workers, .8, and salaried employees, .8; Oslo, 1912–1913, all classes, .8; Oslo and Bergen, 1918–1919, all classes, .9; Finland, 1920–1921, workers, .8; Czechoslovakia, 1927, workers, .85, and 1929, workers, .8; and United States, 1918, all classes .8.

[9] *Ibid.*, London School of Economics, 1932, all classes, .5; Amsterdam, 1923–1924, all classes, .5; Germany, 1927–1928, officials, .7; Basle, 1912, all classes, .7, and 1921, all classes, .6; Czechoslovakia, 1927, officials, .7, and 1929, officials, .7; and United States, 1928–1929, farmers, .7.

[10] *Ibid.*, Copenhagen, 1922, all classes, .3; Denmark, 1922, all classes, .3; Poland, 1929, workers .45.

[11] Colin Clark, *The Conditions of Economic Progress*, (London: Macmillan & Co., Ltd., 1940), pp. 436–439. Clark's calculations are based on data appearing in M. Leven, H. Moulton, and C. Warburton, *America's Capacity to Consume*, Washington, D.C.: (Brookings Institution, 1934).

[12] *Ibid.*, p. 438.

[13] *Ibid.*, p. 437.

[14] Ruth P. Mack, "The Direction of Change in Income and the Consumption Function," *Review of Economics and Statistics*, Vol. XXX, No. 4 (1948).

[15] A. D. H. Kaplan, "Expenditure Patterns of Urban Families," *Journal of American Statistical Association*, XXXIII (1938): 97, 98.

families, Denver, .633; for salaried business families, Chicago, .347; and for salaried business families, Denver, .461. Kaplan points out, however, that the expenditures for food in the higher income families include more services: " . . . the percentage spent for food declines but gradually for incomes between $1,500 and $5,000. With increasing income, the food bill takes on the expenses of eating out and entertaining, as well as the introduction of delicacies into the food budget."[16] Gold and Enlow[17] give the elasticity of expenditure for food for the population as a whole (based on the Consumer Purchase Study of 1935–1936), as follows:

Income class	Elasticity of expenditure
Under $500	.5
$ 500–$1,000	.5
1,000– 1,500	.4
1,500– 2,000	.4
2,000– 3,000	.4

One additional computation deserves attention at this point; it is based on data given by Hildegarde Kneeland.

Income range per capita	Expenditure range per capita	Elasticity of expenditures with respect to income	
$465–$ 560	$142–$156	.4826[a]	.5064[b]
560– 674	156– 171	.4722	.4962
674– 830	171– 189	.4546	.4821
830– 1,038	189– 201	.2533	.2764

[a] Elasticity $= \dfrac{\Delta E/E_1}{\Delta \Upsilon/\Upsilon_1}$ [b] Elasticity $= \dfrac{\Delta E/(E_1+E_2)}{\Delta \Upsilon/(\Upsilon_1+\Upsilon_2)}$

ΔE = increment in expenditure per capita in the expenditure range.
E_1 = expenditure per capita of the lower expenditure range.
E_2 = expenditure per capita of the higher expenditure range.
$\Delta \Upsilon$ = increment in income per capita in income range.
Υ_1 = income per capita of the lower income range.
Υ_2 = income per capita of the higher income range.
SOURCE: Hildegarde Kneeland, *Consumer Expenditures in the United States, Estimates for 1935–1936*, National Resources Committee (Washington, D.C.), 1939, Table 18, p. 6.

INCOME ELASTICITY—USE OF TIME SERIES

In this section, three sets of data will be drawn upon: (1) consumer studies, (2) a study estimating the income elasticity of farm products, and (3) some data on expenditures for farm products.

[16] *Ibid.*, p. 85.
[17] Norman L. Gold and Maxine Enlow, "The Demand for Food by Low Income Families," *Quarterly Journal of Economics,* LVII (1943): 602, Table 1.

Clues from Consumer Studies of Consumption of Food over Time. These studies fall into two distinct groups consisting of those with relatively high estimates which are based on food expenditures and those with much lower estimates based on the "physical" quantities of food consumed as measured by the Bureau of Agricultural Economics index of food consumption.

	Elasticity
Tobin, 1913–1941 (restricted by budget data)[a].	.56
Stone, 1929–1941[b]	.53
Mack, 1929–1940[c]	.54
Tobin, 1913–1941 (unrestricted)[a].	.27
Girschick and Haavelmo, 1922–1941[d]	.25
Bureau of Agricultural Economics[e]	.21
Working, 1922–1941[f]	.28

[a] James Tobin, "A Statistical Demand Function for Food in the U.S.A.," *Journal of the Royal Statistical Society*, Vol. CXII, Part II (1950).

[b] Richard Stone, "The Analysis of Market Demand," *Journal of the Royal Statistical Society*, Vol. CVIII, Parts III–IV (1945).

[c] Ruth P. Mack, "The Direction of Change in Income and the Consumption Function," *Review of Economics and Statistics*, Vol. XXX, No. 4 (1948).

[d] M. A. Girschick and Trygve Haavelmo, "Statistical Analysis of the Demand for Food: Examples of Simultaneous Estimation of Structural Equations," *Econometrica*, Vol. XV, No. 2 (1947).

[e] *Consumption of Food in The United States, 1909–1948*, BAE, *Misc. Pub.* 691, August, 1949, Table 49, p. 142.

[f] E. J. Working, "Appraising the Demand for American Agricultural Output during Rearmament." Read before joint sessions of American Economic and American Farm Economic Associations. Boston, Mass., December, 1951.

An Evaluation of Income Elasticity Estimates. Estimates of the income elasticity of food based on time series represented by the Bureau of Agricultural Economics index of food consumption are substantially less than are estimates derived from data measuring food expenditures. The two estimates are not, however, inconsistent with one another. They are based on two very different concepts of food, and, therefore, if the estimates were the same, they would be highly suspect. The difficulty lay not in economic logic or methods used in analyzing these data, as was Tobin's belief in undertaking his study. Moreover, the procedures which he used to bring them together were not only unnecessary but inappropriate.

Elementary as it may be, sight has been lost of the fact that "more labor and art" is required to prepare food as people become richer. Food when it leaves the farms is one thing. Food when acquired by people at retail is quite another quantity, both larger and different; and food when it is consumed, some of it at home and some away from home, is still something else. We have the following data for the United States for 1947.[18]

*In billions
of dollars*

1. *Farm food* consisting of United States farm products used for food by United States civilians valued at point of farm sales 18.23
2. *Farm food at retail* is the retail value of (1) above consisting of 18.23 + 8.84 (trade) + 5.26 (processing) + 1.83 (transportation). 34.16
3. *BAE food index* includes imported food, food of nonfarm origin, and United States farm food used by civilian sector. (Value implicit at retail prices.) . . 43.13
4. *Department of Commerce food expenditures*
   a. Excluding expenditures for beverages 47.74
   b. Including expenditures for beverages 56.60

Before turning to Table 5–5, which provides a framework for interpreting the studies of income elasticity of food now available, let us take our bearing on several analytical issues. First, there is the notion that inasmuch as food expenditures and cash farm receipts from the sales of farm food commodities, presumably in the short run, rise or fall in about the same proportion as do per capita disposable incomes, food expenditures and, also, farm foods, therefore, have a "dynamic income elasticity" which is very high (at or near 1.0). This notion is mainly an admixture of both price and income elasticities.[19] It can give rise only to confusion because the (low) price elasticity of the demand of farm foods does not make the income elasticity of this food either high or dynamic.

In this study we shall infer the income elasticity of United States farm foods, used by the civilian sector, from an analysis based on food represented by the Bureau of Agricultural Economics index of food consumption. How reliable is such an inference? We shall examine briefly three possible difficulties. There is first the fact that some of the food in the

[18] Derived from paper by Karl A. Fox and Harry C. Narcross, "Agriculture and the General Economy," *Agricultural Economics Research*, Vol. IV (January, 1952), Bureau of Agricultural Economics; from *Survey of Current Business*, U.S. Department of Commerce; and from Bureau of Agricultural Economics food consumption index, the aggregate value implicit when the 1935–1939 price quantities are adjusted to 1947 circumstances.

[19] The otherwise useful paper of Marguerite C. Burk, "Changes in the Demand for Food 1941 to 1950," *Journal of Farm Economics*, Vol. XXXIII (August, 1951), espouses this notion of a "dynamic income elasticity." (See especially pp. 294–295). There are "income sensitivity" problems which Ruth Mack has considered. See also, Clement Winston and Mabel A. Smith, "Income Sensitivity of Consumption Expenditures," *Survey of Current Business*, January, 1950, pp. 17–20.

Bureau of Agricultural Economics index is imported or does not originate in United States agriculture, for example, coffee, tea, off-shore sugar, spices, fishing products, and others. This class, however, is small, probably in the neighborhood of 6 per cent, and what is more, this part has not shown a tendency either to expand or contract enough relative to United States farm foods to affect the index appreciably. Another difficulty could arise from substantial changes in the proportion of the farm foods which is "lost" in conversion in processing, transportation, and distribution. But, here again, it appears that the linkage between farm foods and food at retail has not been affected appreciably, say, since 1935–1939 by changes that have occurred in these conversion factors.[20]

We encounter a more serious difficulty in dealing with the effects of changes in the value relations (1) among foods at retail, (2) among farm foods, and (3) between food at the farm and food at retail. We need to bear in mind throughout that the Bureau of Agricultural Economics index is based on quantities of food consumed, specifically on pounds of food at retail, and that an aggregate is obtained at present by using 1935–1939 retail prices. (See Appendix D, BAE, *Misc. Pub.* 691.) Since we have already commented on the physical conversion factors relating farm quantities to retail quantities,[21] we now turn to the price weights. How satisfactory are the 1935–1939 retail prices in measuring the aggregate consumption of food of civilians given the pattern of retail prices of the late forties? Among others, meat prices at retail had risen relatively, while fats and oils, for example, had declined somewhat. But a tentative calculation, using 1947–1949 consumption quantities and 1949 prices, did not alter appreciably the aggregate consumption from that obtained by using 1935–1939 price weights.[22]

But how satisfactory are the relative prices of food at retail in gauging

---

[20] See Appendix B, BAE, *Misc. Pub.* 691, for the conversion factors used.

[21] The index is so constructed that shifts in food purchases at retail among the 11 principal food groups and also within some of them are measured satisfactorily. But shifts within other groups, for example, within the meat, flour, and sugar categories, are not represented. Marguerite C. Burk has pointed out that the later shifts would have added $5 in 1939 and $15 in 1947 to the average retail value of food consumed per capita in current prices.

[22] A tentative test made for the writer by the Bureau of Agricultural Economics indicated a change of about 1 per cent, which certainly is small. We are of the view, however, that when prices have adapted themselves more fully to the marked inflation that has occurred, the rise in per capita incomes will increase the aggregate by more than 1 per cent over the level obtained by using the 1935–1939 prices as weights. The basis for this belief is discussed below.

the farm food aggregate? We know, for instance, that in 1947 United States farm foods used by United States civilians had a value of about $34 billion at retail, whereas at the farm this aggregate had a value of about $18 billion. Even though relative prices of food at retail stayed about the same, it does not follow that the structure of farm food prices remains unaltered. There is, in fact, much room for such price changes in view of the large differences in the two aggregates.

The total pounds of food consumed per capita tends to stay about the same whether incomes rise or fall. Accordingly, the income elasticity of food may be represented as an "elasticity for quality" and, if it were true that foods which are low in "quality" were to decline in price relative to foods which are high in "quality," the price weights of a particular base period, for example, of 1935–1939, would become increasingly unsatisfactory as per capita incomes rose and the price of low and high "quality" foods moved apart. But except for meat the relative prices of major farm product groups have not changed substantially;[23] moreover, it is likely that the relatively high price of meat will largely disappear as agriculture readjusts its production.

The relative prices of major groups of farm foods tend to remain about the same in the long run because of the possibilities of transferring resources (inputs) from one product to another in farming, taking agriculture as a whole and in a long setting. The range and elasticity of substitution among inputs and products appears to be such that when a rise in income, let us say, increases the demand for animal products and decreases it for potatoes and cereals, while the price of these farm products will, in the short run, reflect these shifts in demand, the transfer of inputs in farming will in the longer run reestablish approximately the former relative prices among animal products, potatoes, and cereals. It is necessary, however, also to take into account the effects of long-run changes in relative factor costs within agriculture. If there were no advances in technology or if these advances were such that they did not alter the relative amounts of the several factors employed, no difficulty would arise. However, new techniques are likely to increase the output per unit of input for some farm products while more or less by-passing others. There is also the effect of more general changes in factor costs—the rise in the cost of human effort relative to the unit cost of capital inputs as an economy develops—which will alter the relative costs of farm

[23] From 1935–1939 to 1949, taking the farm value of the "market basket" unit, it appears that while the meat group rose 171 per cent, dairy products rose 101 per cent; poultry and eggs, 101 per cent; bakery and other cereals, 115 per cent; and fruits and vegetables, 125 per cent.

products to the extent that these sets of two inputs are not employed in the same ratio in producing the various farm products.

The following indexes of prices received by farmers give some clues to the drift in relative farm food prices from 1909–1914 to 1935–1939 and to 1948–1950; but the relative prices indicated for meat and oil crops in 1948–1950 are substantially out of line with long-run costs and will be corrected as farmers adapt their production plans.

	1909–1914	1935–1939	1948–1950
All farm products.	100	100	100
Meat animals	101	110	128
Dairy products	100	110	101
Poultry and eggs	101	101	80
Oil-bearing crops	98	99	110
Truck crops	. . .	95	77
Food grains	100	88	88
Fruits	99	77	73

On changes in the value of farm foods resulting from, say, a rise in per capita income, we conclude that a set of price weights based on a period which prevailed prior to the rise in income will appear to underestimate the quantity of farm food in the short run, but since our concern is with the allocation of resources in agriculture in a long-run setting, this particular attribute of such price weights is not important because it largely disappears in the long run.

We still must consider the relation between the value of farm food at the point of farm sales and the value of this food at retail. Although the relative prices within each of the two sets of prices—farm foods at the point of farm sales and this food at retail—were to remain about the same, the level of one set may rise or fall relative to the other. It is well known that the proportion of the dollar spent by consumers at retail, for United States farm foods which represents the farmers' "share," varies widely from time to time; in 1933 it was 32 cents; in 1935–1939, 40 cents; and in 1950, 48 cents.[24] Seen in terms of prices, with 1935–1939 as 100, the index of retail prices of United States farm foods in 1950 was 189, whereas that of prices received by farmers for these foods was 228. While the Bureau of Agricultural Economics index of food consumption sails smoothly over all these waves, is it possible to determine whether the two sets of prices—that for the farm and that for the nonfarm components—necessarily move apart over time as a consequence of economic development? Are there reasons for believing, under con-

[24] In 1945 this share was 54 cents, the highest annual figure recorded.

TABLE 5-5. APPROXIMATE VALUES OF THE INCOME ELASTICITIES OF FOOD IN THE UNITED STATES

Population	(1) Food in pounds at retail, U.S. civilian sector	(2) U.S. farm foods for U.S. civilians at point of farm sales	Food based on food consumption represented by BAE index			Food based on food expenditures as reported by cross-sectional surveys or by USDC			(9) Food eaten away from home, including services
	(1)	(2)	(3) Current income	(4) Previous years' income	(5) (3) + (4)	(6) Current income	(7) Previous years' income	(8) (6) + (7)	(9)
Farm, cross-sectional								$.35\ (F_a, I_2, 1941)^a$ $.37\ (F_a, I_2, 1936)^a$	
Rural nonfarm, cross-sectional								$.53\ (F_a, I_2, 1941)^a$ $.55\ (F_a, I_2, 1936)^a$	
Urban, cross-sectional		$.25\ (C, I,$ Fox, 1948$)$			$.28\ (C, I,$ Fox, 1948$)$			$.42\ (C, I,$ Fox, 1948$)$ $.51\ (F, I,$ Fox, 1948$)$ $.57\ (F_a, I_1, 1918)^a$ $.61 (F_a, I_1, 1935-1936)^a$ $.64\ (F_a, I_1, 1941)^a$ $.68\ (F_a, I_1, 1927-1928)^a$	$1.12\ (F, I,$ Fox, 1948$)$ $1.14\ (C, I,$ Fox, 1948$)$
All of population, cross-sectional								$.48\ (C, I,$ Burk, 1935-1936$)$ $.49\ (C, I,$ Burk, 1941$)$ $.52\ (F, I,$ Mack, 1935-1936$)^b$ $.56\ (C, I,$ Tobin, 1941$)$	

Time series	.0 (BAE, 1909–1949)			.21 (C, I, BAE, 1922–1941) .28 (C, I, Working, 1922–1941) .27 (C, I, Tobin, 1913–1941) .30 (C, I, Girshick-Haavelmo, 1922–1941)		.54 (I, Mack, 1929–1940) .56 (C, I, Tobin, 1913–1941) .59 (C, I, Stone, 1929–1941)	
		.27	.0		.44		
		.25	.05		.12		1.25
Approximate values (based on civilian population and disposable income of 1949)	.0	.25		.30		.50	

Types of information:
C, per capita bases
F, per family bases
F_a, adjusted to family size of 3.5 persons
I, disposable income
I_1, disposable income + imputed rent
I_2, disposable income + imputed rent + other income in kind including food.
[a] Study adjusted to family size of 3.5 for families of two or more persons as reported by Tobin.
[b] Applies to nonfarm families only.

SOURCES:
Consumption of Food in the United States, 1909–48, BAE, *Misc. Pub.* 691, August, 1949.
Marguerite C. Burk, "Changes in the Demand for Food from 1941 to 1950," *Journal of Farm Economics*, Vol. XXXIII (1951).
Karl A. Fox, "Factors Affecting Farm Income, Farm Prices, and Food Consumption," *Agricultural Economics Research*, Vol. III (July, 1951), Bureau of Agricultural Economics.
M. A. Girshick and Trygve Haavelmo, "Statistical Analysis of the Demand for Food," *Econometrica*, Vol. XV (April, 1947).
Ruth P. Mack, "The Direction of Change in Income and the Consumption Function," *Review of Economics and Statistics*, Vol. XXX (November, 1948).
Richard Stone, "The Analysis of Market Demand," *Journal of the Royal Statistical Society*, Vol. CVIII (London, 1945).
James Tobin, "A Statistical Demand Function for Food in the USA," *Journal of the Royal Statistical Society*, Vol. CXIII (London, 1950). See also discussion by Richard Stone following Tobin's paper.
E. J. Working, "Appraising the Demand for American Agricultural Output during Rearmament," paper read at joint session of the American Economics Association and the American Farm Economics Association, Boston, Dec. 26, 1951.

ditions of full employment and as the economy develops, that the price of farm food per unit will fall or rise relative to the price of the non-farm services per unit employed in processing, transporting, and distributing such farm foods? There are, as far as we can see, no convincing reasons pointing one way or the other; the strong Ricardian belief on this point is not supported by the experiences of Western countries. However, even though in the long run the relative prices of these two components were not to change substantially, we would expect from past experiences the demand for nonfarm services to grow (shift to the right) somewhat more than that for farm services as a consequence of rises in per capita income. This is simply another way of indicating that it appears that the income elasticity of the nonfarm component is not quite as inelastic as is that of the farm component. If these extra nonfarm services were to be added in about the same proportion relative to the farm component to each major class of food, as seems plausible, the Bureau of Agricultural Economics index of food consumption would continue, despite such adaptations in consumption, to gauge the farm component satisfactorily although it would underestimate total food consumption at retail.

We now turn to Table 5–5. Take first the two concepts of food at each end of the scale. As we have said earlier, food of United States civilians, measured in pounds at retail, clearly has an income elasticity of zero for all intents and purposes. At the other end of the scale, in column 9, we have the food which United States civilians eat away from home, where food is defined to include all the services which go with such consumption; it undoubtedly has an income elasticity of unity or higher. Since family budget studies underreport the expenditures for food away from home and in view of other information, our estimate of 1.25 may well be somewhat too low.

Between these two concepts of food, we have:

1. Food measured by expenditures for food consumed at home and away from home and for alcoholic beverages. These expenditures amounted to $58.6 billion in 1949 as estimated by the U.S. Department of Commerce.

2. Food as defined in (1) minus expenditures for alcoholic beverages (an expenditure of $50.7 billion in 1949). The income elasticity of food thus defined, under conditions which characterized the civilian population and disposable income of the United States in 1949, appears to be approximately .5 (see column 8, Table 5–5).[25]

---

[25] Leaving aside differences in the concepts of food used in measuring the consumption of food, the problem of reconciling, at least on formal grounds,

3. Food as measured by the Bureau of Agricultural Economics index of food consumption. The income elasticity of food under this concept and, again, under 1949 population and income conditions, may be taken to be approximately .3 (see column 2 of Table 5–5).

4. Farm food commodities which are used by United States civilians measured at the point of farm sales. This aggregate was about $17.6 billion for 1949. The income elasticity of farm foods thus defined appears to be approximately .25 (see column 12 of Table 5–5).

The approximate values of the income elasticity of food given above for concepts 2, 3, and 4 are likely to be fairly dependable attributes of the demand for food under normal conditions of economic development to which the economy has become attuned. The following conditions, therefore, would appear to be favorable to the use of these values: (1) a long period of gradual and steady rise in per capita disposable income during which the composition of the civilian population did not undergo important changes; or (2) in gauging the shift of the demand schedule from one period to another arising from a change in per capita disposable income where each of the two periods represents a series of years characterized by economic stability, and, again, with no important changes in the composition of the civilian population.[26]

Income Elasticity of Farm Products from Tintner's Model. Tintner has taken the 24 observations provided by the years 1920 to 1943 and by using five variables—prices received by farmers, national income, agricultural production, time, and prices paid by farmers—has been "reasonably successful in estimating the demand function for agricultural

---

the results from cross-sectional budget data and those from time series remains. Haavelmo, in addressing himself briefly to this issue, looks upon these as a set of special problems in aggregation which arise out of changes in distribution of income and changes in the joint distribution along with characteristics associated with such changes. "The ordinary family-expenditure functions or Engel curves, as obtained from budget data, cannot be assumed to remain invariant under transformations of the income distribution, . . . one has to operate with a much larger number of independent variables than is commonly used in order to make the individual units in a cross-section sample comparable." See Trygve Haavelmo, "Family Expenditures and the Marginal Propensity to Consume," *Econometrica*, XV (October, 1947).

[26] Before leaving the different concepts of food considered in the preceding section, let us call attention to a valuable study for 1939 and 1948 by Marguerite C. Burk, "Distribution of the United States Food Supply," appearing in the July, 1952, issue of *Agricultural Economics Research*, Bureau of Agricultural Economics, which includes the following data on the sales value and the estimated retail value of United States civilian food by channels of distribution. See data on p. 64.

Channel of distribution	1939 Sales or market value, in billions of dollars	1939 Estimated retail value — Value, in billions of dollars	1939 Estimated retail value — Per cent of total	1948 Sales or market value, in billions of dollars	1948 Estimated retail value — Value, in billions of dollars	1948 Estimated retail value — Per cent of total
Total food distributed to civilians, estimated retail value . . .	....	18.0	100.0	....	49.0	100.0
Total value of food sold as food and as meals, *i.e.*, food expenditures	15.0	....	.....	43.7		
I. Eating places:						
Sales and food furnished .	3.5	2.3	12.8	10.2	6.7	13.7
Sales only	3.2	1.9	10.6	9.5	5.7	11.6
A. Public eating places .	3.0	1.9	10.6	8.6	5.5	11.2
1. Meals and fountain items sold . . .	2.7	1.5[a]	8.4	8.1	4.8[b]	9.8
2. Food furnished civilian employees and withdrawn by proprietors	0.3	0.4	2.2	0.5	0.7	1.4
B. Private eating places						
1. Clubs, institutions, schools, etc., sales .	0.2[c]	0.2	1.1	0.8	0.5	1.1
2. Clubs, institutions, schools, etc., food furnished employees				0.2	0.3	0.6
3. Boarding houses .	0.3	0.2	1.1	0.6	0.4	0.8
II. Institutions and transportation agencies						
A. Supplied to customers or patrons (meal value)	0.2	0.2	1.1	1.0	1.1	2.2
B. Furnished civilian employees	0.1			0.3		
III. Sales for off-premise consumption						
A. Food sales of retail stores	10.7	10.7	59.5	32.0	32.0	65.3
B. Food sales of commissaries, service trades, and other establishments	0.2	0.2	1.1	0.8	0.8	1.6
C. Direct sales to consumers by farmers, marketers, manufacturers, wholesalers. . .	1.2	2.0	11.1	2.3	4.0	8.2
Total	12.1	12.9	71.7	35.1	36.8	75.1
Less retailers' sales to eating places[d] .	0.3	0.3	1.7	0.9	1.0	2.0
Sales to consumers, net	11.8	12.6	70.0	34.2	35.8	73.1
IV. Food consumed on farms where produced. . . .	1.1	2.9[e]	16.1	2.8	5.4[e]	11.0

[a] Food cost estimated at 7 per cent of sales based on National Restaurant Association Survey; markups of 20 per cent used to retail.

[b] Food cost estimated at 50 per cent of sales; markup of 19 per cent used for cost to retail sales value.

[c] Included with public eating places. Probably less than $100 million.

[d] Rough approximations only.

[e] Estimated farm values of farm food products sold in 1939 and 1948 were 38 and 52 per cent of estimated retail values, respectively.

products in the United States."[27] He has derived and computed the income elasticity for agricultural products using the average of each of the variables in the period and in doing so has obtained the following estimate: 0.307. Tintner has interpreted his results thus, "If the conditions are on the whole the same as during the period considered, and also if other things remain equal, then an increase of 1 per cent in income will be followed by an increase of about 3/10 of 1 per cent in the demand for farm products."[28]

There are three aspects of Tintner's study to which we wish to call attention: (1) it includes all farm products and therefore is not restrictive to food as are most of the studies herein reported; (2) it endeavors to measure the effects of changes in income on farm prices at the point where farmers sell their products and not prices at retail or at some other stage in the production process; and (3) it includes years when incomes fell as well as years when they rose. The magnitude and number of such changes may offset each other approximately and to the extent that they do, the "color" that income fluctuations may introduce into time-series data is lessened. Furthermore, it should be observed that Tintner's estimate of .307 is based on a period of years when the per capita income of the United States was at least one-third less than that attained by 1950.

Clues from Crude Expenditures for Farm Products, 1870–1919. The economic development from the Civil War to World War I offers some data for gauging the effects of rises in income on the demand for farm products, inasmuch as real incomes per capita (in terms of 1929–1934 prices rose from $311 in 1870 to $574 in 1910, a rise of virtually 85 per cent.

In Table 5–6 we have a very rough measure of the proportion of the income of American people that went into farm products during each census year from 1870 to 1910. This table rests on the assumption that farm incomes adjusted for agricultural exports and imports are an approximate measure of the "expenditure" of Americans for farm products. In 1870, with a per capita income in real terms of $311, 34 per cent was "spent" for farm products. In 1910, when the per capita income had risen to $574, the proportion "spent" for farm products fell to 19 per cent. As a consequence of this significant decline of almost one-half in the proportion "spent" on farm products, the per capita dollar expenditures on farm products were only slightly greater in 1910 than in 1870, though real per capita income had risen 85 per cent. In comparing 1870 and

[27] Gerhard Tintner, "Multiple Regression for Systems of Equations," *Econometrica*, Vol. XIV (January, 1946); and also "Scope and Method of Econometrics, Illustrated by Applications to American Agriculture," a paper read before the Statistical and Social Inquiry Society of Ireland, Mar. 21, 1949.

[28] Tintner, *op. cit.* Tintner also provides a test of significance.

TABLE 5-6. UNITED STATES NATIONAL INCOME AND "EXPENDITURE" ON FARM PRODUCTS ADJUSTED FOR AGRICULTURAL EXPORTS AND IMPORTS, PER CAPITA, 1870-1910

	(1)	(2)	(3)	(4)	(5)
Year	National income per capita, current prices[a]	"Domestic expenditures" on farm products per capita, current prices[b]	Proportion (2) is of (1), per cent[c]	National income per capita in real terms, 1925-1934 prices[d]	"Domestic expenditures" on farm products per capita, in real terms, 1925-1934 prices[e]
1870	$180	$61	34	$311	$106
1880	160	52	32	358	115
1890	206	45	22	431	95
1900	254	44	17	528	90
1910	341	66	19	574	109

[a] *Cf.* Colin Clark, *The Conditions of Economic Progress* (London: Macmillan & Co., Ltd., 1940), pp. 78–79. Based on W. I. King, *Wealth and Income of the People of the United States* (New York: The Macmillan Company, 1915), p. 129. The only adjustment is the inclusion of the annual value of rents from dwelling houses. The population figures are from the *Statistical Abstract of the United States, 1942*, U.S. Department of Commerce, p. 11.

[b] Based on farm income minus the value of agricultural exports plus the value of agricultural imports minus the value of imports of crude rubber and raw silk. Value of agricultural exports and imports at the port overvalues these somewhat relative to farm income, which is determined by farm prices. However, since neither exports nor imports bulked large or changed considerably relative to the total farm income, no appreciable error is introduced by this overvaluation. Frederick Strauss and Louis H. Bean, *Gross Farm Income and Indices of Farm Products and Prices in the United States, 1869–1937*, U.S. Department of Agriculture, *Tech. Bull.* 703, Table 7, p. 23; and *Statistical Abstract of the United States, 1942*, U.S. Department of Commerce, p. 548.

[c] The per cent that column 2 is of column 1.

[d] From the same source as column 1, converted from money income to real terms by use of a retail price index for 1925–1934. *Cf.* Colin Clark, *op. cit.*, p. 78.

[e] Obtained by multiplying columns 3 and 4.

1910, we find that although prices generally declined (they dropped sharply from 1870 to 1896, after which they rose substantially), the relative position of the price of farm products to that of all commodities did not change markedly (farm prices rose somewhat, relatively).[29] Leaving changes in taste aside, the inference is that the very marked rise in real per capita income was accompanied by a marked decline in the pro-

[29] All commodity prices dropped from an index of 135 in 1870 to 103 in 1910. The index for the price of foods dropped from 139 to 101, and farm products from 112 to 104, during the same period. Accordingly, farm prices rose somewhat relative to nonagricultural commodities at wholesale in the United States during the period 1870–1910. See W. F. Warren and F. A. Pearson, "Index Numbers of Wholesale Prices in the U.S., 1786–1931," *Prices*, New York, 1933, Table III, p. 26.

TABLE 5-7. UNITED STATES NATIONAL INCOME AND "EXPENDITURES" ON FARM PRODUCTS
ADJUSTED FOR AGRICULTURAL EXPORTS AND IMPORTS, PER CAPITA, 1922-1939

	(1)	(2)	(3)	(4)	(5)
Year	National income per capita, current prices[a]	"Domestic expenditures" on farm products per capita, current prices[b]	Proportion (2) is of (1), per cent	National income per capita in real terms, 1929 prices[c]	"Domestic expenditures" on farm products in real terms, 1929 prices[d]
1922	$522	$ 84	16.1	$553	$89
1925	656	101	15.4	644	99
1929	716	96	13.4	716	96
1934	392	50	12.8	491	63
1937	547	75	13.7	625	86
1939	552	64	11.6	673	78

[a] Computed from Simon Kuznets, *National Income and Its Composition, 1919–1938* (New York: National Bureau of Economic Research, Inc., 1941), Vol. I, p. 139; Simon Kuznets, *National Product War and Prewar*, Appendix Table 7, p. 46; *Statistical Abstract of the United States, 1942*, p. 11.

[b] Frederick Strauss and Louis H. Bean, *Gross Farm Income and Indices of Farm Products and Prices in the United States, 1869–1937*, Table 7, p. 23; *Statistical Abstract of the United States, 1940*, p. 668; *Statistical Abstract of the United States, 1942*, pp. 11, 548, 745.

[c] Simon Kuznets, *National Income and Its Composition, 1919–1938*, Vol. I, p. 153; Simon Kuznets, *National Product War and Prewar*, Appendix Table 7, p. 46; *Statistical Abstract of the United States, 1942*, pp. 11, 372.

[d] (3) multiplied by (4).

portion of that income that was "spent" for farm products. Thus, it would appear that the elasticity of expenditure for farm products with respect to income was in the neighborhood of zero; certainly at best it had a very low positive value.[30]

1922–1939. For a later period than 1870 to 1910, it is less easy to gauge the effects of rises in income on the demand for farm products. However, from the apparent relationship between national income and "expenditure" for farm products from 1922 to 1939 (see Table 5–7), we may guess that for this period also the income elasticity of farm products was very low.[31]

[30] What we have is an increase of 85 per cent in real income accompanied by a 3 per cent increase in "expenditures" for farm products. If other factors had remained constant, this would have been an income elasticity for farm products of .03.

[31] Between World Wars I and II, incomes fluctuated widely, as is evident from Table 5–7. But here, again, the proportion of the national per capita income presumably "spent" for farm products declined, dropping from about 16 per cent in 1922 to 11.6 per cent in 1939. The per capita income, in terms

INCOME ELASTICITY OF SERVICES ADDED TO FARM PRODUCTS

Once we know the income elasticity of food at retail and of farm products entering into food and the proportion of the services entering into food that were contributed by farm products, we can readily calculate the income elasticities of the nonfarm services entering into food. Suppose that the income elasticity of food is .5 and that of farm products entering into food .25, and that one-half of the value of food is contributed by agriculture and the other half by nonfarm resources after farm products leave the farm. Under these circumstances, the income elasticity of the nonfarm services added to food is .75. An indirect procedure, such as this, is, of course, vulnerable because it depends on the validity of each of the other estimates, two of which are very difficult to establish. It is, therefore, very desirable to obtain an independent estimate of the income elasticity of nonfarm services added to food and to other products made from farm products. But the task is even more difficult than that of estimating the income elasticities of either food or farm products. The data available, at best, are not inconsistent with the hypotheses that the income elasticity of these nonfarm services is not as low as that for farm products.

Certain commodities tend to stay fairly constant in their physical composition as farm products, but may change substantially in value at the point at which consumers buy them, reflecting the amount and kind of nonfarm services added in processing, handling, delivering, and serving these products as food. Examining the expenditures for such products, we can obtain another approximation of the income elasticity of food products at the farm level. Cheese is a good example. Whether cheese is prepared as common Cheddar or whether it is eventually made into a highly refined Blue cheese, the raw materials do not vary greatly, nor, consequently, do the claims made on agricultural resources. In Table 5–8, a number of commodities of this type have been selected, and their elasticities have been ascertained, both for physical consumption (quan-

---

of 1929 prices, rose about 30 per cent from 1922 to 1929, and the amount "spent" for farm products, also in 1929 prices, rose about 8 per cent. Since prices that farmers received increased fully 20 per cent from 1922 to 1929, and since all commodity prices at wholesale dropped slightly, the 8 per cent rise in the amount "spent" for farm products was larger on account of the changes in the relative position of farm to other prices than it would have been had prices remained constant. For the entire period, from 1922 to 1939, the per capita income (in 1929 prices) rose about one-fifth, yet the amount "spent" for farm products (in 1929 prices) dropped from $89 to $78, a decline of nearly 13 per cent. Farm prices, however, dropped about 28 per cent from 1922 to 1939, while all commodities at wholesale declined about 20 per cent.

tity) and for value of consumption (quantity plus quality) against income. In each case the elasticity of physical consumption is less, and considerably less, than the elasticity of the value of consumption of the product. For the products listed, the average difference for the lower-income range ($1,233–$1,707) appears to be nearly 25 per cent, that is, the elasticity based on physical consumption is about a fourth less than it is when based on value of consumption.

TABLE 5–8. THE ELASTICITY OF PHYSICAL CONSUMPTION AND THE ELASTICITY OF THE VALUE OF CONSUMPTION WITH RESPECT TO INCOME OF UNITED STATES NONRELIEF NONFARM FAMILIES, MARCH–NOVEMBER, 1936

Family income range	Commodity	Elasticity of physical consumption	Elasticity of the value of consumption
$1,233–$1,707	Tomato juice	1.6311	1.8579
	Cheese	0.4654	0.5902
	Milk	0.3587	0.4138
	Butter	0.3072	0.3681
	Bananas	0.2952	0.3220
	Eggs	0.1625	0.3080
	Canned tomatoes . .	−0.0128	0.1038
	Beans	−0.4180	−0.2890
$1,707–$2,396	Tomato juice	1.2740	1.3763
	Cheese	0.3538	0.4070
	Milk	0.2611	0.3146
	Butter	0.2094	0.2675
	Bananas	0.1803	0.2098
	Eggs	0.1457	0.2834
	Canned tomatoes . .	−0.9046	0.0000
	Beans	−0.5587	−0.4645

SOURCES: Data used are from *Consumer Purchases of Certain Foods, U.S. Non-relief Nonfarm Families, March–November, 1936*, U.S. Department of Agriculture, Washington, D.C., Division of Marketing and Marketing Agreements, March, 1940. The income figures were derived by calculating the average income per family in the income levels $1,000–$1,500, $1,500–$2,000, $2,000–$3,000, respectively. *Cf. Family Expenditures in the United States, Statistical Tables and Appendixes*, National Resources Planning Board, Washington, D.C., June, 1941, p. 29.

The elasticity formula used is

$$\frac{\Delta x}{\Delta y} \frac{y}{x}$$

where Δx = the increment in the average *physical* consumption of all families in the first case, and the increment in the *value* of average consumption per family in the second, Δy = the increment in the mean of the income range.

y = the mean in the lower-income range.

x = the mean of the physical consumption of all families in the lower-income range in the first case, and the mean of the value of average consumption per family in the lower-income range in the second.

TABLE 5–9. ELASTICITY OF EXPENDITURES ON 21 MEALS AT HOME BASIS, UNITED STATES
URBAN FAMILIES, SPRING, 1948

	Elasticity		Relative importance, per cent of total expenditure
	Expenditure	Quantity purchased	
All food (excluding alcoholic beverages and coffee)	.28	.14	100
All livestock products	.33	.23	50.8
Fruits and vegetables	.42	.33	19.0
All other food	.08	−.12	30.2
Total	. . . . .	. . . . .	100.0
Meat, poultry, and fish	.36	.23	29.2
Dairy products (excluding butter) . .	.32	.23	16.9
Eggs.	.22	.20	4.7
Leafy green and yellow vegetables . .	.37	.21	4.9
Citrus fruit and tomatoes.	.41	.42	5.2
Other vegetables and fruit	.45	.35	8.9
Grain products.	.02	−.21	11.4
Fats and oils	.13	−.04	9.8
Sugar and sweets	.20	−.07	5.2
Dry beans, peas, and nuts	−.07	−.33	1.5
Potatoes and sweet potatoes	.05	−.05	2.3
Total	. . . . .	. . . . .	100.0

SOURCE: Karl Fox, "Factors Affecting Farm Income, Farm Prices, and Food Consumption," *Agricultural Economics Research*, Vol. III (July, 1951), Table 10, Bureau of Agricultural Economics.

A recent study by Fourt[32] offers the conclusion that the "income elasticity of farm products is about .4, of marketing services, .8, and of food, .6. Each of these is composed of diverse elements of high and low elasticities." His estimate of .8 for marketing services is essentially a residual based on the other two estimates and the proportion of food that is contributed by farm products. Fourt, however, provides a number of estimates of particular segments of the marketing sector which are valuable clues and they are not inconsistent with the belief that the

[32] L. A. Fourt, *Economic Progress, Income and the Marketing of Farm Products*, an unpublished manuscript reporting results obtained under the University of Chicago-RMA study. Fourt's estimates reflect his measure of food consumption which allows price changes to enter and which places restrictions on quantity changes.

income elasticity of marketing services is substantially higher than that of farm products.

Fox has placed the food consumption survey of urban families, spring, 1948, on a "per 21 meals at home" basis and has obtained the results shown in Table 5–9.

INCOME ELASTICITIES OF PARTICULAR FOOD GROUPS

Whereas agriculture, as a whole, produces and sells a collection of products the demand for which is quite inelastic against income, approximately .25 at the beginning of the decade of the fifties, there are important variations among farm products. The demands of some products gain substantially from increases in income while others lose ground. Salt sides, dry beans and peas, potatoes, flour, and lard and margarine have become inferior foods against income and, accordingly, the demand shifts to the left as incomes rise; while such products as ice cream, turkey, citrus fruit, the better (lean) cuts of beef, lamb, and hogs are in a strong position as incomes move up.[33] The implications of these differences in income elasticities to agricultural production are, of course, clear. They set the stage for shifts in the use of agricultural resources away, for example, from wheat as food to the production of feeds or the use of wheat as feed. Where the supply is essentially "joint" like lard and pork chops, slowly ways are found of producing a "new and better model" hog having less fat and more lean meat.

From many bits of information and from the studies that have been made of the demand of various foods, it is possible to get a rough approximation of these income elasticities. It is our belief that the empirical data at hand point to a classification of food groups for consumers in the United States at retail about as follows:

Inferior Foods against Income. The following foods have negative income elasticities:

> Dry beans and peas—very negative
> Salt sides and lard—very negative
> Potatoes and sweet potatoes—quite negative
> Flour and cereal products—slightly negative as a group
> All fats and oils—slightly negative as a group
> Sugar and sirups—zero or slightly negative

---

[33] An index of the *leanness of meat* is relevant and may prove useful in classifying meats. Such an index is indicated by the study by Gerald Engelman, Austin A. Dowell, Evan F. Ferrin, and Philip Anderson, *Marketing Slaughter Hogs by Carcass Weight and Grade*, Univ. Minn. Agr. Exp. Sta. Tech. Bul. 187, April, 1950.

Low Elasticity Foods. These foods have income elasticities of .25 and less at retail:

Coffee, tea, and cocoa, as a group
Meats, poultry including eggs, and fish as a group
Vegetables and fruits other than tomatoes and citrus
Milk products on nonfat solid basis

Upper Elasticity Foods. The following foods have income elasticities higher than .25 at retail:

Tomatoes and citrus fruits
Fresh cream and ice cream
Turkey
Better cuts of beef, mutton, and pork
Some tree nuts
Some fresh and canned vegetables and fruits.

Waite and Trelogan[34] took the 1935–1936 data and calculated the "income-consumption" elasticities for a number of foods. They restricted this study to households in the North and West in the United States and reported the results shown in the table on page 73.

The Twentieth Century Fund[35] drew heavily upon the talent and data of the U.S. Department of Agriculture and came up with the following very suggestive estimates of increases in the per capita demand for foods that would result from a 25 per cent rise in incomes above the 1940 level:

Food groups[a]	At 1940 income	At income 25 per cent higher than 1940	Income elasticity
Milk (nonmilk solids)	213	232	0.36
Tomatoes and citrus fruit	88	102	0.63
Leafy, green, and yellow vegetables	83	84	0.05
Potatoes and sweet potatoes	137	153	0.47
Dry beans, peas, and nuts	16	10	−1.50
Other vegetables and fruits	197	255	1.17
Eggs	25	25	0
Meat, poultry, and fish.	147	163	0.43
Flour, cereals	201	212	0.22
Fats and oils.	72	71	−0.06
Sugar and sirups.	75	76	0.05

[a] Milk is in quarts, eggs are in dozens, and other foods are in pounds, kitchen weight.

[34] Warren C. Waite and Harry C. Trelogan, *Introduction to Agricultural Prices* (Minneapolis: Burgess Publishing Co., 1948), p. 25.

[35] J. Frederic Dewhurst and Associates, *America's Needs and Resources* (New York: The Twentieth Century Fund, Inc., 1947), Table 37, p. 103.

Commodity	Income elasticity negative	Commodity	Income elasticity 0–.37	Commodity	Income elasticity .38–1.00	Commodity	Income elasticity 1.00 and over
Evap. milk	−.126	Whole milk	.284	Cheese	.503	Cream	1.12
Margarine	−.833	Butter	.327				
Lard	−.299	Vegetable shortening	.318				
Beef		Ground beef	.000			Beef sirloin	1.32
Chuck roast	−.037	Beef					
Boiling roast	−.211	Round steak	.206				
Salt side	−.185	Sausage, pork	.151	Pork chops	.522	Lamb and mutton	1.77
		Bacon, sliced	.137	Ham, sliced	.607		
White flour	−.236	Wheat cereals, uncooked	.250	Ready-to-eat cereal	.769		
Canned tomatoes	−.371			Fresh tomatoes	.576	Tomato juice.	1.38
Dried navy beans	−.522	Canned baked beans	.093	Fresh carrots.	.675	Celery.	1.01
		Canned peas	.034	Fresh peas	.898	Fresh asparagus.	1.14
White potatoes	−.036						
Rice	−.098	Granulated sugar	.054	Oranges	.425	Chocolate.	1.04

SOURCE: Warren C. Waite and Harry C. Trelogan, *Introduction to Agricultural Prices* (Minneapolis: Burgess Publishing Co., 1948).

In retrospect, these estimates appear to have overshot the mark for several food groups, especially for potatoes and for flour and cereals. A mere inspection of the record from 1940 to 1950, during which per capita disposal income rose somewhat more than 33 per cent (in constant dollars) and relative prices had moved back, in part at least, toward their prewar more "normal" relationships, suggests that the demand for food did not rise against income nearly as much as is indicated by these projected estimates. The per capita consumption of potatoes and sweet potatoes fell from an index of 95 in 1940 to 84 in 1950; flour and grain products, from 98 to 88; and meats, poultry, and fish rose only from 108 to 116; in fact, the per capita consumption of all food (Bureau of Agricultural Economics index) increased only from 106 to 111 when we compare 1940 with 1950 during which incomes per capita rose 33 per cent.[36]

NOTE : CLASSIFICATION OF INDUSTRIES

A classification must start with a purpose. Our purpose is to study the direction of resource reallocation in a long secular context, covering the long run when all inputs may be taken as variables. Industries may be classified on the basis of supply or demand attributes. The older English economists chose supply characteristics, using differences in underlying cost conditions. Agriculture was placed in the increasing-costs and manufacturing in the decreasing-costs category. A constant costs class was also at hand. It was one thing to construct the boxes and to label them "increasing," "decreasing," or "constant" costs; yet it was quite another to identify the industries in order to put each into the proper box. Analytically the boxes are required, but empirically they have been either empty or the industries placed in a particular box have not behaved according to the label.

Agriculture is a notable case in point; it "belonged" in the "increasing costs" box no matter what had happened or might happen. Marshall's final statement on the secular tendency to diminishing return is relevant, namely, " . . . whatever may be the future developments of the arts of agriculture, a continued increase in the application of capital and labour to land must ultimately result in a diminution of the extra produce which can be obtained by a given extra amount of capital and labour."[37]

[36] It should be noted, however, that some substitution undoubtedly occurred because of high food prices, since food prices to consumers rose from an index of 97 in 1940 to 204 in 1950, while all items in the consumers' index increased from 100 to 171 during that period.

[37] *Principles of Economics*, 8th ed. (London: Macmillan & Co., Ltd., 1930), Book IV, Chap. III, Sec. 1, p. 153.

Two difficulties continue to exist in employing in empirical analysis a classification of industries based on underlying costs conditions. In the first place, it is exceedingly hard to identify this supply characteristic, and second, the various cost conditions change, and in the really long run all tend to become more alike than otherwise.

There is, so it appears, a strong case for classifying industries in terms of the demand attributes of the products each produces. The income elasticity of the product affords a useful basis for classification because the effects of increases in income over a long span of time are exceedingly important for resource allocation, because it is empirically possible to estimate the income elasticity, and because the income elasticity appears to show a considerable constancy. As we have suggested elsewhere, in such a classification, *primary* industries might be taken to include those "firms" that produce products (services) with an income elasticity, say, of .5 or less; *secondary* industries are those falling between 1.0 and .5; and *tertiary* industries, those with products with an income elasticity greater than 1.0.

NOTE : THE RISE IN THE LEVEL OF INCOME

One index of changes in fundamental factor supplies and product demands is income. A rise in income may be taken to represent economic development. Economic development may be viewed either (1) as an increase in the total income of a community with per capita income settling to a stable subsistence level (the classical formulation of economic progress) or (2) as a rise in both total and per capita income (a) with no restriction on its personal distribution, (b) with no segment of the population and no community in the economy worse off than it was prior to the rise in income, and (c) with all segments of the population and all communities in the economy somewhat better off as a consequence of the rise in income. Of these, (2b) and, as time goes on, (2c) appear to reflect the conception of development (preference) of people of Western countries viewed as a community.

As one reaches for an index to measure income changes, the difficulties of determining income come to the fore. There are difficulties in the concept of income of an individual and of a community whether for a particular date or over time. There is no satisfactory method of passing from the income of individuals to the income of the community.

As better production possibilities emerge, individuals and the community will prefer to take some of these gains in additional leisure; the increase in leisure made possible by economic development and preferred and enjoyed by individuals and the community is not represented in income data. The marginal rate of substitution between leisure and income may be low but it is important, nevertheless. Colin Clark has put the elasticity of leisure against income at somewhat less than .1, meaning by this that out of an increase of 10 per cent in real product a little less than 1 per cent is taken in the form of additional leisure and the rest as additional "real" income.[38] Nor do income data include all the income which individuals produce for themselves and for their families. The useful and valuable work of housewives as housekeepers in their own homes is left out, and over time circumstances change importantly, for example, as more married women take part-time or full-time jobs for pay. There is also the problem of variations in the self-sufficiency of families, particularly of farms—farm households not only over time but also cross-sectionally within a community as large and diverse as the United States. Nor can one be unmindful of the effects of such major institutional changes as the high progressive income tax rates upon the possibility of substituting productive effort for income that is taxable for that which does not enter into tax accounting. Meanwhile, the complex of products and services is constantly undergoing change as new ones are added and old ones are dropped.

Per capita income data give rise to additional difficulties. The composition of a population changes over time, and it differs importantly looked at cross-sectionally at a particular date, in terms of age, sex, race, occupation, location, economic area, proportion working, and in terms of other attributes. The composition of the consuming unit also bristles with difficulties when one comes to gauge the income elasticity, for example, of food. Then, too, there is the personal distribution of income, important on welfare grounds and largely neglected in available income data and in their interpretation.

For all these reasons, it is exceedingly important in any appeal to particular income data, at least to endeavor to judge their shortcomings for the purpose at hand. Income data, at their best, may help one to approximate one of the consequences of changes in fundamental factor supplies and in product demands but they can never measure such changes precisely and accurately.

With these introductory remarks on the difficulties inherent in income data whether they represent comparisons based on a particular date or over time and whether they are restricted to a particular country or entail a comparison among countries, two sets of data will be included. One of these is a bold attempt at international comparisons and the other is restricted to the United States.

[38] Colin Clark, *The Conditions of Economic Progress* (London: Macmillan & Co., Ltd., 1951), rev. 2d ed., pp. 42–44.

TABLE 5–10. LEVELS OF REAL NATIONAL PRODUCT PER MAN-HOUR

Country	1800–1825	1825–1850	1850	1860	1870	1880	1890	1900	1910	1920	1925	1930	1935	1940	1947
United States	0.21	0.21	0.24	0.28	0.24	0.28	0.34	0.42	0.51	0.61	0.75	0.77	0.83	1.00	1.19
New Zealand	...	...	...	...	...	...	...	0.52	...	...	0.66	0.61	0.75	0.81	1.07
Canada	...	...	...	...	...	...	...	0.55	0.51	0.41	0.54	0.57	0.60	0.71	0.96
Australia	0.09	...	...	...	...	...	0.43	0.43	0.49^a	0.43	0.59	0.64	0.68	0.63	0.67
Argentina	...	...	...	...	...	...	...	...	...	...	...	...	0.35	0.39	0.42^b
Britain	0.17	0.17	...	0.22	0.23	0.29	0.31	0.30	0.36	0.37^a	0.48	0.51	0.54	0.57	0.59
Germany	0.05	0.08	...	...	0.17	0.20	0.23	0.26	0.29	0.31^a	0.27	0.34	0.41	0.47	0.49^c
France	0.07	0.08	0.10	0.12	0.14	0.15	0.17	0.19	0.21	0.24	0.32	0.31	0.30	0.34	0.35
Switzerland	...	...	...	...	...	...	0.15	0.16	0.23^a	...	0.31	0.36	0.38	0.37	0.42
Sweden	...	...	...	0.10	0.11	0.12	0.14	0.17	0.21	0.30	0.29	0.33	0.34	0.41^d	0.39^c
USSR	...	...	...	...	...	...	...	0.15	0.17^a	0.10^e	0.15	0.15	0.12	0.18	0.14
Italy	...	...	...	...	...	...	0.10	0.13	0.13^a	...	0.15	0.14^f	0.20^g	0.14^h	0.14
Japan	...	...	...	...	...	...	...	0.03	0.04	0.06	0.11	0.14	0.17	0.19	0.18^c
India	...	...	...	0.03	...	...	...	0.05	...	0.07^e	...	0.08^f	...	...	0.09^c

^{a} 1913. ^{b} 1945. ^{c} 1944. ^{d} 1939. ^{e} 1921. ^{f} 1931. ^{g} 1938. ^{h} 1942.

SOURCE: Colin Clark, "Levels of Real National Product per Man-hour," *Review of Economic Progress*, Vol. I (Brisbane, Australia: April, 1949).

Some International Comparisons

The broad sweep of economic development is reflected in Colin Clark's data on real income per man-hour worked measured in his "international unit." This unit is in terms of goods and not in money; it is the quantity of goods and services exchangeable for $1 in the United States during the base period 1925–1934.

The United States

When one seeks his bearing on United States income, one turns to Simon Kuznets's work for the National Bureau of Economic Research. Kuznets's data show that from 1869 to 1938 the national income increased at a rate of almost 19 per cent per quinquennium while the population grew somewhat more than 8 per cent and the per capita income increased at an 8.5 per cent rate. From the mid-point of 1869–1878 to that of 1929–1938, the national income expanded eightfold; although the population grew almost threefold, the income per capita virtually tripled.

TABLE 5–11. National Income of the United States, 1869–1938 by Decades

Period	Average per year			Per cent of change from decade to overlapping decade		
	National income, in billions of dollars	Population, in millions	Per capita, in dollars, (1) ÷ (2)	National income	Population	Per capita
	(1)	(2)	(3)	(4)	(5)	(6)
1869–1878	9.3	43.5	215			
1874–1883	13.6	48.8	278	+45.6	+12.2	+29.3
1879–1888	17.9	54.8	326	+31.4	+12.1	+17.3
1884–1893	21.0	61.2	344	+17.7	+11.7	+ 5.5
1889–1898	24.2	67.6	357	+14.9	+10.6	+ 3.8
1894–1903	29.8	74.3	401	+23.1	+ 9.8	+12.3
1899–1908	37.3	81.5	458	+25.5	+ 9.8	+14.2
1904–1913	45.0	89.6	502	+20.5	+ 9.9	+ 9.6
1909–1918	50.6	97.7	517	+12.4	+ 9.0	+ 3.0
1914–1923	57.3	105.0	546	+13.3	+ 7.4	+ 5.6
1919–1928	69.0	112.8	612	+20.6	+ 7.5	+12.1
1924–1933	73.3	120.6	607	+ 6.1	+ 6.9	− 0.8
1929–1938	72.0	126.0	572	− 1.7	+ 4.4	− 5.8

Source: Simon Kuznets, *National Income, A Summary and Findings* (New York: National Bureau of Economic Research, Inc., 1946), major part of Table 10, p. 32.

INCOME CHANGES SINCE 1929 AND BELIEFS ABOUT PROSPECTS

The period since 1929 is instructive because it makes evident how difficult it is to gauge the secular shift. The road which United States income traveled during the thirties and forties was especially tortuous.

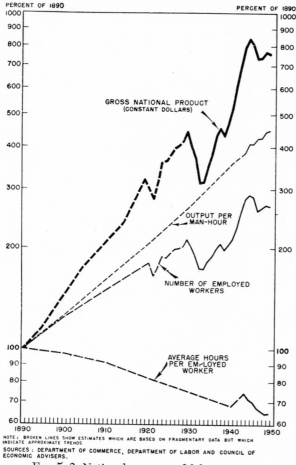

FIG. 5–2. National output and labor inputs.

Per capita disposable personal income dropped 26 per cent from 1929 to 1933 (from 952 to 706 in 1950 dollars) and it did not recover to the 1929 level until 1939. The per capita disposable income in constant dollars rose markedly during the war years and in 1950 was 33 per cent above that of 1940.

The economic experiences of the thirties and forties may be of some value in studying the relation of wide variations in income to other economic variables but they provide little guidance on the secular drift of the economy measured in terms of changes in per capita income. The depression of the early thirties was like an unprecedented drought— it occurred, its effects were vast and tragic, but it is an isolated event.

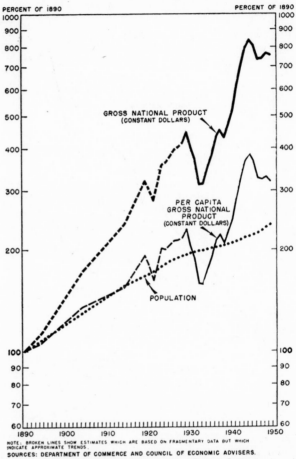

FIG. 5–3. National output and population.

The upsurge of one-third in per capita income during the forties is on a similar footing as a unique event. It is, therefore, not surprising that "estimates" of the anticipated increase in per capita income are easily colored by either of these two events. Those who ventured "calculations" on the prospective rise in incomes during the middle forties, still very mindful of the dismal thirties, were soon proved in error in that

TABLE 5–12. TOTAL AND PER CAPITA DISPOSABLE PERSONAL INCOME IN CURRENT AND 1950 PRICES, 1929–1950

Year	Total disposable personal income, in billions of dollars		Per capita disposable income, in dollars		Population, in thousands
	Current prices	1950 prices	Current prices	1950 prices	
1929	82.5	115.9	678	952	121,770
1930	73.7	108.5	599	882	123,077
1931	63.0	103.6	508	835	124,040
1932	47.8	89.5	383	717	124,840
1933	45.2	88.6	360	706	125,579
1934	51.6	95.6	408	756	126,374
1935	58.0	104.9	456	824	127,250
1936	66.1	118.0	516	921	128,053
1937	71.1	122.4	552	950	128,825
1938	65.5	115.3	505	888	129,825
1939	70.2	124.7	536	953	130,880
1940	75.7	133.0	574	1,008	131,970
1941	92.0	152.3	691	1,143	133,203
1942	116.7	172.4	867	1,280	134,665
1943	132.4	179.4	970	1,314	136,497
1944	147.0	189.9	1,065	1,375	138,083
1945	151.1	188.4	1,082	1,350	139,586
1946	158.9	183.9	1,125	1,302	141,235
1947	169.5	178.8	1,177	1,241	144,024
1948	188.4	188.6	1,285	1,287	146,571
1949	187.4	190.1	1,256	1,274	149,215
1950	202.1	202.1	1,332	1,332	151,772

SOURCE: *The Economic Report of the President,* January, 1951, which includes the Annual Economic Review by the Council of Economic Advisers, Table A–8, p. 178.

they underestimated the rise. The Twentieth Century Fund, *America's Needs and Resources,* completed in 1946, selected assumptions about prospective economic conditions that resulted in per capita income, measured in constant prices, about 26 per cent higher in 1950 than in 1940. The realized increase turned out to be substantially more than this; in fact, the estimate given for 1960 was achieved in 1950.[39] The

[39] J. Frederic Dewhurst and Associates, *America's Needs and Resources,* (New York: The Twentieth Century Fund, Inc., 1947), Table 20, p. 63.

Long-range Agricultural Policy study of the Bureau of Agricultural Economics also underestimated the prospective rise in per capita income given the experience since the report was published.[40] Other and earlier estimates were even more "pessimistic" on this aspect of economic development.

By the close of the forties, the continued high production and the high realized per capita disposable personal income, after allowing for the vast expenditures for national security and high taxes, gave rise to substantially more "optimistic" views with regard to the prospective rate of increase in income. The Council of Economic Advisers, looking ahead from the vantage point of late 1949, anticipated a further expansion in output sufficient to assure an annual rate of increase of 2½ per cent—specifically a 12½ per cent per capita increase by 1954 over that achieved by 1949.[41]

[40] *Long-range Agricultural Policy,* Bureau of Agricultural Economics, published as a committee print by the Committee on Agriculture of the House of Representatives, Mar. 10, 1948.

[41] See *The Economic Report of the President,* January, 1950, p. 78.

6

EFFECTS OF NUTRITION UPON
DEMAND AND SUPPLY

The young science of nutrition has given rise to an active and important development affecting the value of farm products. There is, however, much confusion about the economic effects of nutrition. Better
nutrition is a "good" thing; but under what conditions and at what
price? All too frequently the goal of better nutrition is approached in
altogether too narrow a physical-biological framework with no clear
conception of the possibility (costs) or of the preference and how they
are related one to the other. In some circles, nutrition has provided an
excuse to "puff and push" the more expensive foods unto consumers.
Better diets, as specified by nutrition, have seemed to others a way of
enlarging the demand for farm products, a way of getting rid of the
stocks and surpluses accumulated by governmental programs or to provide additional outlets for the more expensive foods.

The new technical and social insights associated with nutrition express themselves in two ways:

1. As advances in technical knowledge about food adopted by consuming and producing units.

2. As modifications in social objectives which a community endeavors
to achieve by means of social action.

Much depends, accordingly, on how nutrition is put to use. It is not
in any sense predetermined what nutrition, either as new knowledge or
as a social movement, will do to the value of farm products. Education
to inform people about nutrition may induce them to place a higher
value on food, relative to other goods and services; even with incomes
remaining constant they may be taught to spend more of their incomes
for food. Such changes in consumers' choices are fundamental. They are
not likely to occur rapidly.

A common belief is that more complete knowledge regarding nutrition will induce people to consume more of the expensive foods, costlier
in terms of land, labor, and other resources required to produce them.
Much of the promotion in behalf of better nutrition is of this nature.

83

It fits in well with the social conditions that determine the food habits of people, and with those public policy makers who wish to enlarge the market for farm products.

Public measures can, of course, alter diets by various direct and indirect means. Lessening the inequality of incomes among families is one of the more indirect approaches. Because the income elasticity of food is higher in the lower-income groups than it is in the upper-income groups, a more equal distribution of personal income will increase the aggregate demand of food, other things remaining unchanged. Public policy to achieve this goal, whether by progressive income taxes or by other means, is likely to be slow and gradual of realization. Even under favorable conditions such indirect approaches are not likely to add appreciably to the demand for farm products during the course of a decade or two.[1]

There are, however, more direct measures to aid consumers to attain better diets. Governments will undoubtedly do much in this sphere if present agricultural surpluses persist. Food-stamp plans, food grants and aids, in-factory feeding, and school-lunch programs are some of the measures for doing this task.

The economics of nutrition relevant to our study consists of the following parts: (1) What are the supply effects of increasing the efficiency of food? (2) What are the demand effects of this new technical knowledge about food? (3) How much more food is required in the United States to close the existing nutritional gap?

INCREASING THE EFFICIENCY OF FOOD: SUPPLY EFFECTS

The supply effects of this development originate at two points: one, the gains in efficiency that come from the application of the advances in nutrition within producing units, and the other, the gains in efficiency that are achieved in the better handling of food in consuming units. This classification means that households also perform operations which are of the nature of production and they, therefore, affect the supply of food, although we do not commonly conceive of households as contributing to production.

Efficiency within Producing Units. The application of new technical knowledge about nutrition is, of course, not restricted to the human population. In the United States, the feeding of animals often comes first in claims on these advances. Farmers, once they find out that it

---

[1] Structural changes of the kind that occurred in the United States from 1940 to 1948 because of war and because full employment was achieved were instrumental in reducing the inequality in personal income appreciably.

pays to feed nutritionally balanced rations to chickens, dairy cows, hogs, cattle, and sheep, are induced by profit considerations to apply the new techniques and compelled to do so by competition. The motivation of consumers is less direct and less effective in applying such new knowledge.

Farmers obtain appreciably higher rates of output per unit of resource than they did formerly in producing livestock. One measure of this advance is the output per breeding unit. It is noteworthy that the production of livestock in the United States per breeding unit increased over 40 per cent during the three decades, 1920–1950.[2] Heavier feeding of better balanced rations was an important technical development contributing to this increase. Advances in nutrition applied to livestock feeding point the way to better balanced rations; increases in protein supplements made available by the rapid expansion in the vegetable-oil crops and by the upward drift in production of legume hay helped to make them possible.

There is still another way in which advances in what we know about nutrition, when applied, increase the supply of food. Suppose it is discovered that the nutritional value of food is a function of the mineral content of soils, varieties of plants, and climatic conditions under which it is produced, and suppose further that scientists are successful in isolating the effects of each of these components upon the nutritional quality of the food. With this information, a new class of technical advances becomes possible. As yet no quantitative estimates of the gains achieved along these lines are available; there are, however, numerous spectacular illustrations. Christensen[3] cites the Nelson apple from New Zealand which "is reported to have a vitamin C content greater than tomatoes and almost as high as citrus fruits," while presumably apples commonly grown in the United States are very low in this important nutrient. Maynard[4] points out that tomatoes upon which we rely for vitamin C range

[2] *Farm Production, Practices, Costs, and Returns,* BAE, *Statis. Bul.* 83, October, 1949, pp. 34–35.

Sherman E. Johnson, *Changes in American Farming,* USDA, *Misc. Pub.* 707, December, 1949, pp. 47–51.

Raymond Christensen, *Efficient Use of Food Resources, in the United States,* USDA, *Tech. Bul.* 963, October, 1948, pp. 18–19.

[3] *Ibid.,* p. 24.

[4] See L. A. Maynard, "Food Production for Better Health and Longer Life," in *Nutrition and Public Health in the Postwar Period,* a conference report, Children's Fund of Michigan (Detroit), 1944, pp. 7–19. Professor Maynard cites data for apples, tomatoes, and cabbages showing the variation in vitamin C; for wheat on its thiamine content; the influence of soil upon the calcium

from 5 to 45 milligrams. This range in content suggests certain possibilities on the supply side; to illustrate, if tomatoes grown in one area of
the country are more valuable in terms of their vitamin C content than
those produced in another area and if the cost of production in the two
areas is the same, the supply can be increased by shifting some or all
of the production of tomatoes to the area having these advantages—be

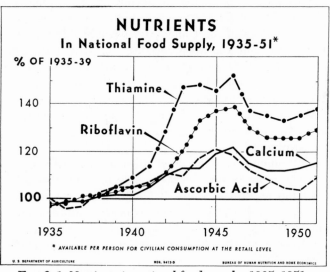

FIG. 6–1. Nutrients in national food supply, 1935–1951.

it in soil, climate, or in some other resource used in the production of
this product.[5,6]

Farmers are not the only producing units who apply nutrition to increase the supply of food. The vast array of firms that buy, concentrate,
handle, store, process, distribute, and market farm products also apply
the advances that are made in knowledge about nutrition in their pro-

---

and phosphorus content of foods; the effects of climate and season, including
light intensity, upon vitamin content, which are very marked; he concludes
that already it is known that these are important genetic, soil, and climatic
factors affecting the nutritive value of foods of plant origin.

[5] Implied, of course, is the assumption that consumers can identify the
superior tomatoes and that they want them; otherwise all this new technical
knowledge is in vain.

[6] There is a vast literature on the technical aspects of nutrition applied to
the production of food. The 1939 *Yearbook of Agriculture, Food and Life,*
U.S. Department of Agriculture, is an exceedingly useful summary, especially
Part 2, on animal nutrition, and the opening paper by Professor E. J. Kraus,
"Sources and Cycles of the Nutritive Elements."

ductive operations. These firms can basically do two things: (1) they can bring about a better utilization of the nutritive contents of the farm products sold by farmers and (2) they can add nonfarm resources to fortify and in other ways increase the nutritive value of the farm-produced supply. Christensen cites the increased use of nonfat solids of milk as an outstanding development during the war years bringing about a better utilization of milk. "The proportion of all nonfat solids in the milk supply used for human consumption was raised from 55 per cent in the prewar period to approximately 70 per cent in 1945." As a result, although the production of milk increased only 16 per cent, the per capita consumption of nonfat solids rose by 25 per cent.[7]

Efficiency within Consuming Units. One of the fundamental postulates of economic theory is the maximizing behavior of consumers. The consuming unit consisting of the household is conceived of as an institution which performs these maximizing operations, and the determinants of these operations are viewed as preferences (and utilities) and constructed into indifference curves on which modern demand analysis rests. A difficulty, however, arises from the fact that consuming units may also perform operations that are of the nature of production. It is, therefore, necessary to identify these production activities of households and determine their supply effects. Usually, studies of demand concentrate on the price paid and quantity taken by consuming units at retail. We are obliged, however, to treat this demand as derived from two sources: (1) from basic consumer preferences and (2) from the household as a producing unit which handles, stores, processes, and combines food elements to increase their value in satisfying the preferences of the individuals it serves.

It is hard to believe that the ratio of input to output is the same for all households or that it remains unchanged for a particular household over time. The efficiency of households in employing the food components that they acquire is subject to many factors and these factors determine the "productive" efficiency of households. Advances in our technical knowledge about nutrition, available to and applied by housewives, are one of the important factors increasing the efficiency of households over time. Pearl's estimates for World War I are cited frequently; they indicate that the wastage of food in the homes resulted in loss of 5 per cent of the proteins, 25 per cent of the fats, 20 per cent of the carbohydrates, and 19 per cent of the total calories.[8,9] The supply ef-

[7] Christensen, *op. cit.*, pp. 21–24.
[8] *Ibid.*, p. 23.
[9] Margaret G. Reid, *Food for People* (New York: John Wiley & Sons, Inc., 1943), reviews the literature on this point in some detail, pp. 250ff.

fects of nutrition as it is applied by the housewife cannot as yet be estimated. All that is possible is to indicate the qualitative aspects of these operations.

DEMAND EFFECTS OF NUTRITION

People are not satisfied when they have achieved subsistence that meets known nutritional requirements at minimum cost. If their preferences were not to take them beyond this point, it would be fairly easy to determine the effects of advances in knowledge about nutrition upon the demand for food. But consumer choices in a high-income community, such as ours, are not geared to physical-biological subsistence. While it would be instructive to find out what combination of foods would provide an adequate diet at minimum cost, given the existing beliefs of scientists about the nutritional value of particular foods, as Stigler[10] attempted to do, such analyses are of little value in determining the demand effects of nutrition. Food is not consumed solely to maintain physical existence or to attain physical comfort. Food serves preferences which are essential parts of our culture and it is the cultural aspects and changes in them that present the real difficulties in the problem at hand.

How is nutrition related to the existing system of preferences? It must

[10] George J. Stigler, "The Cost of Subsistence," *Journal of Farm Economics,* Vol. XXVII (May, 1945): 303. Professor Stigler took the National Research Council's allowances for nutritional requirements seriously to the point of applying them (on paper) to a young college professor for a year at a minimum cost. At retail prices of August, 1939, he succeeded in doing it at a cost of $39.93 and at August, 1944, prices, at $59.88.

Stigler's diets may have a bit more appeal to ruminants than to those who prepare cookbooks but they are nevertheless a challenge to those who are interested in nutritional austerity, as may be seen from his data which follow:

MINIMUM COST ANNUAL DIETS, AUGUST, 1939 AND 1944

Commodity	August, 1939		August, 1944	
	Quantity	Cost	Quantity	Cost
Wheat flour	370, lb.	$13.33	535, lb.	$34.53
Evaporated milk. . . .	57, cans	3.84		
Cabbage	111, lb.	4.11	107, lb.	5.23
Spinach	23, lb.	1.85	13, lb.	1.56
Dried navy beans . . .	285, lb.	16.80		
Pancake flour.	. . . .	. . . . . .	134, lb.	13.08
Pork liver	. . . .	. . . . . .	25, lb.	5.48
Total	. . . .	$39.93	. . . . . .	$59.88

(*Footnote continued on p. 89*)

suffice, in considering this question, merely to indicate certain aspects of the problem that appear to be relevant. One hypothesis would be that the growing emphasis placed on nutrition to maintain health and physical-biological efficiency motivates consumers to reorder their preferences in such a way as to place food higher relative to other goods and services which they consume. This hypothesis would have a good deal of force if it were impossible to satisfy known nutritional requirements with the outlays that consumers are already making for food. It is apparent, however, that the vast majority of consumers in the United States could, if they wanted to, meet nutritional requirements without increasing their outlay for food, provided they were prepared to consume a (slightly) different combination of food. The hypothesis may, nevertheless, be necessary to explain some of the facts, because consumers tend to become aware of the importance of nutritional requirements without acquiring perfect knowledge as to the nutritional value of alternative combinations of food. They respond to this new awareness about nutrition with incomplete information and in doing so seek to improve their diets without modifying appreciably their existing food habits.

When consumers have "complete" information about the nutritional value of foods, the following hypothesis is indicated: Under such circumstances consumers' choice is determined by preferences for particular social and cultural attributes ascribed to particular combinations of food other than their intrinsic nutritional value, because there are available to consumers alternative combinations of food each of which is satisfactory nutritionally, because these alternative combinations are available at costs that vary widely, and because one or more of these combinations fits into the food habits of consumers. This hypothesis assumes: (1) with preferences, prices, and income given, the consumer

---

The low-cost diets that circumstances have imposed on people, for instance, the Irish subsistence on potatoes, should be instructive. How adequate was the Irishman's diet around 1800 when it consisted of about 10 pounds of potatoes and 1 pint of milk a day? An excellent recent study, by K. H. Connell, *The Population of Ireland, 1750–1845* (New York: Oxford University Press, 1950), includes the relevant data (see Table 21, p. 155) and finds that this diet was surprisingly satisfactory. Connell used the National Research Council's Recommendations adjusted downward 30 per cent for minerals and vitamins. To test this typical Irishman's diet of that time against current information on food nutrients and recommendations, the writer obtained the following calculations from the Bureau of Human Nutrition and Home Economics which indicates that this diet, except for Vitamin A, is quite abundant in the nutrients required (see table on following page):

Item	Food energy, cal.	Pro- tein, gm.	Fat, gm.	Carbo- hydrates gm.	Cal- cium, mg.	Iron, mg.	Vita- min A value, I.U.	Thia- mine, mg.	Ribo- flavin, mg.	Nia- cin, mg.	Ascor- bic acid, mg.	Remarks
Potatoes, 10 lb. A.P.	3,176	76.0	4.0	728.0	420	27.0	700	4.00	1.50	44.0	640[a]	Data based on *U.S. Dept. Agr. Handbook* 8, 1950
Milk, whole 1 pint, 588 gm. (⅛ imp. gal.)	399	20.5	22.8	28.7	690	0.6	940	0.23	0.99	0.6	6	
Total potatoes and milk	3,575	96	27	757	1,110	28	1,640	4.2	2.5	45	646	
Recommended daily di- etary allowances, man physically active	3,000	70	....	.....	1	12	5,000	1.5	1.8	15	75	National Research Council, 1948

Nutrients in 100 grams or indicated quantity.

It should also be noted that only about 7 per cent of the calories are supplied by fat, whereas 20 to 25 per cent are considered desirable.

[a] Year-round average.

makes outlays for food that are sufficient, if properly spent, to provide him with an adequate diet; (2) the consumer can acquire a combination of food nutritionally satisfactory that is compatible with his food habits; and (3) the consumer is sufficiently informed and willing to select from among the various foods a combination that is adequate on nutritional grounds. Should we find that this hypothesis explains consumers' behavior that may be empirically observed, we would conclude that the preference system determining the effective demand for food rests on cultural and social conditions and not on nutritional considerations as such. Nutrition would, therefore, be neutral in relation to the demand for food.

Our tentative belief is that, taking the long view, it is likely that nutrition, consisting of advances in our technical knowledge about food, will neither increase nor decrease the demand for food in a country where the people are as rich and as abundantly fed as are the people of the United States.

CORRECTING NUTRITIONAL IMBALANCES

If the diets of all people were adequate, the goal of good nutrition would have been achieved. This statement is in substance a definition of the social purpose of nutrition. Not all people, however, have attained such a diet. Some diets are inadequate because too few of one or more nutrients are consumed and some because too many nutrients are included. Experiences support the belief that a community with an abundant supply of nutritious food well distributed and with high level of income, steady and distributed fairly equally, and with good food habits is more likely to succeed in attaining adequate diets for all people than will a community not so favored. The United States is fairly fortunate in the combination of these circumstances, and as might be expected, the nutritional standard that has been achieved is relatively high.

Stiebeling has called attention to our generous food supply by observing that the "food supply is apparently large enough and varied enough to provide everyone in this country the nutrient allowances recommended by the National Research Council were foods and nutrients to be distributed according to need and selected with discrimination."[11] Stiebeling's appraisal is amply supported by data (see Table 6–1).

The supply of food in the United States is indeed generous, both in

---

[11] Hazel K. Stiebeling, "Family Food Consumption and Dietary Improvement," *Rural Family Living Reports,* Bureau of Human Nutrition and Home Economics, U.S. Department of Agriculture, October, 1949.

its variety and in amount. And while there have been impressive improvements in the distribution of foods and of food nutrients as a result of increases in income, especially in the lower-income brackets, and of changes in food habits for the better, there are nevertheless some deficiencies. These deficiencies in diets can be approached on the de-

TABLE 6–1. NUTRIENTS AVAILABLE PER CAPITA PER DAY IN THE UNITED STATES, AVERAGES 1935–1939, 1941–1945, AND 1950, AND THE RECOMMENDED ALLOWANCES OF THE NATIONAL RESEARCH COUNCIL

Food nutrient	Unit	Average[a]			NRC recommended allowances[c]
		1935–1939	1941–1945	1950[b]	
Food energy . . .	Calorie	3,250	3,408	3,270	2,640
Protein	Gram	89	98	94	65
Fat	Gram	132	141	143	
Carbohydrate . . .	Gram	428	434	403	
Calcium.	Milligram	900	1,018	1,038	940
Iron	Milligram	14	17	17	11.7
Vitamin A	International unit	8,100	9,180	8,600	4,580
Thiamine	Milligram	1.5	2.1	2.1	1.30
Riboflavin	Milligram	1.9	2.2	2.4	1.78
Niacin	Milligram	15	19	19.4	13.0
Ascorbic acid . . .	Milligram	115	129	119	71

[a] Revised estimates for years since 1941 from *The National Food Situation*, Bureau of Agricultural Economics, 42 pp., October–December, 1947. Nutrients indicated are those contained in the food brought into kitchens; they make no allowance for wastes or cooking losses.

[b] Data for 1950 from *The National Food Situation*, Bureau of Agricultural Economics, January–March, 1950.

[c] From National Research Council. Recommended dietary allowances for different age, sex, and level-of-activity groups by distribution of population among groups in 1947, to obtain the average allowances shown here. Recommended allowances are those for nutrients actually taken into the body.

SOURCE: Raymond Christensen, *Efficient Use of Food Resources in the United States*, USDA, *Tech. Bul.* 963, October, 1948, Table 2, p. 9.

mand side by increasing income, by improving knowledge as to what constitutes an adequate diet, and by overcoming existing unwillingness to change customary food habits in order to bring them in line with nutritional knowledge.

The nutritional imbalance is, therefore, a result of the way the food nutrients are distributed. This imperfect distribution is a consequence of the supply of food and on the side of demand of incomes, information, and food habits. Given a generous supply of food at prices consistent with long-run demand-supply developments (relatively low farm product prices), the level, personal distribution, and stability of income are each significant factors affecting the distribution of the food supply. The forward strides that have been made in achieving better diets since the middle thirties may be ascribed largely to changes in income. Before the war, despite the large supply of food and the ease with which

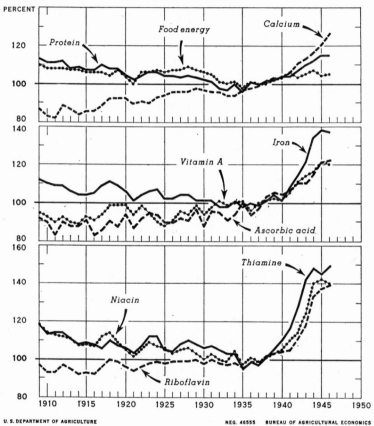

APPARENT PER CAPITA CONSUMPTION OF FOOD NUTRIENTS
IN THE UNITED STATES, 1909-46
INDEX NUMBERS (1935-39=100)

U. S. DEPARTMENT OF AGRICULTURE   NEG. 46555   BUREAU OF AGRICULTURAL ECONOMICS

Fɪɢ. 6–2. Per capita consumption of food nutrients in the United States, 1909–1946.

more food might have been produced, many Americans were short on some essential nutrients in their food. Estimates for 1936 indicated that "fewer than a fifth of the families in this country had diets that met the National Research Council's recommendations for all of the seven nutrients considered (protein, calcium, iron, vitamin A value, ascorbic acid, thiamine, and riboflavin."[12] By 1942 there had occurred a general dietary improvement as families benefited from higher incomes and, of course, also from advances in their knowledge about nutrition. In the case of riboflavin, in 1936 three-fourths of all families had diets that fell below the National Research Council's recommended allowances; in 1942 about one-half were below this mark. In calcium, thiamine, and ascorbic acid, whereas in 1936 only one-half were up to the allowances set by the National Research Council, by 1942 the proportion had risen to two-thirds for calcium, three-fourths for thiamine, and to nine-tenths for ascorbic acid. There were also marked dietary improvements in vitamin A value, iron, and protein.

Real income per capita on the average increased only a little from 1942 to 1948 but that of the low third rose about one-fifth while that of the top third may have dropped slightly. A survey of city consumers indicates:[13]

[That] in 1948 the third of the city families with lowest incomes bought 36 per cent more meat, poultry, and fish than did the third with lowest incomes in 1942. But for the third of the families with highest incomes there was virtually no change in the quantity of meat, poultry, and fish consumed in 1948 as compared with 1942. In the spring of 1948, families at every income level used more milk or milk products other than butter than families at the same dollar income levels in 1942. But even so, increases in milk consumption were greater for the lower than the upper third—31 percent for the lowest income third and 20 percent for the third with highest incomes. Increases in citrus fruit were about 50 percent for the lowest income third, but for the third with highest income, there was little or no change. . . .

. . . that the income elasticities of two groups of foods may have changed between 1942 and 1948. While meat, poultry, and fish and citrus fruits are still consumed in much larger quantities by high as compared with low income families, these foods seem to have a new prominence in city diets at the lower end of the income scale. Thus, the percentage increase in quantities purchased as income rises appears to be smaller than it was at the beginning of the war. . . .

[That the] average quantities of protein, iron, and the five well-known vitamins were above the National Research Council's recommended allowances; and for calcium, averages were less than those

[12] *Family Food Consumption in the United States,* USDA, *Misc. Pub.* 550, 1944, pp. 34–35.
[13] Stiebeling, *op. cit.,* pp. 10–11.

recommended only in the lowest income groups. Among families with diets below recommended levels, calcium, ascorbic acid, and the B vitamins were most often short. Over 4 in 10 city families had less than the recommended amounts of ascorbic acid, thiamine, riboflavin, and niacin when some allowance is made for average losses in cooking.

Diets were improved substantially during the decade of the forties. The deficiencies in food nutrients became small, in fact, very small relative to the abundant supply of food produced in this country. The deficiencies that existed, although small in supply terms, were nevertheless important on welfare grounds.

Clearly, the American community can easily afford diets that are nutritionally adequate; since there are many people who are taking on too many nutrients, the deficiencies among those not receiving enough of them could be corrected without making anyone worse off. If these excess nutrients were sufficient to cover the deficiencies in aggregate, as may well be the case in fact, and if it were feasible to make such transfers, both groups would gain on nutritional grounds, and therefore, on this score a better welfare position could be attained.

The existing nutritional imbalance is, therefore, a problem in the distribution of food and of food nutrients. To place this problem into its economic setting, all that we need to do is to formulate the distribution of food as a function of supply and demand.

To get our bearing in understanding this problem in a relatively rich community with a large supply of food, we need to analyze the factors that determine the demand for food in order to detect why it is that some people still fail to provide adequate diets for themselves. As we do this, we will discover that the conditions that keep people from correcting the nutritional imbalance are mainly on the demand side. The principal task involving both private and social action is to modify the demand for food in ways that will bring about a better distribution of food, better in terms of nutrition. This aspect of the problem can be simplified by concentrating on three types of efforts consisting of (1) more perfect knowledge about food nutrients by consumers and by those who serve them, (2) improvements in food habits, and (3) better incomes.

Clearly these three results are in many ways interdependent in their effects on diets. It is true, however, that the first of these is necessary to achieve the second, but perfect knowledge about nutrition is not sufficient to bring about ideal food habits, nor are such desired food habits the necessary result of high incomes. Better incomes will not of themselves bring about the nutritional objective. In the United States it appears that increasingly the most important factor blocking the further improvement in diets is a combination of ignorance and an unwillingness of people, some of them in every income class, to change their food habits for the better. A recent survey of urban families strongly suggests that many families in each income class consume not only too few of some nutrients but that many other families in each income class consume too many. Table 6–2 provides data for two income classes, the one is next to the lowest and the other next to the highest of urban housekeeping families and shows the per cent of the families in each income class receiving too few nutrients to meet the nutritional allowances recommended by the National Research Council and the per cent with diets that were "excessive," spring of 1948.[14]

TABLE 6–2. GAUGING NUTRIENTS AVAILABLE TO TWO INCOME CLASSES, UNITED STATES URBAN FAMILIES, SPRING, 1948

Food nutrient	Two few nutrients		Too many nutrients	
	$1,000–$1,999, per cent	$5,000–$7,499, per cent	$1,000–$1,999, per cent	$5,000–$7,499, per cent
Calories	23	21	19	17
Protein	17	7	26	32
Calcium	50	36	15	25
Iron	14	12	33	33
Ascorbic acid . . .	20	6	26	42
Thiamine	16	6	46	44
Riboflavin	18	8	29	34
Niacin	12	4	46	57

[14] *1948 Food Consumption Survey, Preliminary Report 12*, Bureau of Human Nutrition and Home Economics, U.S. Department of Agriculture, Nov. 30, 1949.

The income class is based on 1947 income after Federal income tax. 13 per cent of the families included in the sample fell in the $1,000 to $1,999 class interval and 10 per cent in the $5,000 to $7,449. Less than 4 per cent fell under $1,000 and only about 5 per cent of the families had incomes of $7,500 and over. The columns "Too Few Nutrients" give the percentage of the families in each of the two income classes that had diets providing less of the nutrient than the National Research Council's recommended daily allowance. The columns "Too Many Nutrients" consist of the per cent of the families in each of the two income classes taking on excessive quantities of food nutrients: calories, 5,000 and over; proteins, 125 grams and over; calcium, 1.40 grams and over; iron, 20 milligrams and over; ascorbic acid, 200 milligrams

These data indicate that both the "low" and the "high" income families had diets that were deficient. We may look at these deficiencies from two points of view: one, how much better are the diets of the "high" group compared to the "low," and the other, how much or how little are the diets improved when families have $5,000 to $7,499 incomes rather than $1,000 to $1,999 incomes. In calories and iron, the "improvement" was indeed very slight. However, it is noteworthy that on the "excess" side there were no deteriorations; in fact, for calories the "high" income families show up slightly better than the "low," with only 17 per cent of them in an excess position compared to 19 per cent for the "low." One might infer from these data that with incomes at the 1947 level, a further marked increase in incomes of urban families will correct the nutritional deficiencies somewhat but it will also add somewhat to nutritional "excesses." Furthermore, it will by no means correct all the deficiencies. To correct the nutritional imbalance that exists, it is necessary, therefore, to bring other factors in addition to income into play. On the demand side, knowledge about nutrition and a belief that diets that are nutritionally adequate are worth while are factors that cannot be neglected.

A word of caution in interpreting these observations: The inference set forth above to the effect that a higher level of income will not of itself correct the nutritional imbalance does not imply that such an increase in income will not increase the demand for food. Since the income elasticity of food taken as a whole is still positive and since low-income families have a greater income elasticity than do families with high incomes, it follows that a rise in the level of incomes or a more equal distribution of incomes with the level unchanged will increase the demand for food. Education, however, which improves the knowledge that people have about nutrition and which induces them to better their food habits will not necessarily increase the demand for food. There is, first, the offset of the excessive intake of some food nutrients against the deficiencies. Conceivably, these could cancel each other. More important, however, there are the basic determinants underlying consumer preferences. The kinds of food that are consumed depend upon a whole set of preferences which are socially and culturally determined. The evidence seems to show that a rise in the level of incomes brings preferences into play that increase the demand for food requiring more agricultural resources than do those that are lower on the preference scales

---

and over; thiamine, 2.4 milligrams and over; riboflavin, 3.0 milligrams and over; and niacin, 24 milligrams and over. It is not our intention to suggest that intakes of particular food nutrients in excess of these figures are necessarily harmful for normal people; rather our purpose is simply to indicate that such an intake is larger than is necessary.

of consumers. Education regarding nutrition, at least so far, has been oriented mainly in the same direction. Accordingly, on both counts the demand is increased. But education can and should point out the alternative low- and high-cost combinations of food that will provide an adequate diet on the basis of what is known about nutrition and leave it to the existing system of preferences to motivate consumers' choices on how cheap or how expensive a diet to maintain.

7

GAUGING THE NEW AND BETTER
PRODUCTION POSSIBILITIES

The purpose of this chapter is to explain the large increase in agricultural production that has been realized in the United States in recent decades. One starts with a basic fact, that is, agricultural production for sale and home consumption rose about 75 per cent from 1910 to 1950.[1] Since the prices of farm products at wholesale, relative to all commodities at wholesale, were about the same in the two years, it will be convenient to look upon this increase in production as representing a shift of the supply schedule far to the right.[2] Underlying the new and better production possibilities of agriculture are two fundamental developments: (1) the increase in the supply of inputs used in agricultural production and (2) the advances in production techniques increasing in a remarkable way the output per unit of input.

The first part of this chapter consists of a brief study of the changes in the supplies of inputs available to agriculture. The study begins by pointing up one of the basic results of economic development, as it has made its forward thrusts in Western countries, that is, the change in the relative price of inputs (factors) with labor rising relative to "capital"

[1] The index of the Bureau of Agricultural Economics, with 1935–1939 = 100, rose from 79 in 1910 to 138 in 1950. The 1935–1939 weights are not, however, a wholly satisfactory measure of the relative value of farm products, say, in 1948–1950. A preliminary test of the effects of shifting the price weights forward to 1947–1949 indicates only a small change in the level and trend of agricultural production. There is, however, merit in modifying the concept of agricultural production to adjust for interfarm sales and thus make it a measure of "net farm marketings and home consumption." This modification would alter some years but it would not change appreciably the level or the trend observed for agricultural production.

[2] The indices for farm product prices (1926 = 100, BLS) were 74.3, and, of all commodities, 70.4 in 1910; and 170.4 and 161.5, respectively, in 1950. We shall represent this change as a shift of the supply schedule far to the right; a 75 per cent increase in quantity forthcoming at about the same relative price.

99

inputs. One might have expected the price of agricultural land, as an input, to have risen relatively, especially after the completion of land settlement. Land and labor are, of course, very important in farming, with labor representing about 46 per cent and agricultural land 24 per cent of all inputs used in agricultural production in 1910–1914. Other inputs, however, have become available in ever larger quantities from the nonfarm sector of the economy, and these inputs are of a kind that can be substituted for labor and land; moreover, the elasticity of substitution has been increasing.[3]

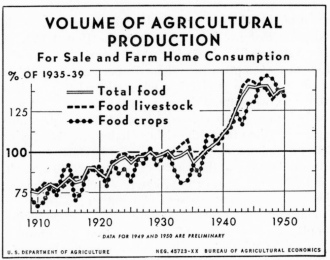

Fig. 7–1. Volume of agricultural production for sale and farm home consumption, 1910–1950.

The second part of the chapter is an endeavor to explain the process of "producing" and distributing new production techniques as it has been institutionalized in the United States in the U.S. Department of Agriculture, the agricultural experiment stations, and the extension services. This is the story of the technical revolution underway in agriculture. We shall, also, attempt to gauge the value of the inputs saved as a consequence of recent advances in production techniques in order to determine whether too few or too many resources are being committed to such agricultural research.

[3] The short-run supply of farm products is highly inelastic because of the supply attributes of the inputs used in farming [see D. Gale Johnson, "The Nature of the Supply Function for Agricultural Products," *American Economic Review*, Vol. XL (September, 1950)]. Our analysis, however, in this chapter is concerned with the long run.

CHANGES IN THE SUPPLIES OF INPUTS

There is no point in belaboring the difficulties in concepts, data, and methods of measurement of price and quantity of these inputs. They are legion; they cannot be fully overcome; much work has gone into the construction of indices to measure both the prices and the quantities of these inputs. We shall use these data in our endeavor to approximate the changes under consideration and we shall indicate, as we proceed, some of the more important shortcomings of the data.

Let us examine, first, changes that appear to have occurred in the relative prices of these inputs. The indices of prices paid by farmers in 1910 and in 1950, with 1935–1939 = 100, are shown in Table 7–1.[4]

How much reliance is one to place in these measures of changes in the price of particular inputs? With this question in mind, let us consider the more important inputs. Labor represents somewhat less than two-fifths of all inputs at 1950 factor costs. Hired labor, however, is only a fourth of the labor force in agriculture because most of the work is done by farmers and members of their families. Even so the wage rates of hired workers are a fairly satisfactory measure of the relative change in the price of labor input because the two sets of earnings tend to move together. The ratio between net farm income per family worker and wage income per hired farm worker has stayed fairly constant, except during World Wars I and II when the ratio turned in favor of farmers and members of their families and during 1920–1923 and 1930–1933 when it turned the other way, that is, the net farm income fell relative to the wage income of hired farm workers on a per person basis. One check is the average net income from farming operations divided

[4] Another study, representing the major components of the national farm product, provides the following price deflators, with 1939 = 100.

	1910	1950	$\frac{1950}{1910}$, per cent
Total value of farm output	106.0	261.3	247
Classes of inputs:			
Intermediate products other than rent	92.1	194.3	211
Rent (based on gross rent paid to nonfarm landlords) .	108.9	273.5	251

Here again, the price per unit of the intermediate products is down relative to land (rent) which rose about as much as did the farm output per unit. See John W. Kendrick and Carl E. Jones, "Gross National Farm Produce in Constant Dollars, 1910–50," *Survey of Current Business*, U.S. Department of Commerce, September, 1951, Table 2.

TABLE 7-1. RELATIVE PRICES OF AGRICULTURAL INPUTS, 1910 AND 1950

	1910	1950	Index (1910 = 100)
Wage rates	79	352	445
Buildings and fencing materials . . .	69	218	316
Farm machinery.	65	180	277
Rental rates	102	280	275
Farm supplies	69	177	256
Seed	78	194	249
Motor vehicles	(88)ᵃ	200	227
Fertilizer	96	141	147
Motor supplies	(125)ᵃ	144	115
Interest rate (farm mortgage). . . .	125	95	76
Interest rate (short term)	144	100	69

ᵃ For 1924, first year in the available price series.

SOURCE: *Farm Cost Situation*, BAE, October, 1951, p. 2, and from data made available to the writer by the Bureau of Agricultural Economics.

by the number of persons in the farm population: In 1910 it was $141 and in 1950, $636,[5] which represents an increase of 450 per cent compared to 445 shown for wages in the table above.

There is some evidence, however, which indicates that the wage rates understate somewhat the rise in the "price" of this input. The wage rates, from 1940 to 1948, rose 341 per cent while money labor returns of all of the labor force in agriculture, as we shall show in Chap. 18, rose from $410 in 1940 to $1,770 in 1948, representing a rise of 431 per cent. We shall proceed on the belief that the money "price" of labor in agriculture was, if anything, somewhat more than 4.45 times as high in 1950 as in 1910.

The second most important input in farming is agricultural land. The net rent per acre for all farm land was $1.76 in 1910 and $4.92 in 1948, a rise of 275 per cent. The question of comparability between the acres in farms currently and four decades ago arises. There were 881 million acres in farms in 1910 and 1,148 million in 1948 (based on the 1945 Census). Most of this increase did not come in cropland harvested but in pasture that is not plowable. The additional land drawn into farms would appear to have been poorer than that in farms in 1910. There have been, however, two developments working in the other direction: (1) the value of farm buildings has increased markedly relative to the value of all farm real estate, representing 18 per cent in 1910 and 33 per cent in 1950 (see Chap. 8), and (2) the irrigated land rose from

[5] *Farm Income Situation*, Bureau of Agricultural Economics, July–September, 1951, Table 4.

about 9 to about 19 million acres during this period.[6] Since the rent per acre includes payment for both of these developments, they probably more than offset any dilution in the quality of land resulting from the expansion in acreage after 1910.

Farm machinery and farm supplies were 277 and 256 per cent higher, respectively, in 1950 with 1910 = 100. It is hard to believe that the quality of these items did not improve substantially despite every effort to adjust for changes in quality in making the indices; motor vehicles, and to a lesser extent, motor supplies also have this attribute. The price rise indicated for each of these inputs, therefore, is likely to be somewhat on the high side because of these improvements.

Without further comment on the prices of particular inputs, let us turn to the effects of the changes in the relative prices of these inputs. (The prices received by farmers, taking 1910–1914 = 100, were 256 in 1950.) Suppose that no advances in production techniques had been made during the period and that agriculture had approximated a long-run equilibrium in 1910; one would have expected farmers to substitute low-priced inputs for high-priced inputs, depending upon the elasticities of substitution. The important changes in relative prices of inputs are clearly as follows: labor inputs became dear relative to other inputs and relative to farm product prices; interest rates on funds loaned, fertilizer, and motor supplies and motor vehicles (the last two from 1922 on) became cheap relative to other inputs and also relative to farm product prices; and a third group consisting of buildings and fencing materials, farm machinery, agricultural land, farm supplies and seeds came to hold an intermediate position, rising in price per unit roughly as much as farm product prices. Two of these, that is, farm machinery and farm supplies, because of substantial improvements in quality, may, however, belong in the second group. Although new production techniques have been many and important, substitution among inputs is clearly evident and it is consistent with the changes that have occurred in the relative prices of inputs. Not that the data reveal the elasticities of substitution; the approximate path, however, can be seen. Labor has been withdrawn while other, cheaper inputs have been added. That land has not become a limitational factor may come as a surprise to those who see secular diminishing returns pivoting on agricultural land.

Data appearing in Table 7–2 are to be interpreted in the following setting: Important advances in production techniques were achieved, to be considered a little later, and the quantity of inputs purchased from

[6] *Irrigation Agriculture in the West,* USDA, *Misc. Pub.* 670, November, 1948. Data taken from Fig. 21.

Economic Development and Agriculture

other sectors of the economy rose sharply. The latter development may be seen in the rise in farm production expenses shown in Table 7–3.

TABLE 7–2. PRODUCTION INPUTS IN AGRICULTURE, 1910 AND 1950

Inputs	1910	1950	Index
Labor.	107	77	72
Interest (horses and mules, motor vehicles, other machinery, crops and livestock)	128	168	131
Land.	83	109	131
Miscellaneous items.	76	118	155
Taxes.	56	98	175
Maintenance or depreciation of buildings, motor vehicles, machinery and equipment	104	196	188
Fertilizer and lime.	69	268	388
Operation of motor vehicles	1	278	278 (fold)
Total inputs	95	108	114
Agricultural production.	79	138	175

SOURCE: Bureau of Agricultural Economics data made available to the writer. The labor input for 1950 differs from the Bureau of Agricultural Economics data, for it has been adjusted downward to reflect the changes in labor force in agriculture since 1940, as indicated by the Bureau of the Census estimate of farm employment. The total input for 1950, accordingly, is also modified by the adjustment in labor. Indices for 1910 and 1950 are centered on 1935–1939 = 100.

TABLE 7–3. FARM PRODUCTION EXPENSES IN RELATION TO GROSS FARM INCOME

Year	Gross farm income, in billions of dollars	Farm production expenses, in billions of dollars	Farm production expenses of gross income, per cent
1910	7.35	3.56	48
1920	15.91	8.99	56
1930	11.42	6.99	61
1940	10.92	6.63	61
1950	32.73	20.02	61

SOURCE: Farm Income Situation, Bureau of Agricultural Economics, July–September, 1950, Table 1. Gross farm incomes for 1940 and 1950 include government payments.

United States agriculture has become increasingly dependent on inputs which are acquired from the nonfarm sector. Kendrick and Jones,[7] in estimating the national farm product in constant dollars, 1939 = 100, place the total value of farm output at $7,080 million, in 1910, and $12,-720 million, in 1950. The increase in production comes out at 79 per cent. The value of intermediate products, that is, of the "nonfarm" inputs used, rose, however, from $1,172 million in 1910 (1939 = 100) to $4,831 million in 1950; in quantity terms, therefore, these inputs were

[7] Kendrick and Jones, op. cit.

TABLE 7–4. FARM PRODUCTION EXPENSES BY CLASSES, 1910 AND 1950

	1910, in millions of current dollars	1950, in millions of current dollars	$\frac{1950}{1910}$, in per cent or fold
Gross farm income.	7,350	32,730	445
All farm production expenses. . . .	3,556	20,024	566
Less			
(a) Hired labor	755	2,858	378
(b) Net rent to nonfarm landlords.	340	1,178	346
Farm production expenses minus (a) and (b) consisting of:	2,461	15,988	650
Operation of motor vehicles . . .	7	2,073	296 (fold)
Depreciation of motor vehicles . .	13	1,388	106 (fold)
Seed purchased	56	585	10 (fold)
Fertilizer and lime	149	821	551
Taxes on farm property	191	865	453
Depreciation of buildings	318	1,380	434
Depreciation of machinery other than motor vehicles	353	1,461	414
Miscellaneous	545	1,839	337
Interest on farm mortgage debt . .	203	262	129
Expenses largely from within agriculture:			
Livestock purchased	200	2,088	10 (fold)
Feed purchased	426	3,226	757

SOURCE: *Farm Income Situation*, Bureau of Agricultural Economics, July–September, 1951, Tables 1, 11, 12, and 14.

fully four times as large in 1950 as in 1910.[8] The major items making up the production expenses of agriculture and the relative increase in each of these items, in current dollars, for 1910 and 1950 are indicated in Table 7–4.

Barton, Cooper, and Brodell[9] of the Bureau of Agricultural Economics

[8] Physical assets other than real estate in agriculture rose sharply relative to total physical assets since 1940. See *1952 Agricultural Outlook Charts*, Bureau of Agricultural Economics, October, 1951, p. 19.

[9] Martin R. Cooper, Glen T. Barton, and Albert P. Brodell, *Progress in Farm Mechanization*, BAE, *Misc. Pub.* 630, October, 1947.

Sherman E. Johnson, *Changes in American Farming*, USDA, *Misc. Pub.* 707, December, 1949.

Farm Production, Practices, Costs and Returns (Foreword by Carl P. Heisig) BAE, *Statis. Bul.* 83, October, 1949.

Glen T. Barton and Martin R. Cooper, "Relation of Agricultural Production to Inputs," *Review of Economics and Statistics*, Vol. XXX (May, 1948).

Ruben W. Hecht and Glen T. Barton, *Gains in Productivity of Farm Labor*, BAE, *Tech. Bul.* 1020, December, 1950.

have advanced substantially the state of information about production inputs in agriculture. These inputs were grouped into eight classes and for each of them there was constructed an index of the quantity used each year beginning with 1910. The eight indices were also combined to measure the aggregate input for each year. Two difficulties are encountered: the underlying data are uneven in completeness and there is the difficulty of aggregating and measuring changes over time. In using these data we have made two important adjustments, that is, the labor inputs after 1940 have been based on the Bureau of the Census farm-employment data and the index of total inputs has been weighted by 1946–1948 input prices.[10]

Our purpose in estimating changes in total inputs is to gauge how much of the increase in outputs has come as a consequence of more inputs and how much from new and better production techniques. It

[10] The measure of labor input used by the Bureau of Agricultural Economics declines from an index of 99 in 1940 to 95 in 1948; the Bureau of the Census, however, indicates a drop from 99 to 83 during this period. The labor input index of the Bureau of Agricultural Economics falls into an intermediate position between the very high Bureau of Agricultural Economics farm-employment estimates and the much lower Census data, and the Census data show more decline relatively since 1940. It appears to us that even the Census data underestimate the "economizing" of labor that has taken place in agriculture since 1940. For an evaluation of the Bureau of Agricultural Economics and Census farm-employment data, see D. Gale Johnson and Marilyn Corn Nottenburg, "A Critical Analysis of Farm Employment Estimates," *Journal of the American Statistical Association,* Vol. XLVI (June, 1951).

The effects of alternative weighting periods on measuring the production inputs for the period 1910–1914 may be seen from the following three sets of input prices:

	Input prices		
	1910–1914	1935–1939	1946–1948
Labor	46.00	46.97	58.59
Land.	23.63	19.58	21.27
Maintenance or depreciation .	10.27	13.30	7.69
Operation of motor vehicles .	0.29	0.18	0.08
Interest .	9.58	9.18	5.68
Miscellaneous .	4.56	5.07	3.33
Taxes	3.21	3.57	2.34
Fertilizer and lime.	2.46	2.15	1.02
All inputs	100.00	100.00	100.00

TABLE 7-5. INDEXES OF PRODUCTION INPUTS IN AGRICULTURE, UNITED STATES, 1910-1950 (1935-1939 = 100)

Year	(1) Fertilizer and lime	(2) Cost of operating motor vehicles	(3) Miscellaneous, excluding horses and mules, seeds, short-term interest	(4) Taxes	(5) Maintenance or depreciation of buildings, motor vehicles, machinery, equipment	(6) Interest, horses and mules, motor vehicles, machinery, crops, livestock	(7) Net land rent	(8) Total farm labor	(9) Total inputs
1910	69	1	76	56	104	128	83	107	95
1911	77	2	76	59	105	139	84	109	97
1912	74	3	83	65	108	125	85	109	98
1913	82	4	82	71	112	134	85	110	99
1914	96	5	88	74	119	142	86	112	102
1915	71	8	85	77	115	152	87	114	103
1916	69	13	79	69	115	137	87	110	100
1917	79	18	83	63	119	116	88	110	100
1918	86	23	90	59	118	129	89	112	102
1919	88	28	86	67	130	137	90	113	104
1920	95	29	103	90	145	139	90	115	108
1921	65	33	95	117	137	162	90	109	106
1922	76	38	97	119	131	130	89	111	105
1923	85	45	104	118	125	127	89	110	104
1924	89	54	103	116	123	124	88	109	103
1925	89	62	103	113	120	114	87	109	103
1926	91	70	110	116	121	123	89	109	104
1927	88	78	102	122	122	128	90	109	105
1928	103	85	103	121	123	129	91	109	106
1929	104	91	103	125	126	138	92	108	106
1930	106	93	102	130	124	154	93	106	107
1931	81	92	109	135	122	151	95	107	107
1932	58	84	104	132	102	145	96	107	107
1933	61	83	104	115	93	113	97	106	104
1934	70	84	96	98	89	94	98	97	96
1935	80	92	97	97	92	81	100	101	99
1936	94	95	100	99	97	101	100	98	99
1937	112	100	104	95	102	94	100	102	101
1938	104	102	105	102	102	111	100	99	101
1939	109	110	95	106	107	113	100	99	101

TABLE 7–5. INDEXES OF PRODUCTION INPUTS IN AGRICULTURE, UNITED STATES, 1910–1950 (1935–1939 = 100). (*Continued*)

Year	(1) Fertilizer and lime	(2) Cost of operating motor vehicles	(3) Miscellaneous, excluding horses and mules, seeds, short-term interest	(4) Taxes	(5) Maintenance or depreciation of buildings, motor vehicles, machinery, equipment	(6) Interest, horses and mules, motor vehicles, machinery, crops, livestock	(7) Net land rent	(8) Total farm labor	(9) Total inputs
1940	124	118	97	103	109	110	100	99	102
1941	135	127	101	99	116	101	102	93	100
1942	146	138	105	87	118	111	104	95	101
1943	162	153	107	81	120	125	105	93	102
1944	181	167	109	79	127	128	107	92	103
1945	199	195	112	88	141	126	109	88	104
1946	240	227	119	91	149	122	109	85	105
1947	241	246	125	88	162	127	109	85	106
1948	231	253	125	85	173	151	109	82	107
1949	245	261	129	97	184	182	109	82	110
1950	268	278	118	98	196	168	109	77	108

SOURCE: Data from the Bureau of Agricultural Economics with two modifications: (1) labor inputs from 1940 on are based on changes indicated by the Bureau of the Census farm-employment estimates and (2) 1946–1948 input prices are used for weighting the several classes of inputs.

is possible to give the approximate upper and lower limits of the changes in aggregate inputs but a more precise estimate is not possible because of difficulties inherent in aggregation. By taking 1946–1948 input prices as weights, total inputs rise from an index of 95 in 1910 to 108 in 1950—*a rise of only about 14 per cent.* This clearly represents the lower limit of the increase in total inputs; labor, the input that has become dear, has been reduced 28 per cent; and other inputs which have become relatively cheap have been expanded, one class, operation of motor vehicles, as much as 278-fold (see Table 7–2). At the other end, by taking 1910–1914 input prices, total inputs rise from 87 in 1910 to 116 in 1950. *This represents an increase of about 33 per cent in total inputs.* This figure may be taken as the upper limit in the increase in total inputs.

Outcome with 1946–1948 *Input Prices.* When we take 1946–1948 input prices for weighting the various inputs, we find:

1. That in 1950, 14 per cent more inputs were employed than in

1910. The output (agricultural production), however, was 75 per cent larger.[11]

2. That a unit of input in 1950, therefore, resulted in 54 per cent more output (production) than in 1910.

3. That when this improvement in the ratio of output per unit of input (*a*) is averaged over the entire period (forty years), it represents an average increase of 1.35 per cent per year, and (*b*) when it is averaged over the last twenty-seven years during which virtually all this improvement actually took place, it represents an average increase of 2.00 per cent per year.

Outcome with 1910–1914 *Input Prices.* When we take 1910–1914 input prices for weights, the outcome in output per unit of input is somewhat less favorable for the following reasons:

1. In 1950, 33 per cent more inputs were employed than in 1910.

2. A unit of input in 1950, under these circumstances, resulted in 32 per cent more output (production) than in 1910.

3. When this (smaller) improvement in the ratio of output per unit of input is spread (*a*) over the entire period of four decades, it turns out to be an average increase of .80 of 1 per cent per year, and when it is spread (*b*) over the last twenty-seven years, it averages 1.19 per cent per year.

New and Better Production Techniques

From the preceding data we infer that from 1910 to 1950 the output per unit of input has improved on the average at least .80 of 1 per cent per year or as much as 1.35 per cent a year. How are we to explain this large advance in production techniques?

New techniques for farmers are the stock and trade of the agricultural experiment stations, extension services, and the U.S. Department of Agriculture. Private firms and individuals also contribute. (We shall for the most part have to leave the research activities of private firms and individuals which contribute new agricultural techniques aside because no reliable information is available.) These new techniques clearly alter the supply; they are far-reaching in their consequences; yet little is known about the underlying economics of the production and distribution of this technology. There are some useful studies of progress in agricultural technology and of changes that occur in farming as a result. These studies, however, do not endeavor to explain the "production"

[11] We may use the 75 per cent increase for 1948 as well as for 1950, as we did earlier, because the production index was the same in the two years.

and use of technology as an economic activity; instead, advances in technology are usually approached as if they were either costless, as something that is made available "free" to the national community and to agriculture, or as a flow (of techniques) that can be described but not explained except in terms of scientific curiosity and as the "accidental" discoveries of minds bent on such inquiry. To look upon new techniques as occurrences that simply happen regardless of economic considerations has led to a serious neglect of the study of the "production" of new techniques.

In examining the conditions that appear to determine the rate at which new techniques are forthcoming, three hypotheses may be indicated.

Hypothesis 1. The discoveries of new techniques are unpredictable. New techniques are not the result of well-laid plans to "produce" them; instead, they are a by-product of scientific curiosity. Their occurrence cannot be foretold; they are "accidental" events; they are not determined by economic considerations. New techniques are, therefore, unpredictable events.

Hypothesis 2. New techniques are an institutional and cultural product. Western *Weltanschauung* and values have placed science in a dominant position. Science makes available many ideas that pave the way for new techniques but science is not motivated by a desire for new techniques. The development of new techniques is, therefore, exogenous in character although it produces at times a large flow of new techniques.

Hypothesis 3. Pure science and its contribution to society are closely interrelated. Modern science is supported mainly for the fruit it will bear measured in terms of new techniques. It is increasingly oriented to this objective. This gives it a strong economic motivation which bulks large in existing (organized) scientific and technological research. New techniques are, therefore, primarily an economic activity subject to economic analysis.

There is room for all three of these hypotheses in explaining the experiences which we have had with science and the development of new techniques. It is our belief, however, that the third of these is necessary to explain most scientific effort that bears technological fruit, and as time goes on, this is becoming increasingly so.

It is our contention that a new technique is a valuable (scarce) resource that has a "price" and that this resource is not given to the community or to the producer as a free good; on the contrary, it entails costs some of which are borne by the community and some by producers as a price that is paid to acquire and apply the resource. Therefore, a new technique is simply a particular kind of input and the economies underlying the supply and use are in principle the same as that of any other type of input. We do not wish to imply that every human activity entering into the development of new techniques can be explained wholly by considerations of cost and revenue; our belief simply is that a large part of the modern process of technological research from "pure" science to successful practice can be explained by economic analysis. Resources of the community, consisting of both public and private funds, are "invested" in research, motivated, it is true, to acquire new scientific insights to be used, however, among other things, mainly to increase the ratio of output from a given input in making something that society wants. Accordingly, the allocation of resources to such research and to the application of the research results is not unrelated to the prospective returns from such effort set against anticipated costs.

Industry and Agriculture Compared. It may be instructive to compare how new techniques are "produced" and applied in industry generally and in agriculture. Two major differences may be noted. First, the basic and applied research in the sciences that contributes to the advances in agricultural technology is not done by farm-firms but primarily by public agencies, that is, by the state agricultural experiment stations and the U.S. Department of Agriculture. In industry most of this research is done by the firm, and since it is usually a large and costly operation, for the most part only large corporations can afford to engage in it. In agriculture, by contrast, most of the necessary research is borne on public account. A typical family farm is obviously in no position to finance, organize, and conduct the highly complicated, costly researches entailed in agricultural chemistry, plant and animal breeding, feeding, agronomy, and the many other applied sciences that enter into farm technology. Most of the costs are borne by the community, through various agencies of government.[12] Since the research is done by public agencies, the results are and should be available to any and all producers.[13] New techniques, therefore, do not become the property of a particular group of farmers. The new knowledge is in substance common

[12] The expenditures of the Federal and state governments on agricultural researches in the United States appeared to have exceeded $100 million in 1951 (see Table 7–7).

[13] There are signs that some university and college organizations are attempting to raise revenue from their discoveries through the sale of patents. Patents in themselves are necessary to protect the public and to assure that the discoveries will not be misappropriated and misused. To use the patent, however, also as a source of revenue, especially in the agricultural processing and merchandising field with its imperfections in competition, raises serious problems in social policy.

information; in fact, much effort and the expenditure of considerable public funds are involved in disseminating such new information to farm people through the Federal and state agricultural extension services.

The competitive structure of agriculture is also conducive to the introduction of new technology. This constitutes the second major difference between agriculture and industry in so far as technological advances are concerned. Much plant and equipment may be made obsolete by the new technology, but the introduction of the new technique in agriculture will not be postponed to maintain the capital value of such obsolete investments. Competition makes it necessary for farmers to adopt the new technology or find themselves at a disadvantage relative to other farmers who do so. The adoption of new techniques in agriculture has back of it the impelling force of competition, with hundreds of thousands of small firms in a highly competitive relationship, one to another, in production.[14] This situation is in sharp contrast to some parts of industry where research is carried on, and where the number of firms in competition with each other is sometimes so few as to give rise to some imperfections in competition that permit the firm to decide whether to adopt the new technique or postpone doing so.

It may be remarked that there are many indications that the improvement in production technique in agriculture, which has been so marked in the last quarter century, has not spent itself. With knowledge already at hand, it would appear that the recent forward surge is still in its early stages because it will take years, perhaps decades, to put into practice in all parts of agriculture what is already known. Farmers in the better situated agricultural areas lead the way; they are already in the vanguard and for many reasons they are quicker, and find it easier, to take on new techniques than do farmers in areas that are already behind in techniques. It will take a long time, therefore, merely to bring such areas as the Appalachians and large parts of the poorer sections of the South abreast.

[14] It is commonly thought that the public appropriations for agricultural research benefit farm people primarily. This is far from true; the gains from these researches are quickly transmitted to those who buy and use farm products in lower prices and in new and better commodities; farmers benefit, when they do, in their capacity as consumers. They do not, as a rule, benefit as producers because of the sluggishness that characterizes the transfer of resources out of agriculture, except that those who first introduce the new technique benefit until the price of the product falls as a result of the expanded output. It should also be noted that some agricultural programs, for example, the acreage allotments and pricing of tobacco, have adverse effects upon the development and adoption of, say, new labor-saving techniques.

"Producing" and Distributing New Techniques. In the United States the community, through the Federal and state governments, allocates a substantial quantity of resources to the "production" and distribution of new agricultural techniques. Is is possible to gauge whether too little or too much is being spent on these enterprises? It is our belief that an economic analysis will show that, while the expenditures are large relative to past outlays and compared to what other countries spend for these purposes, the resources committed annually would have to be increased very substantially before the rate of return from this stream of inputs would not exceed that obtained in production activities generally.

We are here concerned with expenditures for technological research and for the extension of the results to farmers, not over an interval of a year, but with input-output relations in research and extension that are likely to prevail over a decade and longer. Let us assume that the research agency acts like a firm and that the director of an agricultural experiment station, like the entrepreneur that he is, makes decisions that can be explained by economic analysis. The director has presented to him a long list of research projects for financial support. In deciding which ones to approve, he evaluates the expected inputs against the expected outputs of each project, which means that he has some ideas about the necessary production relations. In addition, and prior to this decision-making process, there is the institutional setting in which the director operates which determines his expectations, the availability of funds, developments in farming bearing upon technology, beliefs of experts about fruitful fields for new research in view of advances in the several sciences, and the attitude of farmers and others who have an interest in the research that is undertaken. Undoubtedly other tastes and preferences, other than a "maximization" of economic value of the output, enter into the decision relations determining the director's choices. However, even a casual look at the behavior patterns of directors in approving research projects suggests that economic considerations, broadly conceived and when taken over a span of years, are of primary importance.

There is also the additional assumption that resources, consisting of public and private funds, are allocated in some rough and ready way to such technological research and to the extension of the results to farmers with an eye to expected (marginal) returns that are at least as great as are the expected (marginal) costs. While the governmental process of making appropriations, and the way private gifts and endowments are made for these purposes, are exceedingly crude approximations to the elegant maximizing models that decorate blackboards and textbooks, the empirical observations, nevertheless, can be explained in large part, so it would appear, by this analytical approach. Accordingly, it should be possible to gain substantial insight about the rate at which new agricultural techniques are "produced."

We need also to explain the rate at which farmers adopt new techniques. Clearly the mere availability of such techniques is no assurance that they will be applied in farming. The process by which farmers take on new techniques, as one would expect, is strongly motivated by economic considerations and yet very little is known about this process. In formal analysis, it is customary to neglect this aspect of production by assuming that the producer has complete information about the appropriate (best) techniques of production. (He always knows his production function!) In fact, however, his information is usually very incomplete and constantly subject to change; and because of the rapidity with which new techniques are developed and the trial and error required to demonstrate what can be expected from them in practice, his knowledge about production relations underlying inputs and outputs is not only incomplete but burdened by much uncertainty.

The process by which a farmer takes on a new technique can be explained by treating the technique as a (new) resource which has a supply price to the firm and which has yield potentials that are subject to substantial risk and uncertainty. From this point on the analysis is straightforward and on a par with the determination of the use by the firm of any other productive resource having a given supply price and having a yield expectation that is not single-valued.

When there are marked changes in the supply prices of the different resources used in farming, one may observe the effects of these changes upon the development and taking on of new techniques. For example, when the price of human effort (labor) rose rapidly relative to most capital forms including land, as was the case during the forties, farmers not only found many ways of substituting some of the cheaper resources for some labor inputs, but, in addition, new labor-saving techniques were given the right of way in the recombination of factors in farming. Many such techniques which had been known but which made little or no appeal to farmers up until then were adopted. Furthermore, experiment stations and other research agencies serving agriculture were induced to undertake new research, designed to come up with new techniques that would "save" labor in agricultural production.

AGRICULTURAL RESEARCH: EXPENDITURES AND RETURNS

If all the endowments accumulated by Chicago, Columbia, Duke, Harvard, Hopkins, Princeton, Stanford, and Yale were combined and

Table 7–6. Public Funds Spent for Research in Agriculture for the Fiscal Years
Ending June 30, 1940 and 1949
(In thousands of dollars)

Federal expenditures by bureau or activity	1940	1949
Agricultural Research Administration:		
Office of administrator	134	434
Research on agricultural problems of Alaska.	......	435
Special research fund (Bankhead-Jones Act of June 29, 1934).	1,375	1,274
Office of Experiment Stations (exclusive of payments to states, shown below)	245	378
Bureau of Animal Industry.	1,487	2,919
Bureau of Dairy Industry	691	1,118
Bureau of Plant Industry, Soils, and Agricultural Engineering	5,788	8,911
Bureau of Entomology and Plant Quarantine	2,212	3,331
Bureau of Agricultural and Industrial Chemistry	3,779	6,021
Bureau of Human Nutrition and Home Economics.	362	897
Total, Agricultural Research Administration (exclusive of payments to states and territories, shown below)	16,073	25,718
Research and Marketing Act of 1946 (exclusive of Sec. 9 funds for payment to states and marketing service work).	......	8,756
Bureau of Agricultural Economics	1,437	1,058
Forest Service	2,252	5,051
Soil Conservation Service.	1,713	1,629
Production and Marketing Administration.	503	828
Farm Credit Administration	459	461
Total, all items above	22,437	43,501
Payments to states and territories for experiment station research under Match, Adams, Purnell, and Bankhead-Jones Acts.	6,849	7,406
Additional payments to states and territories for experiment station research under Sec. 9, Research and Marketing Act of 1946.	......	3,148
Total, Federal funds.	29,286	54,055
Non-Federal funds spent by state agricultural experiment stations.	12,635	40,305
Total, Federal and non-Federal funds.	41,921	94,360

Source: The figures on Federal expenditures are from *Department of Agriculture Appropriation Bill for 1951*, Hearings before the Subcommittee of the Committee on Appropriations, House of Representatives, 81st Cong., 2d Sess., Part I, p. 122; and the non-Federal expenditures are from the *Report of the Agricultural Experiment Stations, 1941 and 1950*, U.S. Department of Agriculture.

were earning 4 per cent, the resulting revenue would support only about one-fourth of the agricultural research underway at the beginning of the decade of the fifties.[15]

[15] It would take an endowment of about $2.5 billion to provide enough revenue. The total endowments of these universities in the late forties was about $600 million.

TABLE 7–7. EXPENDITURES FOR AGRICULTURAL RESEARCH BY THE UNITED STATES
DEPARTMENT OF AGRICULTURE AND BY STATE AGRICULTURAL EXPERIMENT
STATIONS DURING 15-YEAR PERIOD FROM 1937–1951

Fiscal year ending June 30	Expenditures for research, in thousands of dollars			
	By agencies of U.S. Department of Agriculture	By state experiment stations		Total
		Federal-grant funds	State funds	
(1)	(2)	(3)	(4)	(5)
1937	16,379	5,617	10,359	32,355
1938	17,853	6,229	11,939	36,021
1939	23,329	6,541	12,397	42,267
1940	21,806	6,848	12,635	41,289
1941	21,127	6,862	13,206	41,195
1942	21,763	6,922	13,519	42,204
1943	22,433	6,871	13,954	43,258
1944	23,106	6,972	15,174	45,252
1945	23,308	6,990	17,343	47,641
1946	24,834	7,190	20,787	52,811
1947	31,143	7,197	27,700	66,040
1948	35,986	8,824	35,350	80,160
1949	43,060	10,604	40,305	93,969
1950	45,864	11,960	45,205	103,029
1951	43,118	12,558	50,972	106,648

SOURCE: The writer is indebted to Harry C. Trelogan of the Agricultural Research Administration, U.S. Department of Agriculture, for these data; also for Fig. 7–2.

Research field	Million dollars	Per cent
Soils	4.35	9.6
Plant production	15.36	34.0
Animal production	4.92	10.9
Economics (of the farm and home)	1.19	2.6
Engineering (agricultural).	0.95	2.1
Marketing (both physical and economic aspects) . .	5.59	12.4
Utilization	12.10	26.7
Over-all administration not included elsewhere. . .	0.78	1.7
Total	45.24	100.0

SOURCE: Data from Harry C. Trelogan of the Agricultural Research Administration, U.S. Department of Agriculture.

In interpreting Tables 7–6 and 7–7 giving public expenditures for agricultural research, several observations are called for:

1. These expenditures have been rising; the upward trend has occurred despite the fact that agriculture is a declining sector of the economy. Compared to 1937 when the Federal and state governments allocated

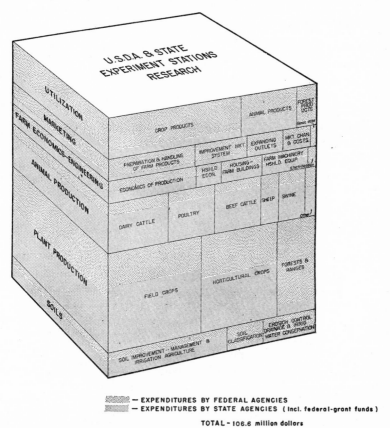

— EXPENDITURES BY FEDERAL AGENCIES
— EXPENDITURES BY STATE AGENCIES (Incl. federal-grant funds)

TOTAL - 106.6 million dollars

Fig. 7–2. Functional analyses of the U.S. Department of Agriculture and State Agricultural Experiment Stations research programs based on estimated expenditures for fiscal year 1951.

about $32 million a year, to 1951 when about $106 million were allocated, the increase has been appreciable in real terms.

2. Congress was strongly inclined at times during the early postwar period to find a way out of its difficulties with agricultural price policy by appropriating more funds for research. The Research and Marketing Act of 1946 can be explained partly on these grounds. Also, for reasons

of national security, research in this area has received some additional support.

3. But the mere appropriation of more funds is no assurance that they can or will be used effectively. One might well ask: Is the United States not reaching a point in all this research of rapidly diminishing returns? While it is necessary to distinguish between solid results and socially acceptable puffing, the vast array of research bulletins and technical papers that appear annually by workers of agricultural experiment stations and by the U.S. Department of Agriculture research staff support the belief that this research is still producing important results; it may well be in its increasing returns phase.

There are undoubtedly some inefficiencies in the ways in which these funds are distributed and put to use. The political mechanism does not cut with a razor's edge; it is a blunt contraption at best; and yet, it appears that in making funds available for agricultural research, with all its imperfections, it compares favorably, for example, with the public and private efforts that went into the settlement of the American frontier. There was indeed much waste in the crude "trial and error" that characterized our settlement, but even so, over a period of decades it gave the United States a pattern of land use which in its main outlines became a fairly good approximation of the proper use of such resources. The parallel between these two operations may be pressed further. For one, it is impossible to plan these research programs for the next decade any more than it was possible for any central agency to have planned the type of farming that should have been undertaken wherever the frontier was being extended. On another score, also, there is a marked similarity: the increase in the social product likely to be achieved is so much larger than the prospective social cost that all the mistakes that are made because of hasty decisions, poorly trained scientific personnel, some overlapping and duplications (much of which is necessary) and the lost motion that has characterized some aspects of this growth in research become quite unimportant when seen against the net gains that are realized despite these "unnecessary" inefficiencies.[16]

We conclude these observations on expenditures for, and returns from, agricultural research by reaffirming a belief about fact on which our analysis rests: The returns from these inputs to society are large; the additions to the social product to be had from a further increase in ex-

---

[16] This obviously is not an argument for poor organization and waste; on the contrary, the gains to be had could be even greater if these inefficiencies were reduced. But sight should not be lost of what appears to be a fact, namely, that despite some operational imperfections the social gains are very large, much larger than are the returns on resources employed in most production efforts.

penditures for agricultural research are substantially larger than are the returns from (most) alternative uses. Vaguely and intuitively the public process realizes this to be true; the public wants these gains and this explains the motivation that supports these expenditures.[17]

GAUGING THE VALUE OF THE INPUTS SAVED

Is it possible to acquire even a feel of the magnitude of the savings in inputs that have been realized as a consequence of improvements in production techniques in agriculture in the United States? A $100 million a year for agricultural research and another $75 million for extension work, on public account alone, is a sizable collection of inputs, even in dollars of the early fifties.

In this endeavor to gauge the value of resources (inputs) saved by new and better techniques, we shall consider only one year, namely, 1950. To produce the 1950 agricultural production (for sale and for farm home consumption), we shall take the value of inputs to have been $30,000 million. The dollar figures that follow are in constant dollars based on this 1950 figure of $30,000 million. We shall attempt to determine how many more resources would have been required to have produced the 1950 agricultural output using (1) 1910 techniques and (2) 1940 techniques.

1910 Techniques for 1950 Production

Two estimates are possible.

Upper Limit in Inputs Saved. This is equal to $16,200 million. When we take inputs at 1946–1948 input prices and techniques represented by

---

[17] We need also to take into account the expenditures for extending information to farm people, the task of the Agricultural Extension Service.

SOURCE OF FUNDS ALLOCATED FOR COOPERATIVE EXTENSION WORK IN UNITED STATES, ALASKA, HAWAII, AND PUERTO RICO FOR THE FISCAL YEARS 1940 AND 1950
(Research and marketing funds not included)

Source of funds	1940	1950
Total Federal funds	$18,584,642	$32,159,840
Total with the states	14,190,453	41,234,647
Grand total	32,775,095	73,394,487

SOURCE: Figures for 1940, *Department of Agriculture Appropriation Bill for 1941*, Part I, p. 206. Figures for 1950, *Department of Agriculture Appropriation Bill for 1951*, Hearings before the Subcommittee of the Committee on Appropriations, House of Representatives, 81st Cong., 2d Sess., Part I, pp. 282–283.

1910 production, the outcome is a savings in inputs of 54 per cent. This follows from data presented earlier in this chapter, that is, total inputs at 1946–1948 prices were 14 per cent larger in 1950 than in 1910; production, however, was 75 per cent larger. The output per unit of input, therefore, was 54 per cent larger in 1950 than in 1910. The inference is that had 1910 techniques been employed to produce the 1950 production and if the 54 per cent additional inputs were available at 1950 input prices, the additional inputs (which were saved) may be represented at a value of $16,200 million.

Lower Limit in Inputs Saved. This is equal to $9,600 million. Weighting the inputs used in agricultural production by 1910–1914 input prices gives the following results: Total inputs are 33 per cent larger in 1950 than in 1910 and, therefore, the output (production 75 per cent larger) per unit of input is only 32 per cent larger. Thus, to have produced the 1950 agricultural production with 1910 techniques with inputs weighted by 1910–1914 input prices, the resources saved become $9,600 million.

The savings in inputs in 1950 alone are much larger, even at the lower limit, than all the expenditures of the Federal and state governments on agricultural research and extension work since 1910. The savings in inputs in agricultural production, at the lower limit, in one year, 1950, stand at $9,600 million and for the upper limit at $16,200 million. Let us suppose that the expenditures had been at an annual rate of $100 million for agricultural research and of $75 million for agricultural expansion. We would then have, for the forty years (175 × 40), a total expenditure of $7,000 million, which is substantially less than the savings in agricultural inputs in a single year, at the lower limit, weighting inputs at 1910–1914 input prices. At 1946–1948 input prices (the upper limit), the savings in inputs in agricultural production *in* 1950 *alone* were more than twice as large as would be forty years of research and extension expenditures at the present annual rate.

1940 *Techniques for* 1950 *Production*

We now turn to a shorter and more recent period. The data should be somewhat better; also one comes closer to a small area and thus less subject to other "disturbances." Again, two estimates are possible.

Upper Limit in Inputs Saved. This is equal to $5,550 million. Production was 25.5 per cent larger in 1950 than in 1940; inputs committed, at 1946–1948 input prices, were 5.9 per cent larger; therefore, output (production) per unit of input was 18.5 per cent larger in 1950 than in 1940. If the 18.5 per cent additional inputs that would have been required to produce the 1950 production with 1940 techniques are valued at 1950 input prices, the savings represent $5,550 million.

Lower Limit in Inputs Saved. This is equal to $1,110 million. As already indicated, production was 25.5 per cent larger. Inputs weighted by 1935–1939 input prices were about 21 per cent larger in 1950 than in 1940. Output (production) per unit of input, therefore, was only 3.7 per cent larger in 1950 than in 1940. Additional inputs of the magnitude of 3.7 per cent to produce the 1950 production indicate $1,110 million of inputs saved.

A double warning is called for in closing this chapter. First, while it has been convenient to treat all the expenditures for agricultural research and extension as if they were used wholly to advance agricultural techniques, some activities for other purposes are financed by these expenditures. While the experiment stations, including most of the researches supported by them in the social sciences, are engaged in "producing" new production techniques, the activities of the extension services are not so restricted and, therefore, by no means all the $75 million being spent by the extension services is used to induce farmers to adopt new and better production techniques. Accordingly, the preceding analysis overstates somewhat the total inputs on public account expended for the purpose of producing and distributing new agricultural production techniques.

A second warning is also required. It would be a mistake to ascribe all the gains from new and better production techniques to the work of the agricultural experiment stations, the agricultural extension services, and to the many agencies of the U.S. Department of Agriculture engaged in research and its dissemination. If that were the case, the returns on these expenditures would be extraordinarily large; indeed they would be many, many fold. By no means all the fundamental research on which these advances in techniques are based is the work of agricultural experiment stations and the U.S. Department of Agriculture. Then, too, account must be taken of the marked improvements in the skills of farm people partly as a result of better education, and partly from cultural developments providing farm people with experiences that are instructive and conducive to the application of such new techniques. It is important, also, not to underrate the research contributions of firms and individuals that serve agriculture by producing for it new and better inputs: power, machinery, fertilizers, insecticides, feeds, and other items. Undoubtedly "external economies" have made important contributions to the observed gains in efficiency in agricultural production. And, yet, allowing for all of these, we are inclined to the view that the returns realized, on the present rate of expenditures on efforts to develop new techniques and to induce farmers to adopt them, are exceedingly large; many times as large as are the returns on "normal" business investments; and therefore, a strong case can be made for a much larger allocation of resources to these organized efforts to provide farmers with better production techniques.

But as this occurs, the revolution in agricultural production will continue; fewer inputs will be required in farming to produce a given farm output. The gains from new techniques during the next several decades are likely to be fully as great as they were during the period on which this analysis has concentrated. Much more, however, could be achieved if the community would reallocate resources in favor of those lines of production which indicate the larger output per unit of input, for this would require that the flow of inputs committed each year to "produce" and "distribute" new agricultural production techniques would be very substantially increased.

TABLE 7–8. INCREASE IN THE RATIO OF FARM OUTPUTS TO INPUTS, UNITED STATES, 1910–1950

(1910–1914 = 100)

Year	Farm output per unit of input[a]	Year	Farm output per unit of input[a]
1910	100	1930	106
1911	98	1931	117
1912	106	1932	117
1913	95	1933	111
1914	101	1934	99
1915	102	1935	119
1916	96	1936	105
1917	104	1937	130
1918	101	1938	125
1919	99	1939	126
1920	102	1940	130
1921	92	1941	138
1922	102	1942	152
1923	104	1943	147
1924	106	1944	151
1925	108	1945	149
1926	111	1946	153
1927	108	1947	146
1928	112	1948	158
1929	111	1949	153
		1950	153

[a] Inputs weighted by 1946–1948 prices.

TABLE 7-9. PER CENT OF THE TOTAL LABOR FORCE ENGAGED IN AGRICULTURE
IN TEN COUNTRIES

Country	1890 or 1891, per cent	1900 or 1901, per cent	1910 or 1911, per cent	1920 or 1921, per cent	1930 or 1931, per cent	1940 or 1941, per cent	1948, per cent
Great Britain[a]	10.3	8.6	7.8	6.8	5.7	4.4	5.5
United States[b]	42.6	37.5	31.0	27.0	21.4	17.6	12.7
Australia[c]	31.1	32.8	30.1	25.7	20.5[d]	....	14.9[d,e]
Switzerland[f]	36.9[g]	30.5	26.3	25.1	20.8	20.0	
Germany[c]	33.3[h]	27.0[i]	....	....	20.4[j]		
Canada[k]	45.5	46.0	39.0	38.0	34.0	32.0	17.0[d]
Sweden[l]	49.6	45.8	42.0	38.4	34.7	29.0	28.0[m]
France[n]	....	41.1	40.7	40.9	35.2	....	36.4[o,d]
Italy[c]	....	59.4	55.4	56.1	46.8	....	48.0[d]
Japan[c]	71.8[p]	....	61.5[q]	53.5	50.3	....	48.0[d]

NOTE: In general, though the definitions for labor force and agricultural labor force vary from country to country and time to time, the proportion of the labor force engaged in agriculture is considered to include all persons economically engaged principally in agriculture, whether as proprietors, managers, paid employees, or unpaid workers assisting in the operation of a family farm or business. Only in the case of Great Britain (except for years prior to 1940), the United States, Canada, and France are workers in forestry and fishing excluded from agriculture. Estimates of labor force include persons in the armed forces and those unemployed.

[a] *Statistical Abstract for the United Kingdom, 1924–1938*, Board of Trade (London), 1940, p. 129; and *Annual Abstract of Statistics, 1938–1948*, Central Statistical Office (London), 1949, p. 97.

[b] *Historical Statistics of the United States, 1789–1945*, Bureau of the Census (Washington, D.C.), 1949, p. 63; and *Annual Report on the Labor Force, 1948*, Series P-50, No. 13, Bureau of the Census (Washington, D.C.), 1949, p. 1.

[c] Colin Clark, *The Conditions of Economic Progress* (New York: The Macmillan Company, 1940), pp. 185–201 and 360–363.

[d] *Yearbook of Food and Agricultural Statistics, 1949*, Food and Agriculture Organization of the United Nations (Washington, D.C.), 1950, pp. 26–27; data for Canada are for 1951; see footnote k.

[e] For 1947.

[f] *Annuaire statistique de la Suisse, 1948*, Bureau Fédéral de Statistique (Basel), 1949, p. 48.

[g] For 1888.   [h] For 1895.   [i] For 1907.   [j] For 1933.

[k] *The Canada Year Book, 1948–49*, Dominion Bureau of Statistics (Ottawa), 1949, pp. 16, 17; data from 1901 to 1951, from Professor David MacFarland.

[l] *Statistisk Årsbok Swerige, 1949*, Utgiven av Statistiska Centralbyran (Stockholm), 1949, p. 39. Agricultural workers and their dependents as a percentage of the labor force and all dependents.

[m] For 1945.

[n] Percentages are computed from figures taken from *Résultats statistiques du recensement de la population effectué March, 1901, 1911, 1921, 1931, and 1936*, Vol. I, France, La Statistique Generale (Paris: Imprimerie Nationale). All persons fourteen to seventy years old in agricultural families in absence of indication of any other occupation are included in the agricultural labor force.

[o] For 1946.   [p] For 1897.   [q] For 1912.

NOTE : LABOR FORCE AND ITS DISTRIBUTION

Fundamental changes in factor supplies and product demand may also be inferred from crude data on the distribution of the labor force within various countries. The proportion of the labor force engaged in agriculture has been dropping not only in the United States and the older countries in western Europe, but also in the larger agricultural countries and in parts of the Orient. This decline has been going on for decades. The magnitude of the decline and the rate at which it has occurred in different countries at different times is instructive. In the United Kingdom most of the decline came before the turn of the century and the proportion of the labor force in agriculture has not dropped much since then, from 8.6 per cent in 1900 to 5.2 per cent in 1948. The patterns of decline in the United States, Canada, and Australia are rather similar. The secular "stagnation" of France and Italy may be inferred from these data. The path of these data for Japan indicates rapid changes in basic factor supplies and product demands.

8

THE DECLINING ECONOMIC IMPORTANCE
OF AGRICULTURAL LAND

We shall now endeavor to gauge and to explain one of the major resource effects of the new and better production possibilities that have
emerged in Western countries, especially in the United States. How have
these developments affected the production possibilities in agriculture?
We shall show that advances in techniques, improvements in skills, use of
more capital and better organization have been about as applicable to
agricultural production as to the production in the rest of the economy.
It will become clear, also, as we proceed, that agricultural land is no
longer the critical limitational factor in economic progress that it once
was. To gain historical perspective, let us begin with Ricardo.

In representing the circumstances of his period, Ricardo assigned a
major role to agricultural land, and quite properly so in view of the
fact that most households in England were spending most of their income for food. It is a long step to R. F. Harrod, who, in 1948 in selecting
the economic variables for his *Dynamic Economics,* saw fit to leave land
out altogether.[1] While it is true that Ricardo sought mainly to determine
the distribution "of the whole produce of the earth" to the various factors
during different stages of economic development, and while Harrod endeavored to explain the occurrence of depressions in an economy like
that of the United States, each reflected the circumstances of his period,
among others, the existing beliefs regarding the place of land in the
economy.

Clearly, in particular countries, land is no longer the limitational factor
it once was; for instance, in such technically advanced communities as
the United Kingdom and the United States and also in many others,
the economy has freed itself from the severe restrictions formerly imposed by land. This achievement is the result of new and better produc-

[1] R. F. Harrod, *Towards a Dynamic Economics* (London : Macmillan & Co.,
Ltd., 1948). On p. 20, Harrod says, " . . . I propose to discard the law of
diminishing returns from the land as a primary determinant in a progressive
economy. . . . I discard it only because in our particular context it appears
that its influence may be quantitatively unimportant."

tion possibilities and of the path of community choice in relation to these gains. This achievement has diminished greatly the economic dependency of people on land; it has reduced the income claims of this factor to an ever-smaller fraction of the national income; and it has given rise to profound changes in the existing forms of income-producing property. The underlying economic development has modified in an important way and relaxed substantially the earlier iron grip of the niggardliness of nature.

Ricardo had in mind a high-food-drain community, while Harrod, the opposite, a difference which may be illustrated by a simple comparison. Take two communities, one representing a situation in which most of the productive effort is required to produce food, a technically undeveloped community with a large population relative to its resources and with a low level of living where rents in agriculture are large relative to total factors rewards. In such a *high-food-drain* community, let us suppose that 75 per cent of the income is used for food and in which, say, $33\frac{1}{3}$ per cent of the cost of food consists of rent (net) for land used in farming. In such a case, one-fourth of the income, at factor cost, would be "spent" for the services obtained from agricultural land. For the second situation, take a *low-food-drain* community, one approximating the United States at its current stage of economic development, and assume that about 12 per cent of the disposable income is expended for farm products that enter into food and that about 20 per cent of the cost of producing farm products is net rent. Under these circumstances only about 2.5 per cent of the income of the community would be spent for the food-producing services of land.[2]

Each of these figures is a significant index of a whole set of attributes of the community from which it is drawn. The social, political, and economic differences between a community in which a fourth of the economic rewards goes for the productive services of land and one where one-fortieth goes for this purpose are so great that it is indeed hard for people living under such diverse circumstances to comprehend each other's problems. The revolutionary implications of land reform in countries where most of the property consists of land, where this property is held not by cultivators but mainly by a small group of families who do

[2] A rough gauge for 1949 would be as follows: Disposable personal income, $187 billion; expenditure on food, excluding alcoholic beverages, $50.7 billion; assuming that one-half of the expenditures for purchased meals represents cost of food at retail, the food expenditure figure becomes $44.9 billion, of which about one-half or 22.5 billion is for the farm products entering into food. 22.5 is 12 per cent of 187. See *Survery of Current Business*, U.S. Department of Commerce, July, 1950, pp. 9 and 24 for relevant figures.

not farm and where most of the political power and social privileges are vested in those who own land, are, for a person living in a technically advanced community, virtually impossible to grasp. Ricardo's economic logic gave little comfort to landowners, but the case for land reform in high-food-drain communities does not necessarily rest on altering the economic relations within agriculture. Basic social and political issues are usually in the forefront in countries where a transfer of land to existing cultivators would not change the size of the operating units or the type of farming. The production process in agriculture need not be altered in such a case; the reform, for instance, by means of taxation might simply absorb the net rent of land, and thus transfer the rent from private individuals to the state as public revenue.

A century ago it appeared to thoughtful men that land firmly held the economic fortunes of all communities in its palms, and that there was no escape from the restrictions imposed by nature. The classical law of (secular) diminishing returns stands as a symbol of this belief about economic history. But circumstances have been altered, for it is clear that the Western communities are now quite free from its grasp. How has this remarkable change come about? It did not occur, of course, by contracting the economy and thus reducing the amount of land required to produce food and thereby making this particular factor relatively more abundant. Such a sequence would be possible if a population were to decline. Yet the record[3] on this score is conclusive; population growth in Western countries was rapid and pronounced during this period, and markedly so during the earlier part, nor has it spent itself.

We shall represent the development underlying the declining economic importance of land in the form of two propositions. The first proposition is restricted to certain changes in the relations between agriculture and the rest of the economy characteristic of communities as they emerge, leaving behind their former high-food-drain status. The second proposition relates to changes in the inputs of land relative to other inputs within agriculture. Land is here restricted to agricultural land used to produce farm products, thus leaving aside minerals, sites, recreational and other services obtained from land.

It is our belief that the following two propositions are historically valid in representing the economic development that has characterized Western communities:[4]

[3] A stage of the history of Ireland may, however, be cited as an exception to this record.

[4] The two propositions can be integrated into a single and more general proposition by simply relating all agricultural land (as an input) to all inputs of the community. Existing statistics, however, are such that it is not possible

1. A declining proportion of the aggregate inputs of the community is required to produce (or to acquire) farm products.

2. Of the inputs employed to produce farm products, the proportion represented by land is not an increasing one, despite the recombination of inputs in farming to use less human effort relative to other inputs, including land.[5]

Whenever these two propositions are in fact valid for a community, it follows that the value added by all agricultural land as an input must necessarily decline relative to the value productivity of all inputs of a particular community. The economic consequences that flow from the first proposition would not suffice, inasmuch as a decline in agriculture by itself would not necessarily mean that the value added by land would fall, because it would be possible under particular conditions for the value contributed by land to rise enough to maintain or even increase its position relative to the aggregate inputs of the community. Also, if the value added by all land were to decline relative to all other inputs in agriculture and if farm products, meanwhile, were to come to claim a larger share of the income of the community, the importance of land, measured in terms of the value added by all agricultural land as an input, could stay constant or even rise. But whenever both of these propositions are valid, land will necessarily decline in importance in the economy. In situations where the first is true and where, in the case of the second proposition, land becomes in fact a smaller proportion of all inputs used in farming, the decline of land, of course, is accelerated.

AGRICULTURE RELATIVE TO THE WHOLE ECONOMY

Let us look briefly at the empirical evidence supporting the first of our two propositions by touching on the United Kingdom and by considering some relevant data about the United States in a bit more detail before turning to the economic assumptions and logic explaining this develop-

---

to get satisfactory data bearing on such a general proposition, while there are some data which permit us to observe the apparent validity of each of the two propositions as we have formulated them.

[5] One may, of course, represent the economic importance of land in different ways. Changes in the relative value per unit is one approach, and when rent per acre declines relative to the rewards of other factors it may be said that the economic importance of land is diminishing. Such a representation is, however, not a complete measure of the changes in land viewed as a price–quantity aggregate. We, therefore, turn to the "value added" by all land relative to all other inputs for our measure, difficult as it is to combine and add together various parcels of land used to produce farm products.

ment. In England just prior to 1800, when England still had most of the characteristics of a high-food-drain economy, worker families may have spent about 75 per cent of their income for food.[6] In 1948 only 27 per cent of the expenditures of consumers in the United Kingdom appear to have been for food.[7] While these figures are not entirely comparable, they leave no doubt that a remarkable change has occurred in the proportion of the income required to obtain food.

The historical record of the United States is fairly easy to interpret in this connection because it has been more nearly self-contained throughout. Some insights may be had from crude property data and the occupations of workers. An estimate of all real and personal property in the United States in 1805 places the total value of this property at $2,505 million of which $1,661 million, or about two-thirds, consisted of land.[8] At that time over 70 per cent of the labor force was engaged in agricultural pursuits.[9] By 1850, farm land, including improvements, was a little less than half of the value of all property, while about 60 per cent of the labor force was agricultural. The 1880 figures are somewhat more precise, since it is possible to separate agricultural land from improvements. In that year, out of an aggregate of $43,642 million, only $8,158 million, or less than one-fifth, was agricultural land and about 50 per cent of the labor force was in agriculture. The national wealth in 1922 was $321 billion, while agricultural land, excluding improvements, was $41.5 billion, or about one-eighth of the total; and 27 per cent of the labor force was engaged in agricultural pursuits.

Another rough check on the first proposition is the downward drift in the proportion of the national income imputed to agriculture. Income estimates for earlier stages of the economic history of the United States are, of course, subject to many limitations and especially for the purpose at hand. The fact that farm families were much more self-sufficient formerly makes it exceedingly difficult to get at all the income produced by agriculture at that time compared to more recent periods, and there-

[6] Sir Frederick Morton Eden, *The State of the Poor*, 1797, Vols. II–III.

[7] *Monthly Bulletin of Statistics*, Statistical Office of the United Nations (New York), February, 1950, p. 3.

[8] *Historical Statistics of the United States, 1789–1945*, U.S. Department of Commerce (Washington, 1949), Table 1, p. 1. The total valuation is reduced by $200 million when the item covering slaves is subtracted, making it $2,305 million, and when land not adjoining or near to the cultivated land is subtracted, the figure for land drops to $759 million, or about one-third of the total.

[9] J. Frederic Dewhurst and Associates, *America's Needs and Resources* (New York: The Twentieth Century Fund, Inc., 1947), Table 215, p. 620.

fore these income estimates understate the contribution of agriculture more as one goes back than they do currently. Some insights, are, nevertheless, possible. We have one set of estimates that goes back to 1799 for the United States based on the realized private produced income. This series provides the following figures:[10]

Selected year	Total private produced income (in millions of dollars)	Produced by agriculture (in millions of dollars)	Per cent produced by agriculture
1799	668	264	39.5
1849	2,326	737	31.7
1879	6,617	1,371	20.7
1900	14,550	3,034	20.9
1920	60,995	10,569	17.3
1938	47,589	6,140	12.9

National-income estimates for more recent years give us a much better gauge of the value added by factors used in agriculture, including land relative to total value productivity of the economy:

Year	Income produced by all industries[a] (in billions of dollars)	Income produced by agriculture[b] (in billions of dollars)	Agriculture as percentage of all industries
1910	30.4	5.2	17.1
1919	68.2	11.8	17.4
1929	87.4	8.4	9.6
1939	72.5	6.4	8.8
1949	216.8	18.1	8.4

[a] U.S. Department of Commerce. The figures for 1910 and 1919 are from the national-income estimates (old series). The others are from the *National Income Supplement to Survey of Current Business*, July, 1947, and also the July, 1950 issue.

[b] *Crops and Markets*, U.S. Department of Agriculture, XXVII (1950): 139; and the *Farm Income Situation*, August, 1950. The commerce series on farm income leaves out rent paid to nonfarm landlords, which makes it less useful for our purposes than the U.S. Department of Agriculture series on which I have drawn.

There is no need to adduce further empirical evidence to support the first of our propositions. The facts, fortunately, are well known and generally accepted. There is, however, no established explanation that is completely satisfactory. We shall endeavor to sketch the essential ele-

[10] *Historical Statistics of the United States*, 1789–1945, *Series* A154–164, p. 14.

ments of such an explanation restricted to the kind of economic development that has characterized Western communities.

In its simplest terms the explanation must answer the following query:
When the effective aggregate inputs of a community increase as a result
of economic development (1) when does a community find it possible
to produce or acquire its farm products with a smaller proportion of its
productive resources and (2) why does it choose this possibility? Our
task here is not that of explaining the increase in aggregate inputs but
the production possibilities and choices that emerge as a result of such
changes.

Figures 8–1 to 8–3 are drawn to represent three sets of production
possibilities. In each figure the particular community is confronted by
the production possibility curve *PP*. The preferred combination of farm

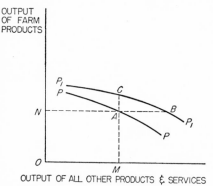

FIG. 8–1. Production possibilities relatively adverse for farm products.

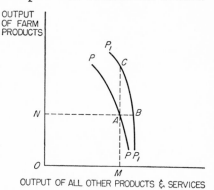

FIG. 8–2. Production possibilities relatively favorable for farm products.

products and of other outputs is represented by *A*, with *OM* indicating
the nonfarm outputs and *ON* the output of farm products (both *OM*
and *ON* in each of the three figures represent logarithmic scales).

Figure 8–1 represents a situation in which the production-possibility
curves are relatively adverse for increasing the output of farm products.
Economic development gives the community a new and improved production situation represented by P_1P_1. The triangle *ABC* indicates the
range of choices open to the community in going from *PP* to P_1P_1 without going below the former level of output of either farm products or of
nonfarm products. The community can now have substantially more
nonfarm outputs in going from *A* to *B*, provided it chooses to restrict itself
to the same amount of farm products it formerly produced. The choice
open to the community in the other directions, however, is very slim. It
can add only from *A* to *C* to its farm products, even though it foregoes
having any more nonfarm products than formerly. Let us suppose that

along with the new and better production possibilities there were to occur a growth in population which required all of *AC* to provide enough food to keep the per capita intake at the old level. In that event, should the community choose to maintain the old level, it would mean stopping at *C* on P_1P_1 with all of the gains in production resulting from the attainment of P_1P_1 being used to produce farm products. This in substance is the Ricardian case.

Figure 8–2 is drawn to represent a situation which is the exact converse of that portrayed in Fig. 8–1. In this case the production-possibility curves are relatively adverse for increasing the output of nonfarm products. In going from *PP* to P_1P_1 the triangle *ABC* again indicates the range of choices, and this time farm products are in a much more favorable position than are nonfarm products. No one to my knowledge has

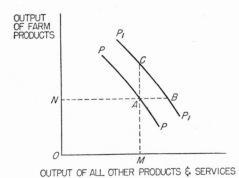

OUTPUT
OF FARM
PRODUCTS

Fɪɢ. 8–3. Improvements in production possibilities neither adverse nor favorable for farm products.

advanced the view that this case can represent a real situation, probably because we are unable to rid ourselves of the specter of hunger embedded in our minds by Ricardo–Malthus–Mill. Looking back, it might be said that the early and middle thirties came close to being a situation of this type; food-production possibilities improved substantially, while industry appeared to be "stagnant" and, at the same time, the rate of population growth dropped sharply.

When we take the long view, however, it is quite clear that improvements in production have been about as favorable for farm products as for other products and services taken as a whole. American data for the period since 1910 leave little doubt on this point. Figure 8–3 has been drawn to represent such a situation; it, therefore, should be more instructive than either Figs. 8–1 or 8–2 in explaining that aspect of our economic history relevant to the problem under consideration. In Fig. 8–3 the shape of *PP* indicates that when resources are shifted from agriculture to other industries or the converse, the substitution possibilities are about the same either way. The new and better production possibility curve P_1P_1 also has this attribute; and the triangle ABC indicates that the community can now have and thus may choose substantially more farm products along AC or nonfarm products along AB, or some preferred combination of the two on P_1P_1 between BC.

With production possibilities like those represented in Fig. 8–3, community choice has considerable room to express itself in going from PP to P_1P_1. As new opportunities have presented themselves, it is clear that Western communities have preferred relatively more of the nonfarm products and services, or to state this another way, as new and better production possibilities have emerged, the preferred combination has become one in which farm products are a decreasing proportion of all products and services.

Why has the Western community preferred these particular combinations? To explain the path of the community choice, we take recourse to the scale of preferences of the community. Taking the long view, as we have in this study, we shall assume that not only products but also the population is subject to the preferences of people. One possible preference scale, which can express itself given a time span of decades, is more people, enough more to absorb all the gains from new and improved production possibilities. (There is no a priori basis for excluding a deterioration in nonfarm products and services, that is, the community choosing less of these in order to make possible the production of more food to feed more people.) There is no way of measuring these scales of preferences directly; at best, we infer their contours and positions indirectly from a process in which we can observe certain effects. The history of the growth of population, at least statistically, is an open book. Western communities have not chosen to behave in accordance with the Ricardo–Malthus–Mill model. Moreover, as the income of people has risen, it is clear they have preferred to spend proportionally less of their incomes for food, and especially for the farm products that enter into food. In other words, the income elasticity of farm products has not remained high, as it was when these communities were of the high-food-drain type; it has become less until, under existing conditions, in a community with as high per capita incomes as exist in the United States, the income elasticity of farm products is now quite low, approximately .25, with many farm products actually in a position of inferior goods against income.

In explaining the circumstances on which the first of our two propositions rests, we have endeavored to show that it is necessary that the new and better production possibilities which emerge as the economy develops do not exclude improvements in the production of farm products. This condition, in general, has prevailed in Western communities because the advances in techniques, improvements in skills, the use of more capital, and improvements in organizations have been about as applicable to agricultural production as to other lines. One of the fundamental consequences of this development has been the favorable choice situation confronting the community. In addition, therefore, it is necessary that the preferences of people, either for more population or for food or combinations of these, do not exhaust the improved possibilities applicable to the production of food. In Western communities it is plain that the preferred combinations underlying the path of community choice that have emerged under these circumstances have called for the production of more nonfarm products and services relative to farm products entering into food.

Relative Position of Land as an Input in Producing Farm Products

Our second proposition about the course of economic development is that the value productivity of agricultural land has not increased relative to that of all inputs used to produce farm products. The evidence supporting this proposition is fairly conclusive for the United States for recent decades with input estimates now available. But before turning to these data, we need to take account of certain difficulties in getting at the empirical proof.

How can land as an input be measured? In 1910, 1,618 million acres were used for agricultural purposes in the United States; by 1945 this acreage had declined slightly to 1,570 million.[11] During that period, the volume of agricultural production for sale and for home consumption increased 70 per cent.[12] From these two sets of facts, we cannot, however, infer either that the aggregate inputs of agricultural land had declined (except in one special and meaningless economic sense, namely, that fewer acres were employed) or that the value added by land had declined relative to all inputs used in farming. We are, here, confronted with a series of difficulties, suggested by the following questions: (1) What is land? (2) Can it be measured and aggregated? (3) Can the other inputs be determined?

It is impossible to standardize land in physical terms; its physical attributes do not permit us to put land into one of several convenient

[11] All land in farms plus all nonfarm land grazed by livestock. From L. A. Reuss, H. H. Wooten, and F. J. Marschner, *Inventory of Major Land Uses in the United States*, USDA, *Misc. Pub.* 663, 1948, Table 16.

[12] Based on *Consumption of Food in the United States, 1909–48*, BAE, *Misc. Pub.* 691, August, 1949, Table 3.

boxes. Land is not only exceedingly heterogeneous physically but also it can be and is altered significantly over time by farming and by nature, even when it is not being farmed. Investment and disinvestment in soil productivity are possible. So what then is land in either a cross-sectional or a secular comparison? Nothing can be salvaged in terms of physical units which are meaningful in determining, say, the supply of land in terms of so many acres, because there is no point whatsoever in adding together the semi-arid, low-yielding acres of parts of Arizona and the highly fertile acres of parts of Iowa. We are, therefore, driven to an index weighted by value components, based either on rent or on the price of agricultural land or on other estimates of the value of the productive service of land. These matters are sufficiently important to deserve special investigation (see note following this chapter).

Before turning to American data on the value added by agricultural land, a brief reference to the United Kingdom and especially to France is in order, given the data made available by a recent study.[13] Had the Physiocrats been confronted by modern France, their *Tableau Économique* would have shown a small, unimpressive "net product." Already

TABLE 8–1. NATIONAL INCOME AND AGRICULTURAL LAND RENT IN FRANCE

Selected years	Agricultural land rent	
	As percentage of national income	As percentage of agricultural income
1901	7.9	25.5
1906	6.8	21.6
1911	6.5	19.5
1916	5.1	24.0
1921	3.2	11.8
1926	3.4	12.0
1931	3.6	15.6
1936	3.7	16.3
1947–1948	Not available	9.0

by 1900 agricultural land claimed only about a fourth of the agricultural income; it has declined to half or less of that figure since then; and the rent imputed to all agricultural real estate has come to represent less than 5 per cent of the national income, as is indicated in Table 8–1.

[13] The data appearing below for France and the United Kingdom are from an unpublished study by Procter Thomson, *Productivity of the Human Agent in Agriculture: An International Comparison.* This study was financed by the Rockefeller Foundation as a part of a research program in agricultural economics at the University of Chicago.

The data for the United Kingdom are quite fragmentary, mainly because of the difficulty of untangling net and gross rent in the way they are reported. Here, again, the study by Thomson shows:

Selected years	Net rent as percentage of net agricultural income[a]
1925	16.8
1938	11.5
1946	5.6

[a] Harkness's figures for gross rent as per cent of net agricultural output in Great Britain are not inconsistent, for they indicate a decline from 39 per cent in 1908 to 26.6 per cent in 1930–1931. See D. A. E. Harkness, "The Distribution of the Agricultural Income," *Journal of Proceedings of the Agricultural Economics Society,* III (March, 1934): 30, Table VI.

American data for recent decades permit one to determine the value added by land as an input in farming with considerable assurance. The Bureau of Agricultural Economics has made estimates of the changes in physical inputs employed for agricultural production going back to 1910. These estimates indicate that land as an input has continued to hold about the same relative position throughout, representing somewhat less than a fourth of all inputs used for agricultural production. Agricultural land, that is land in farms, which we shall define below, was 23.6 per cent of all the inputs used for agricultural production in 1910–1914 and 25.4 per cent in 1945–1948. The composition and combination of inputs, including the land component, have, however, changed substantially. While inputs in the aggregate have increased moderately, the amount of labor has declined. In the case of agricultural land the total acres in farms rose from about 880 million in 1910 to 1,148 million in 1948.[14] Meanwhile, farm buildings and other improvements that are counted as part of the land have come to represent an increasing proportion of the value of agricultural land. Table 8–2 summarizes the relative size of the various classes of inputs, including agricultural land.

A word on the meaning of "agricultural land" in the present context seems necessary at this point. It includes cropland, pasture land, and other land in farms and buildings. It does not include pasture or range land not in farms,[15] but the contribution of this class of land is small;

[14] The earlier acreage figures included all land used for agricultural purposes; while here only land in farms is included. The import of the difference is discussed in the text below.

[15] For a note on the method used in measuring the input of agricultural land, see *Farm Production Practices, Costs, and Returns,* BAE, *Statis. Bul.* 83, October, 1949, Table 27.

TABLE 8–2. RELATIVE INPUTS IN UNITED STATES AGRICULTURE, 1910–1914 AND 1945–1948

Class of input	Relative amounts of inputs employed for agricultural production	
	1910–1914,[a] per cent	1945–1948,[b] per cent
Farm labor.	46.0	42.6
Agricultural land	23.6	25.4
Maintenance and depreciation . .	10.3	10.3
Operation of motor vehicles . . .	0.3	6.3
Interest.	9.6	5.1
Taxes	3.2	3.0
Fertilizer and lime	2.5	2.8
Miscellaneous items	4.5	4.5
Total.	100.0	100.0

[a] Using 1910–1914 cost ratios, from Glen T. Barton and Martin R. Cooper, "Relation of Agricultural Production to Inputs," *The Review of Economics and Statistics*, Vol. XXX (May, 1948), Table 2.

[b] Using 1946–1948 cost ratios, from unpublished data made available to the writer by the Bureau of Agricultural Economics. Labor input from 1940 on based on Bureau of the Census data.

grazing land for which farmers pay fees[16] is a very minor item com- pared to the net rent of all land in farms. In 1948, for example, it was about one-tenth of 1 per cent as large. Two major changes in the com- position of agricultural land can be measured: (1) as already indicated, the acres in farms have increased about 30 per cent during the four decades under consideration and (2) even so, farm buildings have come to represent an increasing proportion of the value of agricultural land, rising from 18 to 33 per cent as set forth below:

Year	Acres in farms, million acres	Value of all farm real estate, in billions of cur- rent dollars	Value of farm buildings, in billions of cur- rent dollars	Farm build- ings relative to all farm real estate, per cent
1910	880	34.8	6.3	18
1920	956	66.3	11.5	17
1930	987	47.9	13.0	27
1940	1,061	33.6	10.4	31
1950	1,148	63.5	20.6	33

[16] These fees are included in the input referred to as "miscellaneous items."

If we assume that the value productivity of farm buildings was roughly the same per dollar of invested value as it was for land in farms minus buildings, after allowing for maintenance and depreciation, and that about half of the farm buildings in value terms represented farm dwellings which we shall, therefore, subtract—the inference is that agricultural land minus farm buildings represented a little more than 19 per cent of all inputs in 1910 and about 17 per cent in 1950.[17]

There are gaps, however, in our information about the various capital components that go to make up agricultural land. In a rough way we can take, as we have taken, account of farm buildings and in doing so separate the buildings used for production from those used for consumption. But there are many other forms of capital embedded and included in agricultural land, for it includes among others such items as fences; windmills, wells, and other water facilities; electric lines serving farmsteads; clearing of land, drainage and irrigation structures; and roads. In addition, there are many components related to soil productivity. Existing social accounting, however, does not permit us to make satisfactory estimates of these items. While there is little doubt that for those capital forms not directly related to the productivity of the soil, the tendency has been upwards relative to the aggregate value of the land in farms as in the case of farm buildings. But it is often alleged that farmers generally have misused the soil, and as a result there has been widespread erosion and depletion, and therefore, in effect substantial disinvestment of the "natural" soil productivity. The evidence offered, however, does not support the generalization. While there are many particular situations where such disinvestments have occurred, these losses appear, judging from informed opinion, to have been more than offset by improvements on other farms. The productive properties of the soil being farmed in the United States are in all probability substantially better today than they were, say, four decades ago, despite the particular soil losses that have occurred.

The following conclusion is warranted: when account is taken of both investments and disinvestments, the input which we have defined as agricultural land has come to an increasing extent to consist of capital components that have been added to the land. We infer, therefore, as a consequence of this development, that the American economy is even less dependent upon the "original and natural properties" of the land than the above figures would indicate.

[17] For estimates of farm buildings and of dwellings and of service buildings used for production, see *Income Parity for Agriculture*, Part II, Sec. 5, U.S. Department of Agriculture, March, 1941; also, *The Balance Sheet and Current Financial Trends of Agriculture, 1950*, BAE, *Agric. Inf. Bul.* 26, October, 1950; also, *Federal Reserve Bulletin*, September, 1950.

The proposition that land as an input in agricultural production has not increased relative to all other inputs used in farming appears to be empirically valid for such technically advanced communities as France, the United Kingdom, and the United States. The input estimates of the Bureau of Agricultural Economics, on which we have based our analysis, make the case on this point quite conclusive for the United States since about 1910.

We realize that land is not for food alone. It is important for other purposes in the community and the economy, purposes which we have neglected throughout this chapter. The conclusion, however, is firm; the economic developments that have characterized Western communities since Ricardo's time have resulted in improved production possibilities and in a community choice that has relaxed the niggardliness of nature. As a consequence of these developments, agricultural land has been declining markedly in its economic importance. Will it continue to do so? Existing circumstances in the United States indicate a strong affirmative answer. Nor is the end in sight. But can existing high-food-drain communities realize a similar economic development? As yet we do not know.

NOTE : LAND AS AN ECONOMIC VARIABLE

Land has played various roles in economics. Like a true Shavian, land has enjoyed a most honorable and versatile career. It is one of the old tripartite division of factors—land, labor, and capital—a classification which made for economy in exposition but not for a satisfactory analysis of the economy. The Physiocrats gave to land not only a leading role but they also made it the hero of their scheme. The belief in the abundances of nature, with rent the gift of God to the landowners, put land in a preferred position in the *Tableau Économique*. Ricardo and the older English economists who followed his casting also gave to land a key role but made it the villain of the piece. The concept of the niggardliness of nature placed landowners in a strategic position in a community with a rapidly growing population. For Marx, the existing landlords became a special species of capitalists of feudal vintage, but obsolete, and therefore soon to be replaced by genuine, industrial capitalists. Again, land was to be cast as the unmitigated villain by Henry George who saw it as the instrument that transfers the unearned social increment of economic progress to landlords.

Before one can study the part that land plays in a developing economy, it is necessary, first of all, to make clear what is meant by land.

Most discussions about land are at cross purposes because of conceptual differences. What is there about land that makes it a relevant economic variable? There is no end of possible definitions. We might endeavor to use the Ricardian conception, that is, take land to be the original and indestructible properties of the soil. How meaningful, however, is this concept in analyzing the conditions affecting the supply of land for producing farm products in a developing economy? The various nutrients in soils on which plants draw are certainly important in farming but these nutrients are neither "original" nor "indestructible."[18] They can be put into a parcel of land and they can be taken out of it; they can be transferred from one parcel of land to another or to some other use; in terms of these nutrients, land can be depleted (exhausted) or developed (restored); nor are the processes of nature entirely neutral, for over geological periods fundamental changes are possible and have occurred. The original and indestructible properties of the soil do not even assure us a continuity of site and surface. But even if they did, what would such a concept amount to for economic analysis? Suppose one were to take the surface of the earth (land and water or both) to be land; the supply would surely be highly inelastic. Suppose we could say with absolute certainty it was fixed (zero elasticity); what of it? This representation of land as an economic variable would have little or no meaning to the problem at hand. Moreover, it is well nigh impossible to conceive of a real problem in which this notion of land would apply.

Land taken to be a *natural agent* does not overcome any of these difficulties. It is, of course, a more flexible concept than that considered above but when is a natural agent pure and free of unnatural elements? It is hard to find a situation where some, and in most cases a great deal, of capital has not been invested and incorporated in land that is being farmed. Even if it were desirable, it would not be possible to separate the two. But no purpose is served in placing "natural agents" into a separate category unless this class of agents possesses some economic attribute which is relevant in solving a particular problem. But even so, should it be impossible to identify a natural agent in practice, there would be little point in ascribing particular attributes to such an agent.

It comes down to this: a particular parcel of land suitable for farming is a complex physical structure in which there is embedded, as one approaches the surface, an intricate biological mechanism. How much or how little of it is natural or original or indestructible has little or no meaningful relation to its productivity. What matters is the useful services that it is capable of rendering. Suppose we tried to base our concept of the supply of tractors on the quantity of natural, original, and

[18] Unless one makes an appeal to physics and its "conservation of energy"; but this belief has no relevancy to the problem at hand.

indestructible elements in tractors. What would we have? A bit of iron ore and few other minerals with very little scrap value at best.

Another approach is to treat land as "pure" capital undifferentiated from all other forms of capital. While the older English economists undoubtedly went too far in their attempts to put land in one box and all other capital instruments in another box, much information about inputs is necessarily lost by going to the opposite extreme, that is, putting them all together and treating the larger aggregate as an undifferentiated variable. When this is done, it is of course true that the supply (of all capital taken as an aggregate) is highly inelastic certainly in the short run. But this fact, while true, is so elementary and, one would suppose, so obvious, that it might be taken for granted. Then, too, this particular attribute of the elasticity of the supply of this aggregate tells one virtually nothing about the supply of land confronting particular farms or a community for producing a particular product or service.

SUPPLY CONCEPT APPLIED TO LAND IN AGRICULTURE

How may we represent land as a variable entering into agricultural production? One can, of course, go back to land as a factor and relate the quantity of this factor to the price that it brings in actual transactions and take this price-quantity relation as the supply. The difficulty is not in the "supply" concept as such but in the "factor" concept applied to land. The difficulty arises in linking one parcel of land with all other parcels used in agriculture when one attempts to construct a meaningful aggregate. Professor Knight and other critics of the classical tripartite classification of factors have repeatedly and cogently pointed out the errors that arise from this practice.

Lumping all parcels of land together in an economic analysis, by counting acres, certainly violates every rule of aggregation. Instead of being similar or related in some meaningful way, acres of land consist of many different kinds of inputs, differing in their technical attributes (physical, chemical, and biological properties) and in the productive services they can render with advantage. Clearly, parcels of land are not, in fact, neatly uniform and standardizable physical units as is, for example, No. 2 yellow corn.[19]

It is unfortunately true that each parcel of land is in some sense unique; and, what is more, the particular technical attribute is usually

[19] Corn in this context can be graded and classified for market purposes; this does not mean, however, that chemists and other physical scientists do not find significant variations within a particular grade.

significant in relation to the physical productivity of land as an input. It is this "unmanageable" heterogeneity of land which makes it exceedingly difficult to group parcels of land into classes which have some semblance of uniformity or to establish a unit of measurement of the input.

PROBLEMS OF CLASSIFICATION AND MEASUREMENT

Soil scientists find certain physical, chemical, and biological properties in land to which they can gear their analytical work. The structure of a soil can be analyzed in terms of such elements. The soil profile is one gauge of its structure. Various combinations of nitrogen, potash, and phosphate can be rated in terms of their yield-producing potentials. Plants and plant growth can be taken as soil indicators. But the variables that go to make up a soil are numerous and the possible combinations stagger the imagination. Attempts to simplify and generalize, for example, as in the Mitscherlick effect law, the Baule units, and the Mitscherlick-Baule equation proposed by Willcox[20] have been without any apparent success. The complexity of the task is indicated by the soil requirements of economic plants as set forth in the following summary:[21]

(1) Suitability for the cultural implements required for most efficient production; (2) effective resistance to destructive soil erosion or soil depletion under the cropping system involved in profitable management; (3) adequate moisture storage to meet the water requirements of the crop, under normal rainfall or irrigation; (4) adequate aeration to a suitable depth to permit the development of a favorable root system for the mature plant; (5) available plant nutrients sufficient for profitable yields; and (6) freedom from adverse chemical conditions such as harmful concentrations of soluble constituents, and from other special soil conditions that favor the development of organisms parasitic to the crop.

Although much thought and work has gone into the art of soil classification and of mapping soils, the results, while useful in many ways, are not satisfactory for measuring the input aspects of land in farming. Agricultural economists have tried to adapt soil surveys and other findings of soil scientists in an endeavor to develop a classification of land

[20] O. W. Willcox, *ABC of Agrobiology* (New York: W. W. Norton & Company, 1937).
[21] M. F. Morgan, S. H. Gourley, and J. K. Ableiter, "The Soil Requirements of Economic Plants," *Soils and Men* (*Yearbook of Agriculture*, 1938), U.S. Department of Agriculture.

that would measure its physical productivity as an input in farming but the results have been quite discouraging.[22]

As is so often the case in economic analysis, it is necessary to rely upon approximations and upon indirect effects for clues in getting at the values of variables entering into the analysis. Land is especially difficult to manage. Several alternatives are open to us, each with its limitations: we can keep on trying to estimate the input of land directly by establishing a technical unit (physical, chemical, or biological, or some combinations of these); we can turn to indirect procedures, such as the market value of land or the rent paid and express the input in terms of an index based on value components (so many dollars' worth) or, even more roundabout, the value of the services produced by the input.

The difficulties of taking rent and the market price of land as indicators of "weights" of the "quantity" of inputs are several. There are the imperfections that characterize the land market. Some land is persistently overvalued while other land is undervalued. Capital rationing affects the price of land in various ways and so does the functioning of the labor market. Then, too, when a parcel of land is purchased its expected physical productivity for growing economic plants is not the only service that the buyer values and acquires. The satisfaction of owning a home enters and so do community facilities and other less tangible considerations, such as personal relations to other families in the community, landscape, hunting and fishing, and other similar possibilities. The rent paid is also not restricted to the physical productivity of the land but often includes a payment for managerial services, expected depletion or development of the soil (which can be plus or minus), and the bearing of various amounts of risk and uncertainty by the landlord, depending upon the nature of the lease and on other circumstances. These limitations may be tolerable in studying changes in the input aspect of land over time when all the "other circumstances" affecting the price of land or the rent paid are presumed to remain essentially unchanged in relation to the physical productivity of the land. But if the problem is to analyze how the land market functions and in so doing determine the nature of, and the reasons for, the existing imperfections in that market, these limitations would preclude using this approach.

Services from Land

Still another route, longer and more difficult in the case of agriculture, is to try to estimate the input of land from the productive contribution

[22] See, for example, *The Classification of Land, Univ. Missouri Agr. Expt. Sta. Bul.* 421, December, 1940.

it makes to the output. Where parcels of land render an identifiable and measurable service and where it is possible readily to determine the value of this service, the road becomes quite passable. When land provides only site, there are situations where the flow of this service affords a useful index of the input of land. Site is apparently the only attribute of land that is at all compatible with the Ricardian dictum that land consists of the original and indestructible properties of soil.

Site is a service of primary importance in urban land economics. Obviously, the nature of the soil, whether red or black, rich or poor, matters little. Most of Manhattan rests on firm rock, much of Chicago on mud, Atlanta on red hills, and Los Angeles is spread over a semidesert terrain. The many technical attributes of a soil that are related to the growth of economic plants give virtually no clue to the type of land that makes up the supply drawn upon for sites. Where land is employed primarily for sites, it is possible to refine this approach greatly, as has been done in studies with regard to urban land. The nature of the services that are being rendered and expected in the further development of a town, city, or metropolitan area provides a significant basis for classifying land resources drawn into this category. Measurement of the supply is, nevertheless, far from easy.

Recreation is another service that some land resources produce. Areas with lakes, woods, and mountains are often chosen as vacation grounds chiefly by urban people during the summer. When winter comes, other areas that are dry and sunny are preferred. Parks, playgrounds, and golf courses are increasingly important in the routine of city dwellers. In all the uses of land associated with recreation, the productivity of the soil in relation to economic plants is of secondary importance, although somewhat more so than it is in the case of sites. Studies already available indicate that land can be classified in accordance to its usefulness and value in producing recreational services. But to establish a unit of supply has not been achieved.

Land from which minerals are taken is on a different footing. The land is always exhausted in the process; the amount of the mineral available can usually be gauged and the output (product) lends itself to standardization. The supply concept applied to mineral lands is fairly straightforward and manageable.

Most of the land used by man is, however, employed to grow plants which are in turn used for feed, food, and fibers. Many farm and forestry products are produced in large volumes. Most of these products are marketed in accordance with well-defined standards and are priced in active and highly competitive markets. These standardized products with meaningful price tags attached to them would appear to offer an excellent point from which to work back to the inputs required, including land, in an attempt to determine the quantity and supply of land available for particular purposes. The principal difficulty arises from the fact that there is no charted path by which one can find one's way through the maze of production activities that characterize agriculture. In the case of some forestry products, where the production activity entails, primarily, the use of land over a long time span, this difficulty does not appear to be too serious. But where the inputs in farming consist primarily of human effort and of capital forms other than land, the difficulties of developing and measuring the input of land are legion and appear to be all but impossible to manage.

We shall conclude this note with these observations: Land as an economic variable is exceedingly hard to get at because of the difficulties that arise when one endeavors to establish and use some unit of measurement. Beliefs about land based on common-sense notions are very misleading. The fact that land is open and aboveboard, physical and concrete, and legally divided into neat, carefully described parcels, or lots, quarter sections, sections, townships, and the like does not help one determine the supply of land. The quantity of land, as it is commonly described, is such a heterogeneous aggregate as to have little or no economic meaning; and, very little has been done in applying economics to land. Where the capital formation of farmers is studied, investments and disinvestments in land are always left out; when factor markets are analyzed, the research on land stops with description; legal, social, and institutional arrangements are stressed while neglecting the economic aspect. Whereas the task is a difficult one, all too little has been done to measure land as an economic variable.

9

DIVERGENCIES IN ECONOMIC DEVELOPMENT
RELATED TO LOCATION

A developing economy draws sustenance from various sources and in the process new branches appear, some old ones grow bigger, others stay about as they were, while still others wither away. Agriculture may expand, stand still, or decline, depending upon the combination of the new factor supplies and product demands that emerge. Under some conditions, it becomes necessary to transfer resources out of farming, some circumstances require no shifts whatsoever, and for still others, transfers into farming are required. Each of these situations is to be found repeatedly in the annals of economic history. Let us, however, leave aside the kind of economic development which the older English school envisaged (for example, in Book IV of John Stuart Mill,[1] "Influence of the Progress of Society on Production and Distribution") which required a transfer of both capital and labor into farming, with agriculture in a position of advantage because of a rise in the price of food relative to other products and because of the increase in the reward to factors specific to farming. Let us consider instead the kind of economic development that has come to characterize Western countries.

Both cross-sectional and time-series data indicate that the process of economic development has occurred quite unevenly not only as among countries but also within a country, for example, within the United States. Agriculture in general has been retarded and within agriculture some major parts have fallen far behind while others have managed to stay abreast. An hypothesis is needed to explain this outcome of economic development; one will be advanced and considered briefly in this chapter, and, then, in the next, some of the income implications will be explored.

[1] John Stuart Mill, *Principles of Political Economy*, W. J. Ashley, editor (London: Longmans, Roberts and Green, 1929), pp. 695–794.

146

An Hypothesis[2]

The divergencies in economic development outlined above, it is assumed, are related to location. On this assumption, the following hypothesis, consisting of three parts, is advanced to explain the divergencies: (1) Economic development occurs in a specific locational matrix; there may be one or more such matrices in a particular economy. This means that the process of economic development does not necessarily occur in the same way, at the same time, or at the same rate in different locations. (2) These locational matrices are primarily industrial-urban in composition; as centers in which economic development occurs, they are not mainly out in rural or farming areas although some farming areas are situated more favorably than are others in relation to such centers. (3) The existing economic organization works best at or near the center of a particular matrix of economic development and it also works best in those parts of agriculture which are situated favorably in relation to such a center; and it works less satisfactorily in those parts of agriculture which are situated at the periphery of such a matrix.

It may be helpful to specify the kind of experiences that would not only cast doubt but would invalidate this hypothesis. If our economic history were to indicate that economic development always occurred evenly and generally throughout the economy, it would deny the validity of the first proposition essential to the hypothesis. However, let us suppose that the facts clearly show that the process is uneven and that there are particular locational matrices of economic growth and progress; but if our economic experience showed that farming areas were primarily the active centers of economic development or that all of them were fully as potent and important as the industrial-urban constellations, such facts would undermine the second part of the hypothesis. It would seem, however, that our economic history strongly supports the first two parts of the hypothesis, but there probably is disagreement with regard to the third, namely, that the existing economic organization is less effective and efficient in locations at the periphery of a particular matrix of economic development than at its center. It is, therefore, on this proposition that our researches should concentrate to determine whether this part of the hypothesis is empirically valid.

On the positive side, the divergency effects that emerge from this formulation of economic development may be restated as follows: In the

[2] This hypothesis was formulated by the writer in "A Framework for Land Economics—The Long View," *Journal of Farm Economics*, Vol. XXXIII (May, 1951), and was referred to as "The Retardation Hypothesis." The title given to this chapter, however, would appear to be a better description.

event the third proposition is consistent with empirical observations, the problem at hand is narrowed substantially and it becomes much more manageable. We can, then, concentrate our study on a set of particular "imperfections" in economic organization, particular in the sense that they can be traced back to the process of economic development as set forth in the first two propositions of the hypothesis. In short, in that case, the uneven development, say, within a particular country is the consequence of particular "imperfections" of the existing economic organization which reduce the capacity of the economy to cope satisfactorily with economic development.

IMPLICATIONS OF HYPOTHESIS

It may be helpful to anticipate in some detail the direction and form of the study which emerges when it is guided by this hypothesis.

Let us take economic development as the type of process that has characterized Western countries, at least, since the industrial revolution.[3] We are, therefore, not endeavoring to explain how an economy functions under stationary conditions or under circumstances resulting in retrogression. Nor are we attempting at this time to get at the essentially short-run economic fluctuations that have occurred repeatedly. In taking the long view, it is, of course, patent that economic development has occurred very unevenly, not only among countries and major parts of the world but also among communities within an economy or country. The very unevenness of this development presents two basic questions: What particular circumstances give rise to the process of economic development? Why does this process occur so unevenly, more especially, why does it by-pass entire communities within an economy, say within a country having well-established internal trade and migration?

We shall consider the first of these questions only in a very general way, for it will suffice to indicate that economic development is a consequence of new and better production possibilities that have been realized by particular communities from advances in technology, accumulation of capital, improvement in skills, growth in population, and improvements in economic organization. We have not found any general

[3] Whereas the hypothesis advanced has been formulated with an eye to the kind of economic development that has occurred since the event of the industrial revolution, the Henri Pirenne study, *Medieval Cities : Their Origins and the Revival of Trade*, translated by Frank D. Halsey (Princeton: Princeton University Press, 1948), presents a thesis that lends support to our hypothesis as also having relevancy in understanding certain economic aspects of the medieval period.

theory that gives a satisfactory explanation of the "causation" of this process taken in its entirety.[4] The second question also raises issues which are challenging; moreover, these issues seem to us to be not only exceedingly important in taking stock of certain shortcomings of our economic organization but to be quite manageable analytically.

We are mindful that there is a host of empirical situations falling within the province of the second of these questions which await a satisfactory explanation. Let us leave aside for the time being the uneven economic development between countries, for example, between the United States and Brazil, Belgium and Portugal, Japan and the Philippines, or the classical economic development of the United Kingdom compared to that, say, of Turkey, both long, well-established communities. Instead, let us take the easier problem of an uneven economic development within a "well-integrated" country in the belief that an understanding of such a situation may give us useful insights into the process that accounts for much, if not all, of the differences between countries. The second of these should be easier to analyze because within a country trade and migration are commonly not restricted by national policy as is usually the case between countries.

What do we find within any major country in this connection? Very significant variations indeed. Take, first, Brazil: The state of São Paulo has pulled far ahead of other states; for example, Minas Geraes, Paraná, or Matto Grosso are certainly far behind. Why? Eastern Canada has not stayed abreast in its economic development with that which has emerged in central and western Canada. This difference within Canada is sometimes "explained" by the historical events which placed some segments of the population in a preferred political position, or by differences in cultural orientation and by social institutions based on these cultural differences. But these "explanations" do not appear to account for the underlying conditions which have been instrumental for the by-passing of eastern Canada by the process of economic development, although some aspects of these "explanations" may throw some light on why trade and migration have not corrected the imbalance more satisfactorily.

The economic history of the United States should be exceedingly instructive in putting elements of this problem into focus. While Canada is beset by low productivity per worker and much poverty as one goes east, within the United States it is the South that has been substantially by-passed by economic development. Here, again, many particular "explanations" are current; there is the Civil War and its aftermath which

---

[4] For example, Joseph A. Schumpeter's *Theory of Economic Development*, or in the eclectic approach of B. S. Keirstead's *Theory of Economic Change*, or in others than can be cited.

left the Southern states greatly impoverished and badly disorganized. The racial difficulties are always advanced as a major part of this problem. But there is Texas, and also North Carolina, substantially in the vanguard. But the more critical facts which throw doubt on such explanations are the very low output per worker and the widespread poverty that characterizes whole farming communities in the areas immediately to the north of the Old South, areas with virtually no Negro population and communities which were spared most of the devastation caused by the Civil War.

To narrow the focus somewhat: Why have communities in central and upper Ohio, Indiana, and Illinois advanced so much more during the last fifty years than have those in the southern parts of these states? Or to take still another area, the northern parts of Michigan, Wisconsin, and Minnesota have been serious "problem areas" compared to the rest of these states. Again, why? The New England states also afford an interesting case study in which the southern part pulled out ahead leaving the northern part substantially behind and yet in more recent decades the gap between them appears to have closed very appreciably and as a result, unlike the developments in Canada, eastern United States is not only in a strong position generally in terms of economic development but is also less differentiated within than are some of the other major sections of the country.

The list of disparities in income among communities within major countries is by no means exhausted by these cases. Is each of these situations a special case which makes it necessary to find the appropriate special explanation? Or are they all essentially variants of a single process which will, once it is put in a suitable framework, make possible a general explanation? It is our thesis that the latter is possible by means of the hypothesis already advanced. In the next chapter, we shall consider the disparities in income that exist among communities and endeavor to show under what conditions income disparities of this type are the consequences of economic development.

To turn now to another set of questions: Once it is established that economic development occurs in a particular locational matrix and unevenly throughout the economy, why should this create any special problems inasmuch as it is the function of the various product and factor markets to correct the resulting imbalance in resource allocation? This matter may conveniently be considered in two parts. First, does economic development of the type that has characterized Western countries place particular strains on the market mechanism? In the case of agriculture, this clearly has been the case as we shall show in subsequent chapters. Second, does economic development either improve or impair the capacity and efficiency of an economic organization dependent primarily upon product and factor markets? Our hypothesis indicates that at or near the center of economic development such markets are strengthened while at the periphery of such a center they are left weak.

A careful study of the various components of economic development will show that as a result of (1) the new and better production possibilities that have emerged in Western countries and (2) the path which the community choice has taken, it has been necessary not only to recombine resources in farming but also to transfer, especially human resources, out of agriculture. The required resource adjustments have not been of the once-over kind, but instead, the effects, in the case of agriculture, have run in one direction and as a result the resource maladjustments have been accumulative.

On the demand side, the growth of population, although still large in absolute numbers, has been occurring at a diminishing rate; the income elasticity of farm products taken as a whole has become low in a country with as high a level of living as is enjoyed in the United States; and consuming units are also taking on new technology that is farm product "saving" in its effects. On the supply side, the rate of population growth in farming communities has been and still is substantially larger than that of industrial-urban communities; the advances in techniques applicable to farming have been fully as effective and rapid as in the rest of the economy; and additional capital improvements in skills and in organization have characterized agricultural production. These components of economic development have placed a heavy and accumulative burden on the existing economic organization. At some locations, the maladjustments that have accumulated have been quite minor while in other areas they have become increasingly more serious to the extent that chronic low productivity and poverty have come to characterize many farming communities.

The hard task that confronts us in this study is to identify the nature and the significance of the particular "imperfections" in the existing economic organization arising out of economic development. Are they to be found primarily in the way the product markets or the factor markets work? Among the various product markets, which ones appear to perform the more satisfactorily, the markets of perishable products such as milk, livestock, fresh fruits and vegetables, and the like, or the markets of such farm products as wheat, cotton, flaxseed, and others, which usually have well-established future markets? In the case of the factor markets, is it possible to determine how economic development affects the labor and capital markets, the extent to which each is under adverse pressure, and how each functions as a consequence?

The purpose of these questions and observations has been to indicate the direction which our inquiry will take as we proceed.

10

INCOME DISPARITY AMONG COMMUNITIES
AND ECONOMIC DEVELOPMENT

Is the low income or poverty that has gradually become embedded in agriculture related to economic development? This chapter presents an affirmative answer to this query. The analysis and argument consists of three parts. The first is an attempt to describe the salient characteristics of the low income (poverty)[1] that has emerged. This characterization is presented in the form of a series of propositions. Next, there is the task of selecting an analytical framework sufficiently comprehensive to include conditions under which economic development can give rise to increasing disparity of income. And, finally, there is the difficult undertaking of determining whether these conditions have necessarily given rise to increasing disparity in income. For the empirical setting we shall take the American scene as it has developed during the comparatively few decades that have elapsed since the settlement of this continent. For the most part, the effects of rapid short-term movements in the main economic magnitudes, for example, movements associated with business cycles and with either of the world wars or with the great depression, will be neglected. Accordingly, in order to make the task at hand manageable, we shall abstract from short term fluctuations in the basic argument. Poverty (low income) is taken to mean being too poor to afford the level of living[2] that has become generally established and that most people can afford. We are not, however, concerned

[1] "Low income" and "poverty" will be used interchangeably throughout this chapter.

[2] The concept of "level of living" refers to the possession of goods, services, and opportunities. It consists in what people have, that is, the opportunities available to them and the goods and services that they use and consume. For the distinction between "level of living" and "standard of living," see Carl C. Taylor et al., *Rural Life in the United States* (New York: Alfred A. Knopf, Inc., 1949), Chap. 17.

Margaret Jarman Hagood, of the Bureau of Agricultural Economics, has made a number of studies concentrating on the level of living of farm people. Her study, *Farm Operator Family Level of Living Indexes for Counties of the United States 1940 and 1945*, May, 1947, is exceedingly instructive. With the

with the poverty of any particular farm family but, instead, with that of an aggregate consisting of all the families located in a given community or neighborhood.[3] More specifically, whenever reference is made to "level of living" or to "income," we shall mean the average level of living or the per capita income of the community. Accordingly, we shall not focus upon isolated farm families, no matter how poverty-stricken they may be, but upon a group of families comprising a community or neighborhood. Thus in any given community one or more families may

---

United States county average for 1945 equal to 100, one finds that her indexes of the level of living for the ten lowest counties in Kentucky range from 5 to 16, as follows:

1945 LEVEL OF LIVING

Counties	Index (ten lowest counties in Kentucky)
Breathitt	5
Leslie	6
Elliott	9
Knott	12
Owsley	13
Magoffin	13
Clay	14
Lawrence	15
Lee	15
Knox	16

Her data for the ten highest counties in Iowa show indexes ranging from 188 to 196, as follows:

1945 LEVEL OF LIVING

Counties	Index (ten highest counties in Iowa)
Ida	188
Buena Vista	189
Hamilton	189
Cherokee	190
Marshall	190
Wright	191
O'Brien	192
Sac	192
Benton	194
Grundy	196

[3] We are inclined to follow fairly closely the idea of a community (or neighborhood) as it is set forth in Taylor *et al., op. cit.*, Chap. 4. For most of the conditions under consideration, the rural neighborhood can be used instead of the community. Accordingly, we shall use the two terms "neighborhood" and "community" as being quite interchangeable.

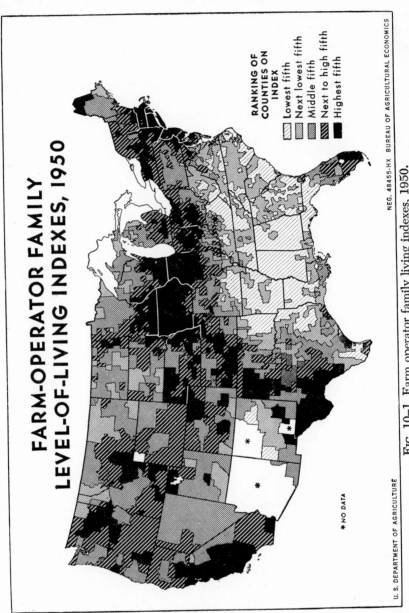

FIG. 10–1. Farm operator family living indexes, 1950.

be beset by poverty as compared to the average level of living of the community. This *within*-community poverty is not, however, the object of this study. The analysis is restricted to *between*-community comparisons. It follows, therefore, that not all the families in a poor community are necessarily equally poor and that some families in such a community may be better off than are many families located in a comparatively rich community.

In order to simplify, let us treat one of the empirical propositions as an assumption at this point. Let it be assumed that these communities had about the same distribution in wealth and natural endowments at the time of settlement or at the time that the developments associated with the industrial revolution began to make their impact. This means that within a community some families had more than average talents while others fell below that mark; for, even at the outset of settlement, it is only reasonable to suppose that some families were poorer than others both in natural endowments and in material possessions, including the "investment" that had already been made in themselves in ways that enhanced their productive capacity. We take it to be a rough approximation of the facts that the distribution of "talents" and "capital" within most, if not all, communities at the time of settlement or at the time that industrialization began to make itself felt was probably not significantly different from one community to another. Meanwhile, they have moved far apart in income, and therefore, on that score, the distributions of families have come to differ greatly. Whether, however, a similar drift has occurred in the case of the endowments of people within communities is a disputed point. Although the evidence is tenuous, it may be held that, whereas there are now poor and rich communities in agriculture, they are still essentially more alike than they are unlike one another in the distribution of natural human endowments.[4]

[4] Dorothy S. Thomas, in reviewing the research that has been done on selective migration, finds that four conflicting hypotheses have emerged as to the direction of this selection and its effects upon rural areas:

1. City migrants are selected from the superior elements of the parent population.
2. Cityward migrants are selected from the inferior elements.
3. Cityward migrants are selected from the extremes, *i.e.*, both the superior and the inferior elements.
4. Cityward migration represents a random selection of the parent population.

Professor Thomas concludes that there is some evidence to support each of these hypotheses. Although the evidence is tenuous, it is nonetheless probable

Simplifying Empirical Propositions

The propositions that follow are intended to direct attention to certain salient characteristics of our economic development. They are an attempt to describe one of the economic aspects of that development, namely, the differences between communities in the rates of growth, expressed in terms of per capita income or level of living. To isolate this aspect, it is necessary to simplify greatly and, in the process, to leave aside many other historical facts and issues. Nor is it our belief that no qualifications are required along the way. These propositions may be stated as follows:

1. In general, the differences in per capita income and level of living among communities were not so great at the time when people pioneered new areas or at the time industrialization began as they have become since then.[5] Poverty of whole communities did not generally exist under pioneering conditions because levels of living were in their essentials quite similar, although, if we look back, people were undoubtedly exceedingly poor by present-day standards.

2. The marked differences in level of living that have emerged within agriculture are not mainly the result of a deterioration on the part of those communities in which people are now living under conditions of poverty but largely the consequences of the increases in per capita incomes that have been realized by people in other communities.[6] This proposition means that families in some localities have been virtually stationary in their level of living. Others have advanced somewhat in their level of living, and still others have shown marked advances. The gap between the first and third types of community has become exceedingly wide, is becoming ever wider, and will continue to increase

---

that "selection does operate positively, negatively, and randomly, at different times, depending on a variety of factors that, up to the present, have not been adequately investigated" [see "Selective Migration," *Milbank Memorial Fund Quarterly*, XVI (October, 1948): 403–407].

[5] Chester W. Wright, *Economic History of the United States* (New York: McGraw-Hill Book Company, Inc., 1949), discusses the agriculture of the late colonial period in these words: "The outstanding feature that characterized colonial agriculture was the fact that the greater portion of the products raised was for the family's own consumption. This was typically the situation except in the regions such as the southern plantations where . . . [tobacco, rice, indigo] dominated" (p. 89). For an account of the level of living about 1770, covering housing, food, clothing, and medical care, see pp. 1010–1022.

[6] A cogent study of this point is that of Mandel Sherman and Thomas R. Henry, *Hollow Folk* (New York: The Thomas Y. Crowell Company, 1933).

as long as the first type remains stationary or advances less rapidly than does the third.

3. These gaps, consisting of differences in level of living, are basically consequences of the way in which the economy of the United States has developed and not primarily the results of any original differences in the cultural values or capabilities of the people themselves.

Each of these propositions is meaningful in the sense that it is possible, by making an appeal to empirical experience, to determine whether each is a valid statement about economic history. Actually, the first two are not essential to the argument proper; for they merely specify a particular set of conditions at the beginning of settlement and outline the changes that have occurred in the relative positions of neighborhoods since that time. It is the third of these that is central and most important to the argument, as may be seen when it is stated as follows: The differences in the per capita income and the level of living that have come to exist *among* neighborhoods in agriculture are basically the consequences of the way in which the economy of the United States has developed.

The principal difficulty that arises in putting this statement to the test is largely in specifying the components that go to make up the way in which the economy has developed and in determining their effects upon the local fortunes of people. Before undertaking this task, however, it should be possible to clear away some misconceptions by calling attention to several fairly obvious implications of this formulation of the problem of poverty within parts of agriculture.

Land Passive in Poverty. If poverty as herein defined is the result of economic development, it cannot be a consequence of the differences in the physical characteristics of land unless it can be shown that the differences in land per se are a significant factor in that development. It will become evident as we proceed that there are strong reasons for believing that the differences in land suitable for farming, in themselves, have not been an important factor in shaping the course of our economic development. The industrial "Ruhr" of the United States developed across the middle states to the north not because the farm land of the corn belt was better than that of the cotton belt generally, but for quite other reasons. The main effect has been the other way around, that is, the economy, essentially as an independent variable, has developed in such a way as to give some farm land a comparative advantage over other land in potential adjustments to economic progress. This statement means that people who settled on poor land located in or near the main stream of economic development have benefited from the economic progress growing out of that development as much as have people situated on highly productive land in or near this stream. On the other hand, people who settled on good land that was located away from the centers of active development, and thus at a disadvantage in terms of making the necessary social and economic adjustments, lost ground relative to those people who settled on either poor or good land located in or near the main stream. The term "disadvantage" in this context is not a matter of physical distances and therefore cannot be measured in miles. It must be expressed in terms of adverse effects upon efficiency and capacity of the entry and exodus of resources that can be transferred, especially of the human agent. The milksheds are a case in point that firmly support these remarks regarding the role of farm land. The milksheds are the closest of all farm land to the active centers of the main stream of economic development because of the overwhelming importance of the industrial-urban sectors in generating economic progress. The differences in the physical characteristics of land among major milksheds are exceedingly great, some of it consisting of rough, hilly, poor land by any standards and some of level, highly fertile land. Yet nowhere within a milkshed, attached to a major industrial-urban area, can it be said that there exist whole communities of poverty-stricken farmers, as is the case in large parts of American agriculture located at the periphery of such centers.

The main import of these remarks on land is simply that studies concentrating on land may describe the location of poverty but cannot analyze its underlying causes, inasmuch as land is essentially passive in the process that has brought about the poverty under consideration.

Effects of Price Drifts. Another implication of the argument set forth above pertains to the drift of prices. It may be stated thus: If poverty is the result of economic development and if this development is not incompatible with changes in the level of particular prices, the long-run decline (or rise) of a farm product price is not necessarily a factor contributing to the poverty that has come to exist among communities in agriculture. Product upon product may be cited in which, over the years, the price has declined relative to other prices and the industry producing the product has prospered in that it has attracted additional capital and labor into its productive effort. On the other hand, there are many cases in which a decline in price has necessitated less output, and the adjustment has been made without generating poverty. It can, therefore, be demonstrated both in theory and in practice that a decline in price is not incompatible with economic development; in fact, on the contrary, it has usually been an essential part of the process.

This is not to argue that prices that fluctuate greatly are as efficient in guiding production as are steadier and more dependable prices.[7] Nor do we wish to imply that contraction is necessarily easy—certainly not in the short run. An appeal may be made to certain obvious empirical observations with regard to agriculture. Take any major farm product, and, regardless of whether the price has declined or risen over the years relative to other farm products, there are farmers—in fact, whole communities of farm families—who are distinctly well-to-do and who are mainly dependent for their income on that product. The view here advanced is simply that long-run price flexibility has not brought about the kind of poverty that is under consideration in this paper. It has, of course, enhanced greatly the efficiency and the size of the national product.

ECONOMIC DEVELOPMENT CAN BRING ABOUT INCREASING DISPARITY IN INCOME

Progress that increases income may be viewed either in the aggregate or in per capita terms. The argument on which this chapter rests presupposes an economy in which both are increasing and in which the per capita income in some communities remains virtually stationary while that of others increases, although the rates of increase may vary. To gain perspective, it may be helpful to look afresh at the classical conception of economic progress. The older economists—Ricardo, Malthus, Mill—conceived of "the dynamics of political economy"[8] as a process in which the aggregate income increases under circumstances where per capita income tends to remain constant. Their analytical apparatus was built around the rates of change of two important magnitudes; they were inclined to call one of these the "power of production" and the other the "power of population."[9] Various rates of increases in production were considered, but, under their assumption, it did not matter whether production moved forward gradually or took a sudden spurt, since extra population soon took up the slack.

[7] The effects of variations in prices (in terms of the economic uncertainty that these impose upon farmers) on the production plans of farmers is the central subject of "Spot and Future Prices as Production Guides," Chap. 14, Theodore W. Schultz, *Production and Welfare of Agriculture* (New York: The Macmillan Company, 1949).

[8] This is John Stuart Mill's phrase in opening Book IV, "Influence of the Progress of Society on Production and Distribution," of his *Principles of Political Economy*. (In this paragraph we restate a part of the analysis set forth in Chaps. 1 and 2.)

[9] Best expressed in David Ricardo's *The Principles of Political Economy and Taxation* ("Everyman's Library" edition), Chap. 5.

Their theory in its main outlines is simple and remains powerful. Whenever conditions are such that the growth in population absorbs any increase in production to the point that per capita incomes tend to remain constant, it necessarily follows that the power of production becomes the limitational factor not only of the size of the population but also of economic progress expressed in terms of increases in aggregate income. The conditions on which this classical conception of dynamics rests are no longer generally applicable, but as a special case they continue to apply to much, perhaps even to most, of the world. And, where they do apply, a great deal of insight can be had by the use of this apparatus.

We need, however, a formulation with greater generality; for it is clear that, when the concept of economic progress is restricted to an increase in aggregate income with per capita income remaining constant, it is conceived altogether too narrowly. The following statement is proposed: *Economic development consists of an increase in aggregate income with changes in per capita income unspecified, except that no community becomes worse off.*

Actually the most important part of this undertaking is to specify and identify the conditions that are necessary in economic development, that generate disparity in per capita incomes, and that perpetuate these inequalities functionally considered, once they have become established.

A few observations on the economic development that has characterized the industrial revolution of western Europe suggest that there is a close parallelism between that development and the central propositions underlying the main argument of this chapter regarding poverty in American agriculture. There is no firm basis for believing that the level of living that existed in most of the communities (or neighborhoods) comprising the bulk of the population of western Europe prior to the events associated with the industrial revolution were as different one from another as they have become since then.[10] The level of living of the mass of the people was obviously very low everywhere compared to levels that emerged subsequently, if we neglect the courts and a few of the trading towns. The levels of living were, with few exceptions, low in virtually all communities and did not differ nearly so much from one community to another as they do at present. The way in which the economy developed by increasing over-all production is noteworthy. The per capita income and level of living began to rise in the countries experiencing the increases in production. One should note also that, instead of a migration of people from other parts of the world toward these

---

[10] In *Review of Economic Progress*, Vol. I, No. 4 (April, 1949), Colin Clark presents data that permit the following comparisons among countries in terms

countries, attracted by the rising per capita incomes and levels of living, there occurred, in fact, an extraordinary migration out of western Europe not only to the United States but to Asia and to other countries overseas.[11] Was it the poor, the people in the communities that were being by-passed by the industrial revolution, who migrated abroad; and did they do so because they found it easier to go abroad than to participate in the growing fortunes of people generally in communities benefiting from economic progress?

This brief reference to the economic history of western Europe since about 1650 suggests that the advances in technology and in economic organization usually ascribed to the industrial revolution gave rise (1) to a much larger aggregate production; (2) to an increase in per capita income and in level of living generally in Europe, despite the fact that the European population has multiplied five times from 1650 to date;[12] (3) to an increasing disparity in per capita incomes and in levels of

---

of levels of real national product per man-hour, showing the period when they reached a specified level (in international units).

At 0.03	0.10–0.15		At about 0.30	
France before 1800	Britain before	1800 (0.14)	Britain,	1890 (0.31)
Germany before 1800	France,	1850 (0.10)	United States,	1890 (0.34)
India by 1860	Sweden,	1860 (0.10)	Denmark,	1913 (0.30)
Japan by 1890	Greece,	1880 (0.13)	Germany,	1913 (0.31)
China by 1930	Eire,	1880 (0.11)	Netherlands,	1913 (0.29)
	Belgium,	1890 (0.11)	Norway,	1920 (0.33)
	Italy,	1890 (0.10)	Spain,	1920 (0.31)
	Norway,	1890 (0.14)	Sweden,	1920 (0.30)
	Switzerland,	1890 (0.15)	France,	1924 (0.30)
	USSR,	1900 (0.15)	Switzerland,	1925 (0.31)
	Estonia,	1913 (0.11)	Eire,	1926 (0.30)
	Hungary,	1913 (0.14)	Belgium,	1930 (0.33)
	Portugal,	1913 (0.11)	Argentina,	1935 (0.35)
	Japan,	1922 (0.10)	Finland,	1937 (0.32)
	Turkey,	1927 (0.10)		
	Ecuador,	1940 (0.11)		
	Brazil,	1946 (0.11)		

---

[11] Dudley Kirk in his book *Europe's Population in the Interwar Years* (Geneva: League of Nations, 1946), Chap. 3, puts the migration out of Europe as follows: "The number of Europeans living outside of Europe was negligible in 1650; it has been estimated that since that time some 60 million Europeans have sought homes overseas. . . . Millions more crossed the low barriers of the Urals to settle in Siberia and the Interior of Asia."

[12] *Ibid.*, p. 17.

living between western Europe (certainly up to World War II) and those parts of the world that had not benefited from the process of industrialization,[13] and (4) to conditions which impeded the migration of non-Europeans into Europe, a development that would have equalized returns to human agents of European and non-European communities had it occurred in sufficient numbers. But what actually happened was a migration of millions of Europeans to other parts of the world.

CONDITIONS RELATED TO THE
INCREASING DISPARITY IN INCOME

There can be no doubt that the industrial development of the Western world, including our own, has brought about a disparity in incomes. Also, the disparity in per capita incomes between the advanced and the undeveloped countries has become ever greater; and, despite the effects of income taxation within a country like the United States, communities at or near centers of economic development have pulled further away in terms of productivity and income per head from some of those communities situated less favorably.[14] We shall endeavor to indicate the conditions responsible for the increasing disparity in incomes.

[13] The increasing disparity in income per head is documented by a wealth of data brought together by Colin Clark, *The Conditions of Economic Progress* (New York: The Macmillan Company, 1940), especially Chap. 4.

[14] It may be of interest to note that, taking Colin Clark's figures appearing in *Review of Economic Progress*, Vol. I, No. 4, and assuming that his $0.03 per hour (in terms of his international unit) is the lowest level of real national product per man-hour, we get the following spread between the low and the high countries:

Year	Number of times highest country is above lowest
Before 1800	5
1800–1825	7
1910	17
1930	25
1940	33
1947	39

The last figure, that for 1947, is obtained by assuming that China has not risen above the $0.03 reported for 1930 and relating it to the $1.19 reported for the United States. That the level-of-living index of farm operators in the United States in 1945 should also show Grundy County, Iowa, thirty-nine times as high as Breathitt County, Kentucky (see footnote 2), is a similarity that should not be dismissed too lightly.

The accumulation of capital that is put to productive uses will, of course, other things being equal, increase the income of those who are the recipients of such earnings. The concentration of productive assets in the hands of people of advanced industrial countries is a common-place; the unequal distribution of such assets among families within a country is also well known. This aspect of the growth of capital and its effects on the distribution of income is certainly not new. Nor has it been neglected in economics. In the formation of policy for agriculture, however, sight is often lost of the fact that many farm families possess valuable property that earns for them very considerable income and that such families are not necessarily poor even when farm prices are low.

Abstracting from changes in income contributed by the growth of capital other than that "invested" in the human agent, there are three sets of conditions inherent in economic development each of which can bring about a disparity in income. They are (1) those that alter the proportion of the population engaged in productive work in one com-munity relative to that of another; (2) those that change the abilities of a population to produce, of one community relative to that of another; and (3) those that impede factor-price equalization of comparable human agents between communities.

Proportion of Population That Contributes to Income. The ratio of contributors to noncontributors becomes larger as communities partici-pate in economic progress. Obviously, this ratio is important; for, if only a few people are active at productive work, there will be less income per head than if many people in a given community are contributors, other things being equal. The conditions that determine this ratio arise out of a number of complex developments; there are (1) the changes in composition of the population associated with economic develop-ment, (2) the changes in the continuity of employment and in the spe-cialization permitted by the division of labor that emerge as a result of economic development, and (3) differences that arise from the way in which income is measured and in which the income accounting is done.[15]

Probably the most important of these conditions is the demographic evolution of the population of a community. There are, from a demo-graphic point of view, basically three population types in the world at present.[16] The first of these is the *pre-industrial type (high food drain:*

[15] The third will not be elaborated in this chapter because it would be some-what afield and would require an entire chapter to do it satisfactorily.

[16] An excellent essay on this subject is that of Frank W. Notestein, "Popula-tion—the Long View," *Food for the World,* Theodore W. Schultz, editor (Chi-cago: University of Chicago Press, 1945); see also Warren Thompson, *Popula-*

Type I) with very high birth and death rates, with a large proportion of the population in the lower-age brackets of the population pyramid, and with a short life expectancy. It fulfils the essential conditions of the Ricardo-Malthus-Mill "model," inasmuch as the potential increase in population is such that it can readily absorb increases in production. The basic consideration in this context, however, is the fact that a large proportion of the population consists of nonproducers. The second type of population is usually referred to as *transitional* (*intermediate food drain:* Type II) with its diminishing birth and death rates but with the death rate dropping first[17] and for a time faster than the birth rate, with a marked increase in population taking place as a consequence. The advanced *industrial type* (*low food drain:* Type III) comes into existence when the birth and death rates are again approaching a balance at rates about one-third to one-half as high as those that characterize the pre-industrial populations. Life expectancy becomes fully twice as high, and the age distribution characterizing the population pyramid is such that a large proportion of the people are in the ages where they can contribute to productive economic effort.

We are inclined to think of the United States as approaching a demographic stage characteristic of an advanced industrial country, but it is true that within agriculture the pre-industrial and the transitional demographic population types predominate. Moreover, one of the major consequences of these demographic differences is to be found in the proportion of the farm population that can contribute to production. For example, in comparing Grundy County, Iowa, with Breathitt County, Kentucky, we find that, in 1940, 62 per cent of the farm population of the Iowa County was twenty-one years of age and over, as against 42

---

tion and Peace in the Pacific (Chicago: University of Chicago Press, 1946), Chap. 2.

[17] To quote Notestein, *op. cit.*, pp. 39–40, on this point: " . . . Fertility was much less responsive to the processes of modernization. So far as we can tell from available evidence, no substantial part of the modern population growth has come from a rise in fertility. On the other hand, neither did fertility decline with mortality. The reasons why fertility failed to decline with mortality are clear enough in general terms. Any society having to face the heavy mortality characteristic of the premodern era must have high fertility to survive. All such societies are therefore ingeniously arranged to obtain the required births. Their religious doctrines, moral codes, laws, education, community customs, marriage habits, and family organizations are all focused toward maintaining high fertility. These change only gradually and in response to the strangest stimulation. Therefore, mortality declined, but a fertility high enough to permit survival in an earlier period began producing rapid growth."

per cent of the Kentucky county.[18] The farm population seventy years of age and over in both cases was slightly more than 2 per cent.

A second development altering the proportion of the population that contributes to income arises out of changes in the continuity of employment and the specialization afforded by the division of labor as economic development has proceeded. Again, it may be assumed that, until industrialization got under way, most communities were essentially alike in this respect; but they have drifted apart because some communities in agriculture have emerged with more continuous employment and with work more specialized than have the communities that have been by-passed in the course of economic development.[19] The result is fairly obvious; in the communities that have been favored, people who can work may do so more of the time during the year; and the division of labor has been carried further, thus permitting them to specialize to better account. Here, again, to illustrate the consequences one needs only to refer to farming in central Iowa compared to that in eastern Kentucky.[20]

We conclude this section with the observation that it would appear from even these brief explorations that the conditions which determine the proportion of a population of a community that contributes to income are a consequence of the social evolution of our society set in motion by the character of our economic development.

Conditions That Determine the Abilities of a Population to Produce. It will be convenient to classify abilities into those with which people are naturally endowed and those which they acquire. As to the first, we have already indicated that it would seem plausible to state that most communities at the time that industrialization began or at the time

[18] Based on data from the 1940 Census. Note that Grundy County had a level-of-living index of 196, while that of Breathitt was 5 in 1945, according to the Hagood study (*op. cit.*).

[19] "Underemployment," which is unproductive employment in the sense that a person produces a smaller product than he could elsewhere in the economy, is not included here, for it properly belongs under the set of conditions that impede factor-price equalization.

[20] There are many clues in the available statistics, although the data are not on a county basis. One comparison may be cited. In the fall of 1945 an attempt was made by the Bureau of Agricultural Economics, by means of an enumerative survey, to ascertain the average hours that farm operators worked during the week September 16–22. These data by type of farming regions show that in the dairy areas farm operators worked nearly twice as many hours (59) as did those in the general and self-sufficing areas (31). For the corn belt, the equivalent figure was 57 hours. The following table has been taken

of settlement were roughly the same in the distribution of native talents. Moreover, communities in agriculture at present may not differ substantially on this score.[21] However, as for the abilities that can be acquired, differences have arisen as a result of the way in which our economy has developed. We can achieve considerable insight into this matter by abstracting from certain social and physical aspects in order to isolate (1) the process by which capital is "invested" in human agents, (2) the amount of capital thus invested, and (3) the effect of this investment upon the productivity of a population.

An analysis of the formation of capital in this sphere is beset by many major difficulties. It is exceedingly hard to draw a line of demarcation

---

from unpublished data made available by Louis J. Ducoff of the Bureau of Agricultural Economics:

AVERAGE HOURS WORKED BY FARM OPERATORS

	Week of September 16–22, 1945	Week of July 14–20, 1946
Regional areas:		
United States.	43	48
General and self-sufficing areas	31	37
Cotton belt.	35	35
Western specialty-crop areas	48	50
Range and livestock areas	53	58
Corn belt	57	65
Dairy areas	59	65
Wheat areas	59	69
Type-of-farming areas:		
South, general and self-sufficing areas.	25	29
South, cotton belt	35	34
North central, general and self-sufficing areas	40	46
West, wheat areas	44	60
Western specialty-crop areas	48	50
Northeast, general and self-sufficing areas	48	59
Northeast, dairy areas	52	59
West, range and livestock areas	55	57
North central, corn belt.	58	65
North central, dairy areas	64	67
North central, wheat areas.	65	76

[21] Howard W. Beers, *Mobility of Rural Population*, Kentucky Agr. Expt. Sta. Bul. 505, June, 1947, p. 40, advances the hypothesis that rural-urban migration has selected the less able youths, leaving on farms those who are most capable. For a more comprehensive review, see Thomas, *op. cit.* (discussed in footnote 4 above).

between inputs for consumption and those that act as capital. Many of these inputs undoubtedly make contributions both ways; and, when it comes to measurement, the existing capital market gives us little or no information because it is not organized to finance "investments" that enhance the abilities of people as producers. Where men are not slaves but free, a mortgage on capital which in the process of formation becomes embedded in a person requires the kind of instrument that has had no appeal to financial institutions, even though the earnings on such investments in many cases would prove very attractive.[22] Consequently, as one would expect, the supply of capital employed to improve the abilities of a population has come from two major sources—from the family and from the community in which a person lives.

Furthermore, with few exceptions, the capital is made available without recourse, that is, the individual is under no obligation to repay his family or community. In substance, then, we have, for all practical purposes, no capital market serving this need. The institutions that exist, namely, the family and the community, bear the brunt of this function, and the results are all too evident.

The amount that is invested per human agent is extremely unequal from one community to another. Where the community is poor, families are also poor, and therefore neither of them can afford to make these investments; the converse, of course, is true in a rich community. The implications of this process to our argument are clear; economic development has been uneven; some communities have been left behind; these communities and the families in them have at hand few resources per head and fewer still per child to train and rear their children, while the communities and families situated in the main stream of economic development have many resources available for these purposes.[23]

There is not much that one can say on the amount of capital that is invested in human agents except to express the belief that it has become very large indeed in countries with an advanced industrial economy and especially so in the best-situated communities in the United States. Any attempt to measure this outlay encounters major obstacles, for reasons already touched upon.

There remain, then, the effects of investments of this nature upon the

---

[22] Professor Earl Hamilton has called my attention to the excellent observations of Marshall on certain aspects of this problem [*Principles of Economics*, 8th ed. (London: Macmillan & Co., Ltd., 1930), see especially pp. 560–563].

[23] In 1938, Mississippi allocated about 5.4 per cent of its income to the support of secondary and elementary schools, while Iowa used about 3.9 per cent of its income for this purpose; and yet the amount that was available per enrolled student was about $22 in Mississippi compared to $74 in Iowa.

productivity of a population. It will be useful to distinguish between
(1) the effects that alter the comparability of human resources in terms
of abilities to do a given type of work equally well and (2) the effects
that express themselves in awareness of alternative opportunities, in the
capacity to communicate, and in willingness to migrate. In the case of
the first of these two effects—that pertaining to comparability—it is evident that where the investment consists of preparing an individual for
a task that requires years of careful and systematic training, such as
is necessary to become a doctor, a lawyer, a scientist, or a skilled tech-
nologist, the person who has received this training is no longer comparable to a person who has not had similar preparation. What about
the bulk of the work in agriculture, where advanced technology is employed, and in industry generally? It appears that in the short run a significant difference in productivity exists between those who have had
the advantages that go with this class of investment as compared to
those who have not. To illustrate, a young migrant from eastern Kentucky would probably find himself at some disadvantage on a typical
Iowa farm or in doing a given job in industry compared to a young
migrant from a rich farming community or from a fairly prosperous
family in western Kentucky; but this margin of disadvantage in most
cases is likely to disappear rather rapidly. The two men would differ
appreciably in the short run, that is, for a month or two or even for
as long as a year, but, after that, they would be on about equal footing in terms of the abilities that are required to do such work. The second of these effects involving awareness of opportunities and a willingness to migrate, so it seems, is by all odds the more important of the
two in accounting for the unequal incomes earned per person within
agriculture. These effects, however, are basic in getting at the imperfect
factor-price equalization that exists and therefore takes us to the third
set of conditions underlying the disparity in incomes under consideration.

Conditions that Impede Factor-price Equalization. We have explored
briefly the conditions that increase the proportion of the population
contributing to income and that improve the abilities of a population
to produce, and we have endeavored to show how the forces of economic development, expressing themselves through the existing family
and community institutions, alter these conditions. There still remains
a third set of conditions which appear to play an important role in contributing to the growing disparity in income among communities within
agriculture.

Two questions may be helpful in putting certain aspects of the problem of achieving factor-price equalization into focus. Does economic

development as we have known it require a vast and unprecedented transfer of human agents? The answer is, without qualification, in the affirmative. Does it give rise to major impediments to migration? The answer to this query may seem to be less unequivocal. It will become evident, however, as we proceed that an equally affirmative reply is warranted. What happens in this connection is about as follows: We have seen how economic development sets the stage for the emergence of the advanced industrial demographic type of population alongside what was formerly a common form, that is, the pre-industrial demographic type. As the differences between these two types increase, the cultural impediments to migration become greater. It is these impediments to a transfer of the human factor that bring about a series of short-run equilibria, which, as time goes on, fall increasingly short of achieving an optimum in the allocation of resources.[24]

Two aspects require further elaboration, namely, (1) the comparability of a typical human agent located in a poor, pre-industrial demographic-type community and the typical person situated in an advanced community and (2) the nature of the cultural impediments and their role as costs to the economy. Before touching on these, an observation on factor-price equalization among pre-industrial communities may be

[24] When factor-price equalization is based upon given wants, the cultural differences under consideration are taken as attributes of the existing pattern of wants. When the problem is approached in this way, cultural differences between a community that has been by-passed by economic growth and development and a community located at or near the centers of industrialization are not impediments to factor-price equalization but a part of the existing wants of the people in the two communities. It follows from this formulation that the two communities may be in equilibrium in terms of resource allocation, although great differences in the level of living exist. Another approach, the one on which this analysis rests, proceeds on the assumption that wants are not given and constant but that they are the result of cultural developments which are not independent of industrialization. One may view the changes in wants that emerge as industrialization proceeds as a movement away from a pre-industrial pattern of wants toward new, more dominant industrial-urban patterns and that the differences in wants are the result of lags in this adjustment. It is better, however, in order to simplify the analytical problem, to introduce a value-judgment explicitly in this connection. This value-judgment is simply to the effect that the wants that characterize the communities that have been by-passed by industrial growth and progress are inferior to the wants which are emerging in the main stream of industrialization. Given this valuation, it follows that the cultural factors that isolate the backward community and press upon it the relatively inferior wants operate as cultural impediments and, as such, impede factor-price equalization.

instructive. Let us take two communities of this demographic type wit the same cultural values, including similar standards of living, and le us assume, further, that the fortunes of the one improve. To make thi concrete, let the increase in production come from an irrigation projec without cost to the community. Is it necessary for people to migrat from the less fortunate community to the one that has the windfa afforded by irrigation in order to attain factor-price equalization? Th answer is that, even without a common market for either factors or prod ucts—that is, *without either migration or trade*—factor-price equalizatio will occur as a consequence of the upward surge in population in th community with the new irrigation project under the assumptions a we have formulated them.

Factor-price equalization, however, cannot occur when the communit benefiting from a windfall is of the advanced industrial demographi type and the other a pre-industrial community, unless a transfer of fac tors takes place.[25]

The question of comparability of human agents as factors in this con text raises a number of issues which are exceedingly difficult to resolve Entirely too little work has been done on this problem,[26] and, as is ob vious, the answer must come, in the last analysis, from an appeal to em pirical reality. It seems that most of the people located at present i poor communities within agriculture are essentially comparable to mos of the people situated in rich communities in terms of their capacitie to produce if allowance is made for the short-run acclimatization re quired for the improvement in abilities which we have already con sidered. If this is true, it follows that the cultural impediments are in deed a heavy burden because the income earned by these (human

---

[25] P. A. Samuelson in two recent articles in the *Economic Journal*, "Inter national Trade and Equalization of Factor Prices" [Vol. LXVIII (June 1948)] and "International Factor-price Equalization Once Again" [Vol. LXL (June, 1949)], has attempted to show that free commodity trade will, unde certain conditions, inevitably lead to complete factor-price equalization. Th conditions that are specified in his analysis are, however, far removed fror the hard realities that underlie the existing geographical inequalities.

[26] A major research program made possible by a grant from the Rockefelle Foundation on the malallocation of resources that characterizes agricultur: production is under way at the University of Chicago, being carried forwar largely by Professor D. Gale Johnson. This research program has as one of it objectives the determination of the comparability of resources within agricu' ture and between agriculture and other sectors of the economy and in th connection focusing primarily on the human agent. We shall draw heavil upon this study in Part Three.

factors is very unequal between communities. Is it possible that the cultural impediments can be so great and so costly? Here the researches of the sociologists are making important contributions, and their results indicate quite clearly that it is no easy matter for people to pull up their roots and leave the folk society, with its strong local-personal-informal relations, and transplant themselves into an impersonal-formal, less locally oriented, urban-minded community. The economist must leave it to the sociologist to isolate and identify the nature of these cultural impediments; the economist, however, can and should come to grips with the cost aspects.

The burden of these impediments is obviously a continuing one. If anything, measured in terms of the unequal factor prices that exist, they have become greater over time. If the "price" of eliminating, or even only substantially diminishing, these impediments is a nonrecurring cost for any given migrant, then the probabilities are high that society could achieve a very considerable gain by taking positive actions to diminish the adverse effects of these impediments upon factor-price equalization and, in so doing, diminish significantly the disparity in incomes on which we have concentrated our attention.

PART TWO

ECONOMIC INSTABILITY AND AGRICULTURE

11

CONDITIONS UNDERLYING THE ECONOMIC
INSTABILITY OF AGRICULTURE

In Part One, in analyzing the interplay between economic development and agriculture, it was possible and also necessary to neglect large and abrupt short-term movements in major economic variables. We took the long view and concentrated on factors which explain the slow and gradual shift of the demand and supply. We shall now turn to movements related to the demand or supply of farm products which are essentially short term in character. These movements give rise to an important set of problems represented by price and income instability.

To take our bearing, let us consider briefly circumstances which would make it fairly easy to adjust to particular short-run movements. One such would be a small shift[1] or even a series of small shifts in either the demand or supply of farm products. It is hard to believe that a shift in either of these two schedules, say, of 1, 2, or even 3 per cent from one production period to the next, would give rise to any "instability" problems whatsoever even though the elasticities were quite low. Or in the event these two schedules were relatively elastic, no serious difficulties would arise even from fairly large shifts in either of the schedules. Furthermore, if one or the other of the two schedules were decidedly on the elastic side, in a short-run context, we would not expect any real difficulties although the shifts were substantial and occurred rapidly. These are not, however, the conditions that characterize American agriculture at this stage of our economic development.

HYPOTHESIS EXPLAINING THE PRICE INSTABILITY OF AGRICULTURE

When we leave changes in the general level of prices aside, the rest of the instability that characterizes farm prices may be explained by a very simple hypothesis, namely, that *the price elasticities of the demand and of the supply of farm products are low and that the shift in one or*

[1] We shall speak of a "shift" in the demand or supply and mean by this a movement of the entire, particular schedule either to the right or the left and, unless otherwise qualified, under the assumption that the elasticity of schedule remains unchanged.

the other of the schedules is large and abrupt. How relevant is this simple formulation? To express, first, a belief about the American economy: Both the demand and supply of farm products are quite inelastic in the short run and, therefore, any large shift in one or the other of the two schedules will result in a large rise or fall in price. Large shifts do in fact occur frequently and abruptly. These two propositions —one regarding the relevant elasticities and the other about the number and magnitude of the shifts—are statements about particular attributes of the economy that can be put to test.

What time interval are we to use? For virtually all farm products, two decades would reach well into the long run. But a period as long as this would be quite meaningless in getting at the particular shifts and price movements that occur quickly and are important. A classification of time intervals from the side of production may be as follows: (1) the stock period, (2) one production period, and (3) more than one production period. It will be convenient to refer to the period when the "crop" is given as the *stock period.* We then have (1) the stock period pertaining to the distribution and use of any existing stock, (2) the short run covering one or more production periods during which variable costs affect supply, and (3) the long run consisting of that number of production periods necessary for "fixed" costs to become variable.

The period when the stock is given is especially important in the case of agriculture because of the nature of its production. The technical conditions of production are such that the existing stock of a particular product cannot be altered, once the crop is made, until the next harvest is on hand. In agriculture, almost without exception, the output has a characteristic periodicity. A farm is not like a steel mill which can produce a scheduled tonnage, say, during the next week. Agricultural production does not emerge as a flow from day to day or week to week. On the contrary, the product is garnered during a short period, usually once a year. Agricultural production is highly seasonal and typically there are long intervals between "harvests." Once the crop is harvested, one is necessarily restricted to the particular stock until the next crop becomes available. During that time interval, only the distribution and use of the stock (crop plus carry-over) is relevant. The concept of a stock period permits us to study both the demand and the supply of farm products during the interval between crops (as we shall do in considerable detail in Chap. 14).[2]

[2] These circumstances give us a basis for representing the supply of producers for the stock period by which we mean the supply schedule of producers showing the quantities which farmers will sell at some schedule of prices once the harvest is given.

We have observed that the stock period is dependent upon particular technical conditions underlying agricultural production. We shall find, however, that it is very difficult to specify conditions which can be identified for distinguishing the short run from that of the long run. Not that this problem is hard formally, for as we have done in studying economic development, it is not difficult to take the long run and consider all inputs as variable costs. The short run presumably is dependent upon conditions when only particular inputs are open to decision within the firm. In practice, however, it is exceedingly difficult to establish a line of demarcation between the short and long run. We are driven, accordingly, to a separation which will serve best the purpose of this part of our study. For the time being, we shall take the short run to consist of a time interval of two years.

Shifts That Are Large

Our hypothesis to explain the instability of farm product prices presumes that the elasticities are low and the shifts that occur are sometimes large. Are there in fact large shifts in either the demand or the supply schedule of farm products either within the stock period or in a two-year time interval? At this point we shall merely sketch the general outlines of the picture leaving some of the essential details for later chapters.

Variations in Stocks and Supply Shifts. The stock of a particular farm product, available after the crop is made, does in fact vary substantially from year to year depending upon the weather. It will be convenient to treat any change in production caused by weather that is less than 5 per cent as too small to be of importance in relation to the set of problems under consideration.

A mere glance at the variations in yield will suffice at this point. From 1919 to 1949, the year-to-year variations in crop production per acre of cropland in the United States averaged over 7 per cent per year (Chap. 12, Table 12–1).[3] This average of 7 per cent hides not only many larger changes that occurred in particular years but also the wide fluctuations in the yields of particular crops. For example, the yield of the 18 major field crops fell 14 per cent in 1934, 13 per cent in 1936, 12 per cent in 1913, and 11 per cent in 1916 and rose 34 per cent in 1937, 25 per cent in 1935, and 19 per cent in 1948.[4]

[3] This is a net variation measured as a change from the preceding year, after allowing for the gradual increase in yields, consisting of about 1 per cent per year.

[4] Nor does it take into account variations in the acreage harvested because of weather.

The variations in yield of particular crops for the 1909–1949 period, (Chap. 12, Table 12–4) after allowing for the secular increase in yield, ranged from 3.8 per cent per year for rice to 29 per cent for apples. The more important crops show the following: tobacco, 4.5 per cent; potatoes, 6.8 per cent; soybeans, 8 per cent; wheat, 9.4 per cent; cotton, 10.6 per cent; corn, 14 per cent; oats, 16 per cent; and flaxseed, 19 per cent. Regional, local, and farm variation in yields from year to year are hidden, of course, in each of these averages. They were large indeed as we shall show later.

Variations in yield are in fact large; they are caused primarily by weather;[5] they are of the nature of shocks which originate outside the economic system. As a consequence of the effects of weather, large shifts occur from year to year in the size of the stock with which the economy begins the "crop" year.[6]

In addition to weather, does agriculture experience large shifts in the supply schedule of farm products in a time interval of two years? Can we observe situations, for example, where during the course of two years farmers plan to produce substantially more (less) products at about the same relative prices? A close analysis of the behavior of agricultural inputs will show that changes of as much as 5 per cent from the preceding year occur rarely, even when the price incentive to change is very large. But when we examine particular products, the data indicate that large shifts in the supply schedule do occur. Reoccurring production cycles appear to characterize a number of farm products. The cobweb theorem has been advanced to explain some of these. Others appear to be the consequence of errors in price expectations. But whatever the explanation, large shifts in the supply schedule of particular farm products cannot be ruled out although they are very difficult to observe and measure.

Demand Shifts. The shock of war on the demand for farm products is on about the same footing as is weather in the preceding analysis. The mobilization for war, the waging of war, and the return to peaceful conditions give rise to large shifts in the demand for farm products. These shifts have occurred quickly. There is no doubt that the event of World War I shifted the demand rapidly and very far to the right and then in the aftermath of the early twenties the shift was sharply to the left. World War II brought a repeat performance, except that the leftward shift afterwards was less pronounced; and following June,

[5] We shall qualify this statement somewhat in subsequent analysis because it is true that for a few crops, for instance, in the case of tobacco and cotton, the amount of fertilizer used is a variable that affects annual yields.

[6] The crop year is here taken to mean the stock period.

1950, with the outbreak of hostilities in Korea, the demand, once again, shifted substantially to the right.

Our purpose will be to examine the demand schedule for possibilities of shifts. The concepts for organizing the information, of course, will be the elasticity of the schedule with respect to price and the shifts of the schedule with respect to population, income and, also, other factors. Two different schedules will be considered, one representing the demand of United States civilians for food at retail which we shall refer to as "schedule A," and the other, representing the demand schedule confronting United States farmers for the farm food commodities which they produce and sell, as "schedule B." In order to take account of information usually neglected because it is difficult to embed into per capita income and population concepts, we shall examine particular shifts which have their origin in factors that go beyond such income and population data. It will be convenient to restrict the time interval, at the outset, to two years because of the implications of such shifts in the demand to short-term movements in food and farm food prices.

Let us begin with a situation where population is increasing at a rate of about $1\frac{1}{2}$ per cent a year, where per capita income is rising about 2 per cent annually, where the income elasticity of food is approximately .25,[7] and where these variables result in a shift of the demand schedule for food to the right of about 4 per cent during a two-year interval. Let this situation represent the normal rate of development to which the economy is attuned. Our task now is to examine the possibilities for departures from this situation. In this examination we shall not restrict ourselves merely to factors which may alter the rate of population growth, the rise in per capita income, and the income elasticity of food. Instead, drawing upon any and all relevant information known to us, we now ask: What are the possibilities of particular developments which can bring about important departures from this normal outcome in shifts of the two demand schedules under consideration.

In order to classify and evaluate the importance of particular departures, we shall view a shift of 5 per cent or more from normal as a large departure, because the resulting movement of food prices is sufficiently large with the existing inelasticity of the schedules to create important difficulties, given our economic organization and political arrangements. Meanwhile, a departure from normal of 1 per cent or less will be viewed as a small shift, so small that it is wholly unimportant in this context.

[7] We shall use .25 for both farm foods at the point of farm sales and for this food at retail (the food consumption index of the Bureau of Agricultural Economics) for consumers, although in Table 5–5, Chap. 5, our study indicates .25 and .30, respectively, for these two income elasticities.

Shifts in these schedules of more than 1 per cent and less than 5 per cent are thus classified as being intermediate in character.

Our first task is to examine some observed demand effects of population changes.

Demand shifts related to population changes	Schedule A (demand for food of United States civilians at retail)		Schedule B (demand for farm foods confronting farmers)	
	Normal as defined in text	Possibilities for departures	Normal as defined in text	Possibilities for departures
	(1)	(2)	(3)	(4)
1. Growth (births over deaths plus net immigration)	3%	Small	3%	Small
2. Distribution:				
2.1. Between civilian and non-civilian sectors	None	Large	None	Large
2.2. Among civilians as to location and occupation. . .	Small	Intermediate	Small	Intermediate
3. Composition in age and sex other than in 2.1	Small	Small	Small	Small

How far can the population growth depart in two years' time? More specifically, suppose that with current birth and death rates and net immigration, the population of the United States will increase about 3 per cent during the next two years: Can these variables change so much that the outcome will be, say on the one hand, an increase of 8 per cent or more or, on the other, a decline of 2 per cent or more. The answer is clearly in the negative. (In some parts of the world, mass migrations induced or caused by war and for other reasons have given rise to large population changes.) The main difficulties in population projections arise when they reach into the more distant future. But whether a particular projection for ten, twenty, or thirty years into the future is realized or is far from the mark, is not necessarily important to the economy and to short-term price movements, for in the longer run the economy can and does adjust and adapt itself to such gradual changes in population as they emerge.

Experience in the United States indicates clearly for item 2.1 in the table above that transfers between civilian and noncivilian sectors can occur rapidly and can be large. Because of such transfers, it is not meaningful to treat, for example, the per capita population of

1945 and of 1946 as identical or even tolerably similar. The rapid demobilization of the armed forces from 1945 to 1946 transferred 7.8
million persons to the civilian sector, increasing the size of that sector by
about 5.8 per cent. In addition, however, the per capita composition of
the civilian population was altered importantly, enough to shift schedule
A about 4 per cent to the right, other things being equal.[8] Nor are the
effects on schedule B negligible, because it apparently requires substantially more food to feed a man when he is in the armed services than
he would consume as a civilian. At the peak of mobilization, this additional requirement alone may have had the effect of shifting schedule
B about 3 per cent farther to the right.[9]

What can one say about the demand effects of possible short-term
changes in the distribution within the civilian sector as to location and
occupation for item 2.2 in the table above? Many different occupational
and locational changes are the normal consequences of economic development when income per capita rises 2 per cent a year and when
the population grows at the rate of 1.5 per cent annually. This set of
particular changes is presumably embedded in the concept of normal
to which the economy is attuned. From 1933 to 1940, for example, the

---

[8] One way of estimating this outcome is to take the per capita food energy
recommended for a population of "normal" composition to be 2,640 calories
and that of young men typical of those in the armed forces to be 4,250
calories. (See Raymond P. Christensen, *Efficient Use of Food Resources in the
United States*, USDA, *Tech. Bul.* 693, October, 1948, Table 2, p. 9.) When
mobilization has proceeded to a point that 7½ per cent of these young men
has been withdrawn from the civilian sector, we have:

(1) Normal population $= 2{,}640 \times 100$ (weight) 264,000
(2) Persons in armed forces $= 4{,}250 \times 7\frac{1}{2}$ 31,875
(3) Persons remaining in civilian sector $= 2{,}510 \times 92\frac{1}{2}$ 232,125

Turning, then, to 1945, we have:

(4) 134.2 million persons remaining in civilian sector, $2{,}510 \times 100$ . . 251,000
(5) 7.8 million persons added from armed forces, $4{,}250 \times 5.8$ . . . 24,650
(6) (4) + (5), 105.8 275,650
(7) $275{,}650 \div 251{,}000 = 109.8$
(8) $109.8 - 105.8 = 4\%$

[9] On the assumption that the amount of food required for a person in the
armed forces is about twice as much as is the per capita food consumption
of a normal civilian population. Of this increase about 60 per cent is represented by the larger food energy requirement of young men as civilians, considered in footnote 8, and the remaining 40 per cent represents the still larger
intake of men in service, stocks and supplies held in reserve, and waste that go
with feeding the armed forces. Therefore, with 7.5 per cent of the population
mobilized, we have $7.5 \times .4 = 3$ per cent increase.

farm population declined on the average about 300,000 net per year. From 1942 to 1944 it dropped 3.3 million, or 2.7 million more than would have been expected from the preceding development. This particular occupational change by itself may have shifted schedule A and schedule B about 1⅔ per cent to the right.[10] Other distributional changes, such as a rapid movement to longer hours of work, more physical work, and the like, could also add somewhat to these demand schedules.

It is hard to believe that changes in age and sex distribution of a normal population, except for the developments considered under item 2.1 in the table above can alter the demand schedule other than in the small.

We shall consider, next, some observed demand effects of changes in income.

What information is there at hand about the relations between changes in income and the demand for food? Much has been done to estimate the income elasticity of food based on disposable per capita income. These studies have been summarized and evaluated in Chap. 5.

When the economy is developing gradually and steadily and when, as a consequence, the particular rate of growth is viewed as normal, such estimates of income elasticity are likely to be fairly dependable indicators. Experiences tell us, however, that this income is subject to large and abrupt movements and that the distribution is also subject to important short-term changes.

Large short-term movements in the proportion of resources that are employed can alter the flow of disposable income sufficiently to bring about a large shift in the demand for food. In considering item 2.1 in the table on page 183, it is hard to forget the experiences of the thirties and early forties. The sharp drop in per capita disposable income from 1930 to 1932 may well have shifted the per capita demand

---

[10] On the assumption that a person on the farm acquires about one half of his food from the farm and purchases the other half at retail, we have, say, for 1942 the following figures:

(1) 106.6 million nonfarm people, about 79.3% × 100 (food weight) . . 7,930
(2) 27.9 million farm people, 20.7% × 50 1,035
(3) (1) + (2) 8,965
(4) Let nonfarm become 82.1 × 100 8,210
(5) Let farm become 17.9 × 50 895
(6) (4) + (5) 9,105
(7) 9,105 ÷ 8,965 = 101.67

Thus there is an increase of 1⅔ per cent in food purchased at retail, other things being equal.

Demand shift related to income changes	Schedule A (demand for food of U.S. civilians at retail)		Schedule B (demand for farm foods confronting farmers)	
	Normal as defined in text	Possibilities for departures	Normal as defined in text	Possibilities for departures
	(1)	(2)	(3)	(4)
1. Normal rise of 2% in disposable per capita income.	1%	. . . .	1%	
2. Movements in disposable income:				
2.1 Large movements in the proportion of resources employed (major depressions and subsequent recoveries) .	. . . . .	Large	. . . . .	Large
2.2 Regular business cycles excluding 2.1 (small movements in proportion of resources employed) . . .	. . . . .	Small	. . . . .	Small
3. Distribution:				
3.1 Personal distribution of disposable income	Small	Small	Small	Small
3.2 Changes in the proportion of personal income required for tax payments. . . .	. . . . .	Intermediate	. . . . .	Intermediate
3.3 Personal allocation of disposable income between consumption and asset holdings	Small	Large	Small	Large

for food fully 6 per cent to the left, whereas a normal rate of growth in income would have indicated a 1 per cent shift to the right.[11] From 1935 to 1937 the shift of this schedule was abruptly to the right, probably about 3 per cent, of which, again, 1 per cent would have been normal. Then, from 1940 to 1942, the shift was again sharply to the right, probably around 5 per cent more than the normal shift of 1 per cent.

[11] Disposable per capita income, in 1951 prices (see *Economic Report of the President,* January, 1952, Table B–10), fell from $939 in 1930 to $760 in 1932, a drop of about 20 per cent. (Unemployment, see Table B–11, rose from about 4.3 to 12.0 million persons.) We shall take the normal income elasticity for food to be approximately .25, and in the belief that it would be somewhat more in the event of an abrupt and large drop in income, let us assume that it was about .33. The implications are, other things unchanged, that the demand schedule for food shifted about 6⁶⁄₁₀ per cent to the left instead of 1 per cent to the right, a very large departure indeed, considering the very low price elasticity of the schedules. The disposable per capita

Movements in disposable income related to regular business cycles, leaving aside those movements considered under item 2.1 in the table above, appear to have only a small effect upon the position of the two demand schedules under consideration. This inference is supported by data on *peaks* and *troughs* of business cycles from 1894 to 1914 and the related index of farm product prices which is cited in *Production and Welfare of Agriculture*[12] (see also Chap. 29). Moore's[13] indicators of cyclical revivals and recessions are not inconsistent with this view.

It does not appear that short-term changes in the personal distribution of income are likely to be an important factor in shifts of the demand schedule for food. Tobin's[14] evidence supports this belief; one study shows the share of the total disposable income received by the top 5 per cent of the population to have declined from 27 per cent in 1938 to 17 per cent in 1945.[15] Except for the effects on distribution of large movements in the proportion of resources employed, this factor is likely to have only a small demand effect in the context of a two-year time interval in which our analysis is cast.

Turning to circumstances represented by item 3.2 in the table above, substantial departures in the rate of growth of per capita disposable income can occur as a consequence of short-term changes in personal taxes. However, even the most abrupt and the largest changes in this variable do not appear to have been responsible for large shifts in the

---

income rose from $882 in 1935 (in 1951 prices) to $1,020 in 1937, a rise of about 15 per cent. (Unemployment fell from 10.6 to 7.7 million.) Assuming the income elasticity of food as this rise occurred to have been less than normal, at about .20, the inference is, leaving other matters unchanged, that the demand for food shifted about 3 per cent, of which about 1 per cent would have been normal. The 1940 to 1942 abrupt rise in disposable per capita income, 1951 prices, was from $1,089 to $1,381, up about 27 per cent. (Unemployment dropped from 8.1 to 2.7 million.) On the above assumption, that the income elasticity would, under these conditions, be below normal and at about .20, we have a shift in the demand schedule for food of 5⁴⁄₁₀ per cent, of which, again, only 1 per cent would have been normal.

[12] Theodore W. Schultz, *Production and Welfare of Agriculture* (New York: The Macmillan Company, 1949), p. 74.

[13] Geoffrey H. Moore, *Statistical Indicators of Cyclical Revivals and Recessions* (New York: National Bureau of Economic Research, Inc., 1950), *Occasional Paper* 31. See especially Table 5 and Sec. 5.

[14] Tobin, *op. cit.*, p. 129.

[15] Simon Kuznets, *Shares of Upper Income Groups in Income and Savings* (New York: National Bureau of Economic Research, Inc., 1950), *Occasional Paper* 35. See Table 2 of Appendix.

demand schedules for food. If, for example, the disposable personal income in 1951 had been as large a proportion of total personal income as it was in 1941, it would have been only about 9 per cent larger. The rapid and abrupt change in this relation which occurred from 1941 to 1943 also represented a magnitude of less than 10 per cent. Accordingly, we may infer, *ceteris paribus,* that the resulting shift in the demand schedules for food may be intermediate, but not large.

It is possible to have large and abrupt shifts in the demand for food as a consequence of decisions by consuming units altering the proportion of the disposable income that is spent. For example, from 1945 to 1947, measured in real terms, the disposable per capita income fell about 8 per cent whereas personal consumption expenditures per capita actually rose about 5 per cent. (The three largest changes since 1939, in net savings as per cent of disposable income, were as follows: from 3.9 per cent in 1930 to −2.9 per cent in 1933; from 4.9 per cent in 1940 to 21.9 per cent in 1942; and from 24.1 per cent in 1945 to 7.6 per cent in 1947 on which the data cited above are based.)[16]

Other factors and demand shifts	Schedule A (demand for food of United States civilians at retail)		Schedule B (demand for farm foods confronting farmers)	
	Normal as defined in text	Possibilities for departures	Normal as defined in text	Possibilities for departures
	(1)	(2)	(3)	(4)
1. Commercial sector				
1.1 Changes in industrial uses of food commodities . . .	. . . . .	. . . . .	Small	Small
1.2 Changes in net stocks . .	. . . . .	. . . . .	Small	(?)
2. Foreign sector (exports) . . .	. . . . .	. . . . .	Small (?)	Large (?)
3. Government sector	. . . . .	. . . . .	Small (?)	Large

The additional factors in the above table do not affect schedule A but are important in explaining shifts in schedule B. However, all too little is known about these particular factors. For instance, what role do changes in stocks held by the commercial sector play? Under normal circumstances, as defined in the text, they probably have little or no aggregating effect on the position of the demand schedule for farm food commodities confronting farmers. When, however, strong inflationary

[16] *The Economic Report of the President,* January, 1952, Table B–9.

or deflationary developments are under way, do changes in these stocks become an important variable affecting the position of schedule B? We really do not know. Likewise, the behavior of the export sector is not at all clear. Much statistical work has been done to represent the variations in foreign purchases in terms of an elasticity with respect to price, whereas what may occur is much more akin to large and abrupt shifts in the foreign demand schedule for United States farm food commodities.

Lastly, we have here the government sector which has become exceedingly important for schedule B. But it is not a simple variable to represent. In considering population changes, we found that transfers of persons from the civilian to noncivilian activities (armed forces) shift schedule A to the left, and the government sector is required to provide additional food; the amount required, however, exceeds the reduction in the civilian sector. Schedule B, therefore, is shifted somewhat to the right under these circumstances. Also, much of the United States farm food which other governments and foreign buyers have obtained has come from the government sector. Nor does this complete the functions of this sector.

Experience in the United States indicates frequent shifts in the demand for farm products. Variations in the size of the stock with which we begin the crop year are sometimes large, especially of particular farm products. The demand, again and again, has made large shifts, abruptly caused by mobilization, war, and the return to peace and by major depressions and related recoveries. How readily large shifts of this kind are absorbed will depend upon the elasticities of the relevant demand and supply schedules to which we now turn.

ELASTICITIES THAT ARE RELATIVELY LOW

The price elasticities of both the demand and supply of farm products are, so it appears, far over on the inelastic side. We shall examine each briefly.

Elasticities of the Demand. Unfortunately, however, we know much less about the price elasticity than about the income elasticity attributes of the demand empirically. Clearly, when one endeavors to gauge the income elasticity of a product, both cross-sectional and time-series data can be brought to bear, whereas when one endeavors to estimate a particular price elasticity one is always emmeshed in the tangled web of time-series data. While it should be possible to use differences in prices related to location, this approach has not been applied. We would like to know the price elasticity of the demand for each of the concepts of food examined in Chap. 5 and also for nonfood farm products not only for domestic civilian consumption, but also for export, stocks, and noncivilian uses. We are, however, dependent largely upon qualitative insights at this stage of our knowledge.

It will be helpful to think of the demand schedule as having three segments, that is, (1) middle, (2) upper, and (3) a lower segment. Most of the information at hand is related to the middle segment. Let us take, first, the demand for food of United States civilians at retail. When we take food as measured by the Bureau of Agricultural Economics index of food consumption, it is our belief that the middle segment of this demand schedule has a price elasticity of approximately —.25 (see column 9, Table 11–1; some studies using one equation, leaving supply effects aside, indicate elasticities up to about —.40). We believe that there exists an upper segment where this schedule is somewhat more elastic. Experience suggests, however, that this segment is not reached even though food prices at retail rise, say, 25 per cent relative to other consumer prices. This is the interpretation we place on what happened, for example, from 1940 to 1947. Two implications follow: (1) it is necessary for food prices at retail to rise more than 25 per cent relatively before substantial additional substitution[17] comes into play; and (2) before this turning point is reached, in letting changes in relative prices curtail food consumption, the political process is likely to intervene. There also exists, in our judgment, a lower segment where this demand schedule will become somewhat more elastic. But here, again, it is not likely to be revealed in practice. The large drop in food prices relative to other consumer prices at retail from 1929 to 1933 did not do so. What is more, the political process is not likely to let farm food prices at the point of farm sales, and, therefore, also not food at retail, drop so far relatively before it intervenes.

Before turning to the demand for farm products at the point where farmers sell, it will be helpful to acquire a feeling for the demand at retail in somewhat more detail than for all food taken as an aggregate.

[17] Several possibilities for additional substitution can come into play, that is, consuming units will increase the food intake per unit of food purchased at retail by more efficient conversion in households (reducing so-called waste), some "overeating" will be reduced, and, most important, shifts among food components will occur, that is, as food prices rise relatively, consumers will shift from animal products and other classes of food which are expensive in terms of agricultural resources required to produce them to cereals, potatoes, and other products not so expensive to produce (the last of these, however, represents the consumption effects of a reduction in real income of consumers caused by the marked rise in food prices, other things unchanged, and we are back to differences in income elasticities of the various classes of food).

TABLE 11–1. APPROXIMATE VALUES OF THE PRICE ELASTICITIES OF THE DEMAND FOR FARM PRODUCTS, FARM FOOD, AND FOOD IN THE UNITED STATES

	For all farm products for domestic uses, exports, stocks, at the farm (BAE Agr. Prod. Index)			For all farm foods for sale and for farm home consumption, at the farm (BAE Farm-food Prod. Index)					For food of United States civilians at retail (BAE Food Consumption Index)	For food of United States civilians at retail (U.S. Dept. of Commerce Consumer Expenditure Index)	Food eaten away from home, including service
	Food	Non-food	All (1) + (2)	Domestic	Exports	Gov't.	Stocks	All (4) + (5) + (6) + (7)			
	(1)	(2)	(3)	(4)	(5)	(6)	(7)	(8)	(9)	(10)	(11)
Year-to-year price: Supply effects, considered			–.12 (Tintner, 1923–1943)						–.25 (Girschick and Haavelmo, 1922–1941) –.27 (Haavelmo, 1922–1941) –.28 (Tobin, 1913–1941)		
Leaving supply effects aside			–.40 (Fox, 1922–1941)	–.24 (Fox, 1922–1941)				–.50 (Fox and Mehren, 1949)	–.25 (Burk, 1922–1941) –.25 (Working, 1922–1941) –.31 (Cochrane, 1922–1941) –.33 (BAE, 1922–1941) –.35 to –.37 (Fox, 1922–1941)	–.43 ("Stone-Tobin," 1913–1941) and –.11 for elasticity with respect to nonfood prices –.51 (Tobin, 1913–1941) –.58 (Stone, 1929–1941)	
Approximate values under conditions of full employment without price supports, middle segment only			–.25					–.25	–.25	–.50	–1.00

SOURCES:

Consumption of Food in the United States, 1909–48, BAE, *Misc. Pub.* 691, August, 1949, Table 48.

Marguerite C. Burk, "Changes in Demand for Food from 1941 to 1950," *Journal of Farm Economics*, Vol. XXXIII (August, 1951); see footnotes 16 and 17.

Willard W. Cochrane, *An Analysis of Farm Price Behavior, Penn. State Coll. Progress Rept.* 20, May, 1951. Elasticity cited for Cochrane adjusted as reported by Working.

Karl A. Fox, "Factors Affecting Farm Income, Farm Prices, and Food Consumption," *Agricultural Economics Research*, Vol. III (July, 1951), Bureau of Agricultural Economics. Also, data from Dr. Fox kindly supplied in correspondence.

M. A. Girschick and T. Haavelmo, "Statistical Analysis of the Demand for Food," *Econometrica*, Vol. XV (April, 1947).

Trygve Haavelmo, "Quantitative Research in Agricultural Economics," *Journal of Farm Economics*, Vol. XXIX (November, 1947).

George L. Mehren, "Comparative Costs of Agricultural Price Supports in 1949," *Proceedings, American Economic Review*, Vol. XLI, No. 2 (May, 1951). Also, data from Professor Mehren kindly supplied in correspondence.

Richard Stone, "The Analysis of Market Demand," *Royal Statistical Journal*, Vol. CVIII (1945).

Gerhard Tintner, "Multiple Regression for System of Equations," *Econometrica*, Vol. XIV (January, 1946).

James Tobin, "A Statistical Demand Function for Food in the U.S.A.," *Journal of the Royal Statistical Society*, Vol. CXIII, Part II (1950). See J. R. N. Stone's remarks, pp. 141–142.

E. J. Working, "Appraising the Demand for American Agricultural Output during Rearmament," paper read before joint session of the American Economic Association and the American Farm Economic Association, Boston, December, 1951.

A study by Fox[18] based on the index of food consumption of the Bureau of Agricultural Economics related to disposable income of consumers for 1922–1941 gives the following estimates.

Product	Price elasticity
All food	− .35 to − .37
All livestock products used for food	− .52 and − .56
All meat	− .62 and − .64
Butter	− .25
Eggs	− .26
Milk for fluid use (farm price)	− .30
Turkey (farm price)	− .61
Chicken	− .72
Beef	− .79
Pork	− .81
Lamb	− .91

What, however, is the demand for farm products at the point at which farmers sell? This is what we are concerned about in considering the instability of farm prices. The price elasticity of the demand for farm products is derived from the demand of consumers modified by the operations and behaviors of the marketing sector. Much depends upon how large marketing costs are relatively, the flexibility of these costs, and upon storage and foreign demand. For instance, if these marketing costs were unimportant (close to zero), and if all of the products sold by farmers were taken directly and at once by consumers, the two elasticities, that of farm products and that of food at retail, would be essentially the same. Or, let us suppose that the price (costs) of marketing services were to drop, say, 10 per cent when the food price at retail fell 10 per cent as a consequence of a larger quantity of the farm product being sold by farmers; the two elasticities would come out about the same. Both the behavior of marketing costs and storage, however, operate to make the price elasticity of the demand for farm products substantially different from that of food at retail from which it is derived. A number of studies are available concentrating on farm products at farm prices.

[18] Karl A. Fox, head of the Division of Statistical and Historical Research of the Bureau of Agricultural Economics, has made available to the writer parts of his study, *The Demand for Farm Products*, from which these estimates are drawn. All of these figures, except those for "all food" appear in Fox's paper, "Factors Affecting Farm Income, Farm Prices, and Food Consumption," *Agricultural Economics Research*, Vol. III, No. 3, (July, 1951), Bureau of Agricultural Economics.

The work of Henry Schultz is clearly the most comprehensive. From this study we draw the following estimates.

	1875–1895 (generally falling prices)	1896–1914 (generally rising prices)	1915–1929 with 1917–1921 omitted (war and reconstruction)
Wheat (per capita utilization) . . .	− .03[a]	− .15[b]	− .08[c] − .18[d]
Cotton (per capita consumption) . .	− .51	− .25	− .12
Corn (per capita production). . . .	− .72	− .60	− .48
Potatoes (per capita production) . .	− .68	− .54	− .32

[a] 1880–1895. [b] 1896–1913. [c] 1921–1929. [d] 1921–1934.

SOURCE: Henry Schultz, *The Theory and Measurement of Demand* (Chicago: University of Chicago Press, 1938).

A recent study by Mehren[19] for 1949 gives the following price elasticities of the demand for particular farm products at the farm level.

Product	Price elasticity −.11 to −.40	Product	Price elasticity −.41 to −.60	Product	Price elasticity −.61 to −.89
Peas, dry, edible . . .	−.11	Wheat	−.41	Flaxseed	−.61
Beans, dry, edible . .	−.12	Eggs	−.42	Corn	−.67
Potatoes	−.15	Flue-cured tobacco .	−.45	Cottonseed	−.70
Rosin	−.18	Sweet potatoes . . .	−.45	Mohair	−.70
Burley tobacco . . .	−.20	Honey extract . . .	−.50	Butterfat.	−.75
Tung nuts.	−.30	Barley	−.51	Wool	−.75
Grain sorghums . . .	−.38	Oats	−.55	Hogs (excluding lard) .	−.80
Peanuts	−.40	Turkey	−.55	Beef cattle	−.80
Turpentine	−.40	Cotton	−.60	Mutton and lamb . .	−.80
Honeycomb	−.40	Rice	−.60	Farm chickens . . .	−.89
		Whole milk	−.60		
		Soybeans	−.60		

Fox[20] provides a set of estimates of the elasticity of the dealer demand for fruits and vegetables on the assumption that the production and sales are equal for 1922–1941.

[19] George L. Mehren, "Comparative Costs of Agricultural Price Supports in 1949," *Proceedings, American Economic Review*, Vol. XLI, No. 2 (May, 1951). Mehren points out that these estimates "are not represented as long-run estimates but rather are relevant only to commercial sales and to 1949 conditions."

[20] Fox, *op. cit.* Fox gives these estimates as net regressions of production upon current farm prices.

Product	Demand elasticity of dealers
All fruits.	−0.82
Lemons	−0.35
Grapefruit	−0.40
Cranberries (1922–1936)	−0.57
Oranges	−0.58
Peaches	−1.18
Apples.	−1.21
Sweet potatoes	−0.74
Onions (all)	−0.39
Potatoes (production)	−0.26
Truck crops for fresh market	
Spring.	−0.30
Fall	−0.41
Summer	−0.42
Winter	−0.45

What, then, is the price elasticity of the demand for farm products at the point of farm sales?

Tintner has estimated the price elasticity for all agricultural products taken as an aggregate, using annual data from 1923 to 1943. For these two decades—working with five variables, that is, prices received by farmers, national income, agricultural production, prices paid by farmers, and time—he obtained −.12.[21]

Fox[22] reports that in the case of "all food livestock products" during 1922–1941, year-to-year changes of 1 per cent in the retail price were related to changes of 1.5 per cent in the farm price. This relation suggests for food at retail, having a price elasticity of −.36, a derived price elasticity at the farm of −.24.

How the price elasticities are affected by varying circumstances is another and an important topic. Suffice it to point out that there are good reasons for believing, if other things are the same, that the shorter the time interval, the lower will be the elasticity under consideration; that a major depression will reduce the elasticity of storable products and conversely a recovery will increase it; that the elasticity usually will be greater in both the upper and lower parts of the schedule than it will be where the "normal" supply intersects; and, that for most farm products, the demand at retail will become less elastic as people become richer.[23]

---

[21] Gerhard Tintner, "Multiple Regression for Systems of Equations," *Econometrica*, Vol. XIV (January, 1946).

[22] Fox, *op. cit.*

[23] We have not tried in this section to use and interpret all the demand studies that might be relevant. For a useful summary, see Warren C. Waite and Harry C. Trelogan, *Introduction to Agricultural Prices* (Minneapolis: Burgess Publishing Co., 1948), Table 10.

Elasticities of the Supply. The response of the supply of farm products to prices may be examined under various circumstances. In Part One, we found that, as a consequence of economic development which characterized the United States, say, from 1910–1950, agricultural production for sale and farm consumption increased about 75 per cent although farm prices taken as a whole were about the same relative to other product prices at the end as they were at the beginning of this period. We are now concerned, not with changes that occur over a period of decades, but with price movements that occur in a two-year time interval and with the stock period defined to cover the time interval between harvests.

The supply of farmers during the stock period is necessarily very inelastic when we take all farm products in the aggregate. In Chap. 14, we shall examine both the farm household and the farm business and trace the effects of a change in price upon the amount of products which farmers will sell. The substitution effects in the household are still appreciable, but because so small a proportion of farm output is consumed in the farm household, a 10 per cent change in the amount consumed would alter this supply less than 1 per cent. The income effects in the farm household are near zero or negative because home-produced food is approaching the status of an inferior good against income for farm families. In the farm business, the price effects are large in the case of those farm products that are used in further production. Storage by farmers is difficult to get at because of the way farm programs have operated. Even so, it is clear that the over-all effects of farm storage must be small because for farmers most farm products are quite perishable.

How elastic is the short-run supply of farm products? For particular products where inputs can be transferred readily from other farm operations, it is highly elastic. Some minor crops, like flaxseed, with a small acreage relative to wheat and in areas where either crop may be grown, respond quickly and substantially to changes in relative prices. It is a commonplace to stress the importance of relative prices within agriculture, for there are many situations in farming where large shifts occur readily and quickly among products in response to changes in relative farm prices. Major crops and large categories of livestock products are, however, on a very different footing, and when we take all farm products, in a two-year setting as our short run, the price elasticity of the supply is relatively low.

Some insights about the elasticity of the supply of farm products may be had by studying the changes in agricultural production inputs following a large rise or fall in farm prices relative to other product prices.

This relation between inputs and prices will be considered in some detail in Chap. 13 (see especially Tables 13–1 and 13–3). The large drop in farm prices in 1919–1920 was followed by a 4 per cent reduction in total agricultural inputs by 1924. Table 11–2 gives more recent data relevant to this relation between inputs and prices. For the period 1929 to 1932, a fall in relative prices (based on the parity ratio) of 37 per cent is related to a 6 per cent reduction in aggregate inputs. For 1940 to 1943, a rise in relative prices of 40 per cent indicates an increase in total inputs of 4 per cent. Note, however, that from 1945 to 1947 a small change in relative prices of 5 per cent is related to an increase in these farm inputs of about 2 per cent.[24]

TABLE 11–2. THREE SHORT-TERM MOVEMENTS IN AGRICULTURAL INPUTS

	Wholesale price index[a]		Parity[a] ratio (1910–1914 = 100)	Total production[b] inputs in agriculture (1935–1939 = 100)
	Products other than farm and food (1926 = 100)	Farm products (1926 = 100)		
1929	92	105	92	107 (1930)
1932	70	48	58	101 (1933)
Drop in per cent	24	54	37	6
1940	83	68	81	99 (1941)
1943	97	123	113	103 (1944)
Rise in per cent	17	81	40	4
1945	100	128	109	105 (1946)
1947	135	181	115	107 (1948)
Rise in per cent	35	41	5	2

[a] *The Economic Report of the President and the Annual Economic Review*, Council of Economic Advisers, 1951, Tables A–24, A–25.

[b] *Farm Production Practices, Costs and Returns*, BAE, *Statis. Bul.* 83, October, 1949, Table 27. Two modifications in these data have been made: (1) the input of labor is based on the Bureau of the Census farm-employment changes since 1940 and (2) inputs are weighted by 1946–1948 input prices (see Chap. 7).

A warning is required, however, because of the widely held false belief that agriculture is a watertight compartment, with a great deal of flexibility within but with no resource transferability between agri-

[24] The rise in inputs following 1945 was in considerable part a delayed adjustment to the war period when farmers could not acquire all the capital equipment they were prepared to buy.

culture and the rest of the economy. At a later point, we shall draw on the work of Johnson[25] to show that the supply of farm products is highly inelastic under conditions of widespread unemployment associated with major depressions but that it is probably substantially more elastic under high employment conditions. Suffice it to indicate that it is quite misleading to generalize the experiences of the early thirties, for they are not applicable, when it comes to transferring resources into or out of agriculture, when resources are fully employed.[26]

The burden of this chapter has been to present the belief that United States agriculture is characterized (1) by demand and supply schedules, the price elasticities of which are relatively inelastic, and (2) by frequent and large shifts in a short interval of time in one or the other or in both of these two schedules. The price and income instability of agriculture is to be explained by these characteristics because this instability stems basically from particular large and abrupt shifts and the existing price inelasticities.

[25] D. Gale Johnson, "The Nature of the Supply Function for American Agriculture," *American Economic Review*, Vol. XI, No. 4 (September, 1950).

[26] For a contrary view, see Willard W. Cochrane, first in an article, "Farm Price Gyrations—An Aggregative Hypothesis," *Journal of Farm Economics*, Vol. XXIX (May, 1947), and then substantially elaborated in *An Analysis of Farm Price Behavior*, Agricultural Experiment Station, *Penn. State Coll. Progress Rept.* 50, May, 1951. My criticism of this view is set forth in a note "Farm Price Gyrations by Cochrane," *Journal of Farm Economics*, Vol. XXXIII (November, 1951).

12

YIELD INSTABILITY

In farming, yields are subject to much uncertainty. They cannot be controlled fully. Nor can they be foreseen accurately. While some advances are possible in controlling yields, by using better techniques, through improvements in organization and in forecasting yields, the agriculture of the United States will continue to experience fluctuations in yields of major economic importance because farming in this country is so largely dependent upon a continental climate.

The economic problems arising out of yield instability may be approached along two general lines by representing the particular farm and the micro setting in which it operates and by considering particular aggregative effects which are macro in character. There is little point, however, in considering all conceivable possibilities in each of these two directions; we shall endeavor, instead, to restrict this study to those attributes which appear to be relevant and important to the American setting. The data that follow are required to take our bearing on the year-to-year variations in yields that characterize farming in the United States.

We shall concentrate on crop yields and not on animal products because in producing animals the rate of output from a particular collection of inputs, leaving aside the variations in the yield of feed crops including hay and pasture, is much more subject to control by farmers than it is in the case of crops. The effects of weather are primarily upon crops. From there they are transmitted to other operations and to other sectors of the economy.

As we study yield data, it will be necessary to guard against the inference that all changes in yield are caused by weather or that all effects of weather are represented by changes in yield. For most major crops, there have been substantial improvements in yields; for the 18 leading field crops, this gain has added up to about 1 per cent per year over the last four decades. Some of these improvements have come quite rapidly, for instance, the gains from the adoption of hybrid corn. Short-run variations in the use of fertilizer have at times been large, for example, the amount of fertilizer used (continental United States, *Agricultural Statistics*, 1949, p. 643) fell from 8.4 million tons in 1930 to 6.5 million tons in 1931 and to 4.5 million tons in 1932. When the economic incentives pull the other way, we observe a rise in the use of fertilizer, for example, from 10 million tons in 1942 to 18 million tons in 1949, with large increases occurring in 1944 and 1946. The principal reason why the effects of weather are not fully reflected in existing yield data stems from the fact that in bad years more than normal amounts of the planted acreage are abandoned and that the yield is calculated on the basis of harvested acreage. It should also be noted that in the case of hay and especially of land that is grazed, it is exceedingly difficult to estimate the relevant yield. These and related considerations must be borne in mind in interpreting yield estimates.

The available data permit us to relate variations in yields to location and to particular products. The first, in a rough way, makes it possible to get at the effects of weather upon the output of farms by geographical areas. The second gives us some insight into some aggregative effects of year-to-year variations in production upon specific products caused by weather.

Fluctuations in Yield by Location

The new Bureau of Agricultural Economics index of "crop production per acre of cropland" by major geographic regions running back to 1919 overcomes one of the major shortcomings of the regularly published "crop yield index," for it takes cropland that is abandoned and summer fallow into account.[1] In the discussion that follows, we shall draw on the new index. It will be convenient, however, to refer to this index of "crop production per acre of cropland" as the crop yield. Let us first compare, among the nine regions, the Pacific and the West North Central, the two extremes.

The Pacific Region Is Placid. Here farm output is under control in farming more so than in any other region. Correcting for the gradual increases in yield (fully doubled since 1919), the yearly variations in crop yields (measured from the preceding year) have averaged 2.1 per cent during the three decades, 1919–1949 (see Table 12–1). Moreover, nearly all of the year-to-year changes have been small. Only once, in 1924, was there a large drop consisting of 22 per cent. But even a part of this drop merely reflected the rather high yield of the preceding

[1] For a discussion of the method used in constructing this index and the series, see *Farm Production Practices, Costs and Returns*, BAE, *Statis. Bul.* 83, (October, 1949), p. 25.

ear. And so it was for 1931, the next largest drop, when the yield index ell 7.9 per cent, following a very good year. The upward drift in yield is mpressive; however, except for 1946, when it jumped 15 per cent, the ncreases are in general small. Later when we come to examine produc-ion we shall find that among the crops grown in the region some have quite erratic yields. The food and feed grains and the sugar crops have his characteristic. But for all that, the gross farm production of the egion is even steadier than is the yield which we have been describing.

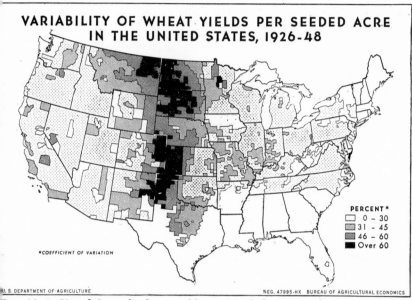

VARIABILITY OF WHEAT YIELDS PER SEEDED ACRE IN THE UNITED STATES, 1926-48

PERCENT*
- 0 – 30
- 31 - 45
- 46 - 60
- Over 60

*COEFFICIENT OF VARIATION

U. S. DEPARTMENT OF AGRICULTURE — NEG. 47995-HX   BUREAU OF AGRICULTURAL ECONOMICS

Fig. 12–1. Variability of wheat yields per seeded acre in the United States, 1926–1948.

The Turbulent West Central Regions both North and South. In this arge area the hand of nature lifts and depresses yields despite all the •fforts of farmers to counteract its influence. Rainfall is a critical, limiting actor, and in all probability will continue to remain so because, for most f the land now used for farming, it cannot be modified appreciably ither by irrigation or by other means. Conceivably, farming may be oncentrated on the valleys and on other flat land which in time can be rrigated; but, this possibility is far removed from the circumstances hat now prevail.

In the West North Central region, after correcting for the secular in-rease in yield which has been quite small, the year-to-year variations in rop yields averaged 18 per cent during the 1919–1949 period (see Table

12–1). The yield experiences of the West South Central region were only slightly better.

These fluctuations in yield are so large that it is hard to believe that no serious difficulties are encountered as a consequence. Moreover, this average figure of 18 per cent for the West North Central and virtually 15 per cent for the West South Central obscures a more important set of problems caused by the large departure from this average, namely, the bunching of bad and good years. Take the yield index for the West North Central region which was running at about 130 in the late twenties when it took the following turn (see Table 12–3):[2]

Year	Yield index
1933	97
1934	49
1935	101
1936	60

Or that experienced during the first part of the forties, as follows (see Table 12–3):

Year	Yield index
1942	161
1943	140
1944	147
1945	144
1946	157
1947	132
1948	168

The very low yields of the thirties came when farm prices fell to very low levels and the bumper crops of the forties when farm prices sky-rocketed—what fortunate circumstances! Unfortunately the assets of most farmers are not adequate for so long a run; assets are soon exhausted and the old set of farmers fades away. A new generation garners the windfalls of a bountiful nature and wartime prices.

Location of Yield Instability—United States. When we average all the crops of all the farmers by regions, which of course hides so many important local differences,[3] we find that the Pacific, New England and

[2] Philip J. Thair, *Stabilizing Farm Income against Crop Yield Fluctuations,* North Dakota Agric. Exp. Sta. Bul. 362, September, 1950, p. 9, reports: "For North Dakota as a whole, during the 70-year period of 1879–1948, there were three separate periods when wheat yields were above average for a run of three or more years, and two of these runs lasted nine years each. In four separate periods, yields ran below average for three or more years in a row; one of these was five and another twelve years long."

[3] To illustrate, the variability of wheat yields per seeded acre for the period

the Middle and South Atlantic regions have the least yield instability while the Mountain and the Central regions are much more vulnerable on this score, as Tables 12–1 to 12–3 show in some detail. But the gap between regional averages and the real yields of a particular farm within a region may be great. In the micro setting in which a farm is located, it is the yield experiences of each parcel of land used for farming that is relevant. Thair, Barber, Schickele, and others have made a start in analyzing the yields of localities in sufficient detail so that the results are applicable to particular farms.[4] A vast amount of data has been ac-

---

1926–1948 exceeded 90 per cent (coefficient of variation) in a number of counties in the hard-wheat area. The Agricultural Experiment Station at Colby, Kansas, had the following yields per seeded acre.

Year	Wheat after fallow, bushels	Continuous wheat, bushels
1928–1931	29.6	14.8
1932	36.8	6.0
1933	0.0	0.0
1934	5.5	0.0
1935	0.0	0.0
1936	0.0	0.0
1937	2.5	1.7
1938	5.2	4.7
1939	4.2	2.5
1940	0.0	0.0

Then came a series of good years.

Year	Wheat after fallow, bushels	Continuous wheat, bushels
1941	23.3	10.0
1942	22.0	15.5
1943	28.7	5.5
1944	31.0	12.7
1945	41.0	7.8
1946	15.8	4.3
1947	46.3	24.7

SOURCE: E. Lloyd Barber, *Meeting Weather Risks in Kansas Wheat Farming, Kansas Agr. Exp. Sta. Agric. Exp. Rept.* 44, September, 1950.

[4] Some insights as to how little and how much a major drought like that of

TABLE 12–1. YEAR-TO-YEAR VARIATIONS IN CROP PRODUCTION PER ACRE OF CROPLAND
1919–1949

United States and regions	(1) Average variations from preceding year, per cent	(2) Variations ascribed to upward trend in yield,[a] per cent	(3) Difference (1) − (2), per cent
United States	8.2	1.1	7.1
Pacific	5.3	3.2	2.1
New England	6.5	1.5	5.0
Middle Atlantic	7.5	1.3	6.2
South Atlantic	8.7	2.1	6.6
East South Central	10.5	1.7	8.8
Mountain	10.3	1.0	9.3
East North Central	10.7	1.3	9.4
West South Central	15.6	0.7	14.9
West North Central	18.5	0.5	18.0

[a] Based on simple average of change per year between average of first three years and the last three years of the 1919–1949 period.

SOURCE: *Farm Production Practices, Costs and Returns*, BAE, *Statis. Bul.* 83, October 1949. For 1947–1949, revised data from the Bureau of Agricultural Economics.

1934 pulls down yields in particular type of farming areas can be obtained from data on family-operated farms.

	Index of crop yield per harvested acre
Type	*(1935–1939 = 100)*
Dairy farms:	
Central New York	85
Southern Wisconsin	75
Corn-belt farms:	
Cash grain	55
Hog-beef fattening	49
Hog-beef raising	44
Hog, dairying	67
Spring-wheat farms:	
Wheat, corn, livestock	92
Wheat, small grain	55
Wheat, roughage, livestock.	44
Winter-wheat farms:	
Wheat.	76
Wheat, grain, sorghum	86
Cotton farms:	
Southern plains	43
Black prairie	73
Delta of Mississippi	81
Cattle ranges:	
Intermountain	86

SOURCE: *Farm Production Practices, Costs and Returns*, BAE, *Statis. Bul.* 83, October 1949.

TABLE 12-2. PROFILE OF THE VARIATIONS IN CROP PRODUCTION PER ACRE OF CROPLAND, 1919–1949

Variations in yield per acre from preceding year, in per cent	Pacific	New England	M. Atlantic	S. Atlantic	Mountain	E.S. Central	E.N. Central	W.S. Central	W.N. Central	U.S.
					Number of years					
+30.1 and over	...	1	...	...	...	...	2	3	2	2
+25.1 to 30	...	...	...	...	2	2	...	1	1	...
+20.1 to 25	...	...	2	...	1	1	2	...	2	...
+15.1 to 20	1	1	2	3	2	1	...	3	2	...
+10.1 to 15	3	1	2	7	3	5	3	2	...	2
+ 5.1 to 10	7	4	3	3	4	5	5	3	4	5
0 to ±5	17	18	13	11	9	7	8	5	9	12
−5.1 to −10	1	4	5	3	4	2	6	4	2	6
−10.1 to −15	...	...	2	1	3	4	1	4	2	...
−15.1 to −20	...	1	...	...	1	2	2	2	3	3
−20.1 to −25	1	...	1	2	1	1	1	2	1	...
−25.1 to −30	...	...	...	...	...	...	...	1	2	...
−30.1 and less	...	...	...	...	...	...	...	...	...	...
Number of years	30	30	30	30	30	30	30	30	30	30
Average variation in per cent per year	5.3	6.5	7.5	8.7	10.3	10.5	10.7	15.6	18.5	8.2

SOURCE: *Farm Production Practices, Costs and Returns*, BAE, *Statis. Bul.* 83, October, 1949.

TABLE 12-3. VARIATIONS IN CROP PRODUCTION PER ACRE OF CROPLAND, 1919–1949
(1935–1939 = 100)

Year	United States Index	United States Per cent of change	New England Index	New England Per cent of change	Middle Atlantic Index	Middle Atlantic Per cent of change	East North Central Index	East North Central Per cent of change	West North Central Index	West North Central Per cent of change	South Atlantic Index	South Atlantic Per cent of change	East South Central Index	East South Central Per cent of change	West South Central Index	West South Central Per cent of change	Mountain Index	Mountain Per cent of change	Pacific Index	Pacific Per cent of change
1919	96	.....	87	.....	82	.....	88	.....	117	.....	81	.....	87	.....	112	.....	85	.....	66	.....
1920	106	10.4	81	−6.9	94	14.6	93	5.7	138	17.9	92	13.6	92	5.7	128	14.3	108	27.0	67	1.5
1921	90	−15.1	83	2.5	74	−21.3	79	−15.1	122	−11.6	72	−21.7	82	−10.9	98	−23.4	106	−1.8	67	0.0
1922	98	8.9	78	−6.0	90	21.6	88	11.4	133	9.0	80	11.1	92	12.2	101	3.0	106	0.0	72	7.5
1923	98	0.0	88	12.8	82	−8.9	89	1.1	131	−1.5	88	10.0	83	−9.8	99	−2.0	112	5.7	81	12.5
1924	97	−1.0	92	4.5	89	8.5	84	−5.6	130	−0.8	85	−3.4	90	8.4	113	14.0	101	−9.8	63	−22.2
1925	100	3.0	89	−3.3	86	−3.4	94	11.9	128	−1.5	87	2.4	101	12.2	102	−9.7	108	7.0	72	14.3
1926	101	1.0	90	1.1	88	2.3	92	−2.0	108	−15.6	96	10.3	107	6.0	103	29.4	102	−5.5	80	10.1
1927	100	−1.0	88	−2.2	87	−1.1	84	−8.7	132	22.2	93	−3.0	89	−16.8	103	−22.0	121	18.6	84	5.0
1928	103	3.0	90	2.3	90	3.4	93	10.7	136	2.9	92	−1.0	89	0.0	112	8.7	118	−2.5	84	0.0
1929	100	−2.9	99	10.0	85	−5.6	88	−5.4	124	−8.8	97	5.4	103	15.7	102	−8.9	103	−12.7	83	−1.2
1930	94	−6.0	102	3.0	87	2.3	80	−9.1	118	−4.8	94	−3.0	85	−17.5	89	−12.7	109	6.0	89	7.2
1931	103	9.6	102	0.0	101	16.1	100	25.0	110	−6.8	99	5.3	108	27.0	129	45.0	85	−22.0	82	−7.9
1932	99	−3.9	96	−6.0	92	−9.0	99	−1.0	128	16.4	75	−24.0	85	−21.3	111	−14.0	96	13.0	87	6.1
1933	89	−10.0	98	−2.0	91	−1.0	79	−20.0	97	−24.2	90	20.0	97	14.1	92	−17.1	88	−8.3	85	−2.3
1934	73	−18.0	96	−2.0	90	−1.0	72	−8.9	49	−49.5	88	−2.2	91	−6.2	66	−28.3	71	−19.3	88	3.5
1935	96	31.5	95	−1.0	100	11.1	99	37.5	101	106.1	98	11.4	88	−3.2	89	34.8	92	29.6	95	8.0
1936	81	−15.6	97	2.1	89	−11.0	76	−23.0	60	−41.0	90	−8.2	93	5.7	80	−10.1	83	−9.8	95	0.0
1937	111	37.0	105	8.2	104	16.8	106	39.5	110	83.3	104	15.6	119	28.0	124	55.0	102	22.9	102	7.4
1938	105	−5.4	99	−5.7	103	−1.0	106	0.0	115	4.5	97	−6.7	106	−10.9	104	−16.1	119	16.7	104	2.0
1939	107	2.0	104	5.0	104	1.0	113	6.6	114	−0.9	111	14.4	94	−11.3	103	−1.0	104	−12.6	104	0.0
1940	111	3.7	110	5.8	104	0.0	106	−6.2	124	8.8	110	−0.9	95	−1.0	112	8.7	115	10.6	110	5.8
1941	113	1.8	109	−0.9	102	−2.0	114	7.5	132	6.5	98	−10.9	105	10.5	106	−5.4	128	11.3	112	1.8
1942	124	9.7	116	6.4	110	8.0	118	3.5	161	22.0	112	14.3	112	6.7	115	8.5	134	4.7	113	1.0
1943	115	−7.2	119	2.6	97	−11.8	106	−10.1	140	−13.0	106	−5.3	108	−3.6	108	−6.1	130	−3.0	113	0.0
1944	122	6.1	100	−15.6	101	4.0	106	0.0	147	5.0	123	16.0	120	11.1	126	16.7	125	−3.8	122	8.0
1945	121	−0.8	105	5.0	101	0.0	113	6.6	144	−2.0	126	2.4	124	3.3	108	−14.3	122	−2.4	119	−2.5
1946	130	7.4	122	16.2	123	21.8	121	7.1	157	9.0	139	10.3	122	−1.6	111	2.8	125	2.5	137	15.1
1947	122	−6.1	118	−3.3	115	−6.5	104	−14.0	132	−15.9	134	−3.6	122	0.0	128	15.3	132	5.6	131	−4.4
1948	137	12.3	124	50.8	121	5.2	130	25.0	168	27.3	137	2.2	147	20.5	127	−0.8	137	3.8	130	−0.8
1949	130	−5.1	121	−2.4	114	−5.8	128	−1.5	139	−17.3	132	−3.6	127	−13.6	151	18.9	122	−11.0	132	1.5

SOURCE: *Farm Production Practices, Costs and Returns*, BAE, *Statis. Bul.* 83, October, 1949.

cumulated in connection with the various crop-insurance plans of the government, which should be useful in studying the locational aspects of this problem.

FLUCTUATIONS IN YIELD BY PRODUCTS

A particular farmer is concerned about the yield attributes of each parcel of land which he farms; the community is affected by yield and production in the aggregate. Poor yields in some regions may be com-

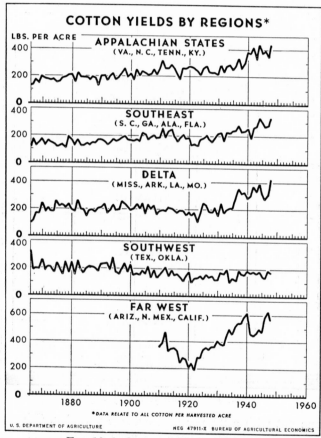

FIG. 12–2. Cotton yields by regions.

pensated by good yields elsewhere and as a result the total production of the particular product will be unaffected despite wide regional variations in yield. Or, on the other hand, large yields of a particular crop may offset the small yields of another crop in each region, and thus the yield index of each region is unaffected, while large fluctuations may occur in the output of particular products in the country as a whole. No crop for which we have data has as steady a record in yields as does the Pacific region; for example, rice from 1909–1949 showed an average year-to-year variation of 3.8 per cent, after allowing for the gradual improvements in yields, while the Pacific region for the period of our data, 1919–

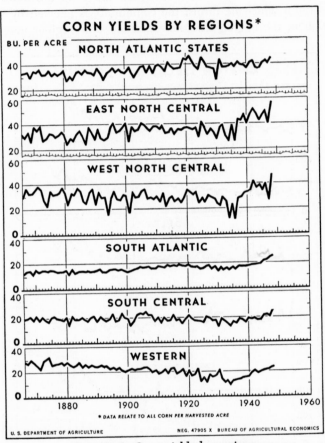

FIG. 12–3. Corn yields by regions.

1949, came out with a 2.1 per cent average variation. Other crops, for instance, flaxseed and apples, have had yield fluctuations exceeding even that of West North Central.

Again we need to repeat the caution that when yield data are based on harvested acres, as in the case in this section, by no means all of the effects of weather are represented. In the summary table that follows for 1909–1949, two highly durable products—rice and tobacco—lead the list

TABLE 12–4. SUMMARY OF VARIATIONS IN CROP YIELDS PER ACRE HARVESTED,
UNITED STATES, 1909–1949

	(1) Average deviation from preceding year, per cent	(2) Average annual improvement or decline, per cent	Net Deviation (1) − (2), per cent
Crop:			
Rice	4.6	0.80	3.80
Tobacco	5.6	1.19	4.41
Sugar beets	6.9	0.90	6.00
Sweet potatoes	6.3	0.11	6.19
Potatoes	9.7	2.85	6.85
Peanuts, picked and threshed	7.4	−0.35	7.05
Soybeans	11.0	3.10	7.90
Beans, dry, edible	8.8	0.73	8.07
Hay, all	8.6	0.43	8.17
Wheat, all	10.0	0.58	9.42
Cotton	12.1	1.45	10.65
Barley	14.0	0.64	13.36
Corn, all	15.2	1.01	14.19
Rye	15.0	−0.12	14.88
Oats	16.6	0.55	16.05
Sorghum grain	18.6	−0.17	18.43
Flaxseed	20.1	1.01	19.09
All apples	30.1	0.80	29.30
Commercial apples	33.5	1.86	31.64
Group of crops:			
18 field crops	7.0	1.00	6.00
28 crops	7.3	1.07	6.23
10 fruit crops	14.7	2.52	12.18
4 feed grains (corn, oats, barley, sorghum grain)	13.4	0.74	12.66
3 citrus fruits	19.6	1.19	18.41

SOURCE: *Crops and Markets,* Bureau of Agricultural Economics, Vol. XXVII (1950).

n having had the least yield instability while apples, a very perishable
ood, appear at the bottom.

The more perishable products show the following yield variations (see
Table 12–4).

Crop	*Yield variation,* *per cent*
Sweet potatoes	6.2
Potatoes	6.8
Three citrus fruits	18.4
Commercial apples	31.6

TABLE 12–5. PROFILE OF VARIATIONS IN CROP YIELDS PER ACRE HARVESTED, UNITED STATES, 1909–1949

Variations in yields per acre from preceding year, per cent	Rice	To-bacco	Sweet pota-toes	Sugar beets	18 field crops	28 crops	Peanuts, picked and threshed	Hay, all	Beans, dry, edible	Pota-toes	Wheat, all	Soy-beans
	Number of years											
+50.1 and over												
+40.1 to 50	....	....	....	....	....	....	....	1				
+30.1 to 40	1	....	....	....	1	1	1	1	....	1	....	1
+25.1 to 30	....	....	....	....	1	....	1	....	2	1	....	1
+20.1 to 25	....	....	1	1	....	1	....	2	....	2	2	
+15.1 to 20	....	1	....	....	1	1	....	....	4	2	1	2
+10.1 to 15	....	3	3	5	4	4	4	1	2	5	5	5
+ 5.1 to 10	6	11	8	8	4	3	7	7	6	4	9	2
0 to ±5	30	17	20	16	21	21	17	15	14	15	12	10
− 5.1 to 10	1	5	4	6	4	4	7	6	7	5	2	
−10.1 to 15	....	3	2	4	3	4	2	5	3	2	3	1
−15.1 to 20	1	....	2	....	1	1	1	1	1	3	5	1
−20.1 to 25	1	....	....	....	....	....	....	1	1	....	....	2
−25.1 to 30	....	....	....	....	....	....	....	....	....	....	1	
−30.1 to 40												
−40.1 to 50												
−50.1 and less												
Number of years	40	40	40	40	40	40	40	40	40	40	40	25
Average variation, per cent	4.6	5.6	6.3	6.9	7.0	7.3	7.4	8.6	8.8	9.7	10.0	11.0

TABLE 12–5. PROFILE OF VARIATIONS IN CROP YIELDS PER ACRE HARVESTED, UNITED STATES, 1909–1949. (*Continued*)

Variations in yields per acre from preceding year, per cent	Cotton	4 feed grains	Barley	Other fruits	10 fruit crops	Rye	Corn, all	Oats	Sorghum grain	3 citrus fruits	flaxseed	All apples	Commercial apples
								Number of years					
+50.1 and over		1			1	1	3	2	1	4	2	5	3
+40.1 to 50		1		1		2		1	1			2	3
+30.1 to 40	2	1	2	2	4	1			2	1	4	1	
+25.1 to 30		1	2	2	1			2	1	1	1		
+20.1 to 25	3		3	3		2	1	4	2	1	3		
+15.1 to 20	3		2	2	5	2	2	2	2	4	2	1	1
+10.1 to 15	6	6	5	4	2	3	5	2	1	4	2	1	1
+ 5.1 to 10	4	6	3	2	4	3	7	3	3	2	6	1	
0 to ±5	8	9	10	8	8	12	8	5	5	8	3	4	1
− 5.1 to 10	7	5	2	8	6	4	5	5	1	3	5	2	
−10.1 to 15	1	4	2	3	4	2	3	5	3	3	2	3	1
−15.1 to 20	5	3	4	3	2	1		3	2	3	4		1
−20.1 to 25		2	2	2		4	4	4	5	1	1	2	3
−25.1 to 30	1	1	3		2	2				1	2	2	
−30.1 to 40					1	1	2	2	1	1	1	1	1
−40.1 to 50											1	1	
−50.1 and less											1	1	
Number of years	40	40	40	40	40	40	40	40	30	40	40	27	15
Average variation, per cent	12.1	13.4	14.0	14.2	14.7	15.0	15.2	16.6	18.6	19.6	20.1	30.1	33.5

SOURCE: *Crops and Markets*, Bureau of Agricultural Economics, Vol. XXVII (1950), p. 6.

The more storable crops range from rice at 3.8 per cent and wheat at 9.4,[5] to flaxseed at 19.1 per cent. As might be expected, each of the major feed grains is more erratic in yields than is the aggregate of the four. But even at that, these four feed grains had a 12.7 per cent yield variation.

[5] For wheat, two studies by V. P. Timoshenko are very useful: "Variability in Wheat Yields and Output," *Wheat Studies*, Part I in Vol. XVIII (April, 1942) and Part II in Vol. XIX (March, 1943), Food Research Institute (Stanford, California).

13

STABILITY OF AGRICULTURAL INPUTS
AND PRODUCTION

The data on which this chapter is based contain three lessons: (1) the behavior of production inputs in agriculture viewed as aggregates, (2) the resulting outputs as national aggregates and also by products and regions, and (3) the divergencies between these inputs and outputs.

We shall examine the stability attributes of the input data[1] already considered in another context in Chap. 7. The input data of the Bureau of Agricultural Economics, it will be recalled, were modified as follows: (1) 1946–1948 input prices were used as weights and (2) the labor inputs from 1940 on were based on the Bureau of the Census estimates for farm-employment changes.

The best known production series is the widely used index of agricultural production[2] for sale and for home consumption on farms. This concept of production is quite appropriate in analyzing, for instance, how nonfarm storage and consumption are related to production. It does not, however, take account of changes in inventories on farms. Nor does it include that part of production which is used as producer goods in farming. Another concept of production, intended to represent the production of agriculture which becomes available eventually for human use, is the new Bureau of Agricultural Economics index referred to as farm output.[3] This index, however, is not a satisfactory one in gauging year-to-year changes because, among other things, it excludes all outputs of farms which are used by farmers as producer goods. The third concept, gross farm production,[3] is clearly the best for the purposes at hand. It represents all the production of crops, pasture consumed by livestock, and the products added in the conversion of feed and pasture into live-

---

[1] *Farm Production Practices, Costs and Returns*, BAE, *Statis. Bul.* 83 (October, 1949), Table 27; and Glen T. Barton and Martin R. Cooper, "Relation of Agricultural Production to Inputs," *Review of Economics and Statistics*, Vol. XXX (May, 1948). Also see Chaps. 3 and 7.

[2] A useful account of this concept and the index appears in *Consumption of Food in the United States, 1909–48*, USDA, *Misc. Pub.* 691, August, 1949.

[3] See Barton and Cooper, *op. cit.* for a more precise formulation.

stock and livestock products for human use and into farm-produced power by horses and mules. Gross farm production comes closest to accounting for all the year-to-year changes in production of farmers because it represents all outputs that are sold, that are consumed in the farm household, that are accumulated as farm inventories, and that are employed as producer goods by farmers. The importance of this more inclusive concept is readily apparent when one looks at the allocation and use of a given stock available at the outset of a crop year following, say, a bad yield. The various uses are interdependent because it is possible to transfer a part of the then existing stock from one use to another.

Stability of Production Inputs in Agriculture

The quantity of inputs committed to farm production from one year to the next is the most stable economic variable in agriculture. It is doubtful that one could find another major variable in the entire economy that is as steady—come depression followed by recovery, or mobilization, war and peace, or bumper crops, or a run of bad yields.[4] Variations in total inputs from year to year in agriculture, measured in terms of the change from the preceding year, corrected for the slow upward drift that has taken place, *averaged about 1 per cent per year* from 1910 to 1950. Gross farm production fluctuated on the average four times as much, although it is also one of the more stable variables in our economy.

In Chap. 7 we found that total inputs, when 1946–1948 input prices are used as weights, changed as follows:

Years	Input index
1910	96.9
1910–1914	100.0
1915–1919	103.5
1920–1924	107.1
1925–1929	106.8
1930–1934	104.8
1935–1939	101.9
1940–1944	103.4
1945–1949	108.6
1950	109.7

To recall the basic shifts among inputs, considered in Chap. 7, the data (shown on p. 211) are presented, again using 1946–1948 input prices as weights.

Let us now examine the year-to-year changes in the quantity of all inputs. The average variation, allowing for the secular increase, was, as

[4] The other side of this coin is the inelasticity of supply schedule of farm products, say, in a time interval of one to three production periods.

	Change from 1910 to 1950
Class of input	(1910 = 100)
Farm labor	72
Interest (horses, mules, motor vehicles, other machinery, crops and livestock)	131
Agricultural land	131
Miscellaneous (seed, short-term interest, and others) . . .	155
Taxes	175
Maintenance and depreciation	188
Fertilizer and lime	388
Operation of motor vehicles	278 (fold)
All inputs	114

has been said, about 1 per cent per year. In no year did farmers either increase or decrease inputs by more than 5 per cent from that of the preceding year. On four occasions, inputs were increased by 3 per cent or more: 1914 by 3.0 per cent; 1920 by 3.8 per cent; 1935 by 3.1 per cent; and 1949 by 3.0 per cent. Decreases of more than 3 per cent occurred only once; in 1934 inputs were 5 per cent less than in 1933, and this was largely an unplanned reduction caused by the widespread drought of 1934.

There is no need in belaboring the point, for even a cursory inspection of Table 13–12 will suffice to demonstrate that production inputs in American agriculture in the aggregate are extraordinarily stable from year to year. There is, however, another lesson in these data that should not be overlooked which contradicts a widely held belief regarding the planned contraction and expansion of agriculture: the belief that, no matter how adverse the farm price situation becomes relative to other prices, farmers do not and cannot contract their operation is fundamentally false. Clearly there have been two contraction periods.

The 1920–1924 period was adverse for agriculture because of the large drop in farm prices, absolute and also relative, following World War I. During the course of four years following 1920, total inputs were de-

TABLE 13–1. CONTRACTION IN AGRICULTURE, 1920 TO 1924

Year	Input index	Decrease from preceding year, per cent
1920	108	
1921	106	−1.9
1922	105	−0.9
1923	104	−1.0
1924	103	−1.0

TABLE 13–2. QUANTITY OF INPUTS IN AGRICULTURE, 1920 AND 1924

Class of inputs	Inputs measured in 1946–1948 dollars, in billions of dollars		Change in inputs from 1920 to 1924 (1920 = 100)
	1920	1924	
Farm labor	13.52	12.80	94.7
Agricultural land	5.00	4.86	97.2
Maintenance and depreciation	2.24	1.90	84.8
Interest (horses, mules, motor vehicles, other machinery, crops and livestock)	1.30	1.76	89.2
Miscellaneous	0.93	0.93	100.0
Taxes	0.71	0.92	129.6
Fertilizer	0.27	0.25	92.6
Operation of motor vehicles	0.19	0.35	184.2
All inputs	24.16	23.17	95.9

creased more than 4 per cent (see Table 13–1), not a large contraction to be sure, but a decline nevertheless which must be seen in a long-run context of rising inputs which not only was halted but reversed. The principal contraction was made in labor inputs, some in agricultural land and in interest, while taxes increased (unplanned) as did motor vehicles.

The years 1931–1933, the second period of contraction, are more important and also more instructive as indicated in Table 13–3.

TABLE 13–3. CONTRACTION IN AGRICULTURE, 1931 TO 1934

Year	Input index	Decrease from preceding year, per cent
1931	107	
1932	104	−2.8
1933	101	−2.9
1934	96	−5.0
1935	99	+3.1

Farm prices dropped about 40 per cent relative to other product prices and total production inputs were reduced nearly 6 per cent (or an elasticity of .15 in a three-year time interval); 1935 is included in Table 13–3 because a larger part of the 1934 decrease in inputs was unplanned. Inasmuch as most of the contraction in inputs was achieved by 1933 in examining the adjustment by classes of inputs, we shall restrict ourselves to 1931 and 1933 in Table 13–4.

TABLE 13–4. QUANTITY OF INPUTS IN AGRICULTURE, 1931 AND 1933

Class of input	Inputs measured in 1946–1948 dollars, in billions		Changes in inputs from 1931 to 1933 (1931 = 100)
	1931	1933	
Farm labor	12.66	12.15	96.1
Agricultural land	5.23	5.37	102.7
Maintenance and depreciation	1.74	1.44	82.8
Interest	1.42	1.06	74.6
Taxes	1.07	0.91	85.0
Miscellaneous	0.98	0.94	95.9
Operation of motor vehicles	0.59	0.54	91.5
Fertilizer and lime	0.23	0.17	73.9
All inputs	23.92	22.58	94.4

Among the particular inputs, fertilizer was reduced from an index of 106 in 1930 to 58 in 1932, a cut of over two-fifths when we take the two years indicated. Each class of inputs was reduced except agricultural land. Taxes (unplanned) also came down. Almost half of the total reduction in inputs was in farm labor.

The year 1916 stands out as a year when inputs were decreased substantially, a curtailment of 2.9 per cent from that of 1915. This reduction in inputs was, however, largely unplanned, for most of it came as a consequence of the very poor crops of that year when the production of food grain fell 44 per cent; feed grains, 20 per cent; and that of all crops, 10 per cent.

In periods when price incentives clearly call for expansion, as they did during World War I, 1917 to 1920 (with 1920 inputs planned on the bases of 1919 and early 1920 prices), the indications are that farmers increased production inputs 8 per cent. Production, however, was much less responsive than during World War II. The 1917–1920 period may be characterized as one of "diminishing returns" while 1939–1949 stands out as a period when marked advances in technology were achieved.

The 1939–1949 period requires more analysis. Let us compare the increase in inputs and in agricultural production:

	1939	1949	Increase, per cent
All inputs (index)	101	110	9
Gross farm production (index)	107	141	32

Despite the very favorable price situation for agriculture, in only one year during this period did farmers increase total inputs by more than 2 per cent from that achieved in the preceding year. The data clearly indicate that they proceeded to commit more inputs, but the yearly increases were small. Farmers concentrated heavily on the adoption of better production techniques and thus increased substantially the rate of output per unit of input.

The major inferences to be drawn from the data and analysis of inputs advanced in this section are (1) any instability that exists in the production of farm products as a whole is not the consequence of planned changes by farmers of the quantity of inputs which they commit to the production of farm products from one year to the next. In any short-run setting, the data indicate that the quantity of agricultural inputs committed by farmers is remarkably stable. (2) While some adjustment in the quantity of all inputs occurs in response to favorable and unfavorable turns in farm prices, contractions and expansions occur slowly but sight should not be lost of the fact that they do take place, given the appropriate economic incentives.

STABILITY ATTRIBUTES OF FARM PRODUCTION

There exists in agriculture a large uncontrolled element in production in any particular year because yields, especially in the case of crops, vary because of weather. We know from the preceding section, however, that the total inputs committed by farmers are seldom changed from one year to the next by as much as 3 per cent,[5] even when we include the unplanned adjustments in inputs made necessary by widespread crop failures or by bumper crops.

In this chapter, under the heading "Divergencies between Agricultural Inputs and Production," we shall consider briefly the more important divergencies between what might be thought of as "planned production" and "realized production." The data on inputs analyzed above give some dependable insights with regard to the first of these. We shall now turn to the farm production that is in fact realized. The data are from the Bureau of Agricultural Economics for *gross farm production* and the reasons for using this concept of production and the index prepared by the Bureau of Agricultural Economics have already been set forth.

Let us, however, examine a little more fully the production operations represented by the data that follow. The gross farm production of the

[5] Only twice during the 1910–1950 period did the change in inputs exceed 3 per cent, namely, in 1920 and 1934. In 1934, the widespread drought is largely the explanation (see Table 13–12).

United States, in any given year, represents not only the output realized from crops harvested that year but also the output of livestock fed, at least in part, on feed produced in the preceding year. The value added to the feed carried forward from earlier crops is credited to the particular livestock operations using them during the year the feed is fed. Feed used for horses and mules represents farm produced power and this feed is also entered into gross farm production on a value added basis. It may be helpful to consider two situations each of which is in a way a limiting case as we interpret the American scene.

Situation 1. Suppose that for a series of years there is no change in the total inputs planned, or in the subclasses of inputs committed to agricultural production, or in technology, and that all yields in each of these years are "normal" and that these yields were expected. The results are (1) that realized production will equal planned production and (2) that production will be the same each year. Suppose further that farmers do not change (1) their inventories of farm products, (2) the amounts of farm products consumed in farm households, and (3) the amounts of farm products employed as inputs in farm production; it then follows from these conditions that the quantity of farm products sold to the nonfarm sectors of the economy will remain the same each year.

Situation 2. Let us suppose, as we did above, that farmers do not change the total inputs planned for the year but that they expect the yield, say, of feeds to vary widely and they, therefore, carry forward as "normal" large inventories of feed and it turns out that the yield of all feeds drops substantially because of bad weather. This situation will reduce the planned inputs allocated to grow feed because fewer inputs are required to harvest a small feed crop than are needed for a normal crop. But the total inputs for animal production may remain unchanged in the event that farmers decide to draw down their inventories of feed enough to maintain the production and sales of livestock and livestock products. Observe the consequences: the amount of farm products sold to the nonfarm sectors will not be reduced from that of the preceding year although gross farm production falls. A situation in which the drop in farm production causes farmers to increase their sales of farm products may arise in the event of a widespread feed crop failure, so severe that feed inventories are altogether too small to maintain the former rate of livestock production and that herds (inventories of livestock on farms) are, therefore, reduced. Under these conditions the actual sale of farm products to the nonfarm sectors will increase as a consequence of the fall in gross farm production caused by the drastic drop in yields of feed crops and the curtailment in livestock operations made necessary by the reduced output of feed.

VOLUME OF FARM OUTPUT, AND PRODUCTION BY GROUPS
OF PRODUCTS, UNITED STATES, 1910-48
INDEX NUMBERS (1935-39=100)

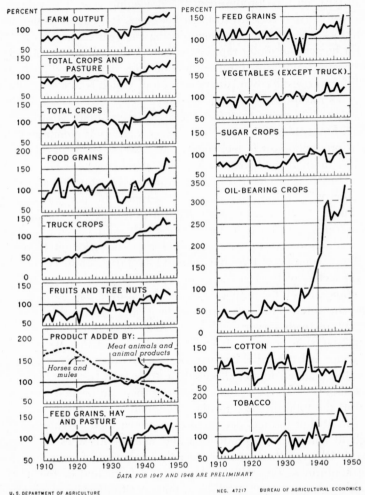

DATA FOR 1947 AND 1948 ARE PRELIMINARY

U. S. DEPARTMENT OF AGRICULTURE   NEG. 47217   BUREAU OF AGRICULTURAL ECONOMICS

FIG. 13–1. Volume of farm output and production by groups of products,
United States, 1910–1948.

Data on farm production permit two general approaches, one by
products and groups of products for the United States as a whole from
1910 to 1950, and the other by major geographical regions from 1919 to
1949. As in the case of our analysis of yields, the first approach prepares
the ground for getting at the effects of variations in farm production
upon the supply available in the stock period of particular farm products

and of farm products taken all together. In the second, we move closer to the effects of these variations in farm production upon location and upon farmers operating in particular regions.

Gross Farm Production in the United States. Despite the large year-to-year fluctuations in the production of cotton, tobacco, food grains, and vegetables other than truck crops, the variations, in total production measured as a change from that of the preceding year, averaged only 5 per cent per year from 1910 to 1950. The figure is reduced to 4 per cent when we correct for the upward trend in production (see Table 13–5). The over-all steadiness of farm production comes about mainly because of the very even rate of operation that characterizes the production of meat animals and of animal products.

TABLE 13–5. YEAR-TO-YEAR VARIATIONS IN GROSS FARM PRODUCTION BY GROUPS OF PRODUCTS, UNITED STATES, 1910–1950

Products	(1) Average variations from preceding year, per cent	(2) Variations ascribed to trend, per cent	(3) Difference (1) − (2), per cent
Total gross farm production . . .	5.1	1.1	4.0
Truck crops	5.6	5.0	0.6
Product added by meat animals and animal products	2.7	1.9	0.8
Product added by horses and mules	3.5	−1.7	1.8
Oil-bearing crops	20.1	18.2	1.9
Total crops and pasture	7.2	1.1	6.1
Total crops	8.0	1.2	6.8
Sugar crops	9.5	0.7	8.8
Feed grains, hay and pasture . .	10.1	0.7	9.4
Vegetables, except truck	11.0	0.7	10.3
Food grains	12.7	1.8	10.9
Tobacco	14.7	2.4	12.3
Fruits and tree nuts	15.1	1.7	13.4
Feed grains	15.4	0.7	14.7
Cotton	17.4	0.0	17.4

SOURCE: *Farm Production Practices, Costs and Returns*, BAE, *Statis. Bul.* 83, October, 1949. Data for 1949 and 1950 supplied to writer by the Bureau of Agricultural Economics.

The profile of variations in Table 13–6 lends additional support to the thesis that farm production taken as a whole is quite stable although it varies four times as much as does total inputs. In twenty-five of the forty years, the variations from the preceding year did not exceed ±5 per cent. In only six years during the entire period was there a fall in excess of

TABLE 13–6. PROFILE OF YEAR-TO-YEAR VARIATIONS IN GROSS FARM PRODUCTION AND GROUPS OF COMMODITIES, UNITED STATES, 1910–1950

Variations in gross farm production from preceding year, per cent	Total gross farm production	Total truck crops	Product added by meat animals and animal products	Product added by horses and mules	Oil-bearing crops	Total crops and pasture	Total crops	Sugar crops	Feed grains, hay and pasture	Vegetables except truck	Food grains	Tobacco	Fruits and tree nuts	Feed grains	Cotton
									Number of years						
+31 and over	....	....	....	....	8	1	2	....	2	1	2	4	3	3	4
+21 to 30	1	....	....	....	4	1	....	1	2	3	3	3	3	2	3
+16 to 20	1	2	....	....	4	....	1	5	....	1	3	2	3	3	4
+11 to 15	1	3	1	....	2	3	3	3	2	6	3	4	2	3	4
+6 to 10	6	7	5	....	4	6	6	8	7	4	5	4	4	3	4
0 to ±5	25	24	33	34	6	22	20	13	15	11	13	10	9	11	9
− 6 to 10	5	4	1	6	3	3	3	4	6	6	2	3	8	5	2
−11 to 15	1	....	....	....	4	3	3	2	3	4	4	4	2	4	1
−16 to 20	....	....	....	....	2	1	2	2	1	4	3	2	1	1	1
−21 to 30	....	....	....	....	1	....	....	2	2	....	1	2	3	3	4
−31 and less	....	....	....	....	2	....	....	....	....	....	1	2	2	2	4
Number of years	40	40	40	40	40	40	40	40	40	40	40	40	40	40	40
Average variation in per cent per year	5.1	5.6	2.7	3.5	20.1	7.2	8.0	9.5	10.1	11.0	12.7	14.7	15.1	15.4	17.4
Trend in per cent per year	1.1	5.0	1.9	−1.7	18.2	1.1	1.2	0.7	0.7	0.7	1.8	2.4	1.7	0.7	−0.1
Difference	4.0	0.6	0.8	1.8	1.9	6.1	6.8	8.8	9.4	10.3	10.9	12.3	13.4	14.7	17.4

SOURCE: *Farm Production Practices, Costs and Returns*, BAE, *Statis. Bul.* 83, October, 1949.

this figure. The largest came in 1934, with a decline of 14 per cent; in 1936 and 1921 it was 10 per cent; and in 1913, 1916, and 1933, only 7 per cent. Even these extreme changes on the downward side look small indeed when compared with the very large drops that frequently occur in industry. The largest increases are partly the result of recovering from a small production, for instance, the 23 per cent jump in 1937 reflects, in part, the recovery from the poor crop of 1936; and the figure for 1935, that from 1934.

But how meaningful an aggregate is farm production taken as a whole when we come to analyze effects of these variations on the supply during the stock period (during a given year after the harvest is completed)? A variation in one product may be offset by an opposite variation in another product and if the two products can be substituted readily the aggregate is, of course, meaningful. Barley, oats, grain sorghum, and corn, the principal feed grains, each show larger variations than do total feed grains. But no such meaningful substitution exists either in further production or in consumption among cotton, tobacco, and the food grains or between these and feed grains except that some food grains are used for feed. Where storage is possible, as in the case of many of these products, substitution over time is possible and important. Clearly, however, the average variations in production per year of many farm products are so large and the profile indicates such a wide scatter that these fluctuations in production must place, so it would seem, a very heavy burden upon storage operations if anything approaching an even flow of product over time is to be achieved.

Gross Farm Production by Regions

Location, and the effects of variations in production upon farmers, is the problem on which this section has a bearing. The series covering 1919–1949, however, is altogether too short, especially in view of the erratic and long series of both good and bad years that occur in the plains states. After correcting for the upward drift in production, four regions indicate low year-to-year variations, less than 5 per cent per year; and two regions show average variations of about 10 per cent. Table 13–7 summarizes these data.

We shall include profile data in Table 13–8 for each of the nine regions but restrict our interpretations to the Pacific and New England regions which have the least variations and to the West South and West North Central regions which have the most.

The Two Stable Ends—the Pacific and New England. The profile of production variations for the Pacific shows only one year (1924) with a

TABLE 13–7. YEAR-TO-YEAR VARIATIONS IN GROSS FARM PRODUCTION BY REGIONS AND
FOR THE UNITED STATES, 1919–1949

United States and regions	(1) Average variation from preceding year, per cent	(2) Variations ascribed to trend, per cent	(3) Difference (1) − (2), per cent
United States	5.3	1.1	4.2
Pacific	4.3	3.2	1.1
New England	3.0	0.8	2.2
Middle Atlantic	4.3	0.4	3.9
Mountain	6.2	1.9	4.3
South Atlantic	6.7	1.4	5.3
East North Central	6.7	1.0	5.7
East South Central	7.8	1.0	6.8
West North Central	10.1	0.7	9.4
West South Central	11.0	0.7	10.3

SOURCE: *Farm Production Practices, Costs and Returns*, BAE, *Statis. Bul.* 83, October, 1949.

decrease of more than 5 per cent from the preceding year. The 14.5 per cent drop in 1924 reflects partly the fact that 1923 was a very good year and partly the 47 per cent drop in food grains, 33 per cent in feed grains, 23 per cent in vegetables other than truck crops, and 21 per cent drop in fruits and tree nuts. The variations on the upward side of more than 5 per cent are, in large part, the result of the pronounced upward trend in production in that region. In New England, production fell more than 5 per cent only three times: 1920, 6 per cent (largely planned); 1938, 5.8 per cent; and 1944, 5.7 per cent. On the other side, there were only four years, despite a substantial upward trend in production, that exceeded 5 per cent: a 5.4 per cent increase in 1923; 6.1 per cent in 1937; 8.6 per cent in 1942 and 7.9 per cent in 1943.

The Unstable Center—West South and West North Central. These two large regions representing fully a third of American agriculture (by production for sale and for consumption on farms) show very large variations in production from year to year even when one takes all farm production together. It should also be noted that the West North Central region includes two states, Iowa and Minnesota, which are relatively stable in production and important in volume, thus dampening appreciably the averages appearing in our data. In this region, only twelve of the thirty years fell within the ±5 per cent range. There were two years when production fell drastically: 33 per cent in 1934 and 24 per cent in 1936. In 1933 it was down 16 per cent and in 1947, 10 per cent. The experiences in the West South Central region were all too similar—a

TABLE 13–8. PROFILE OF THE YEAR-TO-YEAR VARIATIONS IN GROSS FARM PRODUCTION BY REGIONS AND FOR THE UNITED STATES, 1919–1950

Variations in gross farm production from preceding year, per cent	U.S.[a]	Pacific	New England	M. Atlantic	Mountain	S. Atlantic	E.N. Central	E.S. Central	W.N. Central	W.S. Central
					Number of years					
+31 and over	...	...	...	...	...	...	...	...	2	2
+21 to +30	1	...	...	...	...	...	2	2	...	1
+16 to +20	1	...	...	...	1	1	1	...	1	1
+11 to +15	1	1	...	1	2	4	1	2	2	2
+6 to +10	3	7	4	5	7	4	4	5	5	6
0 to ±5	21	21	23	20	15	16	15	13	12	6
−6 to −10	3	...	3	3	3	3	4	4	5	6
−11 to −15	1	1	...	1	2	...	3	3	...	4
−16 to −20	...	...	...	...	...	2	...	1	1	1
−21 to −30	...	...	...	...	...	...	...	...	1	1
−31 and less	...	...	...	...	...	...	...	...	1	...
Number of years	31	30	30	30	30	30	30	30	30	30
Average variation in per cent per year	5.3	4.3	3.0	4.3	6.2	6.7	6.7	7.8	10.1	11.0
Trend in per cent per year	1.1	3.2	0.8	0.4	1.9	1.4	1.0	1.0	0.7	0.7
Difference	4.2	1.1	2.2	3.9	4.3	5.3	5.7	6.8	9.4	10.3

[a] Data for the United States are for the period 1919–1950 and for the regions for 1919–1949.

SOURCE: *Farm Production Practices, Costs and Returns,* BAE, *Statis. Bul.* 83, October, 1949.

TABLE 13–9. VARIATIONS IN GROSS FARM PRODUCTION BY PRODUCTS AND REGIONS, 1919–1949, AND FOR THE UNITED STATES, 1910–1950

(In per cent, net variations)

Products	United States	Pacific	New England	M. At-lantic	Moun-tain	S. At-lantic	E.N. Central	E.S. Central	W.N. Central	W.S. Central
Total gross farm products	4.0	1.1	2.2	3.9	4.3	5.3	5.7	6.8	9.4	10.3
Truck crops	0.6	a	6.3	3.6	a	3.4	3.7	3.5	13.3	7.4
Product added by meat animals and animal products	0.8	0.1	1.3	0.3	2.0	0.0	1.0	1.1	3.9	2.2
Product added by horses and mules	1.8	2.5	1.8	2.2	1.8	0.8	3.0	0.9	2.5	1.9
Oil-bearing crops	1.9	a	....	a	63.0	6.4	a	15.2	12.4	a
Total crops and pasture	6.1	1.4	3.8	6.9	5.8	7.3	9.8	8.0	15.3	14.0
Total crops	6.8	1.9	4.2	8.0	7.7	7.6	10.7	11.6	18.1	15.6
Sugar crops	8.8	16.8	28.2	28.2	17.5	12.2	24.9	14.0	15.5	16.5
Feed grains, hay and pasture	9.4	4.2	4.8	8.1	5.8	6.5	12.5	10.2	19.7	13.9
Vegetables except truck	10.3	7.0	13.0	13.0	9.2	11.8	17.0	13.9	21.9	12.9
Food grains	10.9	14.0	....	11.1	16.2	13.7	22.7	27.7	18.8	25.8
Tobacco	12.3	....	11.7	14.8	....	18.3	13.0	19.3	17.9	....
Fruits and tree nuts	13.4	5.2	25.1	40.8	13.2	17.6	45.8	49.0	53.7	24.4
Feed grains	14.7	18.6	4.3	10.3	19.5	8.1	18.5	13.5	27.3	17.6
Cotton	17.4	a	....	....	3.4	17.1	....	18.6	19.0	23.0

a Figure omitted because large year-to-year increases ascribed to growth clearly overshadow "yield" variations.

SOURCE: *Farm Production Practices, Costs and Returns*, BAE, *Statis. Bul.* 83, October, 1949.

drop of 22 per cent in 1934, 18 per cent in 1921, 15 per cent in 1927, and 13 per cent in 1945 and also in 1938, to cite the extreme cases.

Cross-sectional Data of Product and Region. Meat animals require feed; the variations in production of feed and animals by regions are shown in Table 13–10.

TABLE 13–10. YEAR-TO-YEAR VARIATIONS IN PRODUCTION OF FEED AND MEAT ANIMALS

Region	Average year-to-year variations in production, 1919–1949[a]		
	Feed grains, per cent	Feed grains, hay and pasture, per cent	Meat animals and products, per cent
West North Central	27.3	19.7	3.9
Mountain	19.5	5.8	2.0
East North Central	18.5	12.5	1.0
West South Central	17.6	13.9	2.2
Pacific	13.6	4.2	0.1
East South Central	13.5	10.2	1.1
Middle Atlantic	10.3	8.1	0.3
South Atlantic	8.1	6.5	0.0
New England	4.3	4.8	1.3
United States (1910–1950)	14.7	9.4	0.8

[a] These averages have been corrected for variations ascribable to the trend in each region.

Unless we assume that the efficiency with which feed is fed varies widely from year to year or that large amounts of feed are imported and exported, data appearing in Table 13–10 indicate that feed is substituted over time to a considerable extent to compensate for the instability in yields of feed crops. Feed is also transferred from one region to another. Both the east and west coast areas are normally deficient in feed while parts of the interior—the western fringe of the corn belt and sections of the plains states—usually have a surplus. The deficient areas, however, manage to keep their production of meat animals and of animal products on a much more even keel than do the feed surplus areas. 1934 was a very bad year for feed grains. The production index dropped from 123 in 1932 to 95 in 1933 and then down to 62 in 1934; and that for feed grains, hay, and pasture from 113 in 1932 to 96 and then to 72 in 1934 for the United States as a whole. Where did farmers curtail their livestock operations? Not in the Pacific region although the production of feed grains within that region fell both in 1933 and 1934; on the contrary, meat animal output rose 2.3 per cent in 1934. In five other

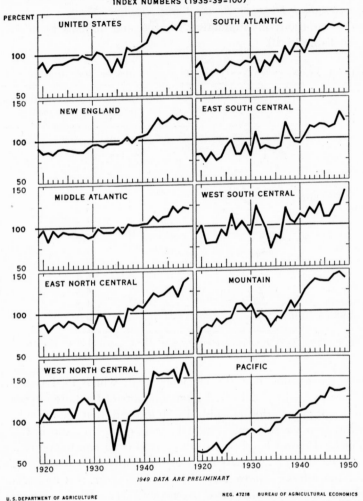

VOLUME OF FARM OUTPUT, BY GEOGRAPHIC
DIVISIONS, 1919-49
INDEX NUMBERS (1935-39=100)

U.S. DEPARTMENT OF AGRICULTURE   NEG. 47218 BUREAU OF AGRICULTURAL ECONOMICS

FIG. 13–2. Volume of farm output by geographic divisions, 1919–1949.

regions the reduction in meat animals and animal products was 3 per cent or less. The three regions that bore the brunt were the West North Central, in which the output was cut 12.5 per cent; the West South Central, 8 per cent; and the East North Central, 6 per cent. Moreover, feed stocks were so depleted and herds sufficiently curtailed that the West North Central regions reduced its output of meat animals and animal products another 9.5 per cent in 1935 and the West South Central by 7.5 per cent, whereas the other regions proceeded to increase their production of these products.

It is significant that 1946 should be the year when the Pacific, New England, South and Middle Atlantic regions made the largest single reduction in meat animal outputs during the three decades, 1919–1949. Feed crops were large and pastures good but the integrating capacity of the market was substantially impaired by price controls.

TABLE 13–11. YEAR-TO-YEAR VARIATIONS IN PRODUCTION OF FRUITS AND TREE NUTS, TRUCK CROPS, VEGETABLES, FOOD GRAINS, AND COTTON

Region	Average year-to-year variations in production, 1919–1949,[a] per cent				
	Fruits and tree nuts	Truck crops	Other vegetables	Food grains	Cotton
Pacific	5.2	[b]	7.0	14.0	[b]
Mountain	13.2	[b]	9.2	16.2	....
South Atlantic	17.6	3.4	11.8	....	17.1
West South Central	24.4	7.4	12.9	25.8	23.0
New England	25.1	6.3	13.0	....	....
Middle Atlantic	40.8	3.6	13.0	....	....
East North Central	45.8	3.7	17.0	22.7	....
East South Central	49.0	3.5	13.9	....	18.6
West North Central	53.7	13.3	21.9	18.8	....

[a] Averages have been corrected for variations ascribable to the trend in each region.

[b] Figure is not used because the upward trend has been so pronounced that it dominates the year-to-year variations observed.

As indicated in Table 13–11, the production realized for fruits and tree nuts is relatively stable in the Pacific region; elsewhere, except perhaps in the Mountain and South Atlantic, it is exceedingly unstable. Truck crops, except for the West North Central, are outstanding among all the crops for their production stability while other vegetables appear to hold an intermediate position between that of truck crops and that of fruits and tree nuts. The food grains and cotton are highly erratic in production in each of the regions in which they are grown (data on cotton in California is dominated by the rapid increase that has occurred).

Nearly all the other farm products than can be identified in our data are concentrated in a few regions and, therefore, cross-sectional analysis by product and regions is not meaningful.

Divergencies between Agricultural Inputs and Production

Both inputs and production are variables. If production were completely controlled by farmers, all inputs could be planned and planned production would equal realized production. Under these circumstances, the relation between the inputs planned and committed and the production realized would simply be a function of a particular technology.

We know, however, that technology in agriculture has not remained unchanged. The gradual rise of the production index relative to the input index suggests that substantial technical advances have been achieved, a process which we have examined in some detail in Chap. 7. The change in technology, however, from one year to the next, it may be presumed, is relatively small and it may therefore be neglected in examining year-to-year changes in the relation between inputs and production. Even under conditions where the technology is known and remains unchanged, as we shall assume is the case in the comparisons of year-to-year variations of inputs and production that follow, the input variable is only partially planned (price determined) in any particular year. In the first place, weather is in substance a complementary "input," an exogenous variable, not price determined, and let us assume, unpredictable for a particular year. In the second place, a change in the weather makes it necessary for farms to alter their planned inputs; for example, in the event of a bumper crop more inputs are required to harvest the crop than would be needed to garner a "normal" crop and conversely in the event of a crop failure.

What are the divergencies between inputs and production from one year to the next? It is convenient to construct a *divergency index* by taking the index of gross farm production and dividing it by the index of agricultural inputs.[6] If we then compare the index of a particular year with that of the preceding year, we can determine whether a divergency occurred and we can also measure the variation. For example, if the inputs were reduced, say about 3 per cent, as they were in 1922, and production also was 3 per cent less, no divergency would have occurred. Or, if inputs were increased, say 2 per cent, as in 1908, and production was the same as that of the preceding year, the divergency index in this instance falls 2 per cent.

The year-to-year variations of the divergency index averaged nearly 4 per cent per year for the 1910–1950 period after correcting for the

[6] More precisely, as is done in Table 13–12, we have taken the gross farm production index ÷ agricultural inputs index × 100. This index may be viewed, also, as a measure of year-to-year changes in over-all yield in agriculture.

variations ascribable to the upward trend in production relative to inputs. The following data permit several comparisons.

	(1)	(2)	(3)
	Average year-to-year variations, per cent per year	Variations ascribable to trend, per cent per year	Difference (1) − (2), per cent per year
Agricultural inputs 1910–1950	1.4	0.3	1.1
Gross farm production 1910–1950	5.1	1.1	4.0
Input-production divergency 1910–1950 . .	4.6	0.7	3.9
Cropland yield 1919–1949.	8.2	1.1	7.1

Column 3 indicates that the year-to-year variation in yield from cropland is nearly twice as great as that of gross farm production. Viewed from the other end of the scale, the year-to-year variation in agricultural inputs (column 3) is only about one-fourth as large as that of production and of the divergency between inputs and production and about one-seventh of that of cropland yield.

A closer examination of the divergency index will show that while it has virtually the same average variation as gross farm production (4 and 3.9 per cent per year as indicated in column 3), the changes in any particular year are not the same. In years of large changes in production, the divergency tends to be less than the changes in production, as may be seen from the following data:

Year	Change from preceding year, per cent	
	Production index	Divergency index
1937	23.0	20.5
1935	18.3	15.3
1934	−13.7	−9.6
1942	10.8	7.2
1936	−10.2	−10.2
1921	−10.0	−8.5
1948	8.3	7.9
1914	8.0	4.5
1913	−7.4	−8.2
1916	−7.2	−4.2
1931	7.1	6.5

TABLE 13–12. AGRICULTURAL INPUTS, PRODUCTION, AND THE DIVERGENCY BETWEEN THEM FROM YEAR TO YEAR, UNITED STATES, 1910–1950

(1935–1939 = 100)

Year	Agricultural inputs[a]		Gross farm production[b]		Input-production divergency[c]		Cropland yield[b]	
	Index	Change from preceding year, per cent	Index	Change from preceding year, per cent	Index	Change from preceding year, per cent	Index	Change from preceding year, per cent
1910	95	.....	88	......	93			
1911	97	2.1	88	0.0	91	−4.3		
1912	98	1.0	95	8.0	97	6.6		
1913	99	1.0	88	−7.4	89	−8.2		
1914	102	3.0	95	8.0	93	4.5		
1915	103	1.0	98	3.2	95	2.2		
1916	100	−2.9	91	−7.2	91	−4.2		
1917	100	0.0	96	5.6	96	5.5		
1918	102	2.0	96	0.0	94	−2.1		
1919	104	2.0	96	0.0	92	−2.1	96	
1920	108	3.8	101	5.2	94	2.2	106	10.4
1921	106	−1.9	91	−10.0	86	−8.5	90	−15.1
1922	105	−0.9	97	6.6	92	7.0	98	8.9
1923	104	−1.0	98	1.0	94	2.2	98	0.0
1924	103	−1.0	97	−1.0	94	0.0	97	−1.0
1925	103	0.0	99	2.0	96	2.1	100	3.0
1926	104	1.0	101	2.0	97	1.0	101	1.0
1927	105	1.0	100	−1.0	95	−2.0	100	−1.0
1928	106	1.0	102	2.0	96	1.0	103	3.0
1929	106	0.0	101	−1.0	95	−1.0	100	−2.9
1930	107	0.9	98	−3.0	92	−3.2	94	−6.0
1931	107	0.0	105	7.1	98	6.5	103	9.6
1932	104	−2.8	102	−3.0	98	0.0	99	−3.9
1933	101	−2.9	95	−7.0	94	−4.1	89	−10.0
1934	96	−5.0	82	−13.7	85	−9.6	73	−18.0
1935	99	3.1	97	18.3	98	15.3	96	31.5
1936	99	0.0	87	−10.2	88	−10.2	81	−15.6
1937	101	2.0	107	23.0	106	20.5	111	37.0
1938	101	0.0	104	−3.0	103	−2.8	105	−5.4
1939	101	0.0	105	1.0	104	1.0	107	2.0

TABLE 13–12. AGRICULTURAL INPUTS, PRODUCTION, AND THE DIVERGENCY BETWEEN THEM
FROM YEAR TO YEAR, UNITED STATES, 1910–1950. (*Continued*)

Year	Agricultural inputs[a]		Gross farm production[b]		Input-production divergency[c]		Cropland yield[b]	
	Index	Change from preceding year, per cent	Index	Change from preceding year, per cent	Index	Change from preceding year, per cent	Index	Change from preceding year, per cent
1940	102	1.0	108	2.9	106	1.9	111	3.7
1941	100	−2.0	111	2.8	111	4.7	113	1.8
1942	101	1.0	123	10.8	122	9.9	124	9.7
1943	102	0.0	120	−2.4	118	−3.3	115	−7.2
1944	103	1.0	124	3.3	120	1.7	122	6.1
1945	104	1.0	123	−0.8	118	−1.7	121	−0.8
1946	105	1.0	126	2.4	120	1.7	130	7.4
1947	106	1.0	121	−4.0	114	−5.0	122	−6.1
1948	107	1.0	131	8.3	122	7.0	137	12.3
1949	110	3.0	129	−1.7	117	−4.1	130	−5.1
1950	108	−2.0	126	−2.4	117	0.0		
Average variation in per cent per year . . .	...	1.4	...	5.1	...	4.6	...	8.2
Variation ascribable to trend	...	0.3	...	1.1	...	0.7	...	1.1
Difference	...	1.1	...	4.0	...	3.9	...	7.1

[a] Based on unpublished data made available by the Bureau of Agricultural Economics. Inputs are weighted by 1946–1948 input prices in agriculture.

[b] *Farm Production Practices, Costs and Returns*, BAE, Statis. Bul. 83, October, 1949.

[c] Gross farm production index divided by input index multiplied by 100 equals the input-production divergency index.

In the eleven years when gross farm production changed 7 per cent or more from that of the preceding year, the divergency index changed less than production except for 1913 when it fell more and 1936 when it fell exactly as much. In years when the changes in production were smaller than this, there were a number when the divergency index varied more than production. In 1911, production was the same as in 1910, but the divergency index fell 4.3 per cent; in 1918 and also in 1919, production was unchanged from the preceding year, while the divergency index fell 2.1 per cent in each of the two years.

We infer from the above analysis the following: Planned agricultural inputs vary even less from one year to the next than do the actual inputs which have varied on the average only about 1 per cent per year. In years of relatively large or small crops, farmers find it necessary to adjust their planned inputs. It is this adjustment in inputs which makes the divergency index less variable in years when the changes in yields are relatively large. The presumption, therefore, is that this attribute of the divergency index provides a clue to the year-to-year variations between planned inputs and realized production. A true measure of the year-to-year differences between planned inputs and realized production, taking account of all agricultural production, would accordingly indicate variation somewhat larger than that of gross farm production but not as large as that of crop yields because of the stabilizing effects of livestock operations generally.

We need to stress once more, however, that we have been analyzing large national aggregates which are like icebergs largely hidden from view. These aggregates hide important differences among regions and among types of farms. The divergencies that have been observed are not spread evenly over agriculture. Some regions and within these, particular groups of farmers, bear the brunt of these variations as was evident from the preceding sections. The aggregates are, nevertheless, useful information for they tell us that, taking the United States as a whole, despite the instability in crop yields, farmers operate their farms in such a way that they counteract and compensate to a substantial extent the adverse effects of crop yields upon gross farm production. As a consequence, the production of agriculture is one of the more stable variables of major importance in the United States economy. The stability of agricultural inputs is even more impressive.

14

PRODUCER SUPPLY DURING THE STOCK PERIOD

Once the crop is made, it does not follow that producers will sell all of it. The price which they receive, or expect to receive, will affect the amount of the product which will be used in the farm household, employed in further production on the farm, held to meet future contingencies, and withheld when price expectations are favorable. Accordingly, these questions arise: When the price of a farm product rises relative to other products, how much substitution will take place in the farm household? Will the increase in income that results from a rise in price reduce or increase the amount of home-produced food which farm families consume? How will the income and substitution effects of a change in price work out in the farm business? How will the amount of farm product which farmers store be affected?

Our purpose is to explain and gauge the substitution and income effects within the farm household and the farm business upon the supply of farm products represented by the sales of farmers to the nonfarm sectors during the interval between harvests. We shall look upon this interval as the *stock period*. We shall find that the concept of a stock period for the supply is both necessary and useful analytically. The information now available, although scanty, will permit us to indicate in a rough sort of way what the relevant price and income elasticities are for farm families in poor and rich communities, although most of our data are for the United States. The importance of substitution in the farm household and farm business will become fairly clear. The nature of the income elasticity of home-produced products for farm families is also quite firm. But the effects of changes in income in the farm business upon inventories with uncertainty present are exceedingly difficult to discern.

We may anticipate one of the major results that emerges, namely, the economic importance of the income effect within farm households upon the slope of the producer supply in different communities. In a rich community, where farmers enjoy a high level of living and where home-produced food has become for them an inferior good against income, both the income and substitution effects of a rise in the farm price contribute to a forward-sloping producer supply schedule. In a poor community, however, characteristic of a high-food-drain economy, where farmers (cultivators) prefer much more food when their income rises, the income effects operating through farm households can be, and frequently are, so powerful that they override whatever substitution may occur and give rise to a backward-sloping producer supply. One of the consequences of this is an unstable market situation.

THE CONCEPT OF THE STOCK PERIOD

It is necessary, especially in agriculture, to distinguish among three types of producer supply. We have the two supply concepts usually employed in economic analysis, namely, the supply in the long and in the short run, to which we shall add the concept of the supply of producers during the stock period, which represents the time interval during which neither variable nor "fixed" costs in production are relevant to the supply of producers. It is the period during which the stock under the control of producers is given by the harvest and the carry-over of producers. The stock period is particularly important in agriculture because of the periodicity of production. The length of the stock period will vary from product to product, depending upon the technical conditions underlying production. It may take a day, a month, a year, or even longer to increase the quantity available by additional production. We shall take the stock period to mean the time interval between harvests and thus distinguish it from the concept of the supply in either its short- or long-run setting, where first variable costs, one class of inputs, and then also "fixed" costs, another set of inputs, enter into the determination of the supply.

In those branches of production where the output approaches that of flow, it may be difficult to identify the supply during the stock period because it will blend almost imperceptibly into current production and into supply adjustments both short and long run. Agricultural products, however, do not for the most part have the attributes of a flow; they have typically a jerky production pattern set by nature with its season for gestation and growth which have been modified as yet only slightly by those who plant, breed, and feed. The seasonality of agricultural production continues to be one of its basic characteristics and the economic system is confronted by a sequence of outputs, each of which becomes a stock for a time. Since the realized production entering into the stock at the beginning of such a period may be larger or smaller than was the planned production, this sequence of stocks also has the attribute of a series of shocks. We shall, however, simplify the analysis in order to make it manageable by leaving yield uncertainty aside and by taking a particular harvest and assuming that it is completed, that the production and farm carry-over are known, and that farmers and all other users of the product proceed to adjust their plans to the stock at hand. It is, of course, well known that the consumption of farm products is not nearly as seasonal or jerky as is production; in fact, many farm products are consumed at a remarkably steady rate throughout the year. We live not like the proverbial grasshopper but like the well-stocked bee.

By Way of Explanation

We shall now outline and examine the ways in which the actions of a farmer will affect the supply during the stock period. There are two sets of such actions; they are the acts involved in operating the farm household and the farm business.[1] Both sets can be identified. The decisions taken by the farmer, or by the farm family, in carrying out these two operations will determine how much of the stock[2] under the control of the farmer will be sold. The farmer along with his other activities is viewed as a seller who determines the amount of the stock which he will sell; and the result is the supply schedule on which we are concentrating. This supply schedule is not necessarily vertical, because the farmer may sell none, some fraction, or all of his stock; the amount he sells will depend upon the price and his response to price will depend, in turn, upon the substitution effects and income effects within the particular farm household and farm business.[3]

A fall in the price of a product induces substitution in the farm household if the product enters into consumption of the farm family; and, also, in the farm business, if it is used as a resource in producing other farm products. In order to see this without becoming involved in the income effects, let us suppose that a large crop of potatoes reduces the price below the normal level but that other products which the potato producer sells are higher in price, sufficiently so that the income of the farmer is not diminished by the fall in the potato price. Given the lower potato price, the farm family is induced to substitute potatoes for other foods, as are other consumers, and in addition the farmer may substitute some potatoes for other feedstuff in his livestock enterprises. The role of the farmer as consumer in this sphere can be seen more clearly if we assume that he exchanges all the product he has produced for money.

[1] We shall not consider at this time the problem of inventories and the structure of assets held by a farmer and the effects of these upon the supply as herein defined.

[2] Stock is equal to carry-over plus realized production.

[3] Uncertainty aside at this point.

He would then be in a position comparable to that of any other consumer with a given income in deciding how much of the product he would want to buy back. Up to this point, the actions of farmers are in no way different from others who are induced to adjust their consumption and uses of the product to that of the particular stock.

The income effects of the price that a farmer receives as a seller of a product are, however, different from what they are for those who buy his product. A fall in price of a farm product will always make a consumer better off, other things remaining unchanged, and this increases his demand unless the product happens to be for him an inferior good.[4] Thus, the substitution effect and the income effect for a consumer arising out of a fall in price always work in the same direction, namely, to encourage additional consumption, except in the case of an inferior good. While this is also the case for substitution for a farmer and his family, the converse is true for income. A fall in the farm price always reduces his income, assuming that the stock under the control of the farmer, is given.[5] The reduction in income will curtail the amount of the product that the farm family will consume, again, with the proviso that the product is not for them an inferior good. Therefore, for the farmer, the substitution effects pull in one direction and income effects in the other, except for inferior goods. Accordingly, unless we know which of these two is dominant, we cannot indicate even the direction of the combined effects on farmers.

There is also another major difference, namely, the income effect of a change in the price of a particular farm product is likely to be "negligible" for consumers in a community with a high level of living, such as is characteristic of most of the United States, because most of them spend only a small part of their income for any particular product. For farmers, however, the income from a particular product is usually exceedingly important because it is, more often than not, the main source of their income.

Before turning to the data, it may be helpful to outline the more important combinations of these effects and to indicate the shape they give to the supply schedule for the stock period. The outline that follows is restricted to the behavior of the farm household.

Backward-sloping Supply Schedule. This schedule will turn back on itself whenever the income elasticity for home-produced farm products

[4] This assumes that the particular consumer receives the same money income as before and that the prices of services and products, other than that of potatoes, are not changed.

[5] Again it should be noted that we are leaving both price and yield uncertainty aside.

is positive and exceeds the pull of whatever substitution occurs. The supply schedule of producers, therefore, for the stock period will turn back most pronouncedly when there is little or no substitution and when the income elasticity is relatively high for farm families as consuming units. With other factors unchanged, it follows that the larger the proportion of the stock that is normally consumed in farm households, the greater will be the change in the amount of stock that will be sold as a consequence of a given increase or decrease in farm income. We, therefore, would expect to find this supply schedule to be decidedly backward in its slope and a matter of economic importance in a community where farmers normally consume a large fraction of the crop, where the crop is such that little or no substitution occurs in farm households, and where the consumption of the crop by farm families is sensitive to income (the crop having for them a relatively high income elasticity).

Vertical Supply Schedule. It will be vertical, that is, have an elasticity of zero, when none of the farm product is consumed by farm families.[6] It will also be vertical when the substitution effects are exactly as powerful as are the income effects and their pulls are in the opposite directions, that is, whenever the two sets cancel each other. A fairly long list of farm products that are not used in the farm household (or in the farm business) fall into this class for these products are not subject to either of the two effects. Also, when substitution does occur and it is exactly offset by positive income effects—the product cannot be for farm families an inferior good—the supply schedule for the stock period is vertical in character.

Forward-sloping Supply Schedule. This will be the outcome whenever the pull from substitution within the farm household is more powerful than is a positive pull from income. Whenever a product is in the position of an inferior good in the farm household, the slope of the supply curve will be upward and forward, even though no substitution were to occur. The conditions most favorable for this type of supply curve will exist whenever, within the farm household, the substitution effects are large and the income effects are negative and large.

We shall now endeavor to apply the preceding analysis to particular situations, for it is possible to narrow somewhat the range of the net results on the supply of producers for the stock period of the two classes of effects as they express themselves through the actions of farmers.[7]

---

[6] We are leaving aside here the farm business and all storage induced by yield and price uncertainties.

[7] We shall not enter into an analysis of storage by farmers or of yield and

DATA AND SOME INFERENCES

Since the farm household may be an important factor affecting the supply of producers in the stock period, we shall begin with it.

Income Effects—the Farm Household

We indicated at the outset that the character of the income effects of a rise in the farm price upon the supply of producers is related to the level of income of the community. We shall, therefore, consider both a poor and a rich community. A poor community means, in this context, among other things, a situation where food consumption has a high elasticity against income.

A Poor Community—the Case of India. The grave food shortage that developed in India in 1946 is instructive on this point.[8] A major factor contributing to the widespread shortage of food was the marked increase in the income of cultivators.[9] Take the small cultivator who produces one product, be it rice, wheat, or one of the millets, and who usually keeps about half of what he produces for himself and his family. The rest he is obliged to sell in order to pay taxes, debts, and other fixed commitments and to buy salt and a few necessaries. He and members of his family seldom have enough food; they urgently want more

---

price uncertainties and their economic effects. It is, of course, true that we shall be dealing with reoccurring stocks, one after each production period is completed. In a more comprehensive analysis, therefore, account must also be taken of the effects of variations in the realized production from one stock period to the next upon the income of farmers unless the price elasticity of the demand is unity. It follows, of course, that the gross income that farmers receive from the sale of a small stock will rise when the demand is inelastic and will fall when it is elastic.

[8] During June and July of 1946 as chairman of the American Famine Mission to India, the writer had the privilege of observing aspects of the Indian economy, especially those touched upon at this point. See *Supplementary Memoranda* 7, "Effects of Changes in Cultivators' Income on Food Consumption in India," *India's Hunger*, the Report of the American Famine Mission to India, issued by the India Famine Emergency Committee (New York), August, 1946.

[9] Other factors that contributed to the serious shortages of food were the unavailability of customary imports of rice from Burma, a number of local crop failures, the disorganization that existed as an aftermath of the war, of which the inflation was exceedingly disruptive including the effect it had on normal price relationships.

to eat; it would appear that for cultivators so situated, home-produced food has an income elasticity as high as 1.0.[10] When the terms of trade of the small cultivator improve, he sells substantially less food in order to have more to eat. To illustrate this, take a typical cultivator who produces 100 units of food grain and assume that as a result of changes in relative prices his real income improves 20 per cent. With an income elasticity of 1.0, he increases his consumption of food grain from 50 to 60 units and thus reduces the amount he sells from 50 to 40 units. This action on the part of the producer diminishes the supply available to others by one-fifth. Here we have a potent force that can easily bring about a grave shortage of food among those dependent on the sales of such cultivators for their food.

The results of a marked improvement in the income of producers under these conditions also point up a most difficult problem in economic organization. A rise in the farm price under the above circumstances, say of wheat, rice, or millet, instead of increasing the amount of the stock which the cultivator will sell, accomplishes the converse because the producer supply curve turns backward and the exchange situation, therefore, becomes unstable. What can and should be done under these circumstances? In a more practical vein, for those families who find their food supply curtailed as the price rises, the situation takes on an ominous implication—famine. To avert such a consequence, supposing no outside supplies are available, it is necessary to check the increase in food consumption of cultivators. But can any economic system dependent solely on relative prices perform a function of this character under these conditions? A rise in price will, as we have seen, not achieve the desired end, for it will only reduce the supply available to people dependent upon the sales of cultivators. An increase in taxes imposed on cultivators would be one means to deal with such a situation. A system of food procurement by direct action based on quotas and thus forcing the cultivator to accumulate his extra income as savings is the approach that appeared most practical to those charged with responsibility of dealing with this grave problem of "economic organization."

In the United States, fortunately, the underlying conditions are such that the results that emerge are the reverse from those observed for a poor community as exemplified by India. The income elasticity of home-produced food, taken as a whole, is certainly not high; it may be nega-

[10] Colin Clark, *Conditions of Economic Progress* (London: Macmillan & Co., Ltd., 1940), includes some data for industrial workers in India which indicate that the income elasticity for food is 0.9 (p. 445). He also includes estimates for food of farm families in China. Quoting from Professor Dittmar's data, he gives the income elasticity for food in this instance as 1.14 (p. 444).

tive, which means that as the income of farm families increases, more, rather than less, of the stock under the control of farmers is sold.

A Rich Community—the Case of the United States. Food is about the only important home-produced product that is used in farm households in amounts having considerable value at this stage of economic development. In 1941 the average farm household used $521 of products and services drawn from the farm consisting of the following items:[11]

Food	$339
Housing	126
Household operations (fuel, ice, etc.) . . .	32
Clothing	18
Furnishing and equipment	6
Total.	$521

TABLE 14–1. HOME CONSUMPTION OF FARM FAMILIES IN RELATION TO AGRICULTURAL PRODUCTION, UNITED STATES, 1949

	(1)	(2)	(3)
	Cash receipts from farming and value of home consumption, in millions of dollars	Value of home consumption, in millions of dollars	Proportion that (2) is of (1), per cent
Vegetables.	2,353	537	22.8
Dairy products	4,516	735	16.3
Miscellaneous crops[a]	728	117	16.1
Poultry and eggs	3,511	473	13.5
Fruits	1,131	69	6.1
Meat animals	8,918	523	5.9
Sugar cane and sirup crops . .	175	9	5.1
Wool, mohair and other . . .	183	6	3.3
Fruits, tree nuts	63	2	3.2
Feed crops.	2,219	21	1.0
Legume and grass seeds . . .	136	1	0.7
Oil-bearing crops	803	3	0.4
Food grains	2,354	8	0.3
Cotton	2,637	0	0.0
Tobacco	904	0	0.0
Grand total.	30,631	2,504	8.2
Total crops	13,504	767	5.7
Total livestock	17,127	1,737	10.1

[a] Forest products in this class accounted for $150 million of cash receipts and $117 million (all) of the home consumption indicated.

SOURCE: *Agricultural Statistics, 1950*, U.S. Department of Agriculture, Table 683.

[11] *Rural Family Spending and Saving in Wartime*, BAE, *Misc. Pub.* 520, 1943, p. 26.

Estimates of the Bureau of Agricultural Economics indicate that the value of home consumption in 1949 represented about 8 per cent of agricultural production.[12] Three classes of products, however, ran higher: vegetables, 23 per cent; dairy products, 16 per cent; and poultry and eggs, 13 per cent. The next two classes of products in this scale were fruits and meat animals both at 6 per cent. In the case of farm products not used for food, such as cotton and tobacco, the farm household, of course, does not affect the supply of producers.

Home consumption by farm families has become a declining part of agricultural production, diminishing from 13 per cent in 1929 to 8 per cent in 1949. The principal factors responsible for this decline are the expansion in production, the decrease in the number of farm families and of farm people, and the rise in farm incomes. Some technical developments have pulled in the other direction, such as the effects of food lockers and refrigeration made possible by the rapid extension of electricity to farms. Declines, however, have predominated and they have been important, as Table 14–2 indicates.

We now turn to some clues on the income elasticity of home-produced food for farm families. The task of estimating this function would not be hard were it not for the shortcomings of existing data.[13] Let us first look at the data on all food, that is, including not only that which is home produced but also that which is purchased by farm families.

The income elasticity of food for farm families is certainly low, substantially less than that for urban families. Budget studies generally confirm this fact. The 1935–1936 and 1941 budget samples for the United States show food consumption, adjusted to family size of 3.5 and to disposable income, as follows:[14]

Study	Income elasticity
Farm, 1935–1936	.37
Urban, 1935–1936	.61
Farm, 1941	.35
Urban, 1941	.65

[12] Agricultural production means cash receipts from farming and the value of home consumption. *Agricultural Statistics, 1950*, U.S. Department of Agriculture, p. 639.

[13] No over-all quantity index is available. The value of home consumption series is so constructed that it does not reflect accurately year to year changes. For example, in the case of meats, the percentage that farm slaughter is of total production is not adjusted every year but usually only once every five years. Another basic difficulty is the determination of an appropriate price index to deflate these value figures.

[14] Taken from James Tobin's study, "A Statistical Demand Function for Food in the U. S. A.," *Journal of the Royal Statistical Society*, Series A, Vol. CXIII, Part II (1950).

TABLE 14–2. CHANGE FROM 1929–1938 TO 1949 IN THE PROPORTION OF PARTICULAR
PRODUCTS CONSUMED BY FARM FAMILIES IN THE UNITED STATES

Commodity	(1) Cash receipts from farming and value of home consumption, 1949, in millions of dollars	(2) Value of home consumption, 1949, in millions of dollars	(3) Proportion that (2) is of (1), for 1949, per cent	(4) M. G. Reid data for 1929–1938, per cent	(5) Decrease or increase between 1929–1938 average and 1949 (4) minus (3)
Sorgo sirup	10.3	4.8	46.6	63.12	−16.52
Sweet potatoes . . .	87	37	42.5	50.04	−7.54
Sugar-cane sirup. . .	11	3.5	31.8	31.9	−0.1
Truck crops	15.81	444	28.1		
Chickens	680	174	25.58	34.76	−9.18
Dairy products . . .	4,516	734	16.25	21.69	−5.44
Eggs (chicken) . . .	2,106	291	13.82	24.57	−10.75
Apples	256	32	12.5	18.37	−5.87
Peaches	107	13	12.15	18.20	−6.05
Hogs	3,662	437	11.93	18.99	−7.06
Maple sirup and sugar .	7.4	0.8	10.8	11.16	−0.36
Potatoes	518	55	10.6	25.18	−14.58
Plums.	12	1.2	10.0	31.46	−21.46
Cherries	44	3.4	7.73	13.78	−6.03
Pears	47	3.6	7.66	15.97	−8.31
Figs	6.7	0.5	7.46		
Buckwheat	1.9	0.1	5.26	15.54	−10.28
Berries other than straw-					
berries	101	4.9	4.85		
Strawberries	88	3.8	4.32	2.93	+1.39
Grapes	98	3.3	3.37	5.77	−2.40
Apricots	14	0.3	2.14	with plums	with plums
Other fruits	10.3	0.2	1.94		
Turkey	270	5.0	1.85		
Cattle and calves . .	4,896	82	1.67	2.36	−0.69
Peanuts	188	3	1.60	3.79	−2.19
Corn	1,380	21	1.52	10.48	−8.96
Sheep and lambs . .	360	5	1.39	1.83	−0.44
Prunes	29	0.3	1.03		
Other poultry . . .	456	4	0.88		
Oranges	202	1.5	0.74		
Grapefruit	55	0.3	0.54		
Wheat	2,175	7.3	0.34	3.13	−2.79
Rice	159	0.5	0.31	0.25	+0.06
Rye	18	0.04	0.22	3.95	−3.73
Lemons	48	0.1	0.21		
Dry edible beans . .	157	0.3	0.19	0.76	−0.57
Other vegetables . .	11	0	0		
Other feed crops. . .	839	0	0		
Other oil-bearing crops .	615	0	0		
Cotton	2,637	0	0		
Tobacco	904	0	0		

SOURCE: Table 683, *Agricultural Statistics, 1950,* U.S. Department of Agriculture; and
data from M. G. Reid, *Food for People* (New York: John Wiley & Sons, Inc., 1943), p. 73.

If we assume that farm people valued home-produced food at retail prices and that the income elasticity for purchased food was for them no higher than it was for urban families, we may infer that home-produced food in 1941 had for farm families an income elasticity of .15.[15] In many ways, a more plausible assumption is to value the home-produced food at farm prices, and if this were the situation, then the income elasticity of home-produced food was *zero* for farm families.[16] There are reasons for believing that farm people rate the food that they purchase higher against income than do urban families. Suppose the income elasticity for this part of their food was .80 instead of .65 and the home-produced food is valued at farm prices, then the income elasticity of the home-produced food becomes .20, decidedly an inferior good against income.[17]

These budget data suggest that the income elasticity for home-produced food for farm families is either very low or at zero. For milk, in the spring of 1942, "income made little difference in the average quantity that was furnished by the farm." For eggs there is some increase with income; for grain products, however, "families with incomes under $1,000 raised far more of these items than those with higher cash incomes; for fats and oils the quantity of home-produced product also declines with income; home-produced beef goes with high income and this is also true for veal and lamb; but "pork, poultry, and fish were produced at home to about the same extent by all income classes."[18]

Some data from farm family accounts, which were collected by the state colleges in four Middle Western states, indicate that the "quantity"

[15] *Family Food Consumption in the United States,* USDA, *Misc. Pub.* 550, 1944, p. 40, giving the results of the budget survey taken in the spring of 1942, indicates that the home-produced food of farm families consumed per family per week was priced at rates paid by families for purchased items amounting to $7.74 out of a total of $12.60. Let the purchased food have an income elasticity of .65, that of urban families in 1941, and with purchased food representing about 40 per cent of all food, we have .40 × .65 = .26. Since the income elasticity of all food consumed by farm families was .35, this leaves income elasticity for the remainder, that from home-produced sources, at .09 ÷ 60 = .15.

[16] When we value the home-produced food at farm prices, it represents about 45 per cent of the reduced total of $8.73, and the $4.86 of food purchased represents about 55 per cent, and .55 × .65 = .357, which fully accounts for the observed income elasticity of all food for farm families.

[17] Here we have 55 × .80 = .44. This makes the remainder, the 45 per cent that is home produced, − .09 ÷ .45 = − .20.

[18] *Family Food Consumption in the United States,* USDA, *Misc. Pub.* 550, pp. 6–21.

of food purchased by these farm families from 1934 to 1947 rose much more than did food consumption generally. These data and the United States per capita food consumption for 1934 and 1947 follow:

	1934	1947	Increase, per cent
United States per capita food consumption (BAE index)[a] . .	99	115	16
"Measures" of food purchased per person of accounting-keeping farm families[b]:			
Southeastern Minnesota	80	111	39
Illinois	70	112	60
Kansas	73	121	66
Iowa	67	122	82

[a] *Consumption of Food in the United States, 1909–48*, Bureau of Agricultural Economics, August, 1949, Table 23.

[b] *Rural Family Living Outlook Charts, 1949*, U.S. Department of Agriculture (processed), from data appearing on p. 29. These figures are simple relative expenditures for food, 1937–1940 = 100 based on farm family accounts of selected farm families in these states. It is only the relative increases that can be compared.

These fragmentary data suggest that the amount of food purchased by farm people per person rose much more than did the United States per capita food consumption from 1934 to 1947.[19] But did the total food consumption per person increase as much on farms as it did for the population generally? Since the per capita consumption of food by farm people normally exceeds that of nonfarm people, we would expect the answer to be in the negative. The inference is that the consumption of home-produced food was reduced by these farm families as they expanded so substantially their purchases of food. The factors responsible for the shift to purchased food were mainly changes in income and relative price. But we cannot untangle the importance of each.[20]

We infer from the data reviewed in this section, especially from the 1941 budget data, that the income elasticity for home-produced food for farm families is either very low, at zero, or negative. If we were compelled to take a position, it would be that home-produced food has become on the average an inferior good against income in American farm

[19] For example, in Illinois, if we take home-produced food as representing half of all food used by these families in 1934, the 60 per cent increase in purchased food, with no change in the amount of home-produced food used, will result in a 30 per cent increase for all food.

[20] The following data, despite their limitations, for 1940 and 1947, covering a period during which farm incomes increased sharply, may be instructive. In the case of home-produced pork (excluding lard), there was no appreciable

households. The implication is, therefore, that the income effects operating through farm households tend to bend the producer supply schedule forward as it slopes to the right.

change in three major farm regions, while in two, where farmers in the main are much poorer, a substantial increase is indicated.

Region	Pounds of pork (excluding lard) per person	
	1940	1947
North Atlantic	45	45
East and West North Central . . .	66	67
West	29	30
South Atlantic	68	80
South Central	58	69

For milk, the results are quite similar.

Region	Quarts of milk per person	
	1940	1947
North Atlantic	200	195
West	189	186
East North Central	236	245
West North Central	251	271
South Atlantic	125	141
South Central	161	206

Home-produced eggs and chickens show no appreciable changes by regions, but in the case of beef and veal, dressed weight, the increase is marked except for the West, which shows a decrease.

Region	Pounds of beef and veal per person	
	1940	1947
North Atlantic	16.2	20.2
East North Central	14.1	27.6
West North Central	18.9	31.5
West	37.6	32.8
South	3.2	4.5

SOURCE: *Rural Family Living Outlook Charts*, U.S. Department of Agriculture, 1949, pp. 41–49 (mimeo.). The data are for "production of farm-slaughtered meat for consumption or for sale, per person per year by persons living on farms."

Substitution—the Farm Household and Business

Budget data give us no information about substitution against price. Available time-series data have serious shortcomings when used to gauge the relevant price elasticities. We are, therefore, compelled at this stage of our economic knowledge to use other approaches, which are at best very rough. For one group of farm products, however, we can infer results that are firm, namely, where none of the product is used on the farm regardless of the price.

Substitution Zero. This group of farm products consists of those that are not used either in the farm household or in the farm business in the form in which they are produced. It follows from these conditions that the substitution effects for this group is always zero. This group includes cotton, wool, and mohair; flaxseed and tung nuts; tobacco; all the legume and grass seeds except cowpeas; beets and cane used for sugar; broom corn, hemp, and flax fiber; hops and, for all practical purposes, greenhouse and nursery products.

Substitution Small and Price Elasticity Low. There is an important group of farm products which are not used as inputs in the farm business and which are produced on farms specializing in their production. The 1945 Census indicates that on all farms classified as "horticultural specialties" only 1.6 per cent of the total value of the production was used in the farm household; for fruit and nut farms the equivalent figure was 2.3 per cent; for vegetable farms, 4.9 per cent; for livestock farms, 6.7 per cent; poultry farms, 7.9 per cent; and for dairy farms, 8.6 per cent. On these specialized farms, which supply most of the commercial product, there is very little possibility for substitution among farm products as far as the farm household is concerned. Nor can there be much substitution between the particular home-produced product on which the farm specializes and all purchased foods in the stock period. In the event, however, that purchased foods rise markedly relative to farm product prices, many farm families will, during the course of one or more production periods, proceed to produce for themselves other food products, especially vegetables and some animal products.

Substitution Important to the Household but Unimportant in Relation to the Aggregate Producer Supply. According to the 1945 Census there were about one and a quarter million farms on which the farm households used 75 per cent of the products that these farms produced.[21] But a more important fact bearing upon our analysis of supply is that these

---

[21] *Statistical Abstract of the United States, 1948,* U.S. Department of Commerce, p. 627. This class of farms produced products valued at $606 million of which $453 million was used by the farm household.

farms did not contribute as much as 1 per cent to the total agricultural production entering into commercial channels. Even though a rise or fall in price were to induce a great deal of substitution in these farm households, it could not alter even appreciably the aggregate supply of farmers in the stock period.

Substitution Effected by the Farm Business. This substitution consists of two classes, namely, farm-produced inputs for purchased inputs and one farm-produced input for another that is also farm produced. The technical conditions of agricultural production are such that there is little room in the stock period for the first class of substitution. When a farmer has both a tractor and horses, as many of them did during the late twenties, a marked fall in the price of feed relative to fuel did induce farmers to curtail tractor operations and do more of the farm work with horses. Some crops can be used to build up the soil and in this way it is possible to reduce in part normal purchases of fertilizer. Feeds, especially protein feed from sources which are nonagricultural or which are in competition with nonfarm uses, are of some importance. Yet taking all the substitution of the first class together, it cannot alter even appreciably the amount of farm products which farmers sell during a particular stock period. The price elasticity of farm-produced inputs, price measured as a relative of purchased inputs, must be low in the stock period.

Substitution among particular farm products used as inputs in farming is, however, on an entirely different footing. Here we have a class where the elasticity of substitution is frequently very high and where substitution plays a very important role. The feed grains on which the large livestock economy of the United States is based are sufficiently close substitutes that in many situations they can be treated as a single product. Corn, oats, grain sorghums, and barley are the principal feed grains; in addition, a large amount of wheat is fed (ranging from about 100 to 500 million bushels in a crop year since 1940); some peanuts are grown for hogs; skim milk is widely used as a feed; rye and rice also are fed under certain price conditions. For this class the producer supply schedule of a particular product is usually highly elastic in the stock period when it is so priced that it is available for feed. Under stable economic conditions, the substitution effects dominate regardless of changes in the income flow which the farm receives.

RESULTS THAT EMERGE

We have found that for farm-produced food the supply schedule of producers in a poor community in the stock period is likely to be a backward-sloping curve.

In a rich community, and in the United States in particular, home-produced food has an income elasticity for farm families that appears to fall within the range of .20 to —.20; taking all home-produced food together, it will have become for farm families an inferior good against income. Among the major classes of farm foods, it seems that only beef, veal, and lamb, as home-produced food, have positive slopes against incomes. The price elasticity of home-produced food, while less firm statistically, is, so it would appear, far over on the inelastic side. For farm foods, therefore, taken as a whole, both the income and substitution effects operating within farm households support a forward-sloping producer supply schedule in the stock period.

We have only touched upon the operations of the farm business as these relate to the producer supply. The substitution effects set into motion by a change in farm price are fairly straightforward. Many farm products cannot be used on the farm in further production and for these, substitution is, of course, zero. For other farm products, notably those used for feed, substitution is important and sufficiently powerful to be predominant regardless of the effect of the altered income of the firm. The effects of variations in income on storage for contingencies and in relation to price expectations is a problem sufficiently complex and important to require separate treatment going beyond the scope of the analysis at hand.

PART THREE

ECONOMIC ORGANIZATION FOR DEVELOPMENT AND STABILITY

15

ECONOMIC ACTIVITIES TO BE ORGANIZED

In studying economic organization we enter upon a difficult terrain where there are no highways over which we can go and come with ease and at our leisure. There are paths but they are unmapped, badly maintained, and hazardous to travel. The peak we are striving to scale may hide another which is higher and which we would try for were our information complete. Economic organization is also the central issue of the great debate of our day. Preferences are at stake. These are put in many ways, all too often as a simple dichotomy: progress or security; freedom or efficiency; decentralization or centralization; and so on. Possibilities, the outcomes of different ways of organizing economic activity, are not established facts, for the lessons to be drawn from the trial and error that characterizes the experiences of communities are not conclusive. The problem of economic organization is with us, however; there is no escaping the issues of choice and of beliefs regarding outcomes.

Propositions about Economic Organization

It may be helpful to endeavor to formulate in an elementary way the underlying propositions on which the analysis of Part Three will rest. If there were no activities having economic attributes, no problem of economic organization would arise. But more than the existence of such activities is required, because if people were wholly indifferent about how these activities were organized, there would be no organizational problem. Furthermore, although such activities and such preferences existed, if the necessary organization were to emerge without effort and were to function automatically and perfectly or if there were one and only one possibility, no problem of economic organization would arise. These statements may be formulated as follows:

1. There is a class of activities in the community which have economic attributes and which require organization.
2. People in the community are not indifferent with regard to the way in which these activities are organized.
3. There are alternative forms of organization and none of these is

achievable without effort, that is, inputs are required to establish and maintain any given organization.

We shall refer to the first of these as the *activity* proposition, the second as the *preference* proposition, and the third as the *possibility* proposition. These are empirical propositions in the sense that it is possible, by making an appeal to empirical experiences, to determine whether the particular attributes ascribed to each is a valid statement about the experience of a particular community.

It should be observed that proposition 1 restricts the analysis to a particular class of activities. Without this restriction, propositions 2 and 3 would have much greater generality in that they would presumably include all efforts which require organization regardless of the nature of the activities. There are many classes of activities which require effort and which can be organized in different ways about which people have preferences but which are not included in this proposition; for example, a group of boys who get together for a game of baseball where the activity is simple play. A particular activity may be formal or informal; it may be recreational, religious, educational, military, or one of many other forms. There is always an economic attribute in each of these activities to the extent that "inputs" are required; it is hard to conceive of any activity that is wholly "free" in the sense that no "inputs" whatsoever are needed. We shall, however, restrict ourselves to that class of activities where the inputs are deemed to be sufficiently important to economize. The scope of this class is, nevertheless, very wide as we shall endeavor to show below.

The preference proposition places no restrictions on what people may prefer by way of organization except that it rules out a complete indifference about organization. The possibility proposition, as it stands, undoubtedly has too much generality, for it includes situations which are not relevant because it is impossible to conceive of a form of organization of a community, which is subject to changes in fundamental factor supplies and in preferences and to uncertainty, that would function automatically and perfectly. There is no point in considering the impossible; nevertheless, much discussion about rules, policies, programs, and how particular activities "should" be organized is wasted because it does not exclude those forms of organization that are clearly impossible.

Classifications of Activities to Be Organized

There exist many different forms of activities in a highly specialized, technically advanced community such as the United States in which it is important to economize and which require organization. These activities may be seen in the small, for example, when a farmer considers how best to rotate crops on a particular farm with an eye to his net worth a decade hence; and in the large, when an entire community, by means of fiscal, monetary, and other policies endeavors to adjust its production, consumption, and savings to the requirements of a much enlarged military. The concept of "economy" is relevant to both of these situations, the fundamental attribute of which is its organizing function because "economy" or "economic efficiency" is *an organizing value.*[1]

How are we to classify existing activities in order to deal with the problems of economic organization? No single classification is likely to be wholly satisfactory because of the weak and shaky bridge that connects micro theory and macro theory, because of the difficulties of separating value considerations (preferences) from possibilities in this area, and because of the emphasis that is often placed on specific *ad hoc* rules, policies, and decisions pertaining to economic organization.

One classification in studying economic organization is in accordance with such functions as follows: (1) the distribution of a given stock of products; for example, in agriculture the distribution of the realized production plus the carry-over during the interval between harvests which may be taken as the stock period. (2) The allocation of a given stock of inexhaustible resources to produce a flow of products and the distribution of these products as a continuous process. (3) The process of production and distribution envisaged in (2) under conditions where some new resources are discovered, "produced," and accumulated while some old resources are exhausted. (4) The process of economic development, implicit in (3), under conditions of risk and uncertainty. And (5) adding to this complex set of functions, particular, relevant, social (including political) variables and taking into account the relations among them and between these social variables and the large set of economic activities implicit in (4).

The difficulties that arise in using this classification lie not in its logic but in the existing state of theory. Virtually all theoretical analysis is confined to the first three of these functions. There is at hand no accepted theory for analyzing the activities and organization of the economy with uncertainty present. Nor is there available a satisfactory general social theory of sufficient scope and power to handle the entire set of important social variables, including the economic subset, on which we are concentrating. The relevance of these difficulties to the two problems to which this study is addressed, namely, agriculture in a developing econ-

---

[1] A. L. Macfie, *Economy Efficiency and Social Welfare* (New York: Oxford University Press, 1943), develops this aspect usefully.

omy and economic instability in relation to agriculture, arises from the fact that these problems are beset by price and yield uncertainty and by major social and political considerations.

Another classification of the functions of economic organization is one that is based on the nature of the operations and not on theoretical requirements in going from simple to more complex situations. The following important activities each entail a flow of inputs, enough so as to give the activity economic relevance: The "production" and "distribution" of (1) information, presumably in as complete a form as is economic,[2] (2) new and better technology, (3) new and "better" taste and preferences, (4) investment in (*a*) human agents and (*b*) nonhuman factors, and (5) products and services.

Here, too, we are confronted by difficulties arising mainly out of the state of economic knowledge. Economists have devoted themselves almost entirely to (5) and (4*b*). Economic instability and development, however, are not independent of what is done with regard to the first three and (4*a*). Moreover, these neglected activities have become increasingly important not only in the effects they have upon (4*b*) and (5) but also in the claims they make upon the total stock of resources available for production.

Still another classification for studying economic organization is to consider the levels at which decisions are made. "Levels" in this context represent the scope of the integrating capacity of the particular organizational unit, some being so comprehensive that they cover the entire community while some are confined to a very small part of a particular activity. The following three classes may be indicated: (1) firm and household units, (2) product and factor markets, and (3) political and social integrating processes. Since we shall rely largely on this classification, some of its more important implications will be considered briefly.

Firm and Household Units. Here it is possible to draw directly upon micro theory. There is the question of how the firm or household should be organized in its entirety to maximize its economic situation. In agriculture it may be a family farm with no, or with some outside labor, or with some other condition specified. It may also be a partnership (father and son lease), cooperative, corporation, or even a "collective." The firm, therefore, may be either a private or a public agency. The household may also take one of several alternative forms ranging from a single individual to a family with one or more members and to an agency or institution acting as a consuming unit for many people. Here, again, public agencies are not excluded. Within the firm or the house-

---

[2] Information is here viewed not as a free service, nor as a service that is given, but as a service which has a price because it takes resources to render the service and because it has utility.

hold, there is usually a vast variety of economic activities, each of which may be studied as a problem in organization. In industry, it may be the plant while in farming it may be any one of many enterprises that go, for example, to make up a typical feed-livestock farm. Both the production function of a typical producing unit and the consumption function of a particular consuming unit are complex aggregates made up of many different activities each of which can be and, to get meaningful insights on certain problems, needs to be identified and analyzed.[3]

Product and Factor Markets. It is necessary to integrate the activities of firms and households in a community in which there exists a division of labor. Only in the exceptional case, of no importance whatsoever in practice, where there is a Crusoe-firm-household, operating wholly independent of all other firms and households, would we find the entire integrating function borne by this particular unit. Economists have devoted much effort to explaining the behavior of the firm and the household, all too much so it would appear in view of their neglect of markets and of the integrating functions borne by the political and social processes. It is our thesis, to which we shall return later, that the mallocations in resources in agriculture associated with economic development are in the main not the consequences of bad farm management per se but of particular imperfections in the way the factor markets work when subjected to the strains and stresses of economic development.

A market is an institution for integrating the activities of firms and of households[4] using the mechanism of relative prices. The organization of a market may be informal or formal; it may be "operated" by either a public or private agency or by a group of such agencies; it may be of local, national, or international scope. Prices are presumed to function in a self-correcting framework. The concept of a market that is wholly "automatic" is an abstraction, often very useful when it is possible to leave uncertainty aside. However, the coordinating function borne by a market, under conditions of certainty, is entirely routine and the required integration can be "automatic" and "perfect" because no meaningful economic decisions need to be made. Such routine behavior implies, however, that only "one" firm is necessary and, as Kaldor has shown,[5] competition disappears because competition and certainty are,

---

[3] Farm management and household economics make this area of analysis their province.

[4] In any particular situation, the larger the firms and the household, the smaller becomes the scope of the markets. The limiting case is a single, comprehensive firm-household, Crusoe once more, where all the integrating functions of markets are absorbed by the particular firm-household.

[5] Nicholas Kaldor, "The Equilibrium of the Firm," *The Economic Journal,* Vol. XLIV (1934).

in this context, inconsistent assumptions. But routine behavior of firms and households with no uncertainty present is not the kind of behavior which confronts product and factor markets. These markets function in a setting where disturbances and uncertainty are "normal." Major depressions and recoveries occur; rapid transformations of the economy are "forced" during mobilization, the waging of war, and the return to peace; the personal distribution of income is altered by legislation; and other major changes and "disturbances" affect markets. How satisfactorily can and do markets function under these conditions?

Political and Social Integrating Processes. Despite the shortcomings of economic theory in coping with economic uncertainty, it nevertheless places the analysis of the first two levels of economic integration, that of firms and households and that of markets, on much firmer ground than is the study of political and social processes in relation to economic activities because there seems to be no meaningful theory of social organization which can handle the relevant political and social variables. Nor do we wish to imply that all political and social processes are necessarily integrating. The outcome is all too frequently disintegration; and extreme case of this is a civil war. Undoubtedly one of the principal reasons why economists shy away from this sphere is the unsatisfactory state of the analytical equipment, and as a result, economists are inclined to abstract from this comprehensive level of integration which must necessarily be performed by the political and social processes. As a consequence, all too frequently the statements of economists leave the impression that markets and firms and households are sufficient in themselves to achieve a workable economic organization.

The preceding comments on "disturbances" give some indication of the problems in economic organization that go beyond markets. There is widespread agreement that fiscal and monetary management is necessary if a moderately decentralized economy is to be kept on an even keel; management, in this sphere, is primarily a governmental function. The political process also carries other important burdens—among them, the important tasks of altering the functional distribution of income so that the personal distribution of income will be socially acceptable; and, of appropriating and allocating a substantial fraction of the national product to the armed services; and, of course, others.

This study of economic organization rests on three elementary propositions: (1) the activity to be organized, (2) organizational preferences, and (3) organizational possibilities. Three classifications of the activities to be organized are at hand; each is useful for particular purposes.

16

ECONOMIC ORGANIZATION: POSSIBILITIES
AND PREFERENCES

Much, and perhaps most, discussion of economic organization is point-less because it does not relate what is possible to what is preferred. The discussion all too frequently considers either what presumably can be done and leaves preference aside, or what appears to be preferred and neglects what is possible. Like a pair of shoes, one without the other is quite useless. We shall consider the more important general attributes of these concepts in analyzing economic organization.

Two Case Studies

To take our bearing and to help clarify the meaning of "possibilities" and "preferences" in this context, we shall consider briefly two real situa-tions, namely, "producing" agricultural production techniques, the work of the agricultural experiment stations, and the production of farm prod-ucts.

"Producing" New and Better Techniques. We shall take it to be a fact that a large collection of inputs is required to "produce" new and bet-ter agricultural techniques; these inputs consist of scientists, tech-nologists, land, and many kinds of materials and apparatus. Let us sup-pose that the community is after big game, namely, the application of promising new hypotheses drawn from physics, chemistry, genetics, and other biological fields to improve plants and animals and to handle ex-isting soils better by new techniques and by advances in engineering. Suppose the community also wants this technical research to be organ-ized on a highly decentralized pattern which would require existing family farms to do the necessary research and experimentation. Experi-ence clearly indicates that a community may satisfy one or the other of these two preferences, but it is pointless to discuss achieving both of them because to achieve both is, in fact, impossible under the conditions specified.

To get a meaningful formulation of this problem, we need to take the alternative forms of research organization and determine how much research output can be achieved by each, say from some fixed expenditure for such research, and then relate these possibilities to the preference of the community. We start with this much information about what the community wants: it prefers from any given expenditure for such research more research output to less and also more decentralized organization of this research to less. Suppose that there existed only four organizational forms which rated in descending order of preference as follows: research so organized so that it is done by family farms, by large specialized private firms, by forty-eight state agricultural experiment stations, and by one national research agency (we shall leave the various combinations of these aside). The research outputs that can be realized are presented in Fig. 16–1 by N_1, N_2, N_3, and N_4.

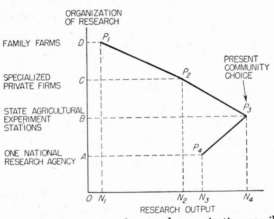

Fig. 16–1. Research output and research organization possibilities.

Figure 16–1 gives us the possibilities which are represented by P_1, P_2, P_3, and P_4 and which permits us to infer: (1) If the community wants to go ahead with agricultural research at all under these conditions, it would be well advised not to commit itself to "one national research agency" because it can attain more decentralization by setting up forty-eight research units and at the same time increase the research output from ON_3 to ON_4; and (2) the choice from among the other three, which are shown by P_1, P_2, and P_3, will depend upon the "quantity" of research results the community is willing to forego in order to have more decentralization in the way the research is organized. In the event the community values decentralization of the kind which puts all such research in the family farms very high, in fact so high that it would be willing to forego all research output except ON_1, the community choice would become P_1. In the United States the political process has settled on P_3.

Producing Farm Products. In this case we shall take it to be a fact that the operations involved in agricultural production in the United States are exceedingly varied and complex and subject to frequent changes because of the wide range of products being produced, because of variations in soil, climate, ability of farm people, and in other conditions and because of yield and price uncertainties confronting those who produce farm products. Suppose that the community wants, under these circumstances, as large an output of farm products as is currently produced from the collection of inputs now committed to agricultural

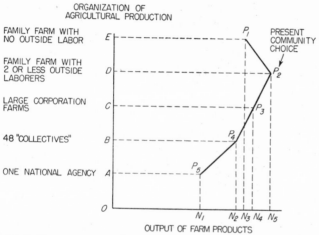

Fig. 16–2. Farm output and organization of agriculture possibilities.

production. And, in addition, for purposes of illustration, let us make an unreal and extreme assumption, namely, that the community wants all of agriculture to be so organized that it will be administered by a single, centralized agency operating by means other than the use of the mechanism of relative prices of products and factors.

Here again, when the matter is put in this way, experience tells us that the community may satisfy one or the other of these two preferences, but under existing conditions (involving resources, techniques, and institutions), it is impossible to achieve both of them. In this particular case, we elected to have the community prefer more centralization to less in order to point up the issue that not all things are possible by merely more centralized organization.

We must, however, turn the organizational preference around in order to make it relevant to the American community. We believe it to be true that the community prefers more farm products to less from any particular collection of inputs committed to agriculture, and it also prefers more decentralized organization of agricultural production to less. To get a meaningful representation of the possibilities that can be related to the community preference, we need to determine the output of farm products that is attainable under each of several types of production organization. In Fig. 16–2 we shall endeavor, also, to throw some light on the standing of the family farm under existing technical conditions and community preferences.

Suppose it were true, starting with a given set of agricultural inputs, that the five particular organizational types would yield a set of possibilities represented by P_1, P_2, P_3, P_4, and P_5, as shown in Fig. 16–2. With this information before it, the community presumably would not choose "one national agency" because it could acquire, by committing itself to "48 collectives," more farm products, namely, ON_2 instead of ON_1 and also more decentralization. This experience would be repeated in going from B to C and then to D putting it at points P_3 and P_2, respectively. The relevant community choice is between P_1 and P_2 and if the community were to value family farms, restricted wholly to the labor of the family, more than it valued the extra output represented by N_3N_5, the choice would be at P_1. At P_2 the community can have the best possible situation on the output scale, and this is about where the political and social process appears to settle at present.

<h3 style="text-align:center">SOME GENERAL ATTRIBUTES</h3>

We shall now consider some of the more general attributes of sets of possibilities that represent various quantities of products and alternative types of organization that are relevant to community choice. The direction of the scale on which each is valued is clear, namely, the Western community prefers more decentralization to less in the way economic activities are organized and it also prefers more products to less from any given set of inputs. The two variables, types of organization and quantity of products, are not only important but we deem them to be fundamental in getting at the organizational problem that besets a community in managing the economic activities in a large, highly specialized, technically advanced economy. Let us now represent the possibilities of an entire economy by the curve P_1, P_2, and P_3 in Fig. 16–3.

A number of observations and inferences may be made on the basis of the curve represented by P_1, P_2, and P_3.

1. If the community were indifferent about economic organization, it would settle for N_2 output of products because at that point it acquires the largest output of products possible from the collection of inputs which we assume are given. Most economic analysis abstracts from organization and when this is done the problem that remains is one of attaining N_2 shown on the horizontal axis.

2. We may, of course, reverse the matter and assume a community which is indifferent about the output of products. In that case, it would settle for C reaching P_1 and realizing N_1 products. There are times in the debates that center on economic organization that one might suppose the only thing that matters is the achievement of a maximum of decentralization. There are also cases where centralization is advanced,

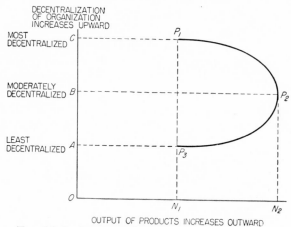

Fig. 16–3. Output and organization possibilities.

so it appears, for its own sake. To do this is to deny both scales of values and forego both more products and more decentralization.

3. In much of the more serious discussion of the problem of economic organization, the issue is not joined because one group, usually implicitly, is considering the P_3P_2 segment of the possibilities curve as relevant to actual circumstances while the other group is taking the P_1P_2 segment. To join the issue, it is necessary to make explicit and agree on which of two sets of possibilities is relevant in fact.

4. The relation of freedom and types of economic organization opens a vast and complex set of issues. Freedom has the attribute of a value which the Western community has come to rate highly. Freedom, however, is also instrumental, and liberal-classical thought has concentrated much attention on this aspect particularly in relation to economic

efficiency.[1] The case for "freeing" households and firms as coordinating units of economic activities and for the opening of exchanges to establish markets and for enlarging their scope was compelling under the historical conditions that existed because these measures made possible a much larger output of products.

It should be observed, however, that this outcome presupposes that the relevant conditions are represented by the P_3P_2 segment of the possibilities curve shown in Fig. 16–3. Whenever the data show that a community is situated anywhere between P_3 and P_2, the community can improve its situation by decentralizing its economic organization, that is, by moving at least to P_2 regardless of how much value it places on some extra output of products in relation to some additional decentralization because it can under these conditions always obtain somewhat more of both in going upward and outward until it reaches P_2. Whenever the P_3P_2 segment is relevant, with the scales of values for organization and for products running in the direction indicated, on which there is little room for doubt in the Western community, it necessarily follows

---

[1] But to protect freedom as a value, restrictions have been placed on "the freedom of an individual to alienate his own freedom," when a contract is made. These restrictions have given rise to impediments to efficiency. The impediments are of various kinds. One of these that is serious is the way in which it blocks the capital markets in providing funds for investment in human agents. As the Western community has become richer, an increasing proportion of its capital is appropriately invested in the development of individuals in terms of knowledge, health, skills, and other experiences that, among other things, enhance their ability as productive agents. Yet these investments are restricted to family and public funds because the individual cannot make a satisfactory contract committing the future earnings from such an investment in himself without contracting away a part of his freedom which is deemed to be inalienable. This impediment has undoubtedly been an important factor causing the community to undertake a more equal distribution of the social product as a corrective to the particular inefficiency arising from this impediment. Still another adverse development closely related to the above is the weak economic position of the individual who has only his own labor to sell. Our social institutions do not permit him to enter into a contract that "impairs his freedom" and the result is that what cannot be sold cannot be pledged and this leaves the individual who has only labor to offer without "property." Professor Frank H. Knight in *Freedom and Reform*, p. 65, puts the matter succinctly: "The inalienability of control over one's own person . . . results in placing in an especially weak position anyone who owns productive capacity only as embodied in his own person in the form of labor power." This impediment has undoubtedly impaired the economic efficiency of the community appreciably.

that the community can improve its position by changing over to a more decentralized type of economic organization. To dispute this conclusion, given the data which have been indicated, is of course pointless, as are most disputes over this matter. The difficulty arises in getting at the data that are required to establish the fact that a particular community is situated somewhere on the P_3P_2 segment. This clearly is a question of fact and not one of inference from established facts.

5. Most problems in economic organization in the United States are represented by the P_1P_2 segment. The case of "producing" new and better argicultural techniques seems to be of this character; the tendency of the political process in the United States to favor the family farm as a producing unit and to restrict its scale gives rise to a set of possibilities that is, at least, closely akin to P_1P_2.

In considering a P_1P_2 segment, the analysis is up against an additional difficulty. Not only is it necessary to determine whether or not the possibilities are in fact in a diminishing relationship one to the other, that is, to acquire more decentralization, it is necessary to forego some output of products, but it is also essential to determine the character of the community preference in this matter. It, of course, will not suffice merely to take the preferences of the investigator. In the organization of technical research for agriculture, the community by a crude process of trial and error "decides" that it prefers the largest possible research output, from a given collection of inputs, and substantial centralization in organization to any other combination of the two. In another area, it reaches for additional decentralization, the case of the family farm, and presumably is willing to forego at least a small amount of output of farm product, as representing the best combination.

PREFERENCES RELATED TO ECONOMIC DEVELOPMENT

A particular community may encourage or it may discourage economic development. It may consider the social adjustments that are required as too high a "price" to pay for the extra production. On the other hand, it may be readily prepared to make the necessary social adjustments because of the relatively high "value" which it places on the additional production. In another direction, when a community has achieved a measure of economic development, it may prefer to have a different combination of "product" and "organization" from that which it had prior to the particular development, as we shall now endeavor to show.

New Combinations of "Organization" and "Product." Let us take a community, which in situation 1, is confronted by a possibilities curve represented by *PP* shown in Fig. 16–4 and which settles at point *A* as the best combination of product and organization under these circumstances. Suppose now that, as a consequence of economic development, a new and improved situation emerges, represented by the possibilities curve P_1P_1. The triangle ABC indicates the path and range of choices open to the community in going from PP to P_1P_1 without going below the former level in "organization" or "product." The community, in going from A to B, can now have AB of additional product, provided it is prepared to restrict itself to the same type of organization which it had under PP conditions. It can have, in the other direction, considerably more decentralization; it can go from A to C, provided the community is willing to get along with the same amount of product as formerly. The inference is that a community can convert, should it prefer to do so, some (or even all) of the gains that are here ascribed to economic development into a more decentralized type of economic organization, which means a better organization because of the nature of the relevant preferences of the community under consideration.[2]

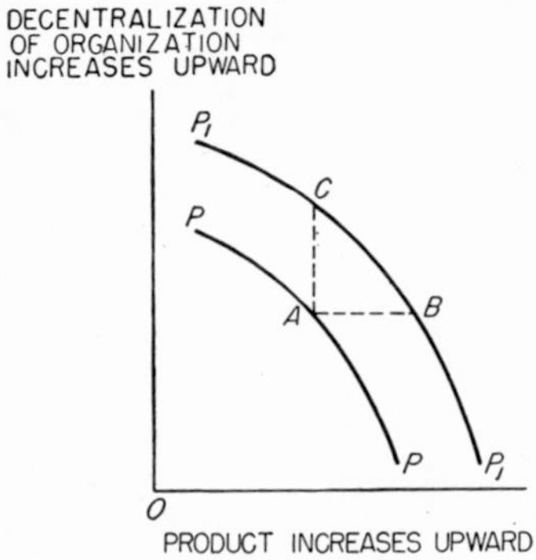

DECENTRALIZATION OF ORGANIZATION INCREASES UPWARD

PRODUCT INCREASES UPWARD

FIG. 16–4. Improvement in output and organization possibilities.

Economic Development and Some Other Social Adjustments. The consequences of economic development, as already pointed out, are not restricted to a mere rise in per capita income. Nor is the type of economic organization and product the whole story although these are fundamental. At this point we wish to consider briefly certain other social adjustments, adjustments which go beyond economic organization, which are relevant and important to economic development.

The broad sweep of the industrial revolution may well be viewed as a long, secular boom in economic possibilities. The real output per unit

[2] It may be argued that economic development always makes it necessary for a community to centralize its organization. Should this outcome happen to be the case in fact, it would require a different representation for P_1P_1. As we have represented P_1P_1 in Fig. 16–4, however, the outcome is such that the community can recombine in accordance with its preferences along the lines indicated. It is hard to believe that the economic development that has characterized the economic history of Western countries has made a more centralized type of economic organization necessary; on the contrary, as a result of economic progress the community can have and can afford more decentralization.

of input of human effort of the United Kingdom increased at least three-fold from about 1800 to 1947 and that of the United States more than five-fold (see Note, Chap. 5) according to some recent figures by Colin Clark.[3] This remarkable advance did not leave the social organization and structure of the community unaltered nor was the community a passive factor merely adapting itself to economic development.[4] The accumulation of capital, the advances in techniques, "discovery" of new resources, and the improvement in skills largely explain the rise in output per person. It is patently clear, however, that these developments have not been either outside or independent of the social organization of the community. The values and the structure of the Western community permitted and induced the required social behavior which has given us the industrial revolution; and in addition, the very appreciable social disorganization that came as a consequence of these developments, costly as it has been, has presumably been socially acceptable.[5] By way of contrast, a community like that of parts of India where tradition and religion have maintained, until fairly recently, a more stationary social structure, there has been less room for an industrial revolution to get underway. Nor has India experienced (as yet) the kind of social disorganization that has characterized the Western countries.

One way of improving the economic possibilities of a community is to engage in trade. We need to remind ourselves that the principal policy objective of classical economics was to enlarge the scope of the market economy by freeing the channels of trade and thereby improving the economic possibilities of the community. But to achieve this objective, it was necessary for England (the community here concerned) to undergo a substantial social change. It may be argued that the landlords' losses were less than were the gains of other classes. But the landlords were not compensated for the losses they sustained from the repeal of the Corn Laws. Welfare economics geared to the principle of compensation applied to this case, after the fact and in view of the circumstances, is a pointless intellectual diversion. What is important in this case is that the community gave its approval to an enlargement of the scope of trade and it accepted the social consequences that this approval entailed. The

[3] *Review of Economic Progress,* Vol. I, No. 4 (April, 1949). The level of real national product per man-hour rose from 17 cents to 59 cents in the United Kingdom and from 21 cents to $1.19 in the United States according to Colin Clark.

[4] See Chap. 1 for relevant concepts of economic development applicable here.

[5] We may, in looking back, feel that too high a price was paid for economic "progress" in the way the social incidences often fell.

losses of the landlords were a mere historical detail in the process. The advantages of a larger market were achieved by the British community because it was willing to make the social adjustments on which the new economic organization was dependent. To express it in another way, trade was freed and this action necessitated social adjustments. In substance, then, we find for the classical case that the scope of the market and the social structure were related variables within a larger social system.

Another way of improving the economic possibilities of a community over the years is to avert the occurrence of major depressions. Largely as a consequence of the severe depression of the thirties, economists have been searching for ways that would avert mass unemployment. It would be belaboring the obvious to recount the losses in national product that a severe depression entails. The analytical problem has not been one of determining the exact amount of this loss because it has been so great that nearly everyone is agreed that such an event *should be averted.* Two sets of problems, however, arise. One is the analytical problem of explaining such depressions and of determining on ways of averting them, that is, on lines of political and social action that are likely to be successful. The other consists of the problem of choice on the part of the community from among the alternative ways that are open to it. A basic consideration often lost sight of is that community choice is concerned about the extent to which "centralization" in organization is required and the kind of social adjustments that are needed. Here again it is quite meaningless to formulate the problem as if it were one of compensating particular "speculators" who might have a vested interest in such fluctuations or the banks who may be required to give up some of their control over the supply of money.

In these observations we have restricted ourselves mainly to the kind of economic growth that has been typical of the Western community, including the gains from international trade and full employment, as representing better economic possibilities. In order that these possibilities can emerge, some social adjustments are required and this in turn calls for a set of social values which sanction the necessary social adaptation. It follows, therefore, that an improvement in economic possibilities does affect (may disturb and upset) the existing social organization of the community. We, therefore, find ourselves concurring in one of the basic social criticisms frequently directed against economic development.

We accordingly must face up to this difficulty. The matter may be put as follows: How are we to deal with the relation between an "improvement" in economic possibilities and social adjustments? There are at least three approaches open to us. One of these consists of disregarding the problem, which is permissible when the changes (improvement) in possibilities are so small that they do not have any appreciable effect upon the social structure of the community. The introduction of hybrid corn on a single Iowa farm, the absorption of one unemployed worker in Chicago, and the importation of 1 pound of wool at Boston duty-free are examples of such small changes. Clearly, however, when hybrid corn is planted on 85 million acres, 9 million unemployed are put to work, or when a Smoot-Hawley tariff is eliminated, the changes become sufficiently large to make this approach inappropriate. Nevertheless, there are many organizational improvements where it is quite proper to proceed on the assumption that they require such small changes in social organization that this aspect of the problem may be neglected.

A second approach involves setting up a general system of analysis which includes among the basic variables not only the national product (and a model to represent the variables within) but also the economic organization and other social adjustments of the community. A procedure of this kind has a strong analytical appeal but it requires a social theory which includes not only the economic behavior of firms and households but also the behavior of the political and social process. Unfortunately, theory at this level of generality appears to be, at least for the present, quite unmanageable when it comes to formulating meaningful hypotheses to explain the kind of political and social behavior on which we are concentrating. It should not be cast aside, however, because of these difficulties. As a way of thinking through the relations between the type of economic changes under consideration and social adjustments, it should provide important insights. What apparently is needed at this stage is a social theory that is restricted to the kind of community that has been developing in Western countries under circumstances that have been favorable to a marked improvement in economic possibilities.

A third approach, on which it is necessary to rely heavily in what economists can do, is to work with a less complete system in order to make the analysis manageable. Such a partial system, however, can go beyond the size of the national product. It can take into account types of economic organization and relate these to output of product and endeavor to get at least some clues that will give insights about the community preference for product and organization. Many social adjustments, however, go beyond changes in economic organization. In the case of economic development, we may proceed on the belief that the Western community is disposed to place a high value on new and better economic possibilities, so high in fact that it is prepared to make particular types of social adjustments that are required to absorb the "gains" that can be realized from new techniques, accumulation of capital, improvement of skills, trade, and full employment. We therefore leave aside these social adjustments, holding on, however, to the basic matter of decentralization in economic organization.

The personal distribution of income, however, is sufficiently important in this context to deserve special attention.

Distribution of Income. One of the unsettled, much neglected, and basic analytical problems confronting economics is the determination of the relation between "improving" the economic possibilities and the personal distribution of income. It is always easy to by-pass the issues by some convenient assumptions, and in that way to avoid dealing with the matter. Unfortunately, the drift has been to separate these two sets of social processes and to deal with them as if they were quite independent one from another. The result has been, as one might expect from such a separation, the adoption of policies to achieve greater equality in the distribution of income without taking into account effects upon either the "product" or "organization." On the other hand, economic analysis has been so engrossed with the function of rewards going to productive services, and in doing so, viewing them as incentives *in the small,* that it has all but failed to consider *the large* social implications of the personal distribution of income.

It is necessary, of course, to acknowledge the development of progressive income taxation and the economic analysis that has gone into it. But it should be noted that in order to get out of the interpersonal utility web, in which it got entangled at the outset, it has become standard practice in economics to leave the rate of progression as a choice to be determined and sanctioned by the community. While this was an advance, it has left the problem of distribution in an unsatisfactory state because of the neglect of the effects of distribution, by whatever social means, upon the "product" and upon "organization." Meanwhile, the community through government has turned to other (additional) devices, including the use of direct controls of product and factor prices, to achieve the socially desired distribution. The consequences of some of these devices upon the "product" are clearly adverse compared to alternative ways of achieving the same goal.

The concept of what it is that is being distributed deserves some elaboration. For our purposes, it is useful to look upon the social product that is being distributed much more broadly than is usually the case when the personal distribution of income is under consideration, for it is essential that we include not only personal disposable income but all want-satisfying activities that have economic content, many of which do not get into our customary income accounting at all. We have reference here not only to the several forms of income that obviously are omitted in our national income data and in income taxation but to such wants as economic security and, even more important, participation in the decision-making process on which economic activities are dependent whether centralized or decentralized. Both economic security and participation are socially significant, want-satisfying attributes of the "social product" which the economy generates. The distribution of this product is a matter of increasing concern to (Western) technically advanced communities where the level of output per head is high and where the desire for a higher level of living is strong and people are "free" and can politically modify the political and social conditions that determine the distribution. While certain attempts at more equal distribution have impaired the "product" of the community, often unnecessarily, it should not be assumed that more equal distribution, especially of investments in human agents and in participation, will not result in a kind of increasing returns of "product." (The community may find itself on the P_3P_2 segment of the possibilities curve, shown in Fig. 16–3, with "product" on the horizontal scale and with "distribution" on the vertical scale.)

A naïve view is to identify the equilibrium distribution of the rewards resulting from any existing pattern of resources ownership and the rewards they earn with the ideal distribution of the social product, as did John Bates Clark. Another view is to restrict economic analysis to the "laws of production," as did John Stuart Mill, and look upon distribution as subject to man-made rules and institutions which are beyond economics and which are not a concern of economics proper. The more "sophisticated" concepts and formulations that now abound do not differ appreciably in their approach from that of Mill. The distribution of the social product is looked upon as a variable that is determined by policy which presumably represents the choice of the community and which, therefore, has its sanction. The attributes of this social choice are then treated like any other choice affecting economic relations. Outside of some of the work in taxation, it has become standard practice to take the distribution as given, that is, determined by decisions outside of the economic system. This procedure, however, leaves an important problem having major economic content unexplored and unsettled as we endeavored to show.

Again, it may be helpful to indicate the approaches open to the economist in dealing with distribution in relation to organizaton. There are economic developments where the changes in distribution are so small that this aspect of the problem may properly be neglected. For example, an improvement in farm management which results in a better utilization of the resources on a few farms would fall into this class. This action would improve the income position of the particular farmers relative to other individuals but the effect on the national income will be so small that it will leave it virtually unchanged.

On the other hand in the case of a major region with much of its labor force underemployed like that of eastern Kentucky and other parts of the Southeast, a recombination of resources with a marked exodus of labor and the "importation" of large amounts of capital would not only lower wages somewhat in the localities receiving the migrants but would also increase the rewards for capital. The distribution effects may turn out to be appreciable under these circumstances. But even here, they present no serious problem because of the strong social sanction for this way of improving the utilization of existing resources. One may put it as follows: The most socially acceptable way of reducing the poverty embedded in agriculture is for low-output farms to produce more, even though it would entail larger farms, fewer farm people in such areas, and more capital, and in addition, more workers in the industrial labor force and less capital for other uses plus some income distribution effects. One can, in fact, generalize this case because it is true that the community is prepared to adapt itself to improvements of this type although the income distribution effects are substantial and adverse for some individuals, some of whom may receive relatively low incomes.

Another way is to take both the income-distribution objective and the particular governmental programs on which the community has hit as determined and proceed to show how the community can under these conditions achieve an economic optimum. One may approach the food-stamp plan or, for that matter, any program "justified" on income-distributional grounds, in this way. It is, however, a weak approach because it fails to take advantage of the fundamental organizational attribute of economic efficiency. The third approach, and by all odds the most relevant to an understanding of the economic aspects of distribution, is to treat income distribution as one of the "values" that the community wants and for which it is prepared to pay a "price." The task of economic analysis then becomes one of setting forth the alternative income distributions and the "price" that goes with each. This formulation focuses attention on the relations among *income distribution, organization,* and *product.*

17

ORGANIZING AGRICULTURE FOR
ECONOMIC DEVELOPMENT

Economic development has come along quite well in the United States
and the record of large parts of agriculture is no exception. Moreover,
there is at hand no theory which gives a satisfactory explanation of economic development. These observations may carry the implications that
it would be prudent to leave well enough alone and, what is more, that
existing knowledge does not provide a satisfactory basis for improving
the process. There is something to be said for this point of view and
those who by temperament are inclined to "conserve" may make a case
for *status quo* in organization.

But the problem-solving mind is all too restless to let matters stand;
for better or for worse it wants to know more. Many are drawn to the
inquiry because economic development is deemed to be important to
countries and to people. The fact that no satisfactory explanation has
emerged is a challenge; we presumably will not rest until we believe
one has been found.

It is easy to say that we want to know what are the necessary and
sufficient conditions of economic development. What are the roles of
business innovators, people who accumulate capital and employ it, individuals who "produce" new and better techniques and of men who
govern wisely and well? What part does private property, social mobility,
competition, and other institutional arrangements play? More fundamental, what values—including the outlook of a community toward
the sciences, experimentation, and induced social changes—are prereq-
uisites of economic development? The classical economists approached
political economy largely as an inquiry to determine how a country may
achieve economic progress. But this important approach has long been
neglected.[1]

Many poor, underdeveloped countries want to "induce" economic de-

[1] The United Nations report, *Measures for Economic Development of
Under-developed Countries* (New York), 1951, prepared by Alberto Baltra
Cortez, D. R. Gadgil, George Hakim, W. Arthur Lewis, and T. W. Schultz,
considers in some detail some of these issues.

velopment; so do the countries of western Europe that led the way in the industrial revolution but during recent decades have not kept pace with the United States and are now anxious to close the gap; and so also the United States, confronted by unsettled international conditions, seeks to expand and strengthen its economy in order to provide additional underpinning for its political power and rising level of living. In many places and in numerous ways, all manner of communities have become concerned about economic development. They want to achieve it; they would like to make large forward strides in a short time; people have come to expect action and quick results. The achievements of the economy of the United States may have been a matter of dull statistics, clouded by economic instability, during the twenties and thirties; but the output attained during World War II, and since then, has surprised many and dramatized for all the enlarged capacity of the economy. The Soviet Union, meanwhile, has "induced" a rate of economic development that has "shocked" most communities out of whatever complacency they may have enjoyed in earlier decades.

Aspects of the inquiry to understand economic development may be narrowed and sharpened. We may profit by restricting the analysis to a cross-sectional examination of particular countries. Canada, like the United States, has made remarkable economic progress; but large parts of eastern Canada have failed to stay abreast of the rest of the economy. The economic development within other major Western countries has also been quite uneven. Surely this has been the case in the United States: the South has been a notable laggard; in recent years the Far West has been in the vanguard; all in all, the great American "Ruhr," from Pennsylvania to Iowa, has experienced growing economic strength and a fairly even development when one considers both agriculture and industry. Why have many communities in the South, in much of the Appalachians, in the Southwest, and in large areas of the intermountain states fallen behind? How are we to explain the very uneven economic development that has come to characterize the United States where both product markets and factor transfers enjoy the essentials of an open economy?

Still another set of issues, the one on which Part One of this study has concentrated, is the effects of economic development upon particular supply and demand relationships. The process of economic development in the long pull appears to give rise to special stresses and strains in segments of the economy such as farming in particular locations. What lessons can we draw from our experiences on these matters and how may we take what we may learn to improve the existing economic organization?

We need to keep in mind that at best the results of these explorations will be tentative. The state of knowledge on these matters does not permit a set of definitive conclusions. Data to gauge the relevant variables and theory to relate one to the other are weak and in the main quite unsatisfactory. Data are fragmentary and usually not suitable for the analysis at hand. Beliefs and intuitions will of necessity carry too much of the burden. But some headway may be made, at least, in staking out the problem.

SOME GENERAL CONCEPTS AND ASSUMPTIONS

There are major difficulties in the concept of community choice whether it be for a collection of products, types of organization, economic development and stability, or for a particular distribution of personal income, or for combinations of these. How can we pass from individual preferences to a community preference to achieve a social maximum in the utilization of resources? Can this be achieved by markets that express consumer sovereignty or by voting? Arrow[2] has advanced the disturbing conclusion that, "If we exclude the possibility of interpersonal comparisons of utility, then the only methods of passing from individual tastes to social preferences which will be satisfactory and which will be defined for a wide range of sets of individual orderings are either imposed or dictatorial." The difficulties are real and basic. To proceed, however, we shall assume that cultural processes have integrated the American community sufficiently (have "imposed" a set of preferences), for all practical purposes, to give us the relevant and required community preference. We shall further assume, as in the preceding chapter, that the American community prefers more product to less and for this reason, among others, wants to encourage economic development; and also, that it prefers more decentralization in economic organization to less in attaining any given measure of economic development.

RATING THE DESIRED DECENTRALIZATION

The concept of decentralization also presents difficulties. Although we have already ascribed particular attributes to decentralization, we have not attempted to define it. A satisfactory definition does not seem possible except in terms of particular situations. Firms and households small

[2] Kenneth J. Arrow, "A Difficulty in the Concept of Social Welfare," *Journal of Political Economy,* Vol. LVIII (August, 1950); see also his *Social Choice and Individual Values* (New York: John Wiley & Sons, Inc., 1951).

enough and numerous enough to permit competition in all product and factor markets may be viewed as the economist's "ideal" in decentralization. But a community may want more decentralization than that required for competition, or it may not be willing to pay the "price" for that much decentralization. The economist's concept is not adequate (1) because there are many situations where this concept of decentralization falls outside of the range of possibilities, namely, where production "cannot" be divided among many firms, (2) because the community may prefer less decentralization and more product, and (3) because the community may prefer (even) more decentralization than is required to satisfy this particular concept of economics.

Why should the household (the family) be taken as the *best* consumption unit? Should a community not at least endeavor to decentralize further by making the individual the decision-taking agent? The community does in practice circumscribe, in many ways, the actions of the "head of the household"; and increasingly so with reference to the economic relations between husband and wife and with regard to children, the aged, and other dependents. Then, too, what are the implications for decentralization when some functions, formerly a part of the normal activities of the family, are taken over by common consent by the community, for example, developments in Western countries with regard to social security, public health, public education, and the like? On the production side, the difficulties are fully as numerous: Why should the firm which happens to represent as a producing unit the best in combination of resources and in scale of operation be taken by the community as the production unit that is most preferred? Why should the community be satisfied with only this much decentralization especially in those situations where the scale of the firm can be reduced substantially from its "economic optimum" with comparatively little loss in productive "efficiency"? Suppose it were possible, in the United States, to increase the number of farms 10 per cent beyond the "optimum" figure without reducing the productivity of factors used in farming by more than 1 per cent, would not this "loss" in productivity be a small "price" for the community to pay for the extra decentralization? In any event, if the community, with complete information at hand, were to choose this combination, it would take priority over the economist's concept of the best size of farms in agriculture. The rub is: Where does the community acquire "complete information" and what are the effects of those preferences which we are inclined to call "vested interest"?

Economic organization, however, goes beyond firms and households. Product and factor markets are required. The political and social process cannot be excluded. Are small markets a sign of decentralization and are they to be rated higher than large markets? Do local markets go above national markets and the latter stand higher than international markets on the decentralization scale? Surely, the economist will balk at such a criterion, but what about the community's conception? Organization is something the community must evaluate, and should the community rate a set of local markets higher than a single national market in terms of decentralization and should it also be prepared to forego as much "product" as is necessary to have this type of decentralization, we presumably must accept this preference as representing the particular attributes which the community singles out and wants in terms of markets. A similar line of argument may be applied in placing national fiscal and monetary management higher than international actions in this sphere.

Despite these conceptual difficulties, we shall endeavor to relate types of organization and "product," in the belief that under particular circumstances it is possible to rate alternatives in economic organization. We shall, however, try to make explicit the nature of the assumptions at various points as we proceed.

Economic organization may be viewed as a social apparatus which the community uses, among other things, *to induce* economic development. Economic organization may also be viewed simply as a set of institutions having the function, among other things, *to adjust* the economy to fundamental changes in product demands and factor supplies that result from economic development the mainspring of which, it may be supposed, is deeply embedded in particular cultural and political conditions. Both views have relevance and may be explored with profit. The two processes, implicit in the terms "to induce" and "to adjust," are not necessarily unrelated one to the other. We shall, however, find it convenient to consider each separately.

ORGANIZATION TO INDUCE ECONOMIC DEVELOPMENT

Neither theory nor data will permit us to explore the nature of the social, political, and economic circumstances that seem to be required for economic development, even if the scope of our study were that comprehensive. The problem implied is, however, a challenging one which should attract serious workers.

In a high-food-drain economy, where most of the income of the community is represented by food, there is little room, except in agriculture, for new and better production possibilities, because the productive efforts required to produce food are so large a part of the whole. Even in a rich country like the United States, a stagnant agriculture would place a heavy burden on the economic development of the rest of the economy. Improvements in fundamental factor supplies within agriculture are an important element in economic development. How may such improvements be achieved? Useful insights may be obtained by considering agriculture as a special case in this context.

Techniques. Take, first, advances in the techniques of production. Improvements in these are important in economic development; they are not a passive element nor are they merely a by-product of the sciences. It is possible, as has been shown in Chap. 7, for a community to organize itself to "produce" new and better techniques; the United States has done so, in fact; and, to the extent that a community engages purposefully in this activity, and the resulting techniques are applied, it may be viewed as a way of inducing economic development.

The "production" of new techniques is becoming a primary economic activity; the amount of inputs required is sufficiently large to make them a matter of economic concern. The inputs are committed to obtain a set of expected outputs and not to do "research for research sake." In the case of agriculture, as indicated in Chap. 7, the "production" of new techniques is an economic activity that requires a large collection of specialized inputs, altogether too large for a small firm to manage. Small family farms are hardly appropriate producing units for this undertaking. Large farms, by existing standards, are also too small for the task. Specialized private firms with large assets, willing and prepared to work for years for salable results, can and do operate in some areas. Economic organization to "produce" agricultural techniques has become (1) largely a public enterprise and (2) not very decentralized by usually accepted criteria. It may be argued, in the case of the United States, that a set of forty-eight state agricultural experiment stations[3] is a relatively decentralized organization; and it is, compared to having one national research agency for this purpose. Nevertheless, a particular experiment station in a major agricultural state is a large operation when it employs not only one but even several million dollars of inputs annually—hardly a small operation when compared with a typical farm.

How satisfactory are the results? The fact that remarkable advances have been made in agricultural techniques in the United States, especially since about 1920, is hardly a relevant datum in determining whether too few or too many resources are being allocated to this particular activity. Let us now leave the organization of the collection of inputs currently allocated and consider only the quantity of resources committed. The value of the new agricultural techniques has exceeded

---

[3] The figure "48" is symbolic because some states really have more than one of these stations and, in addition, there are stations in the outlying territories.

so greatly the value of inputs that have been used to "produce" these techniques that it is hard to believe that enough resources have been and are being committed to this enterprise. We are, so it would appear, a long way from achieving an economic optimum in this field. The political process, which for this undertaking, because of the way in which it is organized, determines the rate of inputs by the funds it appropriates, works quite imperfectly when tested against normal economic standards for maximizing production. (For data and estimates on this point, see Chap. 7.)

Our conclusion is: Too few resources are being committed to this particular enterprise and, inasmuch as new techniques are very important in achieving economic development, more can and should be done to induce economic development by allocating more resources to the "production" of agricultural techniques.

Information. We shall restrict ourselves to "economic information," meaning by this information that is of some relevance in economic decisions. But the analytical lines are not nearly as well drawn as they are in the case of production techniques. For some purposes, techniques may be classified as a particular type of information; however, because production techniques have special attributes and applications, they can be treated separately as we have done.

Our presumptions about economic information may be stated as follows: (1) This information is not assumed for a community (a useful assumption at some points in economic analysis); (2) this information is not a free service; (3) economic information is always incomplete and it can usually be made more complete at some price; (4) economic information can be "produced" and "distributed"; and (5) economic development is dependent to a substantial degree upon the nature and scope of the information which is "made" available.

The state of economic information affects both the organizational possibilities and economic development. In organization the more widely the relevant information is disseminated, the greater the possibilities for decentralization, other things being unchanged. This aspect of information is sufficiently important in itself to make the "production and distribution" of such information a matter of major social concern. In addition, regardless of advances in techniques and increases in fundamental factor supplies whether from savings, improvement in skills, change in the composition of the population, or from some other development, the allocative system cannot take advantage of these unless the necessary information is available. The new allocations, on which economic development is dependent, can be no better than is the information on which they are based.

It is our belief that a community can induce a measure of economic development by making improvements in the information on which economic decisions are based. Moreover, there is some evidence in the American setting to indicate that these contributions may be relatively large; we have in mind here, among others, the work of the agricultural extension services.

It is difficult to classify the information that is relevant in this connection. For firms and household units we may take the following categories: (1) technical information required to farm and to operate farm households. This is an area in which the extension services have made a substantial contribution. (2) Economic information about outputs (farm products and services). The work in standards and grades has helped greatly to classify and identify these outputs. Information about their values, despite the highly organized farm-products markets that exist, is still quite imperfect at the points of decision in farming. The case for forward prices rests, in large part, on the need for better price information which is meaningful in making allocative decisions by farmers. (3) Economic information about inputs (factors). This category of information is the least satisfactory; neither the technical nor value attributes are known satisfactorily. What information exists is poorly organized. We shall point out in some detail later that the existing shortcomings of these factor markets explain in large part why agriculture adjusts so imperfectly to the changes associated with economic development.

It is our belief and thesis that economic information is a valuable service of critical importance in economic organization and in economic development and that this service can be "produced and distributed."[4] The process may be approached and useful insights may be obtained by a representation which endeavors to identify these production operations in order to determine the nature and the value of the inputs committed and of the outputs realized. The activities of the agricultural extension services and of the agencies enforcing and working on standards and grades should be studied from this point of view. It is our belief that the outcome of such an analysis would indicate that "returns" from additional inputs in these and related enterprises, that of "producing and distributing" economic information, are exceedingly large.

[4] Theoretical work in economics has concentrated on the behavior of firms and households under conditions of "complete" information. More recently efforts have been made to deal with "incomplete" information in explaining the behavior of firms and households. A third, and what appears to be a more relevant assumption, is to take information as a service which has value and which can be produced at a cost and then proceed to determine the optimum output of information under various conditions, including meaningful classes of economic uncertainty.

Capital. The accumulation of additional capital by saving and enlarging the productive plant is certainly one of the more powerful engines to be used to induce economic development. We shall, however, leave it here and consider it briefly when we come to analyze the adjustment processes in relation to the capital market.

How should these various activities be organized? The answer depends upon the possibilities and preferences that exist. In the "production" of new techniques for agriculture, we have been willing to forgo substantial decentralization in organization in order to have the larger research output that this makes possible. These research activities, accordingly, have been placed into the hands of large public agencies, chiefly the agricultural experiment stations. To advance the analysis beyond this point, it will be necessary to find ways of improving our knowledge about the shape and position of both the possibilities and preference curves.

The activities that are required to "produce and distribute" economic information are not well defined; possibilities and preferences are not as discernible as they are in the "production" of techniques. Many, and a diversity of agencies, are engaged in these and related activities. A farmer may learn about a new production technique from his neighbors, newspapers, farm journals, the radio, dealers seeking to sell the techniques, the action agencies of the U.S. Department of Agriculture, and from the county agent and the extension service. Economic information about farm products and factors also comes to him from many sources. The experience of the agricultural extension services, organized by states, points to about the same conclusion with regard to organization already advanced for the agricultural experiment stations. Beyond this we cannot go until more study has been given to this subject.

The organization of activities related to the accumulation and investment of capital, while an important process in inducing economic development, will be considered when we take up the functioning of the capital market as it serves agriculture.

ORGANIZATION TO ADJUST TO ECONOMIC DEVELOPMENT

In Part One we considered the effects of the economic development upon agriculture. Our study indicated that economic development places particular stresses and strains on the adjustment processes of the economy, especially within agriculture. Before turning to these adjustments and the implications they have for economic organization, it is necessary to emphasize the growing dependency of agriculture upon the rest of the economy.

Farm families in the United States have become less self-contained; their production and their consumption have been oriented increasingly toward markets and away from production for their own household use. Farm people have gained from the fuller integration of their production and consumption into the exchange system, in so far as they share the benefits that come from the extension of the national and international market, from the specialization that this makes possible, from advances in technology occurring in other fields, and from the increasing range of goods and services made available to them. The level of living of most farm families has improved over the years. In becoming dependent upon markets, farm people have also incurred certain liabilities. These liabilities were not for the most part anticipated; having appeared, they have come to claim much attention in agricultural policy.

As farm families have become more dependent upon selling and buying, they also have become more vulnerable to the unsatisfactory performance in other parts of the economy. The well-being of most farm families is now directly linked with decisions of other "firms" affecting production, consumption, and savings. More specifically, the production and price policies of management and of organized labor, imperfections in competition, the periodic destruction of aggregate demand, the periodic lack of sufficient expansion outside agriculture to provide employment for all available labor, equipment, and plants and to put to account advances in technology, the strangling of world trade by nationalism, and the inadequacy of government policies, especially in the monetary-fiscal sphere—these private and public actions have come to have a direct significance for farm prices and income.

The experiences of the interwar years indicate that American agriculture at times paid dearly for its dependence on the exchange system. In spite of their steady output of a large volume of food and fiber, produced year after year with ever-rising efficiency, farm people have found themselves pitched about by the forward and backward surges of other sectors of the economy. Small wonder that farm people have organized into interest groups seeking ways to lessen the burdens that the exchange economy has placed on them.[5] In their efforts to cope with the emergency of the thirties, farmers accepted production control. In this they

[5] Farmers on the more commercialized farms are organized into commodity groups and into general farm organizations, and their price and income problems have been given strong representation and expression. Commercialized farms are not necessarily large; the greater percentage of them are family-type farms. There are, however, a large group of farm families still comparatively self-sustaining, essentially unorganized, and accordingly less articulate. Their problems, for the most part, receive little or no public attention.

were following the footpaths, so they felt and were told, of industry; the thing to do when the demand shifts to the left is to curtail output and thus, at least, maintain prices. But production control is not a solution either for the underemployment and the attendant low earnings in agriculture or for the instability of farm prices and incomes.[6]

Structural and Locational Attributes of Economic Development. How satisfactorily has the existing economic organization worked in adjusting the allocation of resources to fundamental changes in product demands and factor supplies that have come with development? Has the economy absorbed these changes and, in doing so, has it achieved the new and better optima made possible by development? In turning to these issues, we shall concentrate on the adjustments confronting and affecting agriculture. This study indicates that the process of development has been such that frequently the returns to human agents engaged in farming fall behind and the returns within agriculture become quite uneven. The explanation for this outcome is to be found in two of the basic characteristics of economic development: (1) its structural attributes and (2) its locational attributes.

The structural attributes relevant to this problem may be restated as follows: The demand for farm products, meaning mainly the demand for food, increases less than does the demand for nonfarm products and services; whereas the new and better production possibilities that emerge from economic development are about as favorable for the production of farm products as they are for nonfarm products taken altogether. Then, too, there are the supply effects (quantity of labor) of the relatively high net reproduction rate of farm people. The consequences are that it becomes necessary for people to leave farming and take up

[6] This study does not consider the problem of social security and relief for agriculture. This is a major omission. We have concentrated on economic development and economic instability. We have not, however, dealt with farm relief and social security except in a most incidental manner. Adequate security and relief measures have not yet been developed for agriculture— whether the emergencies arise from sharp curtailment in demand and from depressed prices, or from needs associated with old age, sickness, accidents, and unemployment (in the case of hired farm laborers). In this respect, legislation has not reached the stage that has been attained in providing relief and security for industrial workers. The problems of agriculture in this sphere are so specialized and of such major importance that they deserve special treatment. They have been omitted from this study, since the object here is to examine agriculture in a developing economy and to give some consideration to the problem of price and income fluctuations; measures appropriate for farm relief and social security for farm people are too important to be treated in an incidental manner.

other occupations (the *total* movement, not the net movement, of people out of United States agriculture from 1920 to 1949 may have exceeded 50 million people) and for some classes of capital resources to be drawn into farming (see Chap. 7).

The locational attributes may also be recapituated. The process of economic development does not occur at all points, at the same time, in an economy of any size and diversity; it makes forward thrusts in particular locations (hypothesis advanced in Chap. 9). These locations become centers of economic development; they are increasingly industrial-urban in composition. They are not primarily in agriculture because in the United States and other Western countries agriculture is already a relatively small part of the economy and because the process of development appears to have its mainspring in the industrial-urban complex as such.[7] Some farming areas are situated less favorably than are others in relation to such centers of development.

These two sets of attributes of economic development indicate the nature of the adjustments required. In general the results have been as follows: The existing economic organization works best at or near a particular center of development. It also works best in those parts of agriculture that are favorably situated in relation to such centers; and it works least satisfactorily in those parts of agriculture located at the periphery of such centers.

Why this outcome? Where does the fault lie? Are we to ascribe it to firm and household units, or to product and factor markets, or to the political and social processes? Legislation which attempts to impose on agriculture parity prices which are anchored to the distant past is certainly not the way to adjust farming to economic development. Markets which fluctuate widely are not a satisfactory guide to farmers in allocating resources to accommodate agricultural production to the slow, gradual changes that come with development. Farms operated by farmers who have too few assets available to them are not likely to

---

[7] There are many instances in the literature and notably in the efforts of governments to induce economic development where these locational attributes have given rise to the inference that it is desirable to industrialize and to neglect agriculture, or to industrialize at the expense of agriculture. This inference is entirely unwarranted, for it may be true that unless new and better production possibilities are achieved in agriculture the whole process of economic development in a particular country may be retarded or even stopped, or that at the margin, in the small, the extra productivity from extra capital inputs may be as large as or larger than in other sectors, or that in many countries agriculture is so large a part of the economy that there is little or no room for important advances in productivity unless agriculture is improved.

make the adjustments that become necessary as development proceeds. There are, of course, many particular characteristics of the existing organization at each of the three levels which affect adversely the adjustments on which we are concentrating.

Are there, however, some general characteristics in the organization of agriculture which are important in determining its capacity and efficiency in adjusting to economic development? A comparison of the organization, as we find it at the center and at the periphery of economic development, may be instructive and useful. What we are after, in improving the existing organization, is a performance which is more nearly like that at or near the center. In making this comparison, we shall restrict ourselves to the American scene.

Periphery and Center Compared. Family farms predominate at both the center and at the periphery; therefore the difference in efficiency of the organization at the two locations cannot be ascribed to the family farm as such. Nor is the family farm in itself the corrective for the difference in allocative efficiency. About the same conclusion emerges for the political process. Federal laws for agriculture are usually general in scope; they apply to agriculture whether it is situated at the center or at the periphery of economic development. It is necessary to qualify this statement somewhat because some laws apply to particular commodities which are regional in character and because organized agricultural groups represent primarily those farmers who are favorably located relative to the centers of economic development and these organized groups, of course, press for legislation favorable to themselves. In the main, however, the difference in economic organization, to which we are addressing ourselves, does not have its origin in the political process as such. Nor has the political process, with all the legislation that has been enacted to help agriculture, provided a solution for the uneven economic development that has characterized the United States.

Farm product markets are also on about the same footing whether they serve farmers located at the center or at the periphery of what is a forward thrust in economic development. There is, however, one distinction of some importance, that is, in many instances the prices of the products produced by farmers who are situated at or near these centers are the more stable of the two.[8] This difference in price stability provides at least a clue to the comparative efficiency of the economic organization at the two locations.

[8] For some evidence on this point, see Chap. 14, "Spot and Future Prices as Production Guides," in Theodore W. Schultz, *Production and Welfare of Agriculture* (New York: The Macmillan Company, 1949).

The markets from which farmers buy and to which they sell factors of production work much less satisfactorily at the periphery than they do at or near the centers which characterize economic development. It is our belief that the basic explanation for the relatively poor performance of the existing economic organization in adjusting to economic development is to be found in the factor markets. The uneven rate of economic progress of regions and of farming areas can be traced, so it appears to us, very largely to major imperfections in the various factor markets on which farm people are dependent. If this is a valid interpretation of what has happened in the United States, it follows that much of what has been done by way of legislation has not even touched the root of the problem of achieving a better adjustment to economic development. Most of this legislation has focused on product prices and not on improving the relevant factor markets.

Our next task is to consider how these factor markets function and how they may be improved.

18

FACTOR MARKETS AND ECONOMIC DEVELOPMENT

The factor markets are a key to the retardation that characterizes agriculture and the very uneven development that is typical of agriculture in an economy as large and as diverse as that of the United States. To adjust agricultural production more satisfactorily to changes in fundamental factor supplies and in product demands that come with development, it will be necessary to improve the existing factor markets serving agriculture.

It will be convenient to group the factors into two categories, labor and capital, while recognizing that the capital element "invested" in the human agent is also relevant and important, especially in the long run. Markets related to capital are of three kinds: markets in which particular physical inputs are bought and sold; markets for renting specific resources; and markets for lending fluid resources. Earlier in this study the inputs used in farming were grouped into eight classes, drawing upon the classification recently developed by the Bureau of Agricultural Economics. It may be helpful to comment on these markets in a preliminary way at this point.

The markets for fertilizer and lime and the items required to operate motor vehicles, which together account for 10.6 per cent of all inputs in 1950, vary widely in their efficiency. Farmer cooperatives have entered these fields and, it would appear, they have made contributions of some importance. Even so these markets are not wholly satisfactory. The market for farm buildings is hard to assess. For the most part, it is capital that must be treated as fixed once it has been invested, like improvements in land. It is noteworthy, however, as surplus farm dwellings became available following the shrinkage in the farm population and the farm enlargement, especially in parts of the plains states after the thirties, that many such dwellings were moved, often many miles, and relocated in towns or at the fringes of cities. Here the growth and expansion of such towns and cities was a necessary condition for such a market to develop. The markets for materials used to build and to maintain farm structures are subject to many imperfections. Maintenance (or depreciation) of buildings, farm machinery, motor vehicles, and farm equipment as a class represent 12.6 per cent of all inputs in 1950. The interest imputed to the investment represented by horses and mules, motor vehicles, other machinery, crops, and livestock accounted for about 6.5 per cent of all inputs. A miscellaneous class of inputs should also be mentioned consisting of ginning, irrigation, and grazing (fees); fire, windstorm, hail, and crop insurance; dairy supplies, various greenhouse expenses, the services of veterinarians, and medicine; insecticides, containers, and electricity used for production; tolls for sugar cane, sirup, and sorgo; hardware, blacksmithing, operation of gas and steam engines; and twine—these altogether, however, account for less than 5 per cent of all inputs.

The two really important inputs are, of course, labor (human effort) and land used for agricultural purposes, which in 1950 represented about 38 and 25 per cent, respectively, of all inputs at 1946–1948 input prices. Before turning to these, however, it should be observed that most of the factor markets serving agriculture have a set of limitations in common. First, technical specifications are in the main unsatisfactory. Some are not standardized; some have production effects about which the farmer is not informed, for example, various fertilizers, protein feeds, and insecticides. The farmer, whether he acts as a buyer or seller, finds it exceedingly difficult to determine the technical attributes of the factor. Where specifications are set forth and available, some are so "technical" that the description has little or no meaning to the farmer. It is all too often a pig in a poke that is being priced. Second, the relevant economic information about supply and demand is usually poorly integrated, with the result that prices are often local, particular, and sporadic.

LABOR MARKET SERVING AGRICULTURE

In spite of the decline in the farm population and in the size of the labor force in agriculture, labor continues to be the largest input committed to farming.[1] We shall, accordingly, give major attention to this market because of its economic importance. We shall, first, consider how the labor market serving agriculture functions and then how it may be improved. On how this market functions we shall draw heavily upon the work of Johnson.[2]

[1] In 1910–1914, at factor costs at the time, labor represented 47 per cent of all inputs [see Chap. 7; also, Glen T. Barton and Martin R. Cooper, "Relation of Agricultural Production to Inputs," *Review of Economics and Statistics,* Vol. XXX (May, 1948), Table 2] and 42 per cent of all inputs in 1946–1948 at factor cost then current.

[2] With funds made available by the Rockefeller Foundation, we have for

Functioning of the Labor Market

The total movement of people out of agriculture from 1920 to 1949 may have exceeded 50 million, representing a net movement of farm people to nonfarm areas of about 17.5 million, of which half may have been from the farm labor force. This is an impressive interchange of workers and of other people. Is it possible to gauge from these and related data how efficient the labor market has been in this area, using the criterion that "Labor of equivalent capacities should earn the same real marginal returns in all employment?"

Relative Earnings of Workers. Johnson has found:[3]

1. COMPARABILITY OF FARM AND NONFARM WORKERS. There is probably not much difference between the capacities and skills of farm and nonfarm people, taken as a group. Recent migrants from farm areas earned about 90 per cent as much as the median of the nonfarm residents. Nor

---

some years, at the University of Chicago, been carrying forward major researches in this and related areas endeavoring to explain the low economic productivity that characterizes large parts of agriculture. Most of this research work has been borne by Professor D. Gale Johnson and the results, as the various studies are completed, will appear in due time as a major contribution from his hand. The list of materials already available include:

D. G. Johnson, "Resource Allocation under Share Contracts," *Journal of Political Economy*, Vol. LVIII (April, 1950).

O. H. Brownlee and D. G. Johnson, "Reducing Price Variability Confronting Primary Producers," *Journal of Farm Economics*, Vol. XXXII (May, 1950).

D. G. Johnson, "Nature of the Supply Function of Agricultural Products," *American Economic Review*, Vol. XL (September, 1950).

D. G. Johnson, "Functioning of the Labor Market," *Journal of Farm Economics*, Vol. XXXIII (February, 1951).

D. G. Johnson and M. C. Nottenburg, "A Critical Analysis of Farm Employment Estimates," *Journal of the American Statistical Association*, Vol. XLVI (June, 1951).

D. G. Johnson, "Some Effects of Region, Community Size, Color and Occupation on Family and Individual Income," to be published by the National Bureau of Economic Research.

D. G. Johnson, "Comparability of Labor Capacities of Farm and Nonfarm Labor," Office of Agricultural Economics Research, University of Chicago (mimeo.).

[3] From his paper "Functioning of the Labor Market," *Journal of Farm Economics*, Vol. XXXIII (February, 1951). See also Chap. 6, "Economics of Agriculture," in *A Survey of Contemporary Economics*, Vol. II, Bernard F. Haley, editor (Chicago: Richard D. Irwin, Inc., 1952).

did any important differences appear that could be attributed to the region of origin, provided only white migrants are included.[4]

2. MONEY VALUES OF LABOR RETURNS:[5]

MONEY VALUES FOR THE UNITED STATES

Year	Agriculture	Industry
1940	$410	$1,275
1948	1,770	2,710

MONEY VALUES FOR REGIONS, 1945

Region	Agriculture	Industry
Pacific.	$2,200	
West North Central. . . .	1,745	
Mountain.	1,560	
East North Central	1,455	
Middle Atlantic	1,100	
New England.	1,090	
West South Central	760	
South Atlantic	710	
East South Central	540	
United States	1,135	$2,255

3. REAL VALUE OF LABOR RETURNS. The assumption is made, based on some research,[6] that a dollar earned in a farm area will buy 25 per cent more than it will in a nonfarm area. Accordingly, we arrive at the following figures:

REAL VALUES FOR THE UNITED STATES

Year	Agriculture	Industry	Difference in favor of industry
1940	$510	$1,275	$765
1948	2,210	2,710	500

[4] The statistical difference, if significant, may be ascribed to the relatively short period which the farm migrant had for adjustment and to differences in education (*ibid.*, p. 77).

[5] *Ibid.*, pp. 77, 78.

[6] Nathan Koffsky, paper appearing in *Studies in Income and Wealth,* Vol. XI (New York: National Bureau of Economic Research, Inc., 1949) with comments by Margaret G. Reid, E. W. Grove, and D. Gale Johnson.

Since the average wage income of employed industrial workers was $2,255 in 1945, at least two and perhaps four of the regions show a rough equivalence in real returns for labor on farms and labor in industry. In the others, the real returns to farm labor are less and in three they are far below.[7]

The inference from these data is clear: equality in "real returns between farm and nonfarm occupations requiring equivalent capacities"

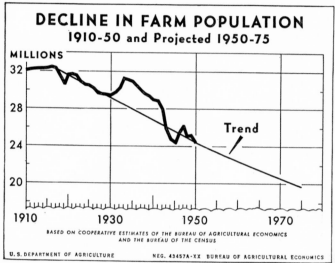

FIG. 18–1. Decline in farm population, 1910–1950, and projected 1950–1975.

had not been achieved "for three regions with about half of the farm population." This inequality in returns to labor, a measure of the failure of the labor market, is the observable outcome after a substantial period of full employment.

An International Comparison. Thomson,[8] studying the productivity of the human agent in agriculture in the United States, the United Kingdom, and France, found that while the real earnings of farm and nonfarm

[7] In 1940, the real returns to farm labor in the region best situated were only 55 per cent as high as those of employed industrial workers (after adjustments for cost of living differences).

[8] Procter Thomson, *The Productivity of the Human Agent in Agriculture: An International Comparison.* Ph.D. thesis, University of Chicago. This study was also financed in large part from Rockefeller Foundation funds. The thesis, however, as filed does not include all the tables, including some of the data appearing in Table 18–1. These data are, however, in a larger, more complete manuscript on file in the Office of Agricultural Economics Research, University of Chicago.

workers have been very unequal in the United States, they have approached equality in France, with the United Kingdom in an intermediate position.

TABLE 18–1. REAL EARNINGS OF WORKERS IN INDUSTRY RELATIVE TO WORKERS IN
AGRICULTURE, UNITED STATES, FRANCE, AND UNITED KINGDOM

Period	United States[a]	France[b]	United Kingdom[c]
1900–1909	1.61	1.10 (1901–1911)	1.74 (1904–1910)
1910–1919	1.36		1.75 (1911–1913)
1920–1929	1.84	1.00 (1921–1929)	1.28 (1920–1922)
			1.78 (1924–1929)
1930–1939	1.82	1.25	1.63 (1930–1934)
			1.38 (1935–1939)
1940–1949	1.23	0.89 (1946–1948)	0.79 (1940–1945)
1900–1949	1.57	1.10 (1901–1948)	1.54 (1900–1945)

[a] Average annual earnings in manufacturing (standardized for differences in age, sex, and racial composition between farm and nonfarm workers), divided by income of the human agent, full-time units, in agriculture and adjusted for differences in cost of living (Table 17, column 3).

[b] Average annual earnings in industry divided by income of human agent in agriculture, full-time units. No adjustment for cost of living differences has been made. Thomson estimates it to be of the order of 10 to 15 per cent, leaving out Paris (Table 33, column 2).

[c] Average wages in industry divided by income of human agent in agriculture, full-time units (Table 45, column 3). No adjustment for cost of living has been made. It is probably quite small. Nor are the industrial units standardized.

SOURCE: Procter Thomson, *The Productivity of the Human Agent in Agriculture: An International Comparison*, Ph.D. thesis, University of Chicago.

The labor market in France, during the first half of the current century, maintained earnings about equal in the two sectors of the economy, whereas in the United States earnings in industry averaged 57 per cent higher than they did in agriculture. The principal contribution of Thomson's study lies in his comparison of the United States and France (United Kingdom data cited are not sufficiently comparable to permit direct comparisons) and the explanation, to which we shall turn later, that emerges for this important difference between the two countries. The variations in the relative earnings of the two groups within the United States, from decade to decade, confirm other available information about the economic history of the period. The 1910–1919 period was a "golden" era for agriculture relatively, with earnings in industry only 36 per cent higher than in agriculture; the forties, however, turned out to be somewhat better, undoubtedly the best period American agriculture has experienced. The twenties and thirties were strikingly adverse for agriculture, with earnings in industry fully 80 per cent above those in agriculture, which helps explain the unrest among farm people which was already widespread before the general debacle of the early thirties.

Low-output Farms in the United States. A study by Wilcox and Hendrix,[9] for the Joint Committee of the Economic Report, approaches the low-output–low-income farms in the United States as a problem of *underemployment* of the farm people situated on such farms.

This study identifies one million farm families, giving essentially all of their time to farming, "where an able-bodied operator of working age produced only one-third as much as workers on the medium-size commercial family farms."[10] The average gross value of the output on these farms, including the value of farm products used in the home, was only $825.

GEOGRAPHIC LOCATION. The million farm familes referred to above were distributed as follows:

	Per cent
South	70
North	26
West	4

Only 165,000 of this group were sharecroppers and, as to tenure, 57 per cent were owner-operator families and 43 per cent tenants. The surprising fact is that the enlargement in farm size and the higher production per acre which occurred during the forties are developments which have in large part by-passed this large group of farm families.

The study also finds 600,000 farm families on small commercial farms where the operator is able-bodied, of working age, and has little or no off-farm work, as substantially underemployed. These farms are located 58, 37, and 7 per cent in the South, North, and West, respectively; and 60 per cent of this group classified as owner-operators.

Throughout the Wilcox-Hendrix study the earnings of human agents on medium commercial family farms (and of industrial workers) are taken as "normal" returns for able-bodied workers, fully employed. The

[9] Walter W. Wilcox and W. E. Hendrix, *Underemployment of Rural Families*, Joint Committee on the Economic Report, Joint Committee print, 82d Cong., 1st Sess. The subcommittee in charge was under the chairmanship of Senator John Sparkman. The hearings before the Subcommittee on Low-income Families which carry the title, *Low-income Families*, 81st Cong., 1st Sess., pursuant to Sec. 5(A) of Public Law 304 held December 12 to 22, 1949, include testimony by Charles E. Brannan, D. Gale Johnson, Margaret Reid, Theodore W. Schultz, and others.

[10] From p. 13 of the report.

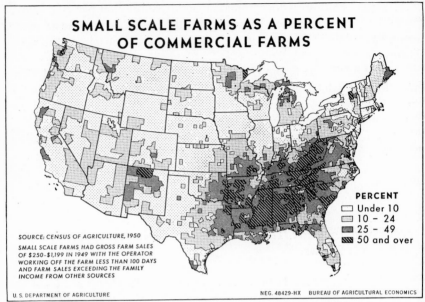

FIG. 18–2. Small-scale farms as a percent of commercial farms.

following figures summarize the basic data for (1) small-scale farms on which the 1,000,000 underemployed farm families were situated, (2) the small-scale commercial family farms on which the 600,000 underemployed families were situated, and (3) the medium community family farms, consisting of 1,173,000 farms, which were taken as the benchmark for the comparative analysis.

	Medium commercial family farms	Small commercial family farms	Small-scale farms
Gross income (1944)	$4,648	$1,874	$825
Labor resources per farm	1.8	1.5	1.3
Gross income per labor resource	$2,588	$1,249	$635
Index for line above	100	48.3	24.5[a]

[a] The capital inputs used on these farms are less than on the medium commercial family farms. Adjusting for this difference in capital places the output per worker on these small-scale farms at about one-third that of workers on the medium class.

SOURCE: Walter W. Wilcox and W. E. Hendrix, *Underemployment of Rural Families*, Joint Committee on the Economic Report, Joint Committee print, 82d Cong., 1st Sess., Appendix A, Tables 4, 5.

BY WAY OF EXPLANATION. Johnson examines particular attributes of the nonfarm labor market for an explanation which may account for the unsatisfactory way in which this market has functioned. Three hypotheses are considered.

1. Farm migrants in the main move short distances; therefore, since returns to labor in agriculture are lowest in the South, if the labor returns for nonfarm jobs in the South were also low relative to nonfarm jobs in other parts of the United States, the failure of short-distance migration to equalize returns within the economy as a whole would be explainable. The results are, however, "that white families in communities of the same size have roughly the same incomes in the South as in any other region in the nation."[11]

2. The possibility exists that unions and firms make entry into nonfarm employment difficult for farm migrants. The available data, however, do not support the hypothesis "that unions have in most cases 'distorted' the wage structure in a way inimical to farm migration."

3. There is also the possibility that minimum wage legislation has had an adverse effect upon job opportunities available to farm migrants, as it has had in Puerto Rico. Johnson has not found any evidence to indicate that existing legislation has had much effect in the United States.

The comparison of the United States and France is highly instructive in this connection. While it does not explain why the labor market fails to adjust labor supplies to the changes in product demands and factor supplies that occur with economic development, it strongly supports the hypothesis that the maladjustments in the allocation of labor are a function of economic development. Thomson's data show, as set forth above, that in France real returns to workers in industry and in agriculture, of presumed equivalent capacities, have not become unequal in spite of dislocations caused by two major wars, serious inflations, and other disturbances, while in the United States the outcome in these two sets of earnings has been very different. In examining the interplay of "progress and equilibrium," Thomson concludes that four factors are primarily responsible: "(1) the relatively slow rate of increase in real industrial earnings in France, (2) the low birth rate in rural areas of France, (3) manipulation of the terms of trade for farm produce by means of the protective tariff, (4) the low rate of technological development in France's agriculture."[12]

---

[11] Johnson, *op. cit.*, p. 80. Johnson also examines the data for subarea effects, which may be hidden in the larger regional averages. The test made indicates negative results on this score.

[12] Thomson, *op. cit.*, Chap. 5, p. 93. Thomson also considers various barriers to migration and concludes: "France has achieved equilibrium because the problems she faced in this respect were less severe, rather than because the barrier index in that country was lower than in the United States."

In the United States, in marked contrast to France, rapid economic progress has been the order of the day which has made possible the rapid rise in real earnings; the birth rate in farming communities has been relatively high; and improvements in agricultural technology have been many and impressive. The organizational price of such progress is adjustments; but the existing economic organization, particularly the labor and capital markets, has not had the capacity to cope satisfactorily with these adjustments.

POSSIBLE EXPLANATION. How, then, are we to explain the substantial failure of the labor market to equalize real returns for equivalent capacities in the United States? The question may be narrowed somewhat: Why has the performance of this market been so uneven as data for the United States appear to indicate? In Chap. 9 the hypothesis was advanced that fundamental divergencies in economic development are related to location. The forward thrusts of economic development are specific to particular locations. Divergencies arise and persist despite free trade and factor transfers within the economy. The various factor markets, especially the labor market, work most satisfactorily at or near the centers of these forward thrusts of economic development and least satisfactorily at the periphery of such centers. At or near these centers economic information is more complete; it is better in quality and quantity; it is better organized. There is, therefore, less uncertainty because the required economic information is more dependable. Product markets also tend to be somewhat more dependable. The cultural process is also affected significantly by economic development. The patterns of wants are modified; changes occur which have important effects upon the growth and composition of the population, upon investments in the human agent, upon the value placed on "leisure," and upon the collection of goods and services which people acquire and utilize. Changes in all these attributes of people's outlook and wants occur at a more rapid rate where economic development has gained its head.

The possible remaining explanation is of two parts, one largely *external* to agriculture and the other *internal* to it. The external aspect consists of uncertainty, uncertainty pertaining to jobs and the conditions related to them; this uncertainty acts as a barrier to migration; and, this particular barrier becomes greater as one leaves a center and proceeds to the periphery. The internal aspect is a function of the different stages in cultural adaptation to the broad stream of events and circumstances that have characterized the industrial revolution. Economic development, therefore, has played an important part in this process of cultural adaptation. People and communities situated at or near such centers reach an advanced stage in this process sooner than do those located at the periphery. To be situated in one of the less advanced stages acts as a barrier to migration. These stages may be viewed as conditions which are indigenous to particular farm people and their immediate environment. Johnson has described this aspect in the following terms:

Most farm people in low income areas may have so limited a set of experiences that they fear the transition to nonfarm life; many may feel strong family or community ties; many may have reached an age that inhibits seeking new experiences; others may reject the values and modes of living that they associate with nonfarm living.[13]

Improving the Labor Market

The preceding analysis establishes two things: (1) the labor market serving agriculture in the United States does not function satisfactorily, even under conditions of full employment; and (2) at least three explanations sometimes advanced to account for this failure do not stand up when tested against the available data. More study is required, however, to determine which part of the possible remaining explanation, or what combinations of the two, will account for the unsatisfactory performance of this labor market. Our endeavor to indicate ways for improving this factor market will be based on the assumption that both parts of this remaining explanation, one external and the other internal to agriculture, are valid.

There are essentially two ways of improving the labor market with regard to the problem before us, namely, (1) eliminate the existing barriers to migration and (2) reduce the necessity for migration. We shall consider briefly three sets of measures to do the first, that is, making the relevant economic information more complete, making grants or loans to move, and investing more in human agents.

Economic Information. The case for more complete information about job specifications, conditions related to employment, and wages rests on a firm foundation. This approach to improve the labor market should make possible more "product" and not less "decentralization" in economic organization, except for the "production and distribution" of the information per se.

There is need to develop a national service that will at least inform workers—not alone in agriculture but also in other occupations—of job opportunities. Farm workers in the more remote farming areas, at the periphery of economic development where output per farm is low, are

---

[13] Johnson, *op. cit.*, p. 87.

especially isolated; they lack knowledge of the type of jobs, working conditions, and earnings that may be available elsewhere.

The *National Agricultural Outlook* has been developed since 1923 into a useful instrument for bringing economic information to farmers and to others interested in agriculture. Under a similar procedure, information about industrial job opportunities could usefully be provided by analyzing the supply-and-demand forces playing upon labor in various industries and in various localities. A *National Outlook* to serve all labor is long overdue. Such an information service should be supplemented by a national and state employment service assisting workers more directly and immediately from day to day, bringing them into contact with jobs.

The United States Employment Service has few offices and it has no special informational programs in the areas where farm earnings are most depressed. Wilcox and Hendrix underscore this lack of informational programs for farm families in areas where underemployment is most acute. They point out, and quite rightly so, that these programs should be broad enough to serve "young adult families, young unmarried individuals, and boys and girls of high school age. Job-training programs are needed to supplement the informational programs on employment opportunities."[14]

Funds to Help People Migrate. This measure to improve the labor market serving agriculture may consist of grants or of loans to families and individuals to cover the costs of moving from an area where returns to workers have fallen into arrears to an area that is better situated relative to such returns.

Investments in Human Agents. Among the important corrective measures that will make for a better distribution of the nation's labor force over the years are certain investments in people, investments that enhance a person's productivity and add to his mobility. Education, medical services, nutrition, and housing all fall into this class. A strong case can be made for greatly enlarged public grants and aids to rural-farm communities and families for such investments. For the most part it is the better equipped young people in rural areas who leave for the cities. Rural-farm people, it may be argued, bear a wholly disproportionate share of the cost of rearing and educating the children of this nation—cost reckoned in terms of food, clothing, shelter, medical attention, and education.

There are no convincing reasons why these necessary replacement

[14] Wilcox and Hendrix, *op. cit.*, p. 11.

costs of the population should be borne so largely by rural-farm people, as is now the case because rural-farm net reproduction rates are higher than urban-industrial. All these costs are borne by the family, except education, which falls, in most of the United States, largely upon the local school district. This means that the necessary cost inherent in maintaining the social efficiency of the individual—a cost that constantly rises as a society becomes richer—is, as things now stand, borne primarily by the family and the local community.

As a consequence, out of their low incomes, farm people now pay a very much larger than proportional share of the replacement cost entailed in bearing, rearing, and educating the next generation. Since people migrate from rural-farm communities in which they are reared to urban-industrial communities, it should be evident that both communities are affected by the character and level of investments made in people. Certainly the urban-industrial communities that receive, and in large measure depend upon, the influx of rural-farm-reared people are interested in adding individuals of good health, who have received a high level of education, and who have, among other things, a social horizon and understanding that make them adaptable to the new environment and thus valuable citizens. Certainly the nation has a vital interest in this matter. Investments of this type enhance very appreciably the economic productivity of the individual and, especially significant in a developing economy demanding considerable labor migration, they increase his mobility as a factor of production.[15]

The report of the Committee on Postwar Agricultural Policy of the Association of Land-grant Colleges and Universities stresses the significance of rural living conditions and social facilities. Emphasizing the fact that the youth from the farms help maintain the urban population, the report points out that the income of many farm families is simply too small to provide an adequate level of living. (It does not, however, relate the public investments, which it deems essential in this sphere, to migration, that is, to bringing about a better distribution of the labor force of the nation.) It urges that rural schools be given more support. To better the quality of teaching personnel, rural teachers' salaries must be raised very considerably and their living quarters improved. Schools in most rural areas will need better sanitary facilities, recreational equipment, and modern buildings, if well-trained teachers are to be attracted

---

[15] For somewhat more extended treatment of this point, see Theodore W. Schultz, *Redirecting Farm Policy* (New York: The Macmillan Company, 1943), section on "Family and Nation," pp. 68–71.

to this work in the future. "The major solution for the financial problems of rural schools," the report concludes, "is greater state and federal aid."[16]

The report does not stress sufficiently, however, that where vocational training is offered, it should prepare farm children as much for nonagricultural employment as for farming. The report makes evident the need for more doctors, dentists, and nurses to serve rural communities, as well as public facilities for medical diagnosis and care, with medical centers and with special ambulance service for rural areas. The provision of school lunches and improvement of education in health and nutrition is urged. Better houses are desirable, electrification is important, telephone services should be expanded, roads are essential, and better recreational facilities are long overdue. All these expenditures are important not only for improving the level of living on farms but also for increasing the mobility of people and thus enabling farm people to improve their lot.

Another approach to this problem is to reduce the necessity for migration and thus lessen the burden that is placed on the labor market. One way would be to stop economic development; this action would remove the underlying cause for the maladjustments in the distribution of the labor supply about which we are concerned.

A slower pace of economic development, it may be presumed, would make it easier for the labor market to function satisfactorily. The economic history of France, since about 1900, supports this presumption. It is very doubtful, however, that this alternative, even if it could be achieved, would be at all acceptable, given the existing community preferences. In the preceding chapter we indicated in some detail the rising interest of governments and people in both the more highly and less well-developed parts of the world in inducing more, rather than less, economic development.

The structural attributes of economic development suggest other ways of reducing the need for people transferring out of farming. Other things unchanged, measures that increase the demand for farm products will lift at least some of the load which otherwise would have to be borne by the labor market. In France, for instance, agriculture has been sheltered by a tariff which has made relatively more of the domestic demand for farm products available to the farmers of France.[17] We shall not con-

[16] *Postwar Agricultural Policy*, Report of the Committee on Postwar Agricultural Policy of the Association of Land-grant Colleges and Universities, October, 1944, p. 51.

[17] In the United States, the early high industrial tariffs presumably had the reverse effect, that is, they curtailed somewhat the demand for American farm

sider the "price" of such tariffs since this aspect of tariffs has received a great deal of attention by economists. There are, however, other ways of increasing the demand for farm products. New uses may be found for some of them. The regional research laboratories of the U.S. Department of Agriculture, cooperating with the state experiment stations, have made advances along these lines, as have private firms and others working in this field. Among the various food products, some have a substantially higher income elasticity than do others. Shifts, for example, to the production of lean meats away from food cereals represent an important adjustment of this kind. Professor J. D. Black and others have from time to time placed much stress on this particular adjustment as a desirable way of "absorbing" the increasing productive capacity of agriculture.[18] Our efforts to gauge the relevant income elasticities and to determine in a rough way the supply and demand effects of advances in nutrition, as set forth in Part One, indicate that the possibilities and preferences in this direction can easily be overrated.

There is another structural attribute; the rate of growth of the supply of farm products may, presumably, be slowed down. Certainly advances in agricultural production techniques can be reduced by allocating fewer resources to the agricultural experiment stations and to the agricultural extension services for disseminating new and better techniques. During the early thirties, when unused resources were everywhere apparent, this approach was seriously advanced. "Why grow two bales of cotton where one grew before if we already have too much cotton?" The full-employment horizon that has come to prevail once more, since the early forties, has made this approach unacceptable.

The supply effects of the relatively high net reproduction rates of the farm population are also relevant. As these decline, the adjustment burden placed on the labor market is reduced, and less migration is required. Here again, the comparison of France and the United States is instructive.

The locational attributes of economic development also point to ways of reducing the necessity for people to move long distances although they

---

products. The cotton-tobacco South has made a great deal of this burden in its political protests" to the tariff laws and their effects. Too much has been blamed on the tariffs, however. More recently, and especially since the price support programs for agriculture were enacted, major farm products, notably cotton and tobacco, have been sold abroad for less than the supported domestic price.

[18] See John D. Black and Maxine E. Kiefer, *Future Food and Agriculture Policy* (New York: McGraw-Hill Book Company, Inc., 1948).

would have to change occupations. If it were possible to induce the economy to develop at the same rate at many points, evenly distributed over the economy, it would greatly reduce the adjustment load now borne by the labor market. Suppose that during the last 75 years in the United States, the centers of economic development had been as numerous and of about the same potential in the South as they have been in the North, it is hard to believe that returns to workers in agriculture in the South would have fallen behind as they have. While there have been many proposals for decentralizing industry, for locating plants and factories more evenly throughout the country, and for development programs that favor the by-passed areas at the expense of the more developed areas, no satisfactory analysis of the "gains" and "losses" which such proposals would entail is available. This is not to contend that this approach to the problem at hand, and also to other serious objectives, for example, national security, is necessarily an undesirable one. It merely implies that the relevant information to gauge the probable economic consequences of such actions is not known. Studies concentrating on this approach are way overdue.[19]

In closing this section, it may be appropriate to call attention once more to aspects of the labor market serving agriculture which urgently require more study. The work to determine how satisfactorily this labor market functions is fairly far along. Barriers to migration, which will explain why it functions so poorly, are not well understood. The barriers *external* to agriculture originating out of the economic uncertainty that clouds job opportunities, conditions of employment and wages, need to be analyzed. The economists should be able to contribute substantially to this phase. The barriers that are *internal* pertain, so it would appear, largely to values, the cultural stage in which the community finds itself, and to other social considerations. Here, workers from other disciplines—sociology, anthropology, and others—are needed. When we come to application, the American scene strongly supports the view that the important existing maladjustments in the distribution of the labor supply are to be found at the periphery of what are the more powerful centers of economic development. More specifically, this means that agriculture in the great Middle West, in most of the middle area, the New England states, and the Far West is favorably situated in relation to these centers and in these areas the labor market serving agriculture, when there is full employment, works quite satisfactorily. Improvements in the labor

[19] See Wilcox and Hendrix, *op. cit.*, pp. 10–11, for recommendations. See also Calvin B. Hoover and B. U. Ratchford, *Economic Resources and Policies of the South* (New York: The Macmillan Company, 1951).

market serving agriculture are required in other major areas, areas which have been by-passed by economic development and which have, as a consequence, fallen behind in terms of the real earnings received by workers in agriculture. Finally, studies will be needed on how to apply this additional knowledge to improve the existing labor market with a due regard for the preference of the community for decentralization in economic organization and for other values.

CAPITAL MARKET SERVING AGRICULTURE

As it was for labor, our query is: How satisfactorily does the capital market work in adjusting the increasing stock of capital to meet the requirements of economic development? Capital is also a powerful agent in inducing economic development. However, since it is not our purpose to explain this development but rather, at this point, to gauge the capacity and efficiency of the capital market to adjust to development, we shall leave aside its contributions to economic growth and progress, although it may well be the more important role of capital. Our task is, nevertheless, a difficult one; in many ways, it is even harder than that of gauging the labor market, because of the pervasive properties of capital and because so little has been done to analyze the allocation of capital. What has been done in this field is primarily descriptive.

This is an area of economic organization, especially when it comes to determining the role of government where controversy abounds and where dependable knowledge is not easy to obtain. Take such simple and fundamental matters as these: What returns does capital at the margins and on the average produce in agriculture? Are there margins where it produces, say, only 2 to 3 per cent and others where the rate of return runs, say, 25 to 30 per cent? If both situations were to exist, is the first necessarily too low a return and the second too high? Where are the relevant data and the criteria for analyzing and interpreting them?

The bare bones of the assets, both physical and financial, of agriculture in the United States are indicated in Table 18–2.

In 1950, all but $12.4 billion of the $127.0 billion represented proprietors' equities. Debts, after a decade of prosperity and inflation, were down to about one-tenth of the total physical and financial assets of agriculture whereas in 1940 this ratio stood at about one-fifth.

Horton's[20] study, based on a 108-county sample, gives the economic

---

[20] Donald C. Horton, *The Pattern of Farm Financial Structure* (New York: National Bureau of Economic Research, Inc., May, 1951), a preliminary draft. Table 4 indicates that the 108-county sample is a satisfactory representation of the United States.

TABLE 18–2. PHYSICAL AND FINANCIAL ASSETS OF AGRICULTURE, 1950
(In billions of current dollars)

Physical assets:
Real estate 63.5
Non-real estate:
    Livestock 13.2
    Machinery and motor vehicles 14.3
    Crops, stored 7.8
    Household furnishings and equipment 6.5
    Subtotal 41.8
All physical assets listed above 105.3
Financial assets:
    Deposits and currency 14.3
    U.S. savings bonds 5.2
    Investment in cooperatives. 2.2
    Subtotal 21.7
    Total 127.0

SOURCE: *The Balance Sheet, 1950*, BAE, *Agric. Inf. Bul.* 26, October, 1950. Also in Roy J. Burroughs, "Balance Sheet of Agriculture: Limitations and Uses," *Agricultural Economics Research*, Vol. II (July, 1950), Bureau of Agricultural Economics.

and financial characteristics of agriculture for 1940, when the total physical and financial assets were valued at 53.8 billions and debts at 10 billions in current dollars (see Table 18–3).

This chain of data for 1940 can be linked to 1950 at several points. Physical assets were about $19,000 per farm in 1950 with non-real-estate

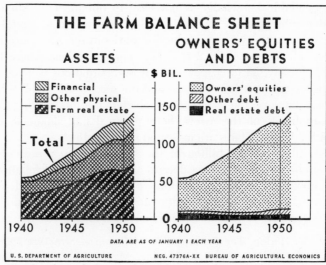

FIG. 18–3. The farm balance sheet—assets and owners' equities and debts, 1940–1951.

Table 18–3. Economic and Financial Characteristics of Agriculture, 1940
(108-county sample, 1940)

Economic characteristics:
Physical assets per farm $8,300
Represented by:
  Land . . . . 52 per cent
  Buildings . . . . 23 per cent
  Non-real estate . . . . 25 per cent
    All three . . . . 100 per cent
Financial characteristics:
Physical assets per farm $8,300
Divided according to interest of
  Operators . . . . 48 per cent
  Landlords . . . . 29 per cent
  Creditors . . . . 23 per cent
    All three . . . . 100 per cent
Farm mortgage debt per farm $1,577
Proportion held by
  Federal land banks and Federal Farm Mortgage Corporation . . 47 per cent
  Insurance and mortgage investment companies . . . . . . 12 per cent
  Commercial and savings banks . . . . 10 per cent
  Individuals and miscellaneous lenders . . . . 31 per cent
    All four . . . . 100 per cent
Non-real-estate loans as per cent of total non-real-estate farm assets of
  Banks and production credit associations . . . . 13 per cent
  Farm Security Administration and emergency crop and feed loans . 8 per cent

items representing about 40 per cent of the total compared to 25 per cent in 1940. Debts relative to assets were down, as already indicated, from about one-fifth to one-tenth. Another important link is the farm mortgage debt: There occurred a marked shift among holders of this debt; the share held by Federal agencies decreased from about 42 to 21 per cent while the share held by commercial banks doubled and that of insurance companies and individuals also increased substantially.

	1940		1950	
	Amount, in billions of dollars	Distribution, per cent	Amount, in billions of dollars	Distribution, per cent
Total	6.59	100.0	5.41	100.0
Federal agencies	2.75	41.7	1.15	21.2
Life insurance companies . .	0.99	15.0	1.17	21.6
Commercial banks	0.54	8.2	0.89	16.5
Individuals and miscellaneous	2.31	35.1	2.20	40.7

Source: *The Balance Sheet, 1950*, BAE, *Agric. Inf. Bul.* 26, Table 20.

A profile of the flows of productive services (expressed as annual rates for 1950, the most recent year for which these data are available) represented by the various classes of inputs used in agriculture are given in Table 18–4.

TABLE 18–4. PRODUCTION INPUTS IN AGRICULTURE IN 1950

	In billions of current dollars	In per cent
Land (net rent)	4.62	24.9
Maintenance and depreciation	4.23	12.6
Operation of motor vehicles	2.07	7.4
Interest (horses, mules, motor vehicles, other machinery, crops and livestock)	1.90	6.5
Miscellaneous items	1.18	4.4
Taxes	0.86	3.2
Fertilizer and lime	0.82	3.2
All nonlabor inputs	15.68	62.2
Total farm labor	9.53	37.8
Total	25.21	100.0

Functioning of the Capital Market

There are no meaningful studies that bring time-series and cross-sectional data to bear on this problem. It is, therefore, not possible at this time to compare the returns to capital used in agriculture in various areas and types of farms with the returns to capital in other sectors of the economy. Until such studies have been made, it will be necessary to rely on indirect evidence and on inferences from more general information.[21]

We observe that in agriculture nearly all the physical assets are individually owned, that is, they are owned largely by individual operators and by individual landlords and not by corporations.[22] The renting of specific factors is important; in 1940, 29 per cent of the physical assets were rented; this figure has declined since then but it still remains large. The loaning of funds is somewhat less important; in 1940 about 23 per cent of the physical assets represented the interest of creditors; by 1950, this figure had decreased to about 12 per cent.

[21] Three studies are under way at the University of Chicago, made possible by funds from the Rockefeller Foundation.

[22] Walter W. Wilcox, "Capital in Agriculture," *Quarterly Journal of Economics,* Vol. LVIII (November, 1943). The individually owned capital in the United States, as distinguished from corporate owned, was placed at $54 billion in 1935 of which $39 billion was in agriculture (p. 51).

The operator who does not own enough assets to organize a farm of optimum scale presumably may rent additional capital goods, mainly agricultural land, or he may borrow funds to purchase additional capital goods and other inputs. How satisfactorily does the renting market and the loanable funds market serving agriculture work in practice?

We take it to be a fact that in the United States there are many farms, probably fully a third of them, which are far below the optimum in the quantity of inputs committed to farming and which employ too few capital inputs relative to the labor that is used. The scale effects in the case of these farms indicates strongly the possibility of achieving increasing returns from farm enlargement. The existing combination of factors means that the returns to labor are relatively low while those to capital are relatively high. One study[23] attempts to determine the marginal productivity of capital and labor employed in agriculture. Using 1939 data, the returns on capital in the Middle Atlantic, East North Central, South Atlantic, and East South Central regions averaged about 12 per cent, and annual returns to workers in agriculture about $390. Unpublished data of Johnson's show the returns on capital in Georgia to have been about 19 per cent, while in a state like Iowa, favored in that there is relatively less capital rationing and also less of an excess supply of labor, returns on capital may have been about 10 per cent in 1939.

Heady,[24] using a random sample of Iowa farms for the year 1939, found decreasing returns to scale; he obtained an elasticity for all inputs of .85 where 1.00 represents constant returns; for the separate inputs, the average percentage increase in total product forthcoming if the particular input were increased by 1 per cent was as follows:

Input	All farms in Iowa sample
Livestock and feed	.48
Land	.23
Equipment	.08
Miscellaneous operating expenses	.032
Labor	.028

Marginal productivities derived from these elasticities gave the following results:

---

[23] See D. Gale Johnson, "Contribution of Price Policy to the Income and Resource Problems in Agriculture," *Journal of Farm Economics*, Vol. XXVI (November, 1944).

[24] Earl O. Heady, "Production Functions from a Random Sample of Farms," *Journal of Farm Economics*, Vol. XXVIII (November, 1946).

	All farms (marginal productivity per dollar of input)
Input	
Livestock and feed	.84
Miscellaneous operating expenses	.39
Equipment.	.20
Labor	.08
Land	.046

One may infer from these data that in Iowa in 1939 more livestock and feed, operating items and equipment should have been employed relative to labor and land. The capital market, however, in Iowa and also elsewhere, is better developed for renting and borrowing funds to acquire additional land than it is to serve farmers in obtaining the other physical inputs listed above.

That a third or more of the farms in the United States are too small in the quantities of inputs employed, under existing technological and economic conditions, is amply supported by data. Wilcox and Hendrix conservatively place the figure at 1,600,000 using 1945 data.[25] They assumed that the medium commercial family farm combined labor and other inputs in about the appropriate proportions and employed approximately enough inputs considering the effects of scale. But there undoubtedly are many farms in this class which would benefit substantially from farm enlargement and from using more capital relative to labor.

The ratio of investment to labor inputs in 1944 was as follows (see also Table 18–5).

Class	Number of farms, in thousands	Investment per man equivalent
Large-scale farms	102	$13,400
Commercial family farms:		
Large.	409	13,500
Medium	1,173	8,300
Small.	1,662	4,560
Small-scale farms	923	2,320

Source: Kenneth L. Bachman and Roland W. Jones, *Sizes of Farms in the United States,* BAE, *Tech. Bul.* 1019, July, 1950, Tables 2, 19.

What then are the effects of renting and of borrowing upon the size of the farm, measured in terms of the physical assets under the control of the operator? If the possibility to rent exists and if the farmer is willing to rent, he can supplement the limited assets which he owns more

[25] Wilcox and Hendrix, *op. cit.*

adequately by renting than by borrowing. In an earlier study this writer concluded:

Within the framework of present institutions and practices, farmers who hire funds from outside sources in order to establish a firm are more likely to obtain sufficient capital to do this by renting rather than by borrowing. Furthermore, ownership of a farm results in the farm family bearing a much larger share of the economic uncertainty that lies ahead than it does when the farm real estate is being rented.[26]

Horton presents four pairs of counties from his sample in order to contrast farm asset size. These data, for 1940, indicate that renting of physical assets is much less important for the counties in which farms are small than it is in those with large farms.[27]

Pairs	Physical assets, per farm	Represented by the interest of		
		Operator, per cent	Landlord, per cent	Creditors, per cent
I. Douglas, Ill.	28,500	31	50	19
Trumbull, Ohio.	5,700	72	11	17
II. Coahoma, Miss.	24,400	23	46	30
Warren, Miss.	3,000	54	24	22
III. Odama, Wash.	39,100	46	39	15
Douglas, Ore.	7,800	70	14	16
IV. Webb, Tex.	37,900	41	46	13
Upshur, Tex.	2,800	60	22	18

Horton stated:

The capital structure of large-unit agriculture is characterized by relatively high outside interests (landlord and creditor); and these outside interests are largely those of investors who operate as part of a relatively broad capital market. Small-unit agriculture, on the other hand, appears to be financed to a greater extent by operator's equity, supplemented by credit from local lenders, notably commercial banks.

[26] Theodore W. Schultz, "Capital Rationing, Uncertainty, and Farm Tenancy Reform," *Journal of Political Economy*, Vol. XLVIII (June, 1940); this also appears as Chap. 12 in Theodore W. Schultz, *Production and Welfare of Agriculture* (New York: The Macmillan Company, 1949).

[27] Horton, *op. cit.*, Table 5.

Propositions about the Capital Market. As already indicated, most of what we know about the capital market serving agriculture is drawn from inferences from rather general information of the kind which we have cited. Studies addressed to the functioning of this market in agriculture are needed and long overdue. Until better information becomes available, it is necessary to formulate such insights as one can obtain. To proceed, we shall outline briefly our presumptions about the capital market serving agriculture. The following propositions are advanced for this purpose:

1. There exists for agriculture both external and internal capital rationing.[28]

2. Both types of capital rationing act as barriers to the transfer of capital into agriculture, which is the normal direction of the flow under conditions of economic development.

3. The transfer of capital into agriculture that is required to adjust to economic development and to reduce the adverse effects of capital rationing will be diminished in economic importance under the following circumstances:

   a. Where the terms of trade of agriculture take a favorable turn (as they did, for instance, during the forties) and conversely where they fall (as was the case in the thirties). This condition is relevant in the comparatively short-run context of a few years to a decade.

   b. Where the reproduction rate of farm people is relatively low and where those who inherit the assets of agriculture remain in (or enter) agriculture.

   c. Where the techniques of production in agriculture are either stationary or are improved slowly.

   d. Where long-run changes in the relative prices of factors (inputs) are small and require, as a consequence, little or no substitution of capital for labor.

[28] For a discussion of aspects of capital rationing, see D. Gale Johnson, "Farm Size, Risk Aversion and Capital Rationing," Chap. V in *Forward Prices for Agriculture* (Chicago: University of Chicago Press, 1947); Theodore W. Schultz, "Capital Rationing, Uncertainty and Farm Tenancy Reform," *Journal of Political Economy*, Vol. XLVIII (1940); this also appears as Chap. 12 in *Production and Welfare of Agriculture* (New York: The Macmillan Company, 1949); Donald C. Horton, "Adaptations of the Farm Capital Structure to Uncertainty," *Journal of Farm Economics*, Vol. XXXI (1949); and Frederick A. and Vera Lutz, *Theory of Investment of the Firm* (Princeton: Princeton University Press, 1951).

4. The adjustments that are required in the allocation of capital will be achieved more satisfactorily in those parts of agriculture that are situated favorably to the centers of economic development than in those at the periphery.

There can be no doubt that the marked improvement in terms of trade of agriculture that characterized the decade of the forties greatly strengthened the financial position of most commercial farmers. The "windfalls" in income made it possible for many farmers to add physical assets of various sorts many of which would have been "profitable" earlier but they were not acquired because of capital rationing. Leaving aside the improvements in farm buildings and other changes in farm real estate, we find that machinery and motor vehicles were more than doubled (in terms of 1940 prices) during this decade (household furnishing and equipment were increased a half). Financial assets at actual value rose from $4.97 billion, in 1940, to $21.7 billion in 1950, while the real-estate debt was reduced more than a billion although this was fully offset by a rise in the non-real-estate debt other than CCC loans.

Some indication of the adverse effects of the financial experiences of the thirties upon the farm capital structure may be seen in the following data.

	Twelve states with	
	Least reduction in real-estate value, 1930–1940, per cent	Greatest reduction in real-estate value, 1930–1940, per cent
Average reduction in farm real-estate value, 1930–1940 . . .	13	41
Interests in real estate in 1940 of:		
Operators	48	37
Landlords.	36	40
Creditors	16	23
All three	100	100

SOURCE: Donald C. Horton, *The Pattern of Farm Financial Structure* (New York: National Bureau of Economic Research, Inc., May, 1951), Chap. 1, p. 8.

Improving the Capital Market

We are keenly aware that existing knowledge about this sector of the capital market is fragmentary and very incomplete. However, there are many indicators which suggest that this market in the case of agriculture has not adjusted satisfactorily the increasing stock of capital to the requirements set by economic development that has characterized the United States. We have advanced a set of propositions to explain this particular outcome; these are, however, at this stage of our knowledge, of the nature of a set of hypotheses to be tested in subsequent research work. The improvements which we shall consider, therefore, depend, in the last analysis, upon the validity of these propositions. The proposed improvements are, in this sense, provisional.

There are, as in the case of the labor market, two general approaches open to us: (1) to increase the capacity and efficiency of this market to adjust and (2) to reduce the necessity for these adjustments. Both approaches, to the extent that they succeed in achieving the objective before us, are ways of overcoming the adverse effects of capital rationing upon the allocation of resources. Inasmuch as the effects of the structural and locational attributes of economic development are, in general, as applicable to the capital market as to the labor market, we shall not recapitulate the particular improvements that fall in this category.

Financial Continuity. Since it is a fact that farming is financed mainly by the operating farmer (the farm family), it is possible by inheritance to strengthen the financial position of those individuals who remain in agriculture. A system of primogeniture is one way of doing this. Other ways have been tried by legislation and by custom. This approach, however, is quite unacceptable to the American community in general because of the high value that it places on equal treatment of children as heirs.

Father-son lease arrangements are also a way of facilitating somewhat the financial continuity under consideration. In the better situated farming areas, in which the capital market normally works the best, father-son leases are receiving considerable attention. But they are not very meaningful in areas where the capital market is least satisfactory.

Substitution of Property for Children. One possible hypothesis for explaining the relatively slow decline of the birth rate and the variations in this rate, as economic development has taken place, is in terms of the possibilities open to families in different occupations of substituting property and the accumulation of property for children. Whether the particular preference implied in this formulation should be viewed as "good" or "bad" is not at issue in testing this hypothesis.[29] Land reform which improves the possibilities of farm people to accumulate farm property may have this outcome should the preference of the farm

---

[29] The relevant data and findings of the excellent study by K. H. Connell, *The Population of Ireland, 1750–1845* (New York: Oxford University Press, 1950), may be explained, so it seems, by the hypothesis here advanced.

people who benefit from the land reform take the form implied. Clearly, over a period of generations, farm families who have few children with most of the children remaining in agriculture represent a cultural adjustment that helps maintain and strengthen the financial position of farm families. A stationary farm population, with most of the farm children becoming farmers in an economy in which there is relatively little economic progress, as has been the case in France, appears to have had this outcome.

There are farming communities in the United States in some of the better situated areas where the net reproduction rates are already quite low,[30] and the implications of this demographic development to the problem at hand is, of course, quite apparent.

Particular Measures to Increase Income. Since nearly all the additions to the physical assets in farming during the forties, for example, were financed not by borrowing or renting but directly out of farm income and since such new physical assets contributed markedly to the "efficiency" of agriculture, it has been argued by some that this outcome justifies measures which will increase the income of farmers, for at least a few years, even though such measures induce, during that period, an unsatisfactory allocation of resources in farming. The tobacco program, for instance, with its high price supports and restrictive production quotas, has been rationalized on this score. It should not be necessary to point out that this approach to improve the existing capital markets is inconsistent with postulates that are fundamental in economics, organization, and welfare. It is an unacceptable approach, despite the observed income effects upon "investments" in agriculture.

Uncertainty Considerations—the Case for Forward Prices. Studies of the relation between price uncertainty in agriculture and capital rationing point to better production possibilities from a program of forward prices. Nearly all production in agriculture requires long-range planning and commitments since it takes months, even years, to complete a production period. Most crops require at least a year, and livestock requires from one to three years. Fruit-bearing trees take a decade and longer, and farm wood lots and other forestry undertakings even more time.

Price uncertainty increases very considerably the compass of capital rationing, checking the enlargement of many farms that are inefficient because they are too small, and inducing farmers to keep their resources too flexible both contractually and technically. Because of the large

---

[30] See George W. Hill and Douglas G. Marshall, "Reproduction and Replacement of Farm Population and Agricultural Policy," *Journal of Farm Economics,* Vol. XXIX (May, 1947). The useful work of Margaret Hagood on replacements should also be cited.

measure of price uncertainty that burdens agriculture (both as to the level of farm prices generally and the structure of farm prices) and the attendant capital rationing (both external and internal for many farms), many farmers are either unable or unwilling to commit themselves to contractual payments, even though the additional resources would improve substantially the efficiency of the farm they operate. Labor inputs on most farms, including that of the family and operator, provide flexibility and thus a kind of "safety" in dealing with price uncertainty, for labor becomes a residual claimant. As a consequence, throughout substantial parts of American agriculture farmers tend to employ too much labor (family labor, the operator, and hired labor) and too few nonhuman resources (machinery, equipment, land, fertilizer, buildings, livestock, and feed inventories). This adjustment to uncertainty and the capital rationing associated with it holds down the per capita earnings of farm people and pushes up the rate of returns on capital, with the marginal-value productivity of capital much higher than its money cost.

Price uncertainty affecting farming therefore has its cost, for it reduces the efficiency of agriculture. Can this cost, this inefficiency and waste, be lessened? In a very real sense, the answer is yes, because many of the farm product price changes occurring within a given production period can be reduced without disturbing trade. There are certain kinds of price changes affecting farmers that are not essential to attain a moving equilibrium, to reconcile the forces affecting supply and demand of farm products. More price certainty for farmers is possible for at least one production period ahead. The additional price certainty that would be gained by reducing these unnecessary price fluctuations would substantially improve the capacity of relative prices of farm products to perform their primary economic function of guiding production. To achieve this greater certainty in prices received by farmers, we have proposed elsewhere[31] a system of forward prices for agriculture.

More Complete Information. We have in this and in the preceding chapter placed much stress on the incomplete nature of both the economic and technical information available to financial agencies and individuals making funds available to agriculture, to firms that supply particular factors, and to farmers who borrow funds or who rent or buy factors. Factor markets serving agriculture are especially burdened by

[31] Theodore W. Schultz, "Ecomonic Effects of Agricultural Programs," *American Economic Review*, XXX (1940): 127–154; and also in *Redirecting Farm Policy*, pp. 43–44; see also Geoffrey Shepherd, "Stabilization Operations of the Commodity Credit Corporation," *Journal of Farm Economics*, XXIV (1942): 589–610. See especially the study by D. Gale Johnson, *Forward Prices for Agriculture* (Chicago: University of Chicago Press, 1947).

TABLE 18–5. NUMBER OF FARMS, AND SPECIFIED CHARACTERISTICS, AVERAGE PER FARM BY ECONOMIC CLASS, UNITED STATES, 1945

Economic class	Number of farms, in thousands	All land in farm, acres	Cropland harvested, acres	All labor resources, man equivalent	Total investment, in dollars	Land and buildings, in dollars	Power and machinery, in dollars	Productive livestock, in dollars	Farm products sold and used, in dollars
Farming units:									
Large-scale farms	102.1	2,906	384	7.2	95,835	78,449	6,992	10,428	39,217
Commercial family farms:									
Large	408.9	514	193	2.5	33,203	26,067	3,264	3,870	10,484
Medium	1,173.0	236	104	1.8	15,135	11,134	1,828	2,176	4,658
Small . . .	1,661.9	125	46	1.5	6,768	5,117	783	870	1,874
Small-scale farms	923.5	72	22	1.3	3,029	2,305	349	375	825
Other units:									
Part-time units . . .	602.2	43	10	.5	3,142	2,587	281	278	574
Nominal units . . .	987.3	65	11	.9	4,042	3,583	249	209	264
All farms	5,858.9	196	60	1.5	10,419	8,100	1,063	1,256	3,113

SOURCE: Kenneth L. Bachman and Roland W. Jones, *Sizes of Farms in the United States*, BAE, *Tech. Bul.* 1019, July, 1950, Table 2.

the unsatisfactory state of information. Information about the technical attributes of different parcels of agricultural land is a notable case in point. The "production and distribution" of this information, so it appears, should be expanded very substantially, for it would pay. The additional "product" and the more decentralized "organization" that such improvements in information would make possible suggest a very large return from the extra resources which we suggest should be committed to the "production and distribution" of such information relevant to factor markets.

Farm-enlargement Programs. Education, technical assistance, and credit are required to facilitate farm enlargement, especially in areas that have been by-passed by economic progress. These programs call for some public action. The Federal and state extension services can make a major contribution. So can the Farm and Home Administration. Additional measures of the kind outlined in *Underemployment of Rural Families*[32] are also needed.

NOTE: LAND REFORM

Land reform may be viewed as a special problem in economic organization. As such, the problem is one of relating the community preference and the possibilities. The possibilities, in this case, represent the outcome of different types of land holdings in terms of "products" and other desired "values." The objective of land reform may, of course, be simply to increase the production of farm products, an exceedingly important goal in view of the inadequate and precarious food supply of most people living in countries where the economy is of the high-food-drain type. Or the objective may be to improve the income position of cultivators by redistributing the existing wealth (mainly property in agricultural land) and thus the income of the community. On the other hand, the purpose of land reform may be primarily to achieve political stability while the resulting effects upon production, upon the personal distribution of property, and upon income are viewed as incidental.

The choice in organization entails a consideration of alternative ways and means, some of which are and some of which are not acceptable to the community, and some will bring about the desired improvements in production, or in income, or in political stability, while others will not do so. Land reform may alter only the legal and administrative rules of landlord-tenant relations: the British Agricultural Holdings Act of 1883 represents a legislative landmark of this kind. On the other hand, land

---

[32] Wilcox and Hendrix, *op. cit.*

reform may consist of breaking up large holdings and transferring the property in land to a new set of (small) farmers or it may transfer the property to existing tenants where the farms are already small and the landlord may be fully compensated or he may be deprived of his property with only partial or no compensation whatsoever. The community values may be such that compensation is deemed essential, as is the case generally in Western countries. Other communities may, however, be quite prepared to expropriate property without compensation.

This note is not addressed to land reform within the United States on the assumption that in the main the types of land holdings that have become established in this country are in general satisfactory to the community. We shall examine, instead, the possibilities of land reform in countries where people are very poor and where most of the income of people is required to acquire food.[33]

Preferred Type of Land Holding

It has become established policy in the United States to support the family farm as the typical producing-consuming unit in agriculture. The farm family may be a full owner, part owner, or tenant. The farm may be small or large ranging from an acre or two in horticulture to several thousand acres in livestock grazing. It should not be a plantation with sharecroppers attached or a corporation with many workers. Instead *the family farm should depend mainly on the labor of the members of the farm family*. This is the fundamental restriction imposed upon the economic organization of the farm by the existing concept of the family farm preferred by the community.

The American community also wants the production in agriculture to be efficient, to be so organized and managed that an optimum output is achieved from the land, labor, and capital that is drawn into farming. The community preference, therefore, consists of two values: (1) a decentralized type of economic organization in farming with the family farm the ideal and (2) a large output to one that is not so large.

We have already indicated, in preceding chapters, how these two values are related one to the other. We actually can have very nearly the best of both, namely, the family farm and also the largest output from a given set of inputs. This outcome turns on technical-economic facts, that is, on the existing transformation possibilities. These possi-

---

[33] There is implicit in this note this query: Should the United States support measures for land reform in such countries? The answer that emerges is in the affirmative.

bilities mean that the family farm can achieve as large, and in many types of farming, a larger, output from a given set of inputs than can alternative forms of economic organization. To the extent that this is in fact true, both values can be realized in combination. The community may be prepared, however, to give up some "product" should that be necessary in order to have the family farm. How much is not a matter that can be determined because the United States has not been confronted with the choice of giving up substantial production in order to maintain the family farm.

The United States, therefore, relying on its own values and economic experience, can make the following statement: *We prefer the family farm because it is a decentralized form of economic organization which has particular social and cultural advantages and because we have found it possible to develop a family farm that is highly efficient in the production of farm products.* It does not follow, however, that people in other communities (countries) place the same value on the family farm that we do or that the economic circumstances are such that it will be as efficient in producing farm products as it has been in the United States. We need, therefore, to consider carefully the preferences and possibilities of each community (country) concerned.

What kind of social and economic organization of agriculture do the poor "underdeveloped" countries prefer? How highly do they rate, for example, the collective, the plantation, the cooperative, some form of corporation, or the family farm, one relative to the other? The control of agricultural land may be highly centralized. Where this is a fact, it does not necessarily mean that it represents the present community preference. Community preference, in this context, is an exceedingly complex matter dependent upon history, information, and expectations. Existing conditions always reflect cultural and political circumstances which may be either highly stable at one extreme or conversely very much in a state of flux.

Production Effects of Land Reforms

In this section, we shall concentrate on increasing agricultural production and, with this objective before us, on what can be done by way of land reform which will contribute to this end. Let us leave aside for the time being the preferred type of land tenure and holdings and consider only the effects of the ways in which land is held upon the output that can be obtained from a given collection of agricultural inputs (land, labor, and capital). Can we identify malallocations of the existing stock of agricultural land? To get our bearing on this problem, the following outline of basic considerations may be useful.

Operating Units That Are Too Small or Too Dispersed

Let us take, first, those situations where the operating units are either too small or too scattered or both.

1. *Fragmentation.* By this we mean a farm consisting of two or more parcels of land so located one to another that it is not possible to operate the particular farm and other such farms as efficiently as would be the case if the parcels were reorganized and recombined. This situation characterized many parts of the world including areas in Europe. It is in part a consequence of postfeudal developments and of earlier land reforms and of other circumstances.

2. *Economic Development.* The economic development that has characterized Western countries because of advances in techniques and because of the substitution of capital for labor, as the value of human effort has risen relative to other inputs, has made farm enlargement necessary. The needed enlargement appears to come slowly. In the United States and in other countries that have experienced substantial economic development one finds many farms that are altogether too small to be efficient. This particular "cause" clearly has not been operative in countries that have not achieved economic development.

3. *Inappropriate Settlement Pattern.* This class includes the 160-acre homestead which happened to be fairly well suited to the better parts of the corn belt but was altogether too small for the plains states. (It should be observed that (2) and (3) above do not apply generally to the Orient.)

Operating Units That Are Too Large

The following are situations where the operating unit (including the amount of land employed) appears to be too large inasmuch as some additional output per unit of input can be achieved by reducing the size of the operating units.

Particular Hacienda. There are in parts of South America many farms that are undoubtedly too large; they exceed the optimum size in terms of scale. This does not mean that all large units fall into this class; on the contrary, in the more arid regions a strong case can be made for relatively large farms both in the amount of land and capital employed.

Plantations. This form of organization is usually associated with operations—for example, in producing sugar, coffee, tea, rubber, bananas, sisal—that require a large amount of labor which can be routinized substantially and where particular technical phases of the production require large investments of capital. In the United States, the plantation is rapidly becoming an obsolete and inefficient form of economic organization. The evidence is, however, not so clear when one looks at the production experiences in the tropics where the plantation type of organization appears most frequently. In any case, throughout the Orient and most underdeveloped countries, plantations account for only a small fraction of all agricultural production. (The problems presented by plantations are usually social and political rather than economic.)

Special Situations. There are a number of additional types, for example, large farms dependent on migratory labor which often are too large when all social and private costs are taken into account; some so-called "suitcase" farms; farms of gentlemen farmers based on urban incomes; and various types of state ventures including the collective farm, not so much perhaps in producing cereals as in the production of livestock and animal products.

Economic Control Too Divided

Let us now consider an important set of circumstances where the operating unit may not be either too large or too small but where the economic control is so divided that the efficiency of agriculture is impaired.

Separation of Ownership and Operation. This is in fact the fundamental problem throughout the Orient and elsewhere. The separation of these two functions need not impair the efficiency of agriculture as is evident in some Western countries, especially in the United Kingdom. The United Kingdom, however, has had for many years enlightened land-tenure laws which safeguard substantially the farmer (also the landlord) in planning the operations of the farm, including investing and disinvesting should economic circumstances require. The United States is decidedly "backward" in its legal and administrative institutions for dealing with this problem. We should have, long ago, taken a leaf out of the experiences of other Western countries which are far advanced in this matter.

Absentee ownership is simply a special case of this separation of functions. Where it creates difficulties, we may have (1) the case of the retired farmer who wishes to have his old farm operated as was his custom despite advances in techniques and major economic developments affecting factor costs and product price; (2) the farmer's widow, not well informed on the managerial aspects of the farm which she owns, perhaps, also, hard-pressed for income and inclined not to approve required investments on the farm; (3) the wealthy townsman who, be-

cause of the limitations of his experience and because of lack of information, fails to see the fine managerial choices entailed in operating a farm
efficiently; and (4) a wealthy urban elite, while often generous in certain symbolic support of farming, delegates the "management" of the
farm property held by it, and absenteeism of the worst sort often becomes established as a consequence. (In India there are situations where
the property rights in agricultural land are held in layers, with not one
but as many as ten or even more individuals owning a *layer* of these
rights, each subsidiary to the one "above" it.)

Credit Control. It is hardly necessary to fill in the details here, for it
may be assumed they are well known and readily understood. Credit
institutions in Western countries have come a long way in correcting
difficulties on this score. The job is, however, not complete. In the Orient
there frequently exists the "scourge" of the moneylender. Credit terms
are not suited to the production periods and processes of farming.

Government Controls. Taxes may absorb most, all, or at times even
more than the economic rent of particular parcels of agricultural land.
The difficulties from this score are many both here and abroad. Crop
controls and acreage and marketing quotas may also impair the efficiency of agriculture. These measures represent a separation of economic control that may affect adversely the production of agriculture.
History is replete with examples where the efficiency of agriculture was
substantially reduced by such measures. It should, of course, be made
clear that there are economic functions which the government can perform better than they can be done by farmers. But there are and have
been many controls which are not compatible with an optimum rate of
agricultural production.

LAND REFORM AND ECONOMIC DEVELOPMENT

It is necessary at this point to call attention to a basic difficulty frequently overlooked and seldom understood. Western countries are no
longer haunted by the *niggardliness of nature.* As we have shown in
Part One, the supply of agricultural land in relation to the food supply
is not nearly so critical a factor as it was in the day of Ricardo-Malthus-
Mill. At that time, in England, about 75 per cent of the expenditures of
people was for food and about 33⅓ per cent of the costs of producing
food was for rent (see Chap. 8). This means that about 25 per cent of
national income was spent for the food-producing services of land. In
the United States today the fraction of the incomes of people spent for
food (farm products entering into food) is so small (about 12 per cent)

and the contribution of agricultural production is such that about 2.5 per cent of the national income is spent for the services of agricultural land.

It is not uncommon in the Orient where people are very poor, where the ratio of people to resources is high, and where little or no economic development has occurred to find between 25 and 30 per cent of the national income represented by the rent of agricultural land. There are situations where this figure is much higher with particular communities indicating a figure as high as 50 per cent.

To restate our belief as already set forth in Chap. 8: The social, political and economic differences between a community in which, say, *one-fourth* of the economic rewards goes for the productive services of land and one where *one-fortieth* is for this purpose are so great that it is indeed hard for people living under such diverse circumstances to comprehend what these differences really mean. The revolutionary implications of land reform in countries where most of the property consists of land, where this property is held not by the cultivators but mainly by a small group of families who do not farm, and where most of the political power and social privileges are vested in those who own land, are, for a person living in a technically advanced community, virtually impossible to grasp.

One of the consequences of economic development has been that it has greatly enlarged the kinds and amounts of property that are productive and in which people can place their capital. Accordingly, people with capital to invest do not concentrate so largely on agricultural land; many other types of investments are at hand; in fact, agricultural land has become distinctly a minor category of property in our economy.

In most of the underdeveloped countries the existing stock of agricultural land is in fact being farmed by "cultivators" who have very small farms, who have very little equipment, and who employ techniques that are anything but modern. Many of these cultivators do not own their farms. Many of them are in a very insecure economic position.

The problem here is not one of breaking up large land-operating units because the actual farms are already very small, often too small, and in some areas also fragmentized. What then can be achieved by way of increasing agricultural production by land reform under such conditions? Three courses of action will be considered.

1. Suppose that the existing landowners are compensated, that the land is sold to the cultivators, and that the annual payments made by the cultivators in servicing the debt are equal to the existing rent. Under these circumstances, could there be any gain whatsoever? The answer is in the affirmative. The cultivator, now that he owns the land, has

an additional incentive to improve his farm in many ways. Ownership has often turned sand into gold. There are numerous studies comparing farm owners and nonowners which show clearly how powerful is the incentive to improve a parcel of land, a piece of property, by investing in it labor and savings, when it belongs to the cultivators. A real difficulty, however, arises out of the effect which the buying of land may have upon the amount of capital available for farm tools, seeds, equipment, fertilizer, and other important inputs. The cultivator may find himself subject to even more acute "capital rationing" than before.

2. If we take the circumstances set forth in (1) and consider a course of action where resources are made available to help this cultivator to acquire some of the most needed tools and equipment, to improve his production techniques, and to enlarge his operations over time (by the growth of industry absorbing some of the present farm population), the stage would be set for advances in agricultural production that are meaningful and significant.

3. Suppose now that when the land is sold to the cultivator he acquires it under terms which require a smaller annual payment than that formerly entailed in the rent that he paid. We now have introduced an income effect. We shall not examine its implications for others (former landowners, the government, and only incidentally for nonfarm consumers) but restrict ourselves to the income effects upon the farmer and his family. The Japanese land reform,[34] because of the general price inflation that occurred in Japan after the land reform, has had in it a very substantial income effect. The cultivator now has more wealth. He, therefore, has a larger income, because in addition to the fruits from his labor and his former meager capital he acquires some income on the additional wealth which has come to him as a result of the land reform. These income effects run two ways: (1) The farm family will be in a position to consume more. The income elasticity of food of these farm families is undoubtedly high, probably in the neighborhood of 1.0. This means that if the family were consuming 50 per cent of its output and if its income were increased, say, by 20 per cent, the farm family would now use 60 per cent of its output, and with the same production, the amount sold, and thus made available to nonfarm consumers, would fall from 50 to 40 per cent, representing a drop of 20 per cent. (2) The

[34] See Mark B. Williamson, "Land Reform in Japan," *Journal of Farm Economics,* Vol. XXXIII (May, 1951); Arthur F. Raper, "Some Effects of Land Reform in Thirteen Japanese Villages," *ibid.;* and Lawrence I. Hewes, Jr., "The Japanese Land Reform Program—Its Significance to Rural Asia," *Proceedings, Thirteenth Annual National Farm Institute* (Des Moines), February, 1951.

other income effect would come in an enlargement of savings, that is, in the amount that can be invested in improving the productive capacity of the farm whether it be used to acquire tools, equipment, seeds, fertilizer, or some other capital form.

It may also be helpful to suggest a number of working hypotheses relevant to the problem of land reform considered in this brief note:

1. When the investment opportunities in agricultural land are opened or are made more attractive to farm families, one of the major social effects in underdeveloped countries is a smaller family, thus checking the growth in population. (See discussion of the substitution of property for children in Chap. 18.)

2. Measures that "suddenly" increase the income of farm families in underdeveloped countries will reduce, often quite drastically, the food supply of nonfarm people.

3. The returns on additional capital invested in agriculture in major underdeveloped countries are usually underestimated by existing governments and public leaders; as a consequence, there is an overemphasis on "industrialization" and a neglect of agriculture.

4. Within agriculture the largest returns are to be obtained from major increases in expenditures in agricultural research and extension work in underdeveloped countries over a period of one to two decades.

5. The components of economic development, namely, advances in technical-economic circumstances and in the level of output per person, reduce the relative claims of agricultural land on the income of families and on the income of a community as a whole.

19

ORGANIZING AGRICULTURE FOR ECONOMIC STABILITY

One of the fundamental characteristics of the economy of the United States has been its instability. Employment and prices are two important attributes of this instability. A satisfactory rate of employment has not been realized at all times; nor has the general level of prices been free from marked trends and sharp short-term movements. The problem of economic instability appeared in an acute form in the mass unemployment of the thirties. This problem has been decidedly in the forefront in the work of economists since then.[1] Many public and private measures have been taken to reduce the existing economic instability or to find ways of adjusting to it.

This chapter and the next are restricted to the organizational problem of coping with the economic instability of agriculture of the United States. Yield, price, and income are the three principal variables; the organizational problem which the fluctuations of each of these present may be considered at the level of farms and farm households, or of product and factor markets, or at the level of political and social processes. Two objectives will be considered: (1) to eliminate or to reduce economic instability and (2) to adjust to the instability which cannot be eliminated or which the community prefers not to eliminate even though it is possible to do so. The second of these two objectives represents the following circumstances: Some of the economic instability cannot be eliminated even though the community preferred to do so, for example, the consequences of bad and good crops and of changes in international tensions; some of the instability, although it can be eliminated, is related to other attributes in such a way that the community does not prefer to eliminate it, for example, some of the instability that is necessarily a part of economic development where the "price" of eliminating or reducing the instability exceeds the social "re-

[1] See "The Problem of Economic Instability, A Committee Report," *American Economic Review*, Vol. XL (September, 1950), prepared by Emile Despres, Milton Friedman, Albert G. Hart, Paul A. Samuelson, and Donald H. Wallace.

turns" from such measures; this leaves a part where possibilities and preferences are such that it can and should be either eliminated or reduced; in this category we are inclined to place, among others, inflationary and deflationary movements which can be counteracted or averted by fiscal and monetary management.

In achieving these two objectives, we shall assume that the community prefers more decentralization in organization to less. Other "values," however, are also involved in relating what is possible and in what is preferred. The size of the "product," economic progress, and the personal distribution of income are not unrelated to economic stability. Nor in the case of the "product" is it only the size that matters, for at times a high value is placed on a rapid transformation from peacetime goods and services to guns and butter, and then again, in going from war to peace. These rapid transformations, under forced draft, are powerful engines of economic instability.

Before turning to the yield, price, and income variability problems of agriculture, let us review briefly the results of our study relevant to the stability with which resources are employed in farming in the United States.

No Marked Short-term Movements in the Employment of Resources in Agriculture

Mass unemployment is a symbol of one important aspect of the economic instability that has characterized the highly developed, technically advanced Western countries, especially the United States. This attribute, however, does not apply to agriculture. It was demonstrated in Part Two that the production inputs, which farmers in the United States commit to farming from one year to the next, are remarkably stable. This particular attribute of agricultural production is clearly observable come depression or prosperity, a series of bad or good crops, and peace or war.[2] The variations in total outputs committed from year to year in agriculture, measured in terms of the change that occurred from the preceding year and corrected for the slow upward drift that has taken place, *averaged only about 1 per cent per year from 1910 to 1950.* Changes in these inputs of as much as 3 per cent in a year have been rare; on two occasions the increase exceeded 3 per cent with 3.8 in 1920 and 3.1 per cent in 1935, and only once was there a decrease of more than 3 per cent, that is, in 1934 when the reduction amounted to 5

---

[2] A question to be explored later is whether it is possible and desirable to achieve somewhat more input response in agriculture when the demand shifts rapidly and substantially.

per cent, but this curtailment was largely an unplanned one caused by the widespread drought of that year (see Chap. 12).

Agriculture and industry are of different temperaments in committing resources to production; one is slow and gradual in its movements and the other sensitive and erratic. The quick rises and falls in industrial employment are well known, but a basic characteristic of the United States economy that is little recognized is that the *production effort* in farming is extraordinarily stable in spite of the price and income variability that confronts agriculture.[3] Many of the more serious economic difficulties that confront agriculture are born out of this difference in the pace of agriculture and industry. The plowman's tread does not allow running for a stretch and then walking, or even stopping altogether. Agriculture has a steady gait, while many other producers in the economy sometimes run and at other times simply stand still. Farmers, in the main, stay in "full production" regardless of the effects of business fluctuations upon the demand for farm products and in spite of governmental efforts to reduce output. This behavior on the part of farmers assures consumers of a large and steady supply of food and of other farm products, but it also has meant great instability in farm prices and farm income.

Differences in Attitudes. Because farmers seldom alter quickly the rate at which they produce and because industry often changes its rate of output very quickly, it is not surprising that farmers have attitudes different from businessmen and laborers about the economic instability facing them as producers.

While managers and workers in industry are haunted by idle plants and idle men, farmers are not worried by a similar possibility in agriculture because farms are not left idle. Not that farm income is unaffected by business conditions—far from it—but farmers are not unemployed during a depression. They stay at their jobs; in fact, they may even work harder as prices decline. Their principal economic devil is the fluctuation of farm prices.

The conclusion of this section is simple and straightforward: In agriculture there are no marked short-term movements in the aggregate employment of resources. No problem with these attributes, therefore, exists. The inference is that on this score the economic organization of agriculture functions satisfactorily, as in fact, it does. A community is well advised not to endanger this important stability attribute of agri-

[3] For an economic explanation, see D. Gale Johnson, "The Nature of the Supply Function for Agricultural Products," *American Economic Review,* Vol. XL (September, 1950).

culture. During the depressed thirties, it was held that one of the functions of acreage allotments and marketing quotas was to make agriculture more "flexible" in adjusting production to the existing business conditions, which meant to the reduced demand caused by the mass unemployment of the time. This was a mistaken view of the problem and an approach, in the case of agriculture, that would have destroyed, had it succeeded, one of the major desirable, organizational achievements of agriculture. Would that other sectors of the economy could be so organized that they too would maintain as steady a rate of resource employment as is normal in agriculture.

Yield Instability in Farming

When it comes to stability of yield, the advantages clearly are with industry. Few farmers can control their output with the certainty that characterizes most industrial firms. The manager of a cement plant, given the inputs of a raw material and labor, can calculate his output with a nicety impossible in agriculture.[4] Agricultural production is subject to many risks and uncertainties that are a major factor in the income instability of the individual farmer. Frost, drought, floods, hail, wind, storms, animal and plant diseases of many types, and a whole array of insects and pests—all conspire to play fast and loose with the production of a particular farm. They determine to no small degree whether yields are large or small, whether flocks and herds increase or are decimated, whether livestock is stunted by disease or whether it gains well while on feed. Over these vagaries of nature the individual farmer has relatively little control. The fortunes and failures of many farmers are determined by these production uncertainties, even in the better situated and more prosperous farming areas.

In any given year there might be hundreds of thousands of farms thus affected, some having their output cut to zero, and yet because of large yields in other sections the aggregate agricultural production of a country as varied and as large as the United States is very steady. The unprecedented droughts of 1934 only reduced total agricultural production (for sale and for farm home consumption) from an index of 96 in 1933 to 93 in 1934.[5]

[4] There are a few minor exceptions to this generalization, for instance, certain dairy farms where all the variable inputs are purchased and all the farmer actually does is to "manufacture" milk, producing none of the feed and engaging in no other enterprises.
[5] This small change in the index of agricultural production for sale and for farm home consumption from one year to another understates, however, the

There is another compensatory factor at work concealing production changes in relation to farm income. The more closely the elasticity of demand approaches unity, the more stable is total farm income, with price changes serving to absorb the deviation between large and small crops. (But where the demand recedes from unity, either in being elastic or inelastic, a differing volume of output gives rise to instability in farm income.)[6] But this does not make for stability in the income of individual farmers. Whole regions may find themselves without crops or livestock to sell. This was the experience of the mass of farmers in the plains states during years in the thirties, but even as they faced an income crisis, the better crops in other areas and, what is more, the higher prices due to the somewhat reduced output because of the crop failure in the plains states contributed to a steadiness in national farm-income figures.

In analyzing the data on yield instability of agriculture in the United States by regions and by products (Chap. 12), we found that it was concentrated in the West North Central and West South Central regions —the plains states mainly—and in the crops which originate primarily in this large area. The variations in crop production per acre are very large; the average was about 18 per cent and 15 per cent for the two regions, respectively, from 1919 to 1949 when one measures the change in yield from the preceding year and adjusts for the upward trend in yield that occurred during the period. Yields of particular farm products varied even more than this.

Functioning of the Economy in Relation to Yield Instability

The basic question again is: How satisfactorily do firms and households, product and factor markets, and the political and social processes work in dealing with the yield instability that is characteristic of agriculture in the United States? Are there some major faults in the existing

---

effect of a drought on production. During a drought year livestock numbers are reduced and feed reserves are consumed, with the result that the production effect of the drought is spread over more than one year. The index for gross farm production fell from 95 in 1933 to 82 in 1934.

[6] This is an elementary proposition: an inelastic demand causes large crops to fetch small incomes, and an elastic demand results in small incomes from small crops.

[7] Four principal corn-belt states (Ohio, Indiana, Illinois, and Iowa) produced, in 1928–1930, a yearly average of 1,640 million feed units; by 1938–1940 this yearly output had risen to 1,916 million feed units, an increase of 17 per cent. Meanwhile, the production of feed in four drought-ridden states (South Dakota, Nebraska, Kansas, and Missouri) dropped from 1,433 million to 950 million feed units, a decrease of 33 per cent.

economic organization in this connection or has the community developed a set of institutions that function rather well? This problem
plainly is one that deserves more study than it has received, although in
recent years several states, notably North Dakota, Montana, and Kansas
(agricultural economists at the land-grant colleges of these states) and
the Bureau of Agricultural Economics have addressed themselves to
some major aspects of this problem.[8] Some studies at the University of
Chicago with the Bureau of Agricultural Economics also bear directly on this problem.[9] However, at present, the available information
and insights are fragmentary and incomplete.

Meanwhile, it will be necessary to state our presumptions about the
relations between yield instability and the organization of economic
activities; formulated as working propositions, they are:

1. The continental climate of the United States is an important exoge-

[8] Most of the August, 1950, issue of the *Journal of Farm Economics*, Vol.
XXXII, was devoted to this problem in one form or another. See especially
the papers by M. M. Kelso, Rainer Schickele, Lloyd Barber and Philip J. Thair,
A. H. Anderson, and by Harry A. Steele and John Muehlbeier. Other contribu-
tions are *Toward Stability in the Great Plains Economy*, Nebraska Agr. Expt.
Sta. Bul. 399, July, 1950 (this is the proceedings of a conference held June
20–22, 1949, at Custer, South Dakota); E. Lloyd Barber, *Meeting Weather
Risk in Kansas Wheat Farming*, Kansas Agr. Expt. Sta. and BAE, *Agr. Econ.
Rept.* 44, September, 1950; Philip J. Thair, *Stabilizing Farm Income against
Crop Yield Fluctuations*, North Dakota Agr. Expt. Sta. and Bureau of Agricul-
tural Economics *Bul.* 362, September, 1950; *Fluctuations in Crops and
Weather, 1866–1948*, USDA, *Statis. Bul.* 101, June, 1951; Harold G. Halcrow,
"Actuarial Structure for Crop Insurance," *Journal of Farm Economics*, Vol.
XXXI (August, 1949); Rainer Schickele, "Farm Business Survival under Ex-
treme Weather Risk," *ibid.*; E. Lloyd Barber, "Variability of Wheat Yields, by
Counties, in the United States," Bureau of Agricultural Economics, September,
1951; and Richard J. Foote and Louis H. Bean, "Are Yearly Variations in Crop
Yield Random?" *Agricultural Economics Research*, Vol. III, No. 1 (January,
1951), Bureau of Agricultural Economics. See also Donald C. Horton, "Adaptation of the Farm Capital Structure to Uncertainty," *Journal of Farm Economics*, Vol. XXXI (February, 1949), and *The Pattern of Farm Financial
Structure* (New York: National Bureau of Economic Research, Inc., May,
1951, preliminary draft).

[9] D. M. Fort, "Fluctuating Hog Supplies and Pork Processing Costs"; W. A.
Frank, "Costs and Gains Involved in Reducing Variability in Hog Supplies";
L. A. Fourt, "Economic Progress, Income and the Marketing of Farm Prod-
ucts"; G. S. Tolley, "Earnings of Labor and Capital in the Food Processing
Industries." (These studies are to be published by the University of Chicago
and the Bureau of Agricultural Economics.)

nous variable to which the economic activities of agriculture are adjusted, as yet, quite imperfectly.

2. Many of the major problems of soil conservation in the United States have their origin in this variable.

3. A series of bad crops represents a disturbance of such a magnitude that the typical family farm in the plains states, and also elsewhere, is unable to cope satisfactorily with the economic consequences of such crops.

4. Product markets do not perform the storage function satisfactorily in counteracting the effects of yield instability, especially upon the livestock production that is dependent upon feed concentrates. Nor do public efforts at storage, as now conducted, provide a satisfactory solution to this aspect of the problem.

5. Many communities located in areas where yields are highly variable are ill adapted to the physical and economic conditions of such areas.

Improvements in Organization to Cope with Yield Instability

There are two classes of organizational improvements, one where the objective is to reduce the existing yield instability and the other where it is to adjust to the instability. Is it possible to reduce or even to eliminate the existing instability in yields? Partly, yes. But considering the problem in its entirety, relatively little can be accomplished along these lines. In the main, it will be necessary to learn how to live more successfully with the year-to-year variation in rainfall which is the critical factor in yields throughout most of the plains states. Three means for reducing somewhat the instability in yields follow.

Close out Particular Areas. One way would be to abandon the areas most vulnerable to the vicissitudes of weather. In the trial and error of settlement and in the adaptations since then, much land has been abandoned. Some has been left idle, some has been put to nonfarm uses, and some once put into crops has been returned to grazing. These adaptations have by no means run their course. The purchases by public agencies of so-called "submarginal" areas is, also, a part of this process of adaptation. Land may also be abandoned periodically, farmed during a series of good years, and then left untilled when bad years appear in sequence. Some very serious community problems arise, however, where farming is of this type, because it is difficult to keep social and private costs and returns from diverging.

New and Better Technology. The development of production techniques applicable to areas subject to wide variations in yield may be viewed as a means of both reducing and adjusting to the yield instability. Better techniques will aid the individual farmer in making his output more constant, in so far as the techniques mean a better accommodation in farming to the natural forces affecting crops and livestock. Drought-resistant crops, dry-land farming, disease-resistant plants and animals, and modern insecticides are a few of the important practices that reduce the incidence of weather, disease, insects, and pests. In the days when corn-belt farmers were dependent upon horses for power, a season as wet as the spring of 1943 would have reduced the corn crop seriously. With tractor power, the field work was done on time and sufficiently well to produce, with favorable weather during the rest of the season, a bumper corn crop.

Advances of this kind come slowly. Some of the technical research of the state agricultural experiment stations and of the U.S. Department of Agriculture is directed to aspects of this production problem. There are, however, regions and areas where the climatic variations are beyond the limits of crop accommodations. Moreover, as farming areas become more specialized, plant and animal diseases and insects present new hazards to the individual farmer.

Application of Water. Since rainfall is the critical, limiting factor in crop yields throughout much of the agriculture of the United States which is most vulnerable to yield instability, the controlled application of water to agricultural land would appear to be, at least in principle, an important way of reducing the existing fluctuations in yields. The Missouri Basin approach is an important development in this connection. More than irrigation is involved. Yet when one considers the magnitude of the problem in terms of area, acres in crops and number of farms, in those parts of the plains states most vulnerable to yield instability alone, it is clear that for the most part, given the existing supply of water and the state of technical knowledge, including "rain making," it will not be possible either to eliminate or even to reduce considerably the instability in yields caused by weather.

Organization to Adjust to Yield Instability

If the existing information about yields for each parcel of land were complete and if this information were freely available, it would not be difficult to organize to cope with variations in yield. Under such circumstances, it is hard to believe that any yield instability problem could continue to exist. One of several solutions or combinations would readily be at hand, for example, (1) embed the costs of the yield instability into the value of each particular parcel of land to which it is related; (2) develop firms that specialize in carrying the particular risk arising from (known) variations in yields; and (3) develop farms with sufficient assets, held in forms which make it possible for them to carry this risk. These organizational solutions, however, are, among other considerations, dependent upon information about yields.

Whether we examine the behavior of firms, markets, or of the political and social processes in relation to yield instability, information about yields is of critical importance. What do the individuals who direct these activities know about yields? How much more is there to be known? This problem consists of two parts: (1) distinguishing between what can be known and what is ultimately unknowable and (2) determining how complete to make the information which can be known.

We know that long sequences of both poor and good crops have occurred in the plains states. But the settlement of the area and the experiences that have accumulated cover too short a period to permit one to determine *wholly satisfactory measures* of the probability of such sequences occurring. It may, of course, prove possible to do this after two or three centuries with the additional weather and farming experiences that such a period will provide. At present, however, alternatives must be formulated on the basis of incomplete information. It is necessary, also, to distinguish between information about yields which can be made more complete at a price and in a time interval which makes it worth while to "produce" and "distribute" such information. There is much that can be done about the problem of yield instability that falls into this category. It must, however, be borne in mind that even where it is possible to acquire additional information, such information may cost more than it is worth.

The proposed organizational improvements which follow are relevant where existing information about yields makes it possible to isolate and adjust to the risk inherent in weather.

Make Each Parcel of Agricultural Land Bear the Yield Risks Inherent in Its Situation. How is it possible to achieve this objective? Can the market of this land be made to price it accordingly? Here, again, it is relatively simple to state the formal requirements: the price of each parcel of land should be equal to the discounted value of the income "stream" which it will produce. But how fine can the marginal razor cut on this kind of face? The realized rent fluctuates widely from year to year and on some of this land the rent approaches zero over the years. Experience in the United States indicates that it is difficult to institutionalize the market of this factor so it will perform satisfactorily where the realized[10] rent fluctuates widely and where the rent is small over the discount period.[11]

Three Private Ways of Carrying Yield Risks. Let us suppose that each parcel of land is valued accurately in relation to its climatic risks; there remains the problem of adjusting to the fluctuations in the realized productivity of the land over time. There are three possible ways: (1) firms that specialize in "yield" insurance; (2) owners of agricultural land who do not farm but who specialize in yield risks; and (3) farms organized to cope with instability in yields.

FIRMS SPECIALIZING IN YIELD INSURANCE. Hail insurance on growing crops had its beginning in 1880; by 1946 the insurance in force reached a billion dollars; from 1947 to 1949 farmers in the United States contracted for about $1,260 million of insurance against hail damage for which they paid annually somewhat more than $50 million in premiums; only a little more than a fourth of this insurance was taken out by farmers in the plains states, as the following data from Ellickson show.

Area	*Crop-hail insurance in force in 1948, in millions of dollars*
Ten plains states	341
Iowa and Minnesota	290
Illinois	270
Five tobacco states	127
Five other North Central states.	102
Three Northwestern states	96
Twenty-two other states	34
United States	1,260

SOURCE: John C. Ellickson, "Hail Insurance on Growing Crops in the United States," *Agricultural Finance Review*, Vol. XIII (November, 1950), Bureau of Agricultural Economics.

On small grains the rates charged in 1950 ranged from $1.50 to $18.75 per $100 of insurance. The chart gives a geographic profile of these rates. Two observations may be made on hail insurance: (1) losses from hail are only one minor factor underlying the instability in yield on which we have been concentrating and (2) information about the

[10] This refers to the economic rent produced and not to the contractual rent paid by the firm under particular leasing arrangements.

[11] The functioning of the land market under conditions where the marginal productivity of land fluctuates widely, where it is often negative, and where it is small over the years requires careful study. This problem has been long neglected. It is a fundamental consideration in determining ways and means, both public and private, to improve the allocation of much land used for grazing and for crops in the intermountain area and in large parts of the plains states.

"probabilities" of losses from hail is still incomplete and unsatisfactory for actuarial purposes.

A comprehensive study by Halcrow[12] indicates that voluntary crop insurance has failed because it has not attracted the majority of farmers where the weather risks are large and because it has not approximated a self-supporting situation. His findings apply to both public and private efforts to provide crop insurance. Halcrow investigated three types of insurance: (1) *all-risk crop insurance* where a base yield is established

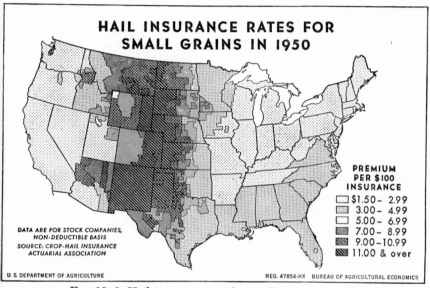

FIG. 19–1. Hail-insurance rate for small grains in 1950.

for each farm and insurance is offered to cover some fraction, say, 50 or 75 per cent of the base yield; (2) *area-yield insurance* where premium and indemnities are based on the yield of particular areas such as a township, county, or even some larger area and where indemnities are paid in any year in which the mean area yield falls below a specified level; (3) *weather-crop insurance* where premiums and indemnities are based on weather records of the area in which the insurance is made available and where indemnities are paid in years in which the weather, in terms of some measurable standards, is adverse.

This study points to the following conclusion:

[12] Harold G. Halcrow, *The Theory of Crop Insurance*, Ph.D. thesis at the University of Chicago, 1948. See especially his paper, "Actuarial Structures for Crop Insurance," *Journal of Farm Economics*, Vol. XXXI (August, 1949), from which the two quotations that follow are taken.

In some low risk regions where the probability of indemnity does not change from year to year and in case of some crops where the current yield is not influenced greatly by a farmer's immediate action, all-risk crop insurance may be used without adverse selectivity or without adverse effects on the efficiency of resource utilization. The same type of insurance may be . . . inadequate and actuarially unworkable in a high risk region like the Great Plains. In such a region area-yield insurance and weather-crop insurance . . . should prove more satisfactory (1) because of the possibilities of providing a higher base for insured yields, (2) because the insurance programs can be made equitable in an actuarial sense and an adverse selectivity can be avoided, and (3) because both types should have a positive, rather than a negative, effect on the efficiency of resource utilization.

In terms of crop-insurance programs, adapted to conditions in the United States, the following proposals emerge:

(1) Since all-risk crop insurance may be appropriate chiefly in low risk regions, . . . its use should be confined to such regions or situations. Empirical studies should be continued to determine the premium-indemnity schedules and the provisions which would be most appropriate for such regions or crops. (2) Since area-yield insurance may be most appropriate for the high-risk crop regions such as the Great Plains, parts of the corn belt, the western cotton area, etc., empirical studies should be undertaken as a basis for instituting the program. These would involve the delineation of areas and the calculation of premium-indemnity schedules for each area. (3) Since weather-yield insurance may be the only type appropriate for large areas of the western United States, especially the ranching areas, investigations should be continued as a basis for determining the specific relationship between weather phenomena, particularly precipitation, and range or forage yields. The weather phenomena then could be used as a basis for writing insurance on range or forage production.

OWNERSHIP OF LAND SPECIALIZED TO CARRY YIELD RISKS. Again, assuming that the yield risks are known, it would be possible to induce owners to specialize in agricultural land which entails high weather risks. Horton[13] has shown that some such adaptation has developed among those having

---

[13] Donald C. Horton, "Adaptation of the Farm Capital Structure to Uncertainty," *Journal of Farm Economics,* Vol. XXXI (February, 1949). See also the preliminary draft by Horton, *The Pattern of Farm Financial Structure* (New York: National Bureau of Economic Research, Inc., May, 1951).

financial interests in the physical assets of farms. Landlords have entered the higher weather risks areas whereas such credit agencies as insurance companies apparently have preferred not to acquire substantial financial interest in agricultural land in such areas. The difficulty of developing further this approach, in addition to the state of information about yields, is the strong community preference for the family farm. While the "ideal" family farm does not necessarily preclude tenant-operated farms, it acts, and probably increasingly so, as a barrier to the kind of specialization that would be required if more of the yield risks were to be transferred to landlords. Moreover, the economic importance of possibilities in this direction is a declining one because farm machinery and equipment are becoming a relatively more important part of the total assets required to farm especially in the plains states.

ADAPTATIONS ON THE PART OF THE FARM-FIRM. In principle, this solution is simple and straightforward. What is needed is a family farm with enough assets so distributed that it can cope satisfactorily with the fluctuations in income caused by variations in yields. Both the interest of the farm business and of the farm household are involved. Two major difficulties arise in practice: The amount of assets required is often too large for a family farm to finance under existing conditions; and most farm families, even if they had sufficient assets, have relatively little experience and information on how to hold such assets in order to manage their activities when confronted by yield instability.[14]

Public Agencies in Relation to Yield Instability. The welfare of the local community in areas of high weather risks is very vulnerable. Community services dependent upon local taxes are in an exposed position. When the realized rent on agricultural land disappears or becomes negative, some property taxes are left unpaid; some land is abandoned, at least temporarily. In some areas, the community finds itself compelled to

---

[14] A serious shortcoming of the studies so far reported dealing with this problem from the point of view of farm-firm adaptations is the lack of data on the amount and kind of assets required to farm satisfactorily in the plains states. The emphasis has been primarily on the income flow and variations in it over time caused by yield instability. But even from cursory observations, it would appear that a wheat-feed-livestock farm of about optimum scale in the northern part of the plains states, say, a farm of about 800 acres with modern machinery and equipment, represents a set of physical assets worth about $75,000 at 1950 factor prices. To "survive" a series of lean crop years of the kind that occurred in the thirties would require about $25,000 of financial assets. In our example, a total of $100,000 is required if both sets of assets are to be provided fully by the operating farm family. It is hard to believe that a typical farm family can command so large a collection of resources under existing conditions.

make additional outlays to reduce the losses from wind erosion on crop-land that has been abandoned because of drought, while education and other public services suffer greatly. Federal agencies have repeatedly provided emergency aids of one kind or another: emergency feed and seed loans, a moratorium on existing Federal loans, cattle-buying pro-grams, public works, and other related measures. The community at local, state, and national levels has in substance come to the relief of farm people; it has been in a residual position in relation to yield risks.

The community might also take a positive approach; it could plan to bear some of these risks on its own terms. Local and state finances could be managed to counteract in part the income instability of agriculture of the locality. Schools and other public construction should not only be undertaken but also paid for in good crop years, and, in addition, local and state surpluses accumulated. Instead, the debt "cycle" of these public agencies appears to run the other way. Federal efforts could also be given a more positive turn. While it is true that the achievements in this connection of Federal agencies in making loans and in obtaining repay-ments has been substantial, they cannot be viewed as a well-conceived way of "carrying" a part of these yield risks. Federal crop insurance has not been developed into a satisfactory program for areas having high yield risks. The Federal income tax has not been adapted to the yield characteristics of the plains states. Nor have the storage programs of the Federal government been designed to counteract yield instability; they have served parity prices—the dead hand of the distant past.

In this section on organization to adjust to yield instability, we have been considering the problem mainly from the point of view of particular farmers and regions. We have related year-to-year variations in yield primarily to weather and to particular parcels of agricultural land. Loca-tion has, therefore, been important and microanalysis of the behavior of particular firms has been in the forefront. The consequences of yield instability also take on certain aggregative characteristics, as we have shown, in studying the year-to-year variations in the output of major crops, the production of which is concentrated in the plains states. This aggregative aspect of the yield problem can be approached primarily by storage.

The possibilities from storage are not restricted to counteracting varia-tions in yield; they are also meaningful in dealing with some variations in demand. Storage operations can have major price and income effects, and for these reasons an exploration of storage will be postponed until the next chapter where we take up the instability of price and income in agriculture.

20

ORGANIZATION FOR PRICE STABILITY

The community, it may be assumed, prefers price stability to price movements, flexible rather than rigid prices, and "free" prices to "fixed" prices. The concept of stable, flexible, and free prices, however, presents many difficulties. Each of these characteristics may represent for a community a particular and distinct preference attribute. The community preference for price stability may be to avert inflation and deflation, business fluctuations, or particular price movements that are deemed to be "undesirable." Flexibility in prices may represent a preference for those changes in relative prices that are required to adjust to economic development as new, fundamental factor supplies and product demands emerge. The preference for "free" prices may be to keep firms, households, and public agencies from "manipulating" prices, to keep economic power from becoming concentrated, and to maintain an open society.

But none of these preferences is unambiguous; there is the ever-present difficulty of passing from individual interests to the welfare of the community in situations where, as is often the case, a conflict of interests exists; nor are these preferences unaffected by changes in circumstance. For example, when a community is at war, it may prefer some inflation to fiscal and monetary measures of sufficient strength to hold inflation completely in check. Then, too, when the tempo of economic development gives rise to major business booms and depressions, the community may prefer to dampen these movements even at the "price" of slowing down somewhat the average rate of economic growth and in the process give up some price flexibility. Or in a situation where very large firms are required to achieve an optimum scale of operation, the community may prefer to forego some free prices and some decentralization in organization in order to obtain the additional product.

The possibilities of achieving a stable or flexible or free price are also beset by difficulties. In some situations, they are complementary and joint; in others, choosing one entails giving up some of the other. To illustrate, taxes to check inflation are not neutral in relation to the distribution, composition, or size of the national product; and monetary management necessarily involves some control over particular (banking) firms. (These banking firms are, therefore, less free.) Flexible product prices that are satisfactory in allocating a particular stock of products (say, crops that have been harvested) can be far from satisfactory in guiding production where the interval between crops is substantial and where production plans are long.

How satisfactorily do farm prices function in relating possibilities to preferences, including the preferences of the community for stable, flexible, and free prices? No meaningful answer can be given to this question because at this stage of our knowledge there is no way of identifying and measuring these particular preference attributes or of determining the possibilities of attaining them. We are, therefore, compelled to restrict this part of our study to a set of particular problems: (1) to the problem of economic instability where mobilization and war are powerful inflationary engines as the economy is now managed and where demobilization and peace may be deflationary; and (2) to the problem of fluctuating farm prices where the price elasticities of the supply and the demand are relatively low and where large and abrupt shifts of one or the other of the schedules occur frequently.

In studying the instability of farm prices, in Chap. 11, two propositions were advanced: (1) that the price elasticities of both the demand and of the supply of farm products are relatively low and (2) that the short-term shifts of one or the other of these two schedules are often large and important.[1] In studying the organizational problem represented

---

[1] We do not wish to imply that this is in any way a complete explanation. We have not attempted to explain why the demand for farm products shifts about as it appears to have done, except in most general terms: because of changes in income where the effects on demand are represented by the income elasticity; because of changes in the distribution of income; and because of variations in foreign demand and purchases by public agencies for the armed services, for other governments, for storage, and for other purposes. Model IV, formulated by O. H. Brownlee and D. Gale Johnson, "Reducing Price Variability Confronting Primary Producers," *Journal of Farm Economics,* Vol. XXXII (May, 1950), represents an approach to a more complete explanation. However, as yet this model has not been put to an empirical test. Such a study should be worth while and should be undertaken. This more complete macroeconomics model represents additional variables and relations which our approach of necessity neglects, for example, the effects of income changes in the farm sector upon the nonfarm sectors and also the converse. But these models are also incomplete. For instance, except for a brief reference (in so-called Model V) the role of price expectations is neglected in the formulations of Brownlee and Johnson. But even so, the empirical analysis (Model IV) may turn out to be very difficult to manage in obtaining usable results. Should this turn out to be the case, one is driven back again to a simpler representation in analyzing the problem at hand.

by the instability of farm prices, we shall consider both the possibility of reducing the price instability and ways of adjusting to it.

REDUCING THE INSTABILITY OF FARM PRICES

Prices received by farmers for all products over the very disturbed period from 1910 to 1946 changed, from one year to the next, on the average 12.3 per cent.[2] In ten different instances these prices either rose or fell over 20 per cent and in three of these, over 30 per cent. This record of large price fluctuations at the farm occurred despite the price stabilization efforts of the Federal Farm Board from 1929 to 1933, the vast network of price supports for agriculture since the New Deal, and the measures taken to hold farm prices in check during World War I and World War II. Table 20–1 gives data on price fluctuations by products and groups of products.

TABLE 20–1. FARM-PRICE CHANGES FROM PRECEDING YEAR
1910–1946

Products	Average change from preceding year, per cent
All dairy products	10.2
Milk at wholesale	11.6
Livestock and products	12.0
Poultry and eggs	12.2
Cattle and calves	13.1
Eggs	13.2
Hay	13.9
All crops	14.2
Meat animals	15.1
Sheep and lambs	15.2
Fruits and tree nuts	15.6
Feed crops	17.8
Food grains	17.9
Wheat	18.0
Tobacco	18.2
Oil-bearing crops	20.6
Corn	21.0
Cotton	22.1
Hogs	22.1
Potatoes	35.2
All farm products	12.3

SOURCE: Theodore W. Schultz, *Production and Welfare of Agriculture* (New York: The Macmillan Company, 1949), Table VI, p. 78. Cattle and calves, hay, corn, sheep and lambs, wheat, and potatoes are for 1910–1945.

[2] Theodore W. Schultz, based on *Production and Welfare of Agriculture*, (New York: The Macmillan Company, 1949), Table VI, p. 78.

There are two sets of problems on which we shall concentrate in examining the instability of farm prices. One is related to the instability of the economy as a whole represented by marked movements in employment and in the general level of prices. The other is related to particular supply and demand attributes of farm products, that is, to the very low price elasticity of these two schedules, the abrupt shifts of the demand, and the variations in production caused by weather and other exogenous factors. The two sets of problems, however, are intertwined in ways that make it difficult to untangle them. For example, the data of the forties are the result of a more than doubling of the general level of prices at wholesale and of farm prices rising sharply relative to other prices because of the large and abrupt shift of the demand to the right. This shift was the consequence partly of the effects of the rise in the price level, partly of the large additional purchases for the military and for other governments, and partly of the growth in population and the rise in per capita income which normally might be expected to occur fairly gradually. It is, therefore, not surprising that some students who are close to agriculture view these price fluctuations primarily as a problem which is particular to agriculture and, on the other hand, that some of those who are concerned about general economic instability, and who are not aware of the supply and demand attributes of farm products, hold the belief that all the instability of farm prices is fundamentally a part of the more general problem.

It should not be hard to demonstrate that many of the most disturbing movements in farm prices have been the consequences of major depressions and subsequent recoveries and of marked deflationary and inflationary movements in prices generally. Those who are bent on the *particular* approach may readily grant this to be a fact, but may contend that it is very unlikely that general economic stability can be achieved and that it is, therefore, necessary to provide particular safeguards for agriculture against some of the adverse effects of this instability in prices. Given this assumption about the "probabilities" of overcoming general economic instability, it is important, nevertheless, that measures which are taken on behalf of agriculture help counteract the general instability and not merely shelter agriculture, especially so since agriculture may be sheltered in ways which will cause serious malallocations in resources within agriculture and which will increase the burden arising from economic instability borne by the rest of the economy.

But what about the belief of those who hold that once general economic stability is achieved, the agricultural pricing problem will also be solved satisfactorily? There is much to be said for this view because marked movements in the general level of prices and in employment do disturb farm prices seriously. Looking back, it seems reasonable to believe that most of the chronic economic problems of agriculture during the seventies, eighties, and into the early nineties, reflected in the Granger-Greenback-Populist movements, would not have arisen had the general level of prices[3] not declined, whereas it fell about one-half during that period. Likewise, most of the farm problems of the twenties and also those of the thirties would not have occurred had prices generally been maintained instead of dropping drastically after 1920 to about three-fifths of the level that had prevailed during 1919 and 1920 and, then, falling once more at the end of the twenties, when prices of all commodities in 1932 and 1933 dropped to about two-thirds of the level of the late twenties. In the other direction, the fact that prices generally more than doubled from 1915 to 1920 and again from 1940 to 1948 distorted the pattern of relative prices appreciably, contributed somewhat to the food problems that arose, and induced many farmers to make bad long-run production plans and financial commitments.

But let us suppose that appropriate fiscal and monetary management had maintained employment and a stable price level, say, from 1920 on. Would there have been no marked, sudden movements in farm prices? The answer is clearly in the negative because variations in agricultural production and shifts in the demand schedule at times were large enough to have caused by themselves large movements in farm prices relative to other prices. To illustrate this outcome, let us examine some of the larger changes in agricultural production occurring since 1920. We shall take the price elasticity of the demand for farm products at the farm to have been about —.25[4] (in the stock period and in the short run, see, Chap. 11) and the changes in the volume of agricultural products sold by farmers to have been the consequences of variations in yield caused by weather. Farm products sold by farmers in 1921 were about 10 per cent below those of 1920;[5] this change by itself points to a 40 per cent rise in farm prices. Bad weather and poor crops, especially of 1934, pulled down the sales of farm products in 1935 about 5 per cent, enough

[3] Price comparisons in this paragraph are based on all commodities at wholesale.

[4] We shall use the —.25 elasticity as applicable over a wide range of the demand schedule in our inferences that follow in order to keep the presentation simple. The demand schedule, however, becomes somewhat less inelastic as one approaches both the upper and lower ranges.

[5] Total inputs committed by farmers in 1921 were about 2 per cent less than those employed in 1920 (see Chap. 7, Table 7–6). This decrease in inputs was in large part, however, unplanned because it came as a result of the poor crops of 1921.

to bring about a 20 per cent rise in prices at the farm. The bumper crops of 1937, on the other hand, resulted in 16 per cent more farm products being sold in that year than in 1935. Allowing for a recovery from the low of 1935 of 5 points, the remaining 11 per cent would indicate a fall in the price at the farm of about 40 per cent, other things unchanged.

We can also identify some large shifts in the demand schedule which presumably would have occurred even though there had been no marked movements in the general level of prices. In 1940, only 2 per cent of the total food available in the United States was exported; the rest was distributed to civilians.[6] In 1942, however, 12.8 per cent of the available food was withdrawn from civilians for exports and shipments and for the military and for other governments. This withdrawal from United States civilians of an additional 10.8 per cent of the food available, in 1942 compared to 1940, points to a price rise at the farm for products used as food of about 40 per cent.[7]

When we come, then, to the organizational task of reducing the instability of farm prices, it will be necessary (1) to improve the stability of the economy as a whole and (2) to modify the relevant supply and demand attributes of farm products in such a way that the particular shifts of the demand and the year-to-year variations in production will not give rise to marked disturbances in farm prices. But to achieve either of these purposes, we come up against the problem of war and peace, because the transformations of the economy in mobilizing, waging war, and demobilizing have been undertaken in ways which have brought about much economic instability in general and large and abrupt demand shifts of farm products in particular. We can, however, learn much from the mistakes which were made during World War I and World War II and, again, from June, 1950, to the early part of 1951 as the military operations in Korea developed, especially in the area of monetary management. With a better understanding of the functions of central banking, it should be possible to reduce substantially the very large

---

[6] Data from The National Food Situation, Bureau of Agricultural Economics, October–December, 1951, Table 2. Also, see Table 20–3.

[7] This inference leaves aside the point that for the general level of prices to have remained unchanged under these circumstances, it would have been necessary for other prices to have declined somewhat.

The price effect of this withdrawal may be put another way. Given the larger production of 1942 and assuming that prices were in equilibrium and not controlled, an increase of 10.8 per cent in the quantity of farm foods available to the civilian sector would have resulted in farm prices about 40 per cent below that which prevailed.

movements of the price level when such transformations of the economy become necessary.

War and Peace with Less Economic Instability

All the large short-term movements of farm product prices in recent decades, except those of the early thirties, were related to the preparing for war, the waging of war, and to demobilization. These particular transformations of the economy were of the nature of severe shocks. In the process, large movements in the general level of prices occurred, and important changes in relative prices also occurred. Farm product prices rose sharply both in absolute and relative terms during World War I and World War II and, again, following the Korean hostilities:

(1910–1914 = 100)	World War I		World War II		Korea	
	1915	1918	1939	1947	1950 (first half)	1951 (first half)
Prices of farm products	99	206	95	275	241	306
Relative prices of farm products . . .	94	119	77	115	96	110

SOURCE: *Agricultural Statistics, 1950,* U.S. Department of Agriculture, Table 678, and *The Midyear Economic Report of the President,* July, 1951, Table B–26.

Farm product prices also fell sharply not only in absolute but also in relative terms after wartime demands had spent themselves after the middle of 1920 and again after 1947, although following World War II the drop was much more moderate and less abrupt:

(1910–1914 = 100)	1919	1921	1947	1950 (first half)
Prices of farm products	218	124	275	241
Relative prices of farm products	111	80	115	96

These transformations of the economy related to the rise and fall in international tensions and to peace and war were made under forced draft; it was deemed very important to make the changes rapidly. These transformations were periods of substantial inflation or deflation with large movements in the level of prices. They were, also, periods of large shifts in the demand for farm products, which explains the relative rise or fall of farm product prices. The price disturbances related to peace and war, therefore, are of two parts: (1) large movements in the general level of prices and (2) large, abrupt shifts in the demand for farm products so timed that they accentuate the movements of the prices of farm products.[8]

A large upward or downward movement of the general level of prices does not leave the relative position of the various demand schedules unaffected. For example, when expectations come to reflect the likelihood of a rise in the general level of prices, some firms and households will shift from money and near money to nonmoney assets.[9] Households buy ahead and in doing so acquire additional "stocks" of goods such as products made of wool, cotton, and leather but not of most foods because they are too perishable. Some firms and individuals, under these circumstances, also buy ahead; they acquire additional stocks or claims on farm products that can be stored and these transactions are facilitated by our well-organized grain and produce exchanges with both spot and futures markets. It is this behavior which explains, under circumstances such as prevailed from 1934 to 1937 and from mid-1950 to early 1951, to take two instances, why the prices of the more durable farm products rose so much more than did those which are more perishable when one allows for differences in price elasticities and changes in production.

But this is not all, because as the rise in the price level proceeds, some of the prices of the resources used to produce the services added to farm products, before they are sold at retail, are relatively slow to advance, for example, transportation costs. As a consequence of this unevenness in the rise in the several relevant prices entering as costs into food at retail, the demand for food, reflecting the larger dollar incomes and expenditures on the part of consumers, made possible and necessary by the general rise in prices, increases the demand for the farm food relative to nonfarm services added to food. There may, also, be some income distribution effects because the rise in the price level may alter substantially the personal distribution of income.

It is our belief that major movements in the price level such as oc-

---

[8] The converse would be a situation, say, where the general level of prices rose because of inflation and where the demand for farm products shifted to the left, thus "offsetting" the price effects of the inflation (in absolute terms) in the case of farm products. Also, of course, a shift in the supply of the same amount as the shift in the demand would leave the relative price unchanged

[9] The monetary authorities in their control of the money supply can check such transfers in the aggregate, but under circumstances when a marked change in the price level has occurred in the past the expansion in the money supply has not only made it possible but has induced firms and household to make these substitutions.

curred from 1915 to 1918, 1920 to 1921, 1929 to 1933, 1933 to 1937, 1940 to 1948, and from mid-1950 to early 1951, in the short run, shifted the demand for farm products at the farm substantially.

Any proposals to reduce the variability of farm prices worthy of consideration must start with the general level of prices. There is not much point in laboring for an enlightened policy covering the relationships among farm prices when the center of gravity of all prices is moving markedly either up or down. These large, general movements in prices submerge the important gains that otherwise could be attained from a better allocation of resources within agriculture. They also, of course, distort the claims and counterclaims of debtors and creditors.[10] Stability in the general level of prices should therefore stand first among objectives in organizing to reduce the instability of farm prices.

The objective is clear enough. But is it possible to transform a major economy with the technical and organizational attributes of the United States from peace to a war basis without an inflationary rise in the general level of prices?[11] Some change (rise) in the general level of prices probably facilitates the conversion process. But must it be a more than doubling of product prices (at wholesale), as was the case from the start to the price peak during both World War I and World War II? There is a growing consensus among economists[12] that it is possible by rational and skillful fiscal and monetary management to make transformations of this kind without large disturbances in the general level of prices.[13]

[10] Many farmers are debtors. To the extent that they own physical assets used in farming, they hold farm commodities, farm machinery and equipment, and title to land. When the level of prices falls, they stand to lose much—many of them are liquidated, including many of the most efficient farmers who have extended their debts to obtain modern machinery and equipment and an efficient combination of resources. Contrariwise, when the level of prices rises, many farmers are the recipients of unusually large windfalls—the kind of prosperity that breeds land booms and seriously distorts values.

[11] In this context, we might view a rise in prices generally of 20 per cent or more, at wholesale, occurring during two or three years as a large disturbance.

[12] For a general statement of important aspects of this issue, see "The Problem of Economic Instability, A Committee Report," *American Economic Review* Vol. XL (September, 1950). The committee agrees on the functions of fiscal and monetary management. It also emphasizes "market policy." Professor Milton Friedman, however, dissents because of his belief that "market policy" is not appropriate to the task (p. 534).

[13] On this possibility in relation to developments following Korea, see Theodore W. Schultz, "Policy Lessons from the Economic Mobilization of the U.S.A.," *Journal of Farm Economics, Proceedings,* Vol. XXXIV (1952).

But what can and should be done about the large and abrupt shifts in the demand for farm products which occur during these peace-to-war conversions? We shall consider this question as part of the more general problem of shifts in demand.

Gradual and Small vs. Abrupt and Large Shifts of the Demand

In Chap. 11 we considered in some detail the possibilities of large shifts of the demand schedule for food at retail and, also, for farm food at the point of farm sales. To provide a working standard, we defined a shift of the demand of 5 per cent or more from normal, occurring in a time interval of two years or less, as a large and abrupt shift, because such a shift implies a rise or fall in the farm price of about 20 per cent, other things unchanged. In examining the possibilities of large shifts in both of the demand schedules referred to above, we found that they have occurred as a consequence of the following circumstances: (1) a marked change in the distribution of the population between the civilian and noncivilian sectors and within the civilian sector as to location and occupation, (2) a large movement in the proportion of the resources of the economy that is employed (that is, major depressions and subsequent recoveries), and (3) a large change in the personal allocation of disposable income between consumption and asset holdings. In addition, there are the effects of the commercial, foreign, and government sectors upon the position of the demand schedule of farm products considered in Chap. 11.

As an objective of economic organization, is it possible and desirable to avert such large and abrupt shifts of the demand schedule? The answer can be drawn in large part from the analysis of possibilities of such shifts occurring, presented in Chap. 11.

Large and Abrupt Demand Shifts Related to Population Changes. Such shifts are possible when the composition of the population is altered as a consequence of marked changes in the distribution of the population between the civilian and the noncivilian sectors. Rapid mobilization of individuals for the armed forces and rapid demobilization of such forces will have this effect.

It should be observed, however, that such large and abrupt shifts of the demand schedule of United States civilians for food and of the demand for United States farm food products at the point of farm sales *are an essential part of the process of mobilizing and demobilizing the economy under such conditions* and under such circumstances the appropriate organizational task is not one of averting these demand shifts but of adjusting consumption and other variables to them. This statement, therefore, implies that under such conditions a rise or fall in the relative price of these products is desirable.

LARGE SHORT-TERM MOVEMENTS IN THE PROPORTION OF RESOURCES EMPLOYED. Although the income elasticity of farm products is relatively low, a rise or fall in per capita income of as much as 20 per cent in two years can set into motion a large and abrupt shift of the demand for these products. Movements in per capita income of such a magnitude, however, have not occurred except in the event of a severe depression, like that of the early thirties, and during a recovery when many unemployed resources have been drawn into place, as was the case during the beginning of the forties. If these are the facts, the solution, at least in principle, is clear; it means organizing the economy so that it will not experience mass unemployment, one of the principal attributes of a severe depression.

What about the effects of "normal" reoccurring fluctuations in business upon the demand for farm products? While no attempts have been made, to our knowledge, to isolate and measure this particular effect of such business fluctuations, studies explaining the demand for food in . the United States, covering periods which were free from marked movements in price levels, suggest that "normal" business recessions and recoveries in the past have resulted in small shifts of the demand for food at retail. The price data in Table 20–2 provide some indirect evidence supporting this inference; from 1894 to 1914 as business fluctuated from trough to peak to trough, the index of farm product prices, correcting for the upward drift of prices, did not show large rises and falls, except perhaps in the rise from May, June, and July, 1908, to December, 1909, and January and February, 1910, followed by the trough that centered on December, 1911, and January and February, 1912.

Instability of Consumer Spending.[14] Large changes have occurred in the distribution of disposable income between consumption and asset holdings, sufficiently large to shift the demand for food at retail substantially during a time interval of two years or less. This particular instability of consumer spending, however, has not given rise to large and abrupt shifts of the demand schedule of food except during wartime circumstances when "forced savings" have become important and then, subsequently, when circumstances again have become more nearly normal. It would appear that most of this particular source of price instability can be averted by appropriate monetary and fiscal management in the event of war and during postwar demobilization.

[14] This very descriptive heading is taken from *The Instability of Consumer Spending* by Arthur F. Burns. The thirty-second annual *Report of the National Bureau of Economic Research*, May, 1952.

TABLE 20–2. FARM PRICES RELATED TO BUSINESS CYCLE STAGES
1894–1914

Period	Stage of cycle	Index of farm product prices[a]
1894 (May, June, July).	Trough	60
1895 (Nov., Dec., and Jan., 1896). . . .	Peak	59
1897 (May, June, July).	Trough	57
1899 (May, June, July).	Peak	61
1900 (Nov., Dec., and Jan., 1901). . . .	Trough	74
1902 (Aug., Sept., Oct.).	Peak	82
1904 (July, Aug., Sept.).	Trough	81
1907 (Apr., May, June).	Peak	86
1908 (May, June, July).	Trough	87
1909 (Dec. and Jan., Feb., 1910)	Peak	107
1911 (Dec. and Jan., Feb., 1912)	Trough	97
1912 (Dec. and Jan., Feb., 1913)	Peak	99
1914 (Nov., Dec., and Jan., 1915). . . .	Trough	98

[a] Warren and Pearson, *Cornell Memoir* 142.

SOURCE: Adapted from Arthur F. Burns and Wesley C. Mitchell, *Measuring Business Cycles* (New York: National Bureau of Economic Research, Inc., 1946), Appendix A, Table A1.

LARGE CHANGES IN PURCHASES OF FARM PRODUCTS FOR PURPOSES OTHER THAN SUPPLYING UNITED STATES CIVILIANS. The demand shifts considered above stem from the behavior of United States civilians as consumers. The demand shifts which arise from large variations in noncivilian uses and purchases of farm products cannot, in the main, be eliminated. Specifically, during World War I and World War II not only the military but other countries, our allies and friendly countries, found it necessary to turn to the United States for large additional amounts of farm products. These purchases represented, in large part, an increase in the demand that was vital to the war effort.

A gauge of the large and abrupt shifts in the demand for farm products from changes in purchases that occurred after 1940 is at hand, although comparable data for World War I are not available.

Suppose that United States civilians had acquired 98 per cent of the food available in 1942, as they did in 1940, in a free market; the price of food at retail instead of rising sharply (nearly 30 per cent) would have fallen appreciably, relative to other prices and, also, somewhat in absolute terms. One also observes from Table 20–3 that the food withdrawn from the United States civilian supply represented 2 per cent in 1940 and 20.3 per cent in 1944 of the food available. The change from 1944 to 1946 is noteworthy; the purchases under discussion were reduced

TABLE 20–3. YEAR-TO-YEAR CHANGES IN THE PROPORTION OF THE AVAILABLE FOOD
ACQUIRED BY UNITED STATES CIVILIANS
1924–1951

Year	Available food acquired by United States civilians, per cent	Changes from preceding year, per cent	Year	Available food acquired by United States civilians, per cent	Changes from preceding year, per cent
1924	93.1				
1925	94.9	+1.9	1940	98.0	+1.0
1926	94.6	−0.3	1941	93.8	−4.3
1927	94.3	−0.3	1942	87.2	−7 0
1928	94.9	+0.6	1943	81.4	−6.4
1929	95.1	+0.2	1944	79.7	−2.1
1930	95.4	+0.3	1945	82.3	+3.7
1931	96.0	+0.6	1946	89.7	+9.0
1932	96.7	+0.7	1947	89.7	0.0
1933	97.3	+0.6	1948	91.4	+1.9
1934	96.6	−0.7	1949	91.1	−0.3
1935	98.2	+1.7	1950	93.2	+2.3
1936	98.9	+0.7	1951	90.2	−3.2
1937	97.7	−1.2			
1938	96.6	−1.1			
1939	97.0	+0.4			

SOURCE: *Consumption of Food in the United States, 1909–48*, BAE, *Misc. Pub.* 691, August, 1949, Table 1, and *National Food Situation*, Bureau of Agricultural Economics, October–December, 1951, Table 2. For the years 1945 through and including 1951, these figures included procurement for relief feeding in areas occupied by our armed forces. The total food available consists of production, imports, and changes in stocks (plus or minus). The total distribution is classified: civilian, military, including military civilian feeding, net purchases of the U.S. Department of Agriculture, and commercial exports and shipments.

sharply, and civilians acquired 9 per cent more of the food available. From 1950 to 1951, as a result of the Korean hostilities, these purchases were increased, again, shifting the demand for food appreciably to the right.

Is there some way by which the shifts in the demand for farm products at the farm arising from this source can be made smaller and thus more gradual? The problem deserves careful study, but it would be a mistake to view these shifts in demand basically as the result of imperfections in economic organization. To endeavor to hold the price of food or of farm products constant relative to other prices under these circumstances is to impair seriously the functioning of economy. It might turn out that storage can be so managed as to counteract some of the price effects of these large and abrupt demand shifts. But even a cursory look at the data indicates that the volume of farm products involved during World War I and World War II was so large that even stocks at the highest level undertaken so far by the Commodity Credit Corporation would have made only a very small dent.

Reducing the Variations in Agricultural Production

Some fluctuations in agricultural production are in some respects comparable in their effects on farm price to large and abrupt shifts in demand. But it would be incorrect to regard these fluctuations as planned shifts of the supply schedule of farm products. In studying the factors underlying the emerging new and better production possibilities in agriculture (in Chap. 7) and the remarkable year-to-year stability of inputs used in farming in the United States (in Chap. 13), we found no evidence to indicate that the supply schedule, like that of the demand, is subject to large and abrupt shifts as a consequence of decisions taken by farmers. There have been periods of contraction, presumably a movement down on the existing, very inelastic supply schedule, and, similarly, some increases in the short run in response to higher relative prices by moving up on the schedule. But the short-run shifts of this schedule have not been either large or abrupt by the standard which we used in gauging such shifts of the demand. Although the supply schedule has shifted far to the right over the years, since at about the same relative price 75 per cent more was being produced in 1950 than was the case in 1910, this shift is the result of many small shifts of this schedule.

But agricultural production has not been nearly so stable, for there have been some large changes from year to year and also some series of good and bad crop years because of weather. While agricultural production as a whole in the United States comes along rather evenly despite the weather, there are, nevertheless, some large and abrupt changes, such as the changes from 1920 to 1921, 1933 to 1935, and 1935 to 1937 (see Chaps. 12 and 13). Data presented in Chap. 13 make it clear, however, that production disturbances from fluctuations in yield caused by weather are restricted mainly to the food grains, feed grains, cotton, and to oil-bearing crops, and to the plains states area primarily.

But not much can be done by way of economic organization to reduce these particular variations in yield (see Chap. 19). It is possible, however, to adjust to these variations in production better than has been the case in the past; and, presumably, some of the price effects can be averted by storage.

Increasing the Price Elasticity of the Supply

The price elasticities of both the demand and supply are very low. If it were possible to increase the elasticity of either or both schedules, changes in output caused by weather and, more important, large shifts in the demand schedule could be absorbed with less pitching of farm prices. If this possibility were attainable without foregoing some "product" and some decentralization in organization, a strong case would presumably exist to increase the relevant price elasticities. How much "product" or decentralization to forego, should this be necessary, would depend upon the nature of the community preference for price stability, "product," and decentralization.

Can agricultural production be organized so that it will be more responsive to changes in relative prices? Are acreage allotments, as used by the AAA, a satisfactory way of contracting output?

Making Farm Output More Responsive to Changes in Relative Prices. This response is characteristically slow and gradual, particularly so during a major depression. The total inputs committed to agricultural production were reduced only about 6 per cent from 1930 to 1933, although relative farm prices fell more than a third. During such a period the supply function of agricultural land has a price elasticity approaching zero; that of capital equipment is also very inelastic because the demand price falls below the price of new equipment and because the old equipment does not have alternative uses outside of agriculture. The supply function of labor shifts with the level of income and employment in the other sectors of the economy, and as unemployment increases in the rest of the economy, farm workers are willing to accept lower wage rates rather than become unemployed.[15] This is the response of farm output during a major depression.

There are, however, convincing reasons for the belief that the aggregate farm output is substantially more responsive to a fall in the relative farm price when resources in the rest of the economy are fully employed and when such conditions have prevailed for some time, that is, long enough to absorb most of the underemployment that has accumulated in agriculture as a consequence of a depression. In analyzing the two primary factor markets, that of labor and of capital serving agriculture,

---

[15] See D. G. Johnson, "The Nature of the Supply Function for Agricultural Products," *American Economic Review*, Vol. XI (September, 1950). Johnson goes on to point out that under such conditions "(1) farm prices, farm wage rates, and land rents would fall in about the same proportion and (2) the employment of land, labor, and machinery would not change appreciably" (p. 548).

in relation to economic development, we found that these markets function much more satisfactorily at the centers of economic development than they do in areas peripheral to such centers; and from this we may infer that the process of regaining and achieving full use of resources also acts to improve the performance of both the labor and capital markets. The supply function of agricultural land will still be highly inelastic in the short run but somewhat less so than during a depression; capital equipment will show little change when it comes to contraction but on the side of expansion it will be appreciably more elastic. The supply function of fertilizer and lime may be viewed as relatively elastic in this context. The most important improvement will occur in labor; the supply function of this input will become substantially more elastic.[16]

The case for greater built-in flexibility in agricultural production rests, first, on the need for a more rapid response when the short-term demand shifts are substantial, for example, as a consequence of mobilization, war, and return to peace and, second, on the better possibilities for expanding and contracting agricultural production. These possibilities have become better as farming has become more dependent upon inputs purchased annually from the rest of the economy, the supplies of which are relatively elastic (see Chap. 7). There is need for a study of the possibilities of increasing agricultural production, say, 5 per cent in two years by means of relative prices inducing farmers to use more agricultural inputs available from the rest of the economy.

Contracting Farm Output by Acreage Allotments. Another way to increase the "elasticity" of the supply of farm products, again focusing upon output, is for the government to ration particular inputs and to establish marketing quotas along lines of the contraction in production which the AAA tried to achieve under the legislation enacted during the early thirties. It will be helpful at this point to review at some length the early experiences of the AAA.

USE OF ACREAGE ALLOTMENTS. Of the many objectives of the AAA, the main objective was to regulate the acreage of certain basic crops. To do this, the AAA developed a system of acreage allotments, entailing the establishing of acreage limits for farms growing the crop. Certain benefits were offered to induce farmers to participate and make the required adjustments in their cropping programs, and at an appropriate time the AAA checked compliance and made its payments to farmers.

Acreage allotments were used for three purposes:[17] (1) to curtail

[16] *Ibid.* The data presented in the latter part of Johnson's paper are not inconsistent with this description of the several input responses.

[17] We are restricting our attention to the effects of acreage allotments, only

production, and thus raise farm prices and income;[18] (2) to reduce misuse of the soil; and (3) as a basis for making government payments to farmers for participation in the program. In this discussion we are concerned chiefly with the first of these objectives. It may be helpful, however, to anticipate our findings to help see some of the essential interplay that was at work. In our judgment, the AAA acreage allotments reduced the acreage planted and harvested of the main crops subject to this technique, but they probably did not affect total production appreciably (except for cotton) and hence had no substantial price or income effect. The program did contribute considerably to soil conservation by reducing the acreage of both cotton and corn, two of our more "erosive" crops, and by inducing better farming practices on the crop side generally. But the procedure of tying most of the AAA payments to acreage allotments made the personal-income effects of these payments regressive, because larger farms and farm families in the better income brackets received proportionately larger payments than did the small farms and poorer farm families.

ESTABLISHING ALLOTMENTS. To understand the function and economic implications of acreage allotments, it is necessary to look at the way in which such a system is established and administered. The AAA found it necessary to do two things for each crop: (1) to determine a total acreage goal and (2) to allot a part of this total to each farm on which the crop was produced. The total acreage, set as the national goal, could be either smaller or larger than that which farmers would otherwise plant and harvest. In principle, acreage adjustments may be either up or down. In practice, however, the AAA machinery was used chiefly to curtail acreage and not to expand it.[19] The acreage goals were set each year not according to any predetermined formula but with an eye to carry-overs, prospective demand, and parity price. The national total was then broken down into state totals, which in turn were allotted to individual farms on the basis of their crop history, thus tying the acreage allotment of each farm to what the farm had been producing.

The benefits offered to farmers for participating were of two kinds: (1) direct benefits consisting chiefly of AAA payments, crop loans, re-

---

one of the several administration techniques employed by the AAA, albeit the most important one.

[18] The effect of curtailed production on income depends, of course, upon the elasticity of the demand. With the demand near or greater than unity, income would be, if anything, reduced. Only with an inelastic demand would farm income be increased.

[19] This discription applies to the period up to the time when World War II demands made it necessary to induce agriculture to expand output.

duced prices for fertilizer and other materials (in some areas), and for a time the privilege to participate in the crop-insurance program (mainly in wheat); and (2) indirect benefits through higher prices (resulting from the collective action of farmers curtailing output), a storage program to reduce the price instability caused by varying crop yields, and soil conservation effected by reducing the most exploitative crops, such as corn, cotton, tobacco, and wheat.

In addition to offering these benefits to induce farmers to participate, the AAA was authorized to institute for some crops a system of marketing quotas with penalties for noncompliance. (Commodity loans and marketing quotas are administrative techniques distinct from acreage allotments which also may be, and have been, employed to regulate production.) For cotton and tobacco, and to some extent wheat, each farmer, each year that marketing quotas were in effect, was given a quota permitting him to market a specified amount. If he exceeded his quota, he was subject to a penalty.

The AAA was operating in a depression with widespread unemployment and only small foreign demand for farm products. Against this background the AAA initiated its program of curtailing basic crops, stressing three major aims: (1) to reduce surpluses, (2) to increase farm income, and (3) to lessen the wastage of soil. In the first stage, up to 1936, the AAA operated on revenue obtained from processing taxes, and it made individual contracts with farmers in which it specified the obligations of the participating farmer and of the government. During this period emphasis was laid upon reducing production, so that it would match more nearly the reduced demand occasioned by the drop in exports and by the depressed domestic market. In 1936, because of widespread drought, the appearance of the dust bowl, and the adverse decision of the Supreme Court in the Hoosac-Mills case, the AAA shifted from reducing production through acreage allotments to conserving soil. Following the extraordinarily large crops of 1937, however, AAA went back to a kind of middle way, stressing both soil conservation and the curtailment of crops. The "ever-normal granary" idea was also given prominence at this time. It appealed both to consumers who had become drought-conscious and concerned about food supplies and to producers who saw in it an outlet for part of their output when crops were as large as in 1937. The storage of crop surpluses was given a larger role in the revised AAA of 1938.

At the time the war started, the AAA was trying to do several things: it was trying to regulate crop production through acreage allotments; it was seeking to facilitate soil conservation by reducing the acreage of the more exploitative crops; it was using the CCC as an agency for leveling big and small crop years through storages; it was asking for and receiving from Congress large appropriations for payments to farmers to induce them to participate in adjusting output to the acreage allotted and for other purposes. Throughout this period, however, no meaningful criteria were developed for measuring the performance of the AAA. All the basic legislation was tied to the concept of price parity. Parity prices, however, remained in practice a rather distant goal, someday to be attained, because prevailing farm prices were far below those called for by the parity formula.

The AAA Act of 1933 had given the Secretary of Agriculture considerable administrative discretion in determining acreage allotments. It was not until the Act of 1938 that Congress began to circumscribe the Secretary's powers, by making the parity-price goal much more binding upon the actions of the administrative agencies in agriculture.

WHAT DID AAA ALLOTMENTS DO TO CROP ACREAGES? As the table below reveals, the four basic crops subject to AAA control were down over 45 million acres, a 21 per cent decrease for the four crops taken together. How much of the reduction was effected by AAA? One study[20] indicates that the drought years pulled corn down about 10 million acres in Nebraska, Kansas, Missouri, and South Dakota, thus accounting for nearly half the reduction in corn. Wheat and cotton, however, were not affected by the drought in the same way as corn, although no similar study has been made for them. Thus, while it is not possible to demonstrate precisely what part of the 45-million-acre cut was brought about by the AAA program, it does seem that most of it may be ascribed to the crop-control features of AAA.

Crop	Acreages without AAA 1931–1933 average, million acres	Acreages with AAA 1940–1942[a] average, million acres	Reduction, per cent
Corn	111.0	89.0	20
Wheat	67.2	58.7	13
Cotton	38.6	23.8	38
Tobacco	1.7	1.4	18
Total	218.5	172.9	21

[a] Acreage planted except for tobacco, which is acreage harvested.

SOURCE: U.S. Department of Agriculture, Washington, D.C. Comparing the change in acreage from the five years 1928–1932 to the five years 1938–1942, these four crops dropped from 216 to 180 million acres, a decrease of about 17 per cent.

[20] Theodore W. Schultz and O. H. Brownlee, "Effects of Crop Acreage Control Features of AAA on Feed Production in 11 Midwest States," *Agr. Expt. Sta. Research Bul.* 298, Ames, Iowa, April, 1942, p. 683.

WHAT DID ACREAGE ALLOTMENTS DO TO CROP PRODUCTION? Acres of land are plainly only one of several inputs that a farmer employs in growing crops. If one of the inputs is rationed (in this case the amount of land allotted for a crop), he has several alternatives open to him should he want to maintain, or even increase, production. (1) He may remove from production his poorest acres (that is, keep his best acres in corn or cotton or whatever crop is restricted). (2) He may intensify the use of the land planted in the restricted crop by applying more capital and labor resources (namely, by using improved seed, more fertilizer, improved tillage, and more labor). (3) On the acres restricted by the AAA allotment he may produce substitute crops (for example, such crops as alfalfa, sorghum, and soybeans may under certain circumstances produce even more feed than corn). (4) He may substitute future outputs for present output by investing in soil resources (for example, by adopting crop rotations and cropping practices that will build up his soil). The production effects of these various types of substitution on a particular farm depend upon the nature of the soil resources, the crop and livestock enterprise, the technology, the relation between the cost of the factors employed and product prices, and the enterprise of the farmer.

What changes did occur in production of the four crops under consideration?

Crop	Production without AAA[a] 1931–1933, in millions	Production with AAA 1940–1942, in millions	Change, per cent
Corn, bu.	2,635	2,757	5
Wheat, bu.	750	910	21
Cotton, bales	14.4	12	−17
Tobacco, lb.	1,318	1,377	4

[a] If the period 1928–1932 is compared with 1938–1942, the average yearly production for corn rose from 2,554 to 2,680 million bushels; wheat from 864 to 878 million bushels; cotton fell from 14.7 to 12.0 million bales; and tobacco rose from 1,427 to 1,480 million pounds.

In spite of the reduction in acres, production actually increased except for cotton. The 17 per cent drop in cotton, however, overstates the reduction because of the very high yields in 1931 (which resulted in a 17-million-bale crop) and the poor crop in 1941 (when less than 10.7 million bales were produced).

The experience in corn illustrates how shifts within the farm will offset production effects of the cut in corn acreage. The Iowa study, analyzing the over-all production of feed in eleven key corn-belt states, indicates:

. . . (1) that aggregate feed production in these eleven states . . .' would not have been significantly different without crop acreage control, (2) that the proportion of the total feed supply comprised by corn has been somewhat smaller as a result of corn acreage allotments, (3) that about the same aggregate amounts of feed concentrates other than corn have been produced as would have been grown without AAA, and (4) that feed roughages were not only greater in absolute amounts but made up a greater proportion of the total feed supply than would have been the case without crop acreage control.[21]

Farmers producing wheat and cotton do not have at hand so wide a range of substitute methods to offset a cut in cotton and wheat acreage. The corn farmer is in a unique position, because he has a number of effective alternatives in recombining his resources and thereby not only has maintained but in many instances increased his total output of feed. Examining the production consequences of the crop allotment feature of AAA, the upshot seems clear: *There was enough substitution of the type described to have made the crop acreage allotments, ruling out the vagaries of weather, ineffective in contracting production.* Drastic cuts in acreage do reduce output the first year or two, but even with programs as severe as those administered in cotton, it appears that within a few crop seasons the total output recovers remarkably even in the face of a 40 per cent cut in acreage.

Our conclusion from this review of the early effort of the AAA to contract farm output is that acreage allotments as practiced by the AAA did not achieve this particular objective. We need not determine whether it was desirable for the community to have tried, for it will suffice to indicate that the AAA approach, purely in terms of past experience, was not effective in making the output of farm products more "elastic."[22]

Increasing the Price Elasticity of the Demand for Farm Products

If this objective were realized, it would reduce the price movements of farm products resulting from particular changes in output caused by weather and from large and abrupt shifts in the demand. The demand for farm products at the farm, as has been pointed out, is a derived demand from (1) consumers at retail, (2) public agencies for con-

[21] *Ibid.*, p. 678.
[22] For a useful analysis of the over-all effects of these programs on burley tobacco from 1933 to 1950, see Glenn L. Johnson, *Burley Tobacco Control Programs, Kentucky Agr. Expt. Sta. Bul.* 580, February, 1952.

súmption in the armed services and in public institutions, (3) nonfarm firms using these products as inputs, some as durable producer goods, (4) processors for stocks and private firms and public agencies for storage, (5) farmers for producer goods, consumption, and for stocks, and (6) foreign governments for various purposes not included in the others.

We shall restrict this section to substitution which occurs as a result of the behavior of consuming units and to the effects of price margins. We have already considered the problem that arises from purchases of farm products for the military and for other governments related to war and peace. The possibilities by way of storage will be explored later.

Substitution Represented by Consumer Behavior. Fundamentally the low price elasticity of farm products has its origin primarily in the behavior of consumers. We have already observed that consumers generally become less sensitive to changes in relative prices of foods as they become richer; substitution rates among products which have their origin in agriculture, and between these and other products and services, become relatively less elastic as the real income of consumers rises. Thus the problem before us, that is, the relative inelasticity of the demand for farm products, becomes more acute as consuming units benefit from economic development.

Does the behavior of consumers represent perfectly the preferences of consumers? The relevant information on which consumers act is certainly far from complete and often quite unsatisfactory. But it is not clear that better information in this context would necessarily make the demand for farm products more elastic, desirable as it is to improve such information.

There exists a substantial lag in consumer behavior in adjusting to particular changes in relative prices, because substitution is at first delayed pending more information to convince the consumer that the change in relative price is likely to persist and that it will be worth while to proceed to substitute. As a result, the relevant elasticities show up more elastic as time passes, other things remaining unchanged. It should be possible to shorten this adjustment period and thus reduce this particular lag in consumer behavior. Uncertainty, like a Damoclean sword, hangs over the consumer; to avert some of the consequences of this uncertainty, consumers strive for flexibility by holding liquid assets and, among other things, by foregoing some substitution over time. It appears highly probable that with less uncertainty, consumers would be prepared to acquire and carry larger stocks than is now the case of some foods and especially of some of the more durable consumer goods, for example, those made from leather, wool, cotton, and the like, when, for

instance, a bumper crop causes the price to fall. Such additional substitution over time would increase the elasticity of the demand, and it
is possible that its effect could become quite substantial.

Behavior of Price Margins. The consumer at retail is rarely confronted
by a situation where he purchases an item which is wholly farm produced. On the contrary, along with the farm-produced component he
buys the services of many firms and individuals who have processed,
transported, distributed, and in many ways have had a hand in the
production of the particular product sold at retail. By price margins we
mean the price paid by consumers for a given collection of nonfarm
services incorporated into or attached to the product purchased at retail.
These price margins are quite inflexible in the short run. As a consequence of this particular inflexibility, the elasticity of the derived demand at the farm is less than it is at retail. One should not infer from
this statement that consumers necessarily prefer fewer nonfarm services
per unit of purchases when the price, say, because of an increase in the
quantity available, falls at retail. Nor do we know the cost effects of a
short-term increase in the quantity of a farm product upon the cost of
producing a unit of these services. With the processing and distributing
capacity large (essentially fixed in the short run), one might presume the
cost per unit would fall. On the assumption that the "preference" of consumers remains unchanged with regard to the preferred combinations
of nonfarm and farm services, the price elasticity of farm products at
the farm would become greater, to the extent that the price per unit of
nonfarm services would decrease when the farm output and sales rose
and conversely when they fell.

In the preceding section, we have tried to gauge the possibilities in
economic organization of reducing the instability of farm prices. We conclude that general economic stability is a fundamental prerequisite, not
only to make it possible for farm prices to function more satisfactorily,
but to enlarge the contribution of the economy to the community. When
the price level and employment are stable, agriculture is spared (1) the
income effects of marked movements in employment which can shift the
demand for farm products far and abruptly, (2) the effects upon the
demand for farm products that arise from the uneven movement in
relative prices when the price level undergoes a marked change, and (3)
the absolute rise or fall of farm prices related to changes in the price
level. To achieve this much would go far in solving the problem of price
instability confronting farmers.

More can be done, however, to improve the existing economic
organization, for it should be possible to increase somewhat the price
elasticity of both the supply and demand schedules of farm products

at the farm. But even with these improvements, the continental climate characteristics of most of the United States will continue to be one of the basic conditions affecting crop output, to which the economy will have to adjust itself. Then, too, international tensions are likely to continue, and as they rise and fall, the purchases of farm products for the armed services, for other governments, and for still other purposes are likely to cause large, abrupt demand shifts.

By Way of Accommodations

What can and should be done, however, for and by agriculture in the event mass unemployment and a major movement in the price level were to occur again? It is only prudent to be prepared for such a contingency for despite the built-in fiscal flexibility of the last two decades the failure in monetary management leaves the outcome highly uncertain. Inflation or deflation, as a result, may be given its head. Then, too, what can be done with regard to the large and abrupt shifts in the demand for farm products and large variations in crop production caused by weather? These short-term changes will continue and they will cause farm prices to fluctuate widely, even though the United States were to achieve general economic stability.

By way of accommodation, we shall consider briefly three organizational approaches: (1) establishing firms, mainly farms, capable of operating more satisfactorily under these conditions; (2) safeguarding the income of agriculture in the event of a major depression in ways that, on the one hand, will help counteract the depression and, on the other, will not disturb trade and the allocation of resources within agriculture; and (3) using stocks to modify the price effects of some of the underlying conditions contributing to the instability of farm prices.

Organize Farms More Capable of Coping with Price Instability

Surely this approach is relevant because it is possible and it would appear to be consistent with the preference of the community for economic decentralization. Moreover, one observes a considerable advance along this line since the late thirties inasmuch as most commercial farmers in the United States have improved their financial position markedly during the decade of the forties. They are, therefore, in a much better position to cope with price fluctuation than they were prior to this. This approach, however, is not without its price.

Several difficulties arise. For one, it would take more capital to enter agriculture and farm. The amount of assets required to purchase or rent the collection of physical resources for an optimum scale and the financial resources to cope with price instability is likely to exceed for many types of farms substantially the financial capacity of the typical family farm.[23] In considering ways to adjust to large variations in yields, in Chap. 19, the possibility of farms with sufficient assets owned by the farm family was explored. Now add to this enough assets to cope with major depressions, a marked drop in the price level, and large and abrupt shifts in the demand for farm products to the left, the amount of capital needed, that is, owned by the farm family, to continue to farm through thick and thin would by and large exceed the financial capacity of the typical family farm. This approach when carried to this point becomes inconsistent with the prevailing community preference for family farms. The "preferred" family farm appears to call for more decentralization in economic organization than would exist if these firms were large

[23] William O. Jones, "A Case Study in Risk Distribution: The California Lettuce Industry," *Journal of Farm Economics*, XXXIII (May, 1951): 241, provides a clue to the critical importance in this industry for those who have come out successfully of "adequate capital reserves" in undertaking the required "program of staggered planting and thus free themselves largely from the impact of frequent price changes." I have tried to find out in this case what "adequate capital reserves" has entailed. William O. Jones has been good enough to supply me with two sets of data from the United States Congress, *Violation of Free Speech and Rights of Labor*, Hearings before the Senate Committee on Education and Labor, 76th Cong., 3d Sess., Part 73, pp. 26989–26991. Total shipments from the district for the 32-week season in 1938 were 20,318 cars. Distribution of shippers by number of cars was:

Number of shippers	Carloads shipped
1	1,713
2	1,250–1,500
4	1,000–1,249
3	750–999
4	500–749
11	250–499
23	Under 250

Another indirect measure of the size of firms in the same years is given by a breakdown by number of employees.

Number of shippers	Number of employees during peak months
4	300 or more
4	250–299
2	200–249
1	150–199
6	100–149
9	50–99
3	10–49
4	Less than 10

enough in the assets they owned to cope with all manner of instability in farm prices.

Another difficulty arises from the adverse effects of price uncertainty upon the allocation of resources. Short-term investments are encouraged because they leave farmers in a more liquid position. Flexibility is achieved in many ways, which reduces the efficiency of farms. The most important effect is upon the size of farms. Farms that are too small to use efficiently the labor resources of the farm families are maintained. Soil-building activities which are in substance long-term investments are not undertaken; livestock enterprises requiring plans and commitments which extend over many years are by-passed for enterprises with a quicker turnover; there are not enough granaries and insufficient storage.

We shall not, however, pursue this problem further because the adverse effects of uncertainty upon the allocation of resources in agriculture, resulting from widely fluctuating farm prices, have been considered in some detail elsewhere.[24]

Safeguarding the Income of Agriculture in Depression

Another accommodation for price instability consists of income[25] payments to farmers by government in major downward movements in employment and general price level. Although altogether too much stress has been placed in public policy, and notably in agricultural legislation, during the past decade and longer, on measures to cope with a major depression, like that of the early thirties, a strong case can be made for income payments to farmers as one of the secondary lines of defense to help counteract a depression that has been allowed to get out of hand. Again, however, it must be emphasized that fiscal and monetary measures are the appropriate ones and, therefore, come first in efforts to achieve economic stability. But a failure to employ these measures in time, in the right direction, and with sufficient force can result in a situation requir-

[24] See especially D. Gale Johnson, *Forward Prices for Agriculture* (Chicago: University of Chicago Press, 1947), Chaps. 4–6; and Theodore W. Schultz, *Production and Welfare of Agriculture* (New York: The Macmillan Company, 1949), Chaps. 12, 14.

[25] When payments of this type were first proposed [Theodore W. Schultz, "Two Conditions Necessary for Economic Progress in Agriculture," *Canadian Journal of Economics and Political Science*, Vol. X (August, 1944)], they were referred to as "compensatory payments" to stress the fact that they were to be used as a countercyclical device. The concept is an important one; moreover, sight may be lost of it when the term "income payments" is used without carefully specifying the conditions under which they are to be made. The author, however, yields to the literature on this point, in which the term "income payments" has predominated.

ing additional measures, among others, the kind of income payments to farmers that are here envisaged.

The case for such income payments to farmers, under these circumstances, rests on the following propositions: that it becomes important to check the decline in aggregate demand and, in doing so, not to disturb the functioning of relative prices in allocating factors and distributing products; that these income payments can keep the aggregate income of agriculture and thus the demand of this sector from falling below some specified level; that the demand of farmers for inputs, both for current production and for capital items is large (farm production expenses totaled 20 billion in 1950) and these expenditures, particularly for capital items, are responsive to changes in farm income; that these income payments can be administered so that the depression will not disturb the allocation of resources within agriculture and that the channels of trade can be kept open, whereas acreage allotments disturb resource uses and support prices disturb both production and trade. It should also be noted that these income payments to farmers, in the event of a depression, are in many ways on a par with unemployment compensation to workers during such a period.

Income payments for this purpose are beset, however, by a number of difficulties. It is not easy to formulate a set of rules that are wholly satisfactory for administering these payments, that is, rules which will specify unambiguously when the payments are to be undertaken, to whom they are to be paid, the amount of the payment, and when the payments are to be terminated. Several proposals have been advanced.[26] In addition, it is difficult, given the nature of the political process, to restrict such income payments to farmers to the particular purpose; experience indicates that income payments to farmers may be advanced for all kinds of purposes other than to help counteract a major depression; then, too, once public attention is focused on this way of safeguarding the income of agriculture against a depression, it may not only

[26] *Ibid.* See also Theodore W. Schultz, *Agriculture in an Unstable Economy* (New York: McGraw-Hill Book Company, Inc., 1945), Chap. 10, especially pp. 220–235; E. J. Working, "Report of Ad Hoc Committee on Agricultural Price Supports," *American Economic Review*, Vol. XXXVI (1946); Committee on Parity Concepts, "Outline of a Price Policy for American Agriculture for Postwar World," *Journal of Farm Economics*, Vol. XXXVIII (1946); William H. Nicholls and D. Gale Johnson, "Farm Price Policy Awards, 1946," *Journal of Farm Economics, ibid.;* L. J. Norton and E. J. Working, "A Proposal for Supporting Farm Income," *Illinois Farm Economics*, No. 127 (1945); and for an appraisal of alternative proposals, see D. Gale Johnson, *Forward Prices for Agriculture* (Chicago: University of Chicago Press, 1947), Chap. 12.

divert attention from the role of fiscal and monetary measures but may be viewed and employed as a substitute for them.

Possibilities by Storage

Storage operations may be organized to serve many different purposes; much of the confusion about storage arises from the failure to distinguish one from the other. The usual textbook case is restricted to the distribution of a product, once it has been harvested, over a part or all of the crop year (always abstracting from economic uncertainty). Stocks may, also, be accumulated in years of bumper crops to be used in years of poor crops; this has been one of the declared purposes of the "ever-normal" granary. Then, too, stocks may be acquired to accommodate the seasonality of the demand or, even, to adjust to large and abrupt shifts in the demand. National security considerations may present still another purpose which entails stock piling and related operations. And last in this list, farm products may be employed as part of a commodity reserve in the management of the money supply. In view of these different purposes, the possibilities and choices that can come into play are numerous; some combinations are exceedingly complex, and some combinations are internally quite inconsistent.

In examining the possibilities of storage in relation to the instability of farm prices, we come up against a major difficulty, because the fundamental attribute which affects storage operations, relevant to the problem at hand, is the fact that such operations are beset by economic uncertainty. If it were possible, for instance, to predict perfectly for the next decade each and every variation in production and shift in demand, it is hard to believe that the substitution of products (factors also) over time would present any difficulties whatsoever. Under such circumstances, that is with no uncertainty present, the amount and distribution of a stock to be carried forward, say, from the harvest of a particular crop, would resolve itself into a routine function of firms and households and such activities could be readily explained in economic terms. But when the underlying conditions have attributes which are associated with economic uncertainty, the function of stocks presents serious difficulties both for analysis and for organization.

In analyzing the functions of stocks for each of the purposes already listed, we need answers to the following questions: (1) What are the appropriate criteria for storage? (2) What has been the behavior of stocks? (3) How satisfactory have stocks been managed when tested against the appropriate criteria for storage? But we shall have to put these basic issues aside because it is not possible to answer them at this time.[27] The best that can be done now is to explore particular possibilities in managing stocks of some farm products in the United States and choices related to such possibilities. Our explorations must be considered highly tentative. We shall advance some proposals, as we proceed, for improving the management of stocks. These proposals, however, will rest on particular propositions which are assumed to be valid. We shall endeavor to make each of these propositions explicit so as to make clear the assumptions on which the proposal is dependent.

Storage to Counteract Variations in Agricultural Production. In Chap. 14 in examining the supply of producers during the stock period, we considered in some detail the fact that agricultural output does not have the attribute of a day-to-day flow because for most products the "harvest" is seasonal. But this seasonality of output, whether the product is perishable or not, would probably not present any important organizational difficulties under conditions of (1) general economic stability, (2) no large and abrupt shifts in demand, and (3) no marked year-to-year variations in production caused by weather and by other exogenous factors. We have attempted to gauge the seasonal behavior of stocks during periods that were relatively stable, for example, 1900 to 1914, and have found that the flow of products into consumption channels is not only much steadier than is output but the output is distributed over the seasons at about the rate consistent with the cost of storage under conditions of economic certainty.

It is our belief that year-to-year variations in agricultural production, also, would be accommodated by storage quite satisfactorily, consistent with the costs of storage, provided the patterns of these variations were known with some assurance and provided no marked movements in the price level and in employment and no large, abrupt shifts in demand were to occur. Leaving the instability of the economy and large and abrupt demand shifts aside, to be considered later, this belief implies that it is very important to analyze past variations in production with a view to isolating the effects of weather and of other exogenous factors in order to provide as complete information as is possible for the management of stocks. Existing information on which farmers, processors, other private firms, and public agencies make their storage decisions is in a most unsatisfactory state. It should prove possible to improve greatly this type of information, a prerequisite for the improvement of storage operations to counteract such variations in production. There are some

[27] A series of studies are being made under a Research and Marketing contract with the Bureau of Agricultural Economics, at the University of Chicago, on the storage of feed grains and of wheat. George Tolley is in charge of these studies.

indications, especially in the case of feed grains, that much larger stocks than have been heretofore carried forward from a series of good crops are called for on the basis of probable costs and returns from such additional stocks.

Storage to Counteract Shifts in the Demand for Farm Products. We shall leave aside seasonal variations in demand, for like the seasonality of production, storage for this purpose appears simple and a wholly routine function when other more important conditions are satisfied. But what about large and abrupt shifts in the demand for farm products of the kind considered in Chap. 11 and earlier in this chapter? Some storage operations appear to be required to counteract the demand effects of large short-term movements in per capita income during major depressions and subsequent recoveries. This problem will be examined briefly later. Shifts in demand related to mobilization, waging of war, and returning to peacetime conditions have been at times very large and abrupt. But one can hardly expect farmers and other private firms to engage in storage operations which will satisfactorily accommodate these shifts unless and until the government has developed, made known, and put into operation a storage program designed to serve the purposes of national security. But thus far, the kind of products, the amounts, and the location of stocks required for purposes of national security are not known.

Storage and General Economic Stability. We have stressed repeatedly that the stability of the price level and of employment is fundamental in improving the stability of farm prices and, also, in improving storage operations to accommodate reoccurring variations in demand and in production whether seasonal, from year to year, or a sequence of good and bad years. Two general questions, however, arise. Is there a role for the storage of farm products in achieving general economic stability? And, in the event of a marked movement in the price level and employment, is it possible by storage operations to counteract some of the adverse effects of such instability?

There have been various proposals to relate the management of the stock of money in part or in whole to a commodity reserve made up in part of some storable farm products.[28] As Professor Friedman has shown, a commodity reserve currency seeks "to gain the countercyclical ad-

[28] See, especially, Benjamin Graham, *Storage and Stability* (New York: McGraw-Hill Book Company, Inc., 1947), and *World Commodities and World Currency* (New York: McGraw-Hill Book Company, Inc., 1944); Frank D. Graham, *Social Goals and Economic Institutions* (Princeton: Princeton University Press, 1942); also, M. K. Bennett and Associates, *International Commodity Stockpiling as an Economic Stabilizer* (Stanford: Stanford University Press, 1949).

vantages of a fiat standard while retaining the physical base of the gold standard" and as a consequence, seems "to fall between two stools and, like so many compromises, to be worse than either extreme. It cannot match the nonrational, emotional appeal of the gold standard, on the one hand, or the technical efficiency of the fiat currency, on the other."[29]

The instability of farm prices is an important economic problem. It is, however, exceedingly difficult to organize the economy so that farm prices will be on the one hand both flexible and free and on the other relatively stable. Farm price supports and efforts to control agricultural production by acreage allotments, marketing quotas, and related public measures are not satisfactory. Diversion operations, subsidized exports, and efforts to shelter the domestic market from foreign competition are also unsatisfactory.

To cope with the instability of farm prices, we have indicated several changes in economic organization. First and foremost, it will be necessary to improve the stability of the economy as a whole, where the objective is to keep the general level of prices on a more even keel and resources fully employed and where the appropriate measures are fiscal and monetary. We have found that large and abrupt shifts in the demand schedule for farm products have occurred frequently and have been important because of the marked price effects of such shifts, given the low price elasticities of both the demand and supply. Where the amounts of farm products required for the military, for other governments, and for other purposes related to mobilization, the waging of war, and demobilization change rapidly, large and abrupt shifts in demand will necessarily occur. For the economy to function satisfactorily under such circumstances, marked changes in relative prices are required. Where, however, the demand for farm products shifts abruptly because of rapid changes in per capita income caused by mass unemployment (a major depression) and by an equivalent recovery, the fundamental problem is one of achieving general economic stability. The substantial variations in agricultural production, which occur from time to time, are also an important factor underlying the instability of farm prices. Not much, however, can be done by way of economic organization to reduce the variations in yield caused by weather. It should be possible to increase somewhat the price elasticity of the demand for farm products and to make agricultural production appreciably more responsive to changes in relative prices. Efforts along these lines deserve much more thought and study than they have received.

Another approach to the organizational problem represented by the

[29] Milton Friedman, "Commodity Reserve Currency," *Journal of Political Economy*, LIX (June, 1951): 232.

instability of farm prices is to find ways of accommodating agriculture. We have given a high priority to the organization of farms more capable of coping with price instability, but we found that this approach is not wholly consistent with the community's desire for a family farm. Also, it is possible and desirable to safeguard the income of agriculture during depression. In addition, there are some possibilities by way of storage, but these have not yet been thought through sufficiently to indicate the appropriate criteria for storage under existing circumstances.

INDEX

367

Date Due